PLAN YOUR ESTATE

by Attorney Denis Clifford

PLEASE READ THIS

We have done our best to give you useful and accurate information concerning estate planning. But please be aware that laws and procedures are constantly changing and are subject to differing interpretations. If you are confused by anything you read here, or if you need more information, check with an expert. Of necessity, neither the author nor the publisher of this book makes any guarantees regarding the outcome of the uses to which this material is put. The ultimate responsibility for making good decisions is yours.

NOLO PRESS • 950 PARKER STREET • BERKELEY CA 94710

IMPORTANT

Nolo Press is committed to keeping its books up-to-date. Each new printing, whether or not it is called a new edition, has been revised to reflect the latest law changes. This book was printed and updated on the last date indicated below. Before you rely on information in it, you might wish to call Nolo Press (415) 549-1976 to check whether a later printing or edition has been issued.

PRINTING HISTORY

New **Printing** means there have been some minor changes, but usually not enough so that people will need to trade in or discard an earlier printing of the same edition. Obviously, this is a judgment call and any change, no matter how minor, might affect you.

New **Edition** means one or more major, or a number of minor, law changes since the previous edition.

First Edition	MAY 1989
Illustrations	MARI STEIN
Cover Illustration	DENIS CLIFFORD
Production	STEPHANIE HAROLDE
Book Design & Layout	JACKIE CLARK
	TERRI HEARSH
	TONI IHARA
Index	SAYRE VAN YOUNG
Printing	DELTA LITHOGRAPH

Clifford, Denis.
    Plan your estate / by Denis Clifford. -- 1st ed.
       p. cm.
    Includes index.
    ISBN 0-87337-050-3 : $17.95
    1. Estate planning--United States--Popular works.   I. Title.
KF750.Z9C59 1989
346.7305'2--dc20
[347.30652]   89-60665
                                             CIP

DEDICATION

To Naomi, Mi Amor

ACKNOWLEDGEMENTS

My thanks to all those friends who helped me with this book, both putting it together and over the years:

Dorcas Moulton, Amanda Cherrin and Naomi Puro, for their contributions to the cover painting; Jake Warner, Mary Randolph and Steve Elias, superb and thorough editors; Mark Peery, Corte Madera, California, a superb estate planning lawyer (and great friend); Marilyn Putnam, San Francisco, another estate planning wizard; Stephanie Harolde, who prepared so many drafts of the book so well; Ken Fischer, Orinda, California, a fine insurance agent; Bill Hudspeth, Austin Trust Co., Austin, Texas; Magdelen Gaynor, another fine estate planning attorney, White Plains, New York; David Marcus; Paul Remack, R.G. Financial Service, San Francisco.

And my thanks and respect to all my other colleagues at Nolo Press, who together make it such a unique and enjoyable place: Jackie Clark, David Cole, Albin Renauer, Ann Heron, Barbara Hodovan, John O'Donnell, Jack Devaney, Lulu Cornell, Amy Ihara, Kate Thill, Leili Eghbal, Sue Fox, Claudia Goodman-Hough, Terri Hearsh, Janet Bergen, Karen Chambers, Monica Kindraka, Susan Quinn, Ken Cober, Lisa Goldoftas, Robyn Samuels, Barbara Kate Repa, Christine Leefeldt, Susan Mather, Renee Rivera, Michael Sigal, Jennifer Spoerri, Susan Stern; and once again, to Toni Ihara, who started it all.

And finally, my continued appreciation to other friends who also helped with the original California version of this book: Dave Brown, Peter Jan Honigsberg, Robert Wood of Athearn, Chandler & Hoffman, San Francisco, members of the Bay Area Funeral Society, Walter Warner; people who helped prepare the manuscript—Sandy Wieker, Christy Rigg, Cathy Cummings and Bethany Korwin-Pawloski; and Keija Kimura, Carol Pladsen and Linda Allison.

Contents

Part I—Introduction to Estate Planning

Here you get acquainted with basic concepts and realities of estate planning, including human, personal concerns, and learn how you can use this book to achieve your goals.

INTRODUCTION
How to Use This Book

CHAPTER 1
Personal Concerns and Estate Planning

CHAPTER 2
An Overview of Estate Planning

Part II—Groundwork

These chapters cover what you need to know to define and inventory your property and choose those you want to inherit it, your beneficiaries, with special focus on concerns about minor children.

Part III—Avoiding Probate

Here you'll learn what probate is, why it's sensible to avoid it, and how you can accomplish this; the materials also show you how to prepare your own living trust, the most popular probate-avoidance device, from a form in the Appendix.

CHAPTER 7

Probate and Why You Want to Avoid It

CHAPTER 8

Chart: Probate Avoidance Methods

CHAPTER 9

Revocable Living Trusts

CHAPTER 10

Joint Tenancy

CHAPTER 11

Bank Accounts as Estate Planning Devices

Part IV—Tax Planning and Controls on Property

These chapters discuss federal estate taxes, state death taxes, gifts and
gift taxes, and using trusts to reduce taxes or impose controls on property.

Part V—Wills

This chapter provides basic information about wills, and shows
you how to prepare a basic will from a form in the Appendix.

Part VI—Practical Matters and Special Situations

This potpourri covers using durable powers of attorney to handle possible incapacity:
funerals, cremation, body-part donations, and burials; special business estate
planning concerns; possible effects of social security benefits on estate planning.

Part VII—Going Further

These chapters discuss two aspects of going beyond the information presented in this book: going further into the law, by doing your own research or hiring a lawyer, and what you need to do after your initial plan is completed—keeping it current.

Part VIII—Sample Estate Plans

This final section discusses several different estate plans, using the concepts and methods discussed in the book.

Glossary

Appendix I: Estate Forms

Appendix II: State Death Tax Rules

PART I

Introduction to Estate Planning

INTRODUCTION

CHAPTERS 1 & 2

How to Use This Book

INTRODUCTION

How to Use This Book

THIS BOOK IS DESIGNED to enable you to understand and prepare for the practical consequences following a death. Primarily, this means arranging to transfer your property and providing for your loved ones after you die. Lawyers call this "estate planning." Your "estate" is simply all the property you own, whatever it's worth. The "planning" required can be understood by normal, intelligent people—you don't have to be an attorney or a nuclear physicist. Indeed, with the aid of this book, many people will learn that they can safely do much, or even all, of their planning themselves, without any need for an attorney.

Warning to Louisiana Residents:
This book is designed for residents of all states except Louisiana, which has a legal system based on Napoleonic Code, different from the other states.

A. What This Book Helps You Do

THIS BOOK WILL ENABLE YOU to accomplish two things. First, you'll understand what estate planning is: what choices you have, how they work, and the advantages and drawbacks of each choice. Second, you may decide to do some, or all, of your own estate planning by using or adapting forms presented in this book, such as simple living trust forms, and basic will forms.

The first thing that comes to most people's minds when they think of estate planning is property. Who gets what? Often as deep is a desire to conserve as much of their property as possible for those who will inherit it, minimizing the amount siphoned off by lawyers and taxes. And, of course, a major concern of people with minor children or dependent adult relatives is providing for their care and support. All of these issues are important aspects of estate planning, but there are other significant concerns explained in this book. Structurally, as you can see by looking at the Table of Contents, the book is divided into eight major units, to take you through all major subjects of estate planning. Here's a brief overview of major subjects covered:

- Making an inventory of your property so you know what you own and what you owe.
- Choosing beneficiaries.
- Arranging for proper care of your minor children and their property should you and the other parent die.
- Avoiding probate—the legal process generally required when property is left by a will. In probate, a court decides whether a will is valid; the deceased person's assets are ascertained, then bills and taxes are paid. Eventually—usually after a long time and outlandish lawyer's fees—the remaining property is distributed as the will directs. Because so many people understand that probate is often little more than a lawyers' racket, probate avoidance is a high priority in this book. The major probate avoidance methods, including living trusts and joint tenancy, are explained in detail.
- Planning to minimize death taxes.
- Using long-term trusts.
- Ensuring that sufficient cash will be immediately available to your close family when you die.
- Using insurance as part of an estate plan.
- Preparing your will.
- Deciding who will handle your medical and financial affairs and make legal decisions for you if you become incapacitated.
- Handling special estate problems facing owners of small businesses.
- Planning for your funeral or body disposition.
- Doing your own legal research or using lawyers.
- Keeping your plan up-to-date.

B. Who Should Use This Book

THIS BOOK IS ESPECIALLY DESIGNED for people with small or moderate estates—those with a net worth less than $600,000. By reading this book, people within this financial range can gain a good understanding of their options. Many will learn they can safely prepare their own estate plans. The key documents for many of these estate plans—a living trust and a will—can be drafted from the information and sample forms in this book.

Many of the methods this book covers, however, are equally useful for estates larger than $600,000. For instance, the probate avoidance methods explained in Chapters 9 through 13 can work well for estates worth millions. Similarly, planning for what happens if you become incapacitated involves substantially the same concerns, no matter what the size of an estate. Also, the book provides an introduction to using trusts to save on death taxes or to manage property left to inheritors. But aside from a simple trust used for leaving property to minor children, I don't cover tax savings or managerial trusts in operational detail. These types of trusts are simply too complicated to be amenable to a self-help format in a general book on estate planning.

Those with estates larger than $600,000 may need the assistance of a lawyer or other expert to investigate or use methods beyond the scope of this book. But even if you eventually decide to get help on some aspect of your estate plan, you'll benefit greatly by comprehending the basic issues and objectives involved. The information you gain reading this book will enable you to deal with a professional to get the help you really need.

C. Emotions and Practicalities

LEGAL MATTERS may often be of minor concern in the face of the overwhelming emotional force and mystery of death. Chapter 1 discusses some of the human realities that can be involved in estate planning. But this book doesn't attempt to deal with the larger meanings of a death; they are appropriately left for philosophers, clergy, poets, and—ultimately—to you. Death is a difficult subject to think about, to talk about, and to plan for. The ancient Greeks believed the inevitability of death could best be faced by performing great deeds. Christian religions offer the promise of eternal life; preparing for death means preparing to "meet your maker." Other cultures have prepared for death in a wide variety of ways.

However anyone chooses to emotionally prepare for death—his own or someone he cares for—there are also practical consequences that someone must deal with. In the U.S., if there has been no planning, the normal result is that the survivors, upset and confused, turn everything over to "professionals." A body must suddenly be disposed of, so a funeral parlor is called. A myriad of financial problems can arise: how are bills to be paid and tax returns prepared? How is title to the family house transferred to the inheritors? Who pays death taxes? Enter a host of highly paid professionals, often including lawyers, CPAs, real estate advisors, and insurance brokers.

While trying to deal with the emotional trauma and the physical reality of death, it's easy for thousands of dollars to be consumed by the excessive or unnecessary fees of professionals. The money wasted comes from the estate of the person who died—money that would otherwise be available for the family, friends or others to inherit. In addition to curtailing this kind of waste, planning can save substantial amounts on death taxes for larger estates. So, in the final analysis, preparing an estate plan is an act of love for your inheritors. Although you don't directly face the consequences of procrastination and avoidance, they will, unless you decide to act.

D. Tailoring Your Estate Plan to Your Needs

YOUR ESTATE PLAN will consist of the methods and documents you've decided on, and prepared, to handle what happens, after your death, to the matters that concern you. For example, you might decide to use a simple will to name a guardian for your minor children and make some minor gifts, a living trust to pass your real estate and other major items to your beneficiaries, and an insurance policy to pay debts, taxes and provide for your family's immediate needs.

The word "plan" can be misleading. It doesn't mean you'll have a document that looks like a map, nor have lots of charts and graphs. Some authorities have attempted to present pre-packaged estate plans that apply to certain "standard" situations. For example, if a husband and wife have minor children and an estate of approximately $200,000, Plan A is proposed, but a husband and wife with no minor children and an estate over $200,000 should use Plan B, and so on. The problem with these off-the-shelf estate plans is that real life isn't standardized. There are many variables in each person's situation. Each individual must take stock of her own needs and desires, and determine what her goals are. Then, with the information and forms presented in this book, you can put together an estate plan geared for your personal situation.

Plan Your Estate should be used as a workbook, not a book to cherish unmarked. It's designed to help you understand and prepare your overall estate plan. While reading this book, you should be actively involved—writing down factual information, making notes, recording your decisions, and perhaps, using the forms presented to draft your own legal documents. A number of worksheets and sample forms are provided to help you do this. You can leave the worksheets in the book while using them, or photocopy them and work on the copies.

How far you delve into the specifics of any one aspect of estate planning is up to you. For example, when you inventory your property, you'll have to determine how detailed you want to be. This will depend not only on how complex your property situation is, but on what type of planning you want to engage in now. If you only want a general understanding of estate planning, or want to leave all your property to your spouse, you may not need to list your specific property and all the gifts you'll make.

Read through the book once before you actually start to complete any of the legal documents. Different aspects of estate planning are often intertwined. Thus, you shouldn't decide what should go in your will until you understand probate avoidance methods. Similarly, if you have a good-sized estate, you'll need to understand how estate taxes work before you can determine the wisest ways to transfer property to your loved ones. The point is, you need to get a good overview of the whole field before you begin to make your plan. Of course you can safely skip those parts of the book which obviously don't apply to you.

E. Will You Need Professional Help?

FOR MOST PEOPLE with moderate estates, the actual process of estate planning isn't nearly as forbidding as many professionals make it seem. For example, one pillar of estate planning is respect for conventional lawyer language and accepted forms. What can be surprising is how simple it often is for nonlawyers to learn how to use these legal tools. As this book shows you, most people who have estates up to $600,000 (and often more), and who have clear desires about their property, can learn how to prepare their own estate planning forms.

After finishing this book, you'll be able to determine whether you want or need help from an expert. Make this judgment carefully, of course, but do remember that lawyers and experts aren't monetary magicians. The costs of hiring an expensive estate planner, for people with a moderate estate, is often greater than any savings or certainty she can achieve, beyond what you accomplish yourself by the methods presented here. Even if you do find it necessary to hire someone to help, it should be much cheaper than having the person design or prepare your plan from scratch. Also, if you educate yourself and do much of your initial planning, you're more likely to end up with something that fully expresses your own desires.

This book doesn't claim to present definitive advice on all aspects of estate planning. Many subjects covered, such as estate taxes, life insurance, probate avoidance, ongoing trusts, or will drafting, are large matters. There are volumes of books on each topic in any good-sized law library. Certainly there are some situations where you'll need the assistance of a professional expert (unless you're willing to do your own research; see Chapter 22). Where appropriate, I recommend seeing an expert. When I do so, I also use the identifying symbol

so you can easily determine an expert is suggested. Though you'll see quite a few of these symbols throughout the book, most readers won't be affected by any of them.

Other Nolo Resources

NOLO PRESS publishes other materials which may be useful to you in your estate planning, including:

- **WillMaker,** Nolo's computer will program, which enables you to prepare a comprehensive will, including a simple trust for your minor children, allowing you to choose the age at which your children inherit property you leave them.

- **Nolo's Simple Will Book,** an in-depth explanation of how to prepare a will that covers all normal needs, including simple trusts for your minor children.

- **The Power of Attorney Book** enables you to prepare a durable power of attorney to appoint, in advance, the person with legal authority to act for you if you become incapacitated.

- **How to Probate an Estate** (California Edition) enables Californians to do normal probate without an attorney.

- **The Deeds Book** (California Edition) explains how to use deeds to transfer real estate for estate planning.

- **Social Security, Medicare and Pensions,** an excellent resource about rights and benefits of older Americans.

Throughout **Plan Your Estate,** I alert you when one of these materials provides more coverage of an aspect of estate planning than this book does. You can order any of these books direct from Nolo, at a special 25% discount. An order form is at the back of this book.

Personal Concerns and Estate Planning

CHAPTER 1

Personal Concerns and Estate Planning

UNDERLYING THE CREATION OF ANY ESTATE PLAN are profound human concerns: a deep human urge for order and the desire to pass on property to loved ones. So, a good estate plan is an accurate reflection of your individual spirit. While much of this book is about mechanics, methods and documents, it's important to remember that no matter how well you deal with the legal technicalities, your estate plan won't succeed unless you take human concerns into account, too.

I make no claim to being an expert on the psyche. Indeed, I'm wary of "experts" who claim they have precise understanding of something as complex and mysterious as human beings. Happily, you don't need an expert to cope with the human realities that can come up in your estate planning. You do need common sense, some candor and an ability to put legal technicalities aside from time to time while you look into your heart.

For many, probably most, people, no serious personal problems arise in their estate planning. They know who they want to give their property to. They do not foresee any possibility of conflict between their beneficiaries, nor threat of lawsuit by someone claiming they should have been been a beneficiary. On the human level, these people can, happily, focus on the satisfactions they expect their gifts to bring.

Other people's situations are not so clear and straightforward. They must deal with more difficult human dynamics, such as possibilities of family conflicts or dividing property unequally between children or providing care for minor children or handling complexities arising from second or subsequent marriages.

Before beginning your legal planning, it's vital that you assess your personal circumstances and resolve any potential human problems that your estate planning might raise. If you're sure you don't face any human problems, wonderful. If, however, you think you might face complications—or if you're not sure what kinds of problems can come up—read the balance of this chapter, which discusses a number of human concerns based on examples drawn from my estate planning practice.

A. Avoiding Conflict

AVOIDING CONFLICT to the extent reasonably possible should be a central goal of estate planning. After your death, you surely don't want the way you distribute your property to result in bitterness, family feuds or fights between former friends. So, one important aspect of creating a good estate plan is to reflect on the potential for conflict in your situation. If this potential does exist, think of what can be done to eliminate or at least reduce it.

A self-evident truth about estate planning is that it involves property—money or things that can be converted into money. Money, as most of us have learned, is strange stuff indeed. It has power to do good in a number of material ways, and can also alleviate anxiety and provide security. Unfortunately, however, human flaws and fears can sometimes become unleashed when substantial sums of money are involved; meanness, greed and dishonesty occasionally surface. Naturally, in making your gifts, you don't want to unnecessarily stir up negative feelings or emotions. But what about your inheritors? Are they clear-headed enough to accept your gifts in the spirit in which you give them, or are some likely to create their own brand of trouble? Sadly, bitterness, strife and lawsuits are far from unheard of upon distribution of property after one's death.

Let's first explore general ways to avoid conflict by looking at three different family situations. Then, in the sections that follow, I will discuss conflict avoidance in a number of typical problem areas.

Patrick and Clara have five children. One, Sean, is a lawyer. Patrick and Clara admit to themselves, though they never reveal it to others, that Sean is their one grasping child, who has always wanted the most, materially, from his parents, and the world. Indeed, by sheer persistence, Sean has already managed to acquire a substantial number of family heirlooms. Sean tells his parents he wants to supervise distribution of their property when the survivor dies, as executor of their wills and successor trustee of their living trust, stating that he's obviously the most professionally qualified.

At first, Patrick and Clara aren't sure what to do. After considerable discussion, they decide they don't want Sean to have sole authority to supervise the distribution of their estate. Basically, they conclude that while they love him as they do their other children, they can't rely on him to be able to put his own desires aside and distribute their property impartially. They'd prefer to have their daughter Maude, the kindest and most level-headed of their kids, be both executor and successor trustee. However, they're afraid that doing this will offend Sean, something they're determined not to do. After much thought, they decide to have three executors and successor trustees—Sean, Maude, and another daughter, Maeve. (Patrick, Jr. lives in Europe and isn't interested, and Polly is still a minor). While this may be a little awkward, and sets up the possibility that Maude and Maeve may have to combine forces to cope with Sean (as they've had to do for 30 years), Patrick and Clara feel they have arrived at a solution that has a good chance of success. Then they need to talk to Maude, Maeve and Sean to try to work things out, including the rules for authority—such as whether two of three can determine what's done, even if one is opposed. While this may involve some conflict with Sean, there's far less risk of serious family strife than if Sean were named sole trustee and executor.

Sol and Bernice have two children in their late 20's, Abel and Alexis, and a combined estate worth about $530,000. Sol also has a 34-year-old daughter, Lilith, from his first marriage, who he's seen very rarely since his marriage to Bernice. Sol wants to give Lilith a gift of $100,000 in his living trust. Bernice says "That's absolutely ridiculous. You're just trying to absolve yourself of the guilt you feel for ignoring Lilith all these years." Sol replies "Isn't it my money?" Bernice points out that half of it is her money, as their property lists both their names as owners (see Chapter 3, State Property Ownership Laws). Sol says, "Yes, but half of $530,000 is $265,000, so I can give $100,000 to Lilith if I want to." But he soon admits that this "divide my estate" approach would mean he would only be leaving Bernice $165,000, with nothing for his other two children, who, in truth, he is closer to. Sol realizes his children from his present marriage would almost surely feel hurt. Sol and Bernice decide to work through this problem together. After some lengthy talks, they decide that Sol will give $50,000 to Lilith, and the rest to Bernice in his living trust (assuming Bernice survives Sol). When Bernice dies, she will pass on everything that's left to Abel and Alexis. They then check with the two children to see if this seems fair to them as well. Happily, it does. Abel says, "Hey, it's your money, Pa." Their daughter adds, "So enjoy." Both convince Sol and Bernice that they think the gift to Lilith is fair.

Al is a widower with three children. Although there's no problem dividing up his big ticket items among his children equally—they all agree on that—all three children have expressed deep attachment to a number of relatively inexpensive family treasures. Al decides they have to talk it out. He gets all three children together and says "You're going to have to work it out among you. Come up with something you all agree on and I'll do it. But don't make me guess, and don't leave me worrying that you'll be fighting amongst yourselves when I'm gone." A family retreat is planned and carried out. It takes longer than any of them anticipate, but the kids stick with it, and eventually, a few flashes of temper and some weary hours later, they've worked out an agreement to divide some items of property and share others. Everyone is in good spirits. Al studies the agreement and, while he secretly thinks it's more complex than necessary, he agrees that it's fair. That evening, everyone drinks, and toasts to Al's good health and long life.

B. Leaving Unequal Amounts of Property to Children

SOMETIMES PARENTS WANT to leave unequal amounts of property to their children, but don't want to give the impression that they favor the child who is given more. Here are some examples of how people have handled this matter.

A widower feels that of his three grown children, one, a struggling pianist, needs far more financial support than his other two, who have succeeded in more conventional and well-paying jobs. He wants to give the pianist the bulk of his money, but decides it might cause problems among his children. So he includes in his estate plan a letter explaining that he loves all three children equally and that his decision to give the pianist more is a reflection of need, not preference. (These letters are discussed in Chapter 5, Section G.) He also leaves most family heirlooms, which are emotionally but not monetarily valuable, to the other two children to emphasize how much he cares for them.

An elderly couple owns a much-loved summer home in the Poconos. Only one of their four children, Skip, cares about the home as much as they do, and they plan to give it to him. But they question whether they should reduce his portion of the rest of their estate by the value of the home, or divide the rest of their estate equally between their four children, and on top of this, give the summer home to Skip. As the family is a close one, they discuss the problem with the kids. One of them doesn't think their last alternative is fair. Skip doesn't think so either. The parents decide to give Skip less than one-fourth of the rest of their estate, but not to reduce his share by the full value of the summer home. They explain their decision to the others on the basis that Skip had helped maintain the summer home for many years, and that his work should legitimately be recognized. It is, and the plan is accepted in good grace by all.

A widow with no children asks her three nieces and two nephews which of her heirlooms they want. Most things are divided in good spirit, but four of the five want her Daumier etchings, and none of them seems willing to give way. The widow discusses this with them, and they eventually agree to all own the etchings and rotate possession every year. The widow secretly thinks the solution is awkward but is proud of herself for coming up with a plan that will keep peace in her family.

Ed's parents have paid for his college and dental school education and helped him purchase his first house. Melinda, their other child, has always been an independent sort who, while a loving daughter, has prided herself on making it on her own. Now they want to equalize their gifts by giving more to Melinda in their estate plan. Some hints of their thinking are enough to disturb Ed, and he argues that he still should get half. The parents retreat, talk it over and decide they'll stick to their original plan, giving Melinda more, and won't discuss the subject with Ed again. In their estate planning documents (a will and a living trust), they'll explain why and how they determined the distribution. They'll emphasize that they love both children equally and are determined to treat them equally. They hope that being fair and firm with Ed will gain his respect in the end.

C. Providing Care for Minor Children

A PRIME CONCERN OF PARENTS of minor children is who will take care of their children if the parents die. If both parents are involved in raising the child (together, or with joint custody, or any involvement of both parents), the worry is what happens if both parents die. If there is only one parent, and the other is dead or has effectively abandoned the child, the sole parent wants to make sure his children will be well cared for if he dies. The primary issues are who will raise the child *and* who will be responsible for supervising property the parent(s) leave to the child. These issues are discussed in depth in Chapter 6, Children. Here I want only to indicate some of the emotional concerns that may be raised when trying to resolve them.

A married couple, Taylor and Sondra, have two grade school age children. Taylor and Sondra discuss who will raise their children if both parents die. Taylor strongly promotes his sister, Beth, as the suitable guardian. Sondra thinks Beth is a snob and declares she doesn't want her children raised in that household. She suggests her older brother, Louis. Taylor retorts that Louis has been known to take a drink and doesn't have the most stable marriage. Taylor and Sondra realize they have to talk seriously to see who they can both agree on as guardian. After considerable discussion among themselves, and a fairly successful effort to feel out the kids, they settle on Sondra's best friend, Hortense, who has children about the same age and is willing to accept the responsibility.

Marcie, a single parent, wants her best friend, Shoshana, to be the guardian for Marcie's nine-year-old daughter if Marcie dies. To Marcie's surprise, Shoshana says she can't accept the responsibility. She has two kids of her own, and that's all she can handle. Marcie is hurt, and worries there's no one she trusts who will do the job. After some reflection and discussion with other friends, Marcie realizes that her brother Alex is willing to be guardian. Marcie is not overjoyed. Alex and she weren't really close as kids and still aren't. But she realizes that Alex is a trustworthy person and that her child would be well cared for with him. She concludes that her best estate plan is to stay alive until her daughter is an adult, but if she doesn't, she will rely on Alex.

D. Second or Subsequent Marriages

PEOPLE WHO MARRY MORE THAN ONCE may face problems reconciling their desires for their present spouse and family with their wishes for children from their prior marriages. Individual situations can vary greatly here, and you must work carefully through your needs.

A couple in a second marriage each have children from their prior marriages. Both spouses want to eventually leave their property to their own children, but both also want to protect the interest of the survivor. The couple owns a house, with each spouse owning half. If the first spouse to die leaves half directly to his or her children, they may want to sell it or use it before the other spouse dies. At best, the surviving spouse will be insecure and, at worst, may be thrown out of the house. Neither spouse wants to risk that. They decide to each leave the other what's called a "life estate" in their one-half of the house. For example, if the husband dies first, the wife can live in the house during her lifetime, but when she dies, the husband's share automatically goes to his children. (These types of trusts are discussed in Chapter 14, Section C, and Chapter 16, Section B.) As the wife's share will presumably go to her kids, this will mean the house will be sold, and the proceeds divided, when the survivor dies.

Ms. Bellows, in her 70's, is wealthy and has three grown children. She remarries Mr. Rice, also in his 70's; they live in her house. Mr. Rice has very little property, and has two children from a prior marriage who Ms. Bellows does not particularly care for. As she plans her estate, Ms. Bellows realizes she wants to allow Mr. Rice to remain in the house if she dies before he does, but doesn't want him to be able to rent out the house, nor be able to sell it and buy another one. She discusses her concerns with him. He is bothered that she doesn't trust him fully. Then she talks with her children, who are concerned that Mr. Rice, or more accurately his children, might somehow consume their inheritance.

Ms. Bellows decides to give much of her property outright to her children. She will create a trust for the house, and leave enough money in the trust to pay for mortgage and upkeep on the house. The trust will be managed by the most responsible of her children. Mr. Rice will have the right to live in the house for the duration of his life. He agrees with this arrangement but asks what happens if he gets ill and must be hospitalized? Will he be thrown out of the house? His concern prompts Ms. Bellows to realize that there are many aspects of the trust to pin down. To do this, she first discusses how the trust will wash with Mr. Rice, and then with her children. She then has the trust document prepared by a lawyer.

E. Long-Term Care for a Child With Special Needs

PARENTS OF DISADVANTAGED CHILDREN may need to provide care and support for those children whether they are minors or adults. Providing this care often requires the help of experts, particularly to coordinate the parents' plan with rules on government benefits.

A family has a disabled child, Bob, who will need care all his life. The parents' primary concern is doing all they can to arrange for Bob's care after they die. They realize this means leaving Bob most of their modest estate. They discuss this with their 17-year-old daughter, Rebecca, who says "that's fine." There are many questions the parents must resolve about Bob. Who will be responsible for Bob's care after they die? How can they best leave money for his use? Will any money left be counted when determining eligibility for government benefits? Arranging for guardians means talking it over with Rebecca and their friends. Only then does the legal work get done. The family decides to establish a "special needs" trust for Bob. They have this trust drafted by an expert who designs it to maintain Bob's eligibility for government assistance programs and to provide control by a trustee over trust property used for Bob's benefit.

F.   Concerns of Unmarried Couples

UNMARRIED COUPLES have no inherent legal right to each other's property. A central concern of most unmarried couples is to make sure each creates a binding legal method to leave property to the other. Happily, people—whether lesbian, gay or heterosexual—have the right to leave their property to whomever they want, as long as they're competent. In case of serious threat by hostile family members, a couple may take action to establish by clear proof that they were competent when they prepared their estate plan.

Ernest and Linda have lived together for several years. Aside from a few small gifts to friends or family, each wants to leave all their property to the other after death. They're concerned with efficiency and economy, but above all they want to be sure that their estate plan can't be successfully attacked by several close relatives who have long been hostile to their life style. Ernest and Linda each prepare a living trust leaving their property as they desire. They videotape their signing and the notarization of this document to provide additional proof they were both competent and not under duress.

G.   Worries About the Effect of Inheriting Money

SOMETIMES PEOPLE WORRY that someone they want to leave money or property to cannot handle it. In other words, they fear their gifts will have destructive results; the beneficiaries may be too young or too immature, for example. Resolving these concerns requires a careful examination both of oneself and the character of the potential beneficiaries.

Ed is quite wealthy, and worried about the effects of his wealth on his children and grandchildren. He grew up poor, worked hard all his life and made a small fortune. Shouldn't his kids, now in their 20's and 30's, and just making their way in the world, continue to work hard, at least until they're old enough to keep a large inheritance in perspective? If Ed dies soon, and each child inherits over $1,000,000, will they decline into sloth and decadence? Wouldn't his best estate plan be to say "Being of sound mind, I spent what I could and I give the rest to charity"? Should he give money only to grandchildren if they follow in his business? (None of his children did.) Before Ed can hope to make a decent estate plan, no matter how much he learns about the intricacies of tax planning and probate avoidance, he needs to do some serious thinking and reflecting on the subject of his money and family, to better understand the complicated nature of his emotions and expectations as pertaining to his money. Once he does, he should be better able to make up a plan to benefit his children and grandchildren. For example, perhaps he will leave the bulk of his wealth in trust for his children. Each child will receive a moderate amount of income for a number of years, only getting the property outright at the age Ed has chosen. (Joseph Kennedy established trusts for each of his children which didn't release the trust property until that child became 50 years old.)

Sylvia, a wealthy widow, has two children in their 30's: Yvonne, the sensible one, and Colleen, who's always been improvident and often more than a little self-destructive. Sylvia wants to leave her estate equally to her two daughters. She'll give Yvonne's half to her outright, but she's troubled by the thought of Colleen receiving several hundred thousand dollars. After reading Chapter 16, Sylvia decides it's sensible to give Colleen her money in what's called a "spendthrift" trust, where a trustee, someone other than Colleen, controls the money (principal), and Colleen receives only the trust income. She can only draw on any of the trust principal if the trustee agrees she needs it for educational, medical or other essential needs.

Sylvia still faces three important problems: first, who is to be trustee of the trust? Second, should she tell Colleen what she's decided upon? Third, when should the trust end? Sylvia discusses both questions with Yvonne, who convinces her mother that she—Yvonne—shouldn't be the trustee. They agree that, given the personalities involved, it's potentially destructive if one sister controls the other's inheritance. So, Sylvia decides to appoint her younger brother as trustee. She also decides the trust will end when Colleen becomes 45, at which point she will get all the money outright. She hopes Colleen will be fully responsible by then. Finally, she decides to tell Colleen her plan, although she's not joyously anticipating that discussion. She does tell Colleen that if, over the coming years, she decides Colleen has matured and can handle money, she will change her estate plan and leave Colleen her money outright.

H. Disinheriting Children

SOME PARENTS WANT TO DISINHERIT A CHILD, or children. Other people want to ensure that certain relations or ex-friends get none of their property. Legally, you can disinherit anyone you want, with the exception, in many states, of your spouse. (See Chapter 3.) But deciding to disinherit a child is often not easy to do.

Steve and Kathy have three daughters and a substantial estate. They are very close to two of the daughters, but bitterly on the outs with the third, Betty. Steve and Kathy had originally intended to leave most of their property to the surviving spouse, with some to the two daughters they're close to. Then, when the surviving spouse dies, the remaining property is to be divided between these two daughters. But they have second thoughts. Do they really want to cut their daughter out entirely? If they do, aren't they creating an incentive for her to sue and try to invalidate their estate plan? They decide that both good hearts and prudence dictate the same decision. Each will leave Betty $25,000 and include a "no-contest" clause in their wills. This clause states that if any beneficiary challenges a will, she gets nothing if her challenge is unsuccessful. The parents expect Betty to take the certain $50,000 she'll receive from both parents rather than the risk and the cost of a lawsuit she's very likely to lose. Also, Steve and Kathy are relieved that they haven't had to formally disinherit one of their own children.

Peter has two grown children, both prosperous. Peter decides he wants to leave much of his estate to his favorite charity, and the rest to his children. He hints at this to them. One child is quite accepting; the other is very upset. Peter decides to stick to his plan, accepting whatever disapproval or conflicts it will cause. In his living trust, he states expressly why he has decided his property is best given to the charity, and that even though he has done this, he loves his children deeply.

I. Communicating Your Decisions to Family and Friends

MOST OF THESE EXAMPLES indicate that talking can help resolve many potential difficulties with family and friends. Among the decisions about communication only you can make about your estate planning are:

- Who do you want to talk to? Obviously, you need to talk to those you're naming to have responsibility for your minor children, or for supervising the distribution of your property after you die. But what about some, or all, of your beneficiaries?

- What do you want to talk about?

- Do you want to tell people what you've already decided and why, or ask for advice, or state that you're open to suggestions? Do you want to discuss the mechanics of your plan with your inheritors? (You should, of course, with your executor and successor trustee.)

- Do you want to give your inheritors copies of your estate plan?

Talking is not invariably a panacea. Certainly, there are times when someone doesn't want to hear or talk, or other times when communication only reveals a deep and unbridgeable gulf. And from the older generation's point of view, there can be risks involved with communication: if they promise money now to beneficiaries, they may feel guilty if some future dire medical necessity eats up some—or all—of that money. They may worry that their opening up will reveal undesirable qualities like greed and hard-heartedness in those promised to inherit.

Still, most of the people I've worked with have been aided by talking about their estate planning. Communication about estate planning isn't necessarily always initiated by the older generation. It can very legitimately be initiated by children (or other possible inheritors). Sometimes it's initiated because a child knows a parent has done no estate planning and understands that dying intestate will mean a lengthy and costly probate proceeding in court. Or, children may wonder what their parents' estate plan is, or perhaps even want to comment on it. Here, too, there can be barriers to candor: a societal code that death is an unmentionable, especially to one's own parents; fear that motives can be misunderstood, and you'll be thought pushy or greedy; the sense that honor lies in not caring about a parent's property, or that of any other loved one. Still, the results of talking openly are usually positive. For one example, I know of a situation in which a child who had done very well financially asked her parents to leave a disproportionate share of their estate to the other children. The children's discussion provided the impetus for their parents to do estate planning they'd intended to do for years; they were quite relieved to finally have it accomplished.

In sum, if you have a personal problem or two, something to work out on the human level, it can require a good deal of thought, understanding and judgment. For these problems, two or more heads do seem better than one.

An Overview of Estate Planning

CHAPTER 2

An Overview of Estate Planning

THERE ARE A NUMBER of ways to leave property to those you want to have it after your death. The peculiarities of our system of inheritance mean that substantial amounts of money and time can often be saved if property is labelled and transferred by certain legal means rather than others. For example, if you leave your affairs to be handled by lawyers, a considerable sum of your money will almost certainly end up in their pockets as fees for that time-consuming and unnecessary legal game called probate. Fortunately, there are safe and understandable methods you can use yourself that will save time and money when your property is passed on. Before plunging into the nitty-gritty details of the different aspects of estate planning, this chapter gives you a general view of its main aspects.

A. The Language of Estate Planning

ESTATE PLANNING is one of the more jargon-ridden areas of law. I've tried to keep use of this lawyer dialect to a minimum, but it isn't possible to eliminate it entirely. Each important term is defined when it's first used in the text. There's also a glossary near the back of the book.

There are some legal terms that anyone who wants to learn about the subject must know. Some are euphemisms. For example, a dead person is referred to as a "decedent." Others are technical terms, including:

- "Testate" means to die leaving a will or other valid property-transfer device, such as a living trust.

- "Intestate" means to die without one.

- "Real property" is real estate—land and the buildings on it.

- "Personal property" is every other kind of property, from stocks to cash to furniture to wedding rings to your pet canary and your old magazines. Of course, land isn't any more "real" than a car or wallet. Nevertheless, it apparently seemed more real to our ancestors; as Mark Twain put it, "Buy land. They aren't making any more of it." So we're stuck with the definition.

- "Gift" means property you transfer freely (not by sale or trade) to a person or institution. Throughout this book, "gift" is used both to describe property you give away during your lifetime, and property you give away at your death, depending on the context. This saves us from having to use the legalese "bequest," "devise" or "legacy."

B. What Is An Estate?

IN COMMON SENSE TERMS, your "estate" includes all the property you own, minus anything you owe (assets minus liabilities). To actually plan your estate sensibly, you first have to estimate the value of your estate. Another way to say this is that you must determine your "net worth." (You'll do this in Chapter 4.) However, as you'll learn in subsequent chapters, there are two other ways to value your estate that can also be important for your planning:

- **The taxable estate:** This is the property that's subject to federal estate taxes (and state death taxes, too, if there are any in your state) when you die. Very generally, this is the same as the value of your estate, or net worth (assets minus liabilities), except that certain property included in your estate is excluded from the taxable estate. For example, for federal tax purposes, property left to a surviving spouse or to charity is excluded from the taxable estate.

- **The probate estate:** This is the portion of your estate that must go through probate before it can be distributed. Most property left by will must go through probate. Everything that is transferred by probate-avoiding methods such as living trusts, joint tenancy or insurance, is not part of the probate estate. For those who plan wisely, the "probate estate" will be considerably less than the taxable estate. Some people will eliminate it entirely.

Maureen's taxable estate amounts to $500,000. She decides to transfer the major items in her estate—her house and stock account worth $460,000—by a living trust, not her will. Thus, her probate estate totals only $40,000.

How to calculate the value of the estate, the taxable estate and the probate estate is explained in subsequent chapters.

C. Deciding Who You Want to Receive Your Property

DECIDING WHO THEY WANT to receive their property is the heart of estate planning for most people. Distributing your property as you choose to is, obviously, a personal decision. Most people approach their estate planning with at least a broad idea of what they want to do with their property. However, as you proceed through the book and move deeper into estate planning, you'll understand options which might affect your ultimate choice of beneficiaries, such as:

- estate tax considerations;
- naming alternate beneficiaries;
- leaving property to an adult for use for a minor, instead of leaving that property to the minor.

D. What Is Probate and How Do You Avoid It?

PROBATE IS THE NAME given to the legal process by which a court oversees the distribution of property left by a will.[1] Probate proceedings are generally mere formalities, since there's rarely any dispute about a will,

but they are nevertheless cumbersome and lengthy. (I explain why in Chapter 7.) During probate, the assets of the decedent are ascertained, all debts and death taxes are paid, fees for lawyers, appraisers, accountants and for filing the case in court are paid, and the remaining property is finally distributed to the inheritors. The average probate proceeding drags on for at least a year before the estate is actually distributed.

The very word "probate" has acquired a notorious aura. Although probate doesn't involve evil officials or outright corruption, it is commonly an institutionalized rip-off of a dead person's estate by lawyers, and sometimes executors, who get large fees for what in most cases is routine, albeit tedious, paperwork. For example, if a parent dies and leaves a will dividing his estate equally among his three children, and no one contests the division, why should a lawyer be paid a hefty sum to shuffle some routine papers through a bureaucratic maze?

Since probate lawyers are so expensive, can you safely handle probate without them? Unfortunately, except in California and Wisconsin, the answer is normally "no," at least not without considerable difficulty.[2] Legally, it's permissible for the executor named in a will to act for the estate, appear in probate court and handle the proceedings without an attorney ("in pro per"). But probate is a technical and tedious area of the law. The forms that must be filled out can seem complicated to the uninitiated. In some situations, there are court proceedings to attend. Learning how to do probate yourself normally takes considerable time—and risks continuing frustration. Worse, the courts and clerks can be unhelpful, or even hostile, to laypeople. (This isn't to defend such bureaucratic hostility—there's obviously no defense—but it's important to note it exists.)

The wiser approach is to plan to avoid probate altogether. This can be done for most estates. Several probate avoidance methods avoid court proceedings,

---

[1] If there was no will or other valid transfer device, such as a living trust or joint tenancy, probate occurs under the "intestacy" provisions of state law.

[2] Simple estates can be probated without a lawyer in California by using Nissley, *How to Probate an Estate* (Nolo Press). Wisconsin provides a simplified probate system, with court clerk assistance for completing forms (see Chapter 13, Section B).

transfer property quickly after a death, and can often be prepared without a lawyer. These methods are:

- Living trusts (Chapter 9);

- Joint tenancy (Chapter 10);

- Informal bank account trusts (pay-on-death accounts) (Chapter 11);

- Life insurance (Chapter 12); and

- Probate exemption or simplification procedures, which are available in many states for small estates in the $5,000 - $60,000 range (Chapter 13).

E. Why You Should Have a Will

EVERYONE SHOULD MAKE OUT A WILL. Even those who plan to transfer all their property by probate avoidance methods, such as living trusts or joint tenancy, should prepare a will to back up these other transfer devices. You need a will to:

- transfer property somehow overlooked when establishing probate-avoidance devices;

- transfer property unexpectedly acquired after probate-avoidance devices are set up (a sudden inheritance, lottery winnings, etc.);

- appoint an executor for the estate; and

- nominate personal and back-up financial guardians for your minor children (discussed in Chapter 6).

Some people decide all the estate planning they want is a will. They prefer the ease of using a will to the more complicated methods needed to avoid probate or reduce death taxes. In other words, they decide to keep things simple for themselves, in spite of the additional complexity and cost probate and death taxes impose on their inheritors.

For some people, limiting estate planning to making a will can make good sense. For example, younger people in good health often want to postpone detailed estate planning for later. A will naming a personal and property guardian for minor children and leaving property to a few close relatives is all they need now. But for older people with a reasonable amount of property, it makes little sense to depend on a will alone. The amount of time and effort it takes to plan to avoid probate is just not that much—certainly far less than inheritors will expend going through it, not to mention the significant costs saved.

Some experts argue that in cases where estate taxes must be paid, or estate tax returns filed, it makes sense to have a probate lawyer, experienced in these tax matters, do the paperwork as part of a formal probate. I don't believe it. There are many tax experts out there, and they'll generally prepare an estate tax return for an estate which avoids probate for far less than the cost of probate.

Finally, in unusual situations, probate can actually be useful. The primary instance is if your estate will have many debts or claims from creditors, probate provides a forum for resolving those claims with relative speed and certainty when compared to regular lawsuits.

F. Death Taxes and How to Minimize Them

DEATH TAXES are taxes imposed on the property of a person who dies. Some people confuse probate avoidance devices, such as living trusts and joint tenancy, with tax-saving schemes. Unfortunately, avoiding probate doesn't have any effect on, or reduce, death taxes.

Death taxes are called by various names. The federal government calls them "estate taxes." Some of the states that impose death taxes (many states don't) call them "inheritance taxes." In theory, these states tax the recipients of a deceased person's property rather than the property itself, but the reality is the same—the taxes are paid out of the deceased's estate.

Whether or not your estate will be likely to be required to pay death taxes depends on two factors:

- the value of your taxable estate (remember your taxable estate is your net estate minus any gifts or expenses that are tax-exempt), and

- the laws of the state where you live.

If the net worth of your estate will be less than $600,000, you'll have no liability for federal taxes—assuming you haven't made large gifts during your lifetime (see Chapter 14, Section B). If your estate is larger than this amount, it will normally owe federal tax. However, certain types of gifts, such as gifts to spouses and many gifts to charity, are exempt from federal estate tax. One caveat: If you're married and the total combined estate belonging to you and your spouse amounts to over $600,000, you will want to consider tax planning if each spouse plans to leave most of his or her property to the other, especially if both spouses are elderly. This type of marital estate tax planning, which usually involves establishing a marital life estate trust, is discussed in Chapter 14, Section C and Chapter 16, Section B. In this situation, if you don't do any tax planning, the estate of the surviving spouse will end up with more than $600,000 and therefore end up paying a hefty tax.

The state where you have your home is, generally, the one which determines if you're liable for state death taxes. Many states have no death taxes. (State death tax rules are discussed in Chapter 14, Section E.) Some states do impose stiff death taxes, particularly on property left to non-family members. This can be a particular problem for unmarried couples.

There aren't as many ways to reduce or avoid federal estate taxes as you might think. The major ones include:

- making gifts while you're alive (Chapter 15);

- leaving property to your spouse or charity (Chapter 14);

- creating certain types of trusts, especially marital life estate trusts or a "generation-skipping trust," saving estate taxes on up to $1,000,000 in the middle generation (see Chapter 16, Section B); and

- transferring ownership of life insurance on your life (Chapter 12, Section F).

G. Choosing Someone to Supervise Your Estate

HOWEVER YOU CHOOSE to transfer your property, you need to name someone who will be responsible for supervising your estate after you die and seeing to it that your expressed desires are carried out. This person is your "executor," if named in a will, or your "successor trustee," if named in a living trust. Since many people use both a living trust and a will, they name the same person in each capacity.

Most people know who they want to be their executor or successor trustee—their spouse or mate. Others select a best friend or close family relation. If there's no obvious person who comes to mind, work through your possible selections, using common sense to decide who would be the wisest choice. Do remember that human concerns are usually more important than technical "expertise." Of course, the person you name must agree to do the job, but the most vital criterion here is trust. Competence and expertise can be purchased, but at the most personal level, trust and honesty cannot.

Some conservative estate planners recommend that you select a "corporate fiduciary" such as a bank, or even a "team of professional experts," to handle your affairs after you die. I strongly recommend against this in most instances. Your personal representative is your link to the future, the one who's in charge of distributing your property after your death. You want someone human, with genuine concern, not an impersonal institution that charges fees for every small act. If your most trusted friend is your banker, name him as executor, but not the bank itself.

H. Providing for Care and Support of Minor Children

IF YOU HAVE MINOR CHILDREN, you'll want to plan ahead for what will happen if you and the other parent (if there is one) die before your children become legal adults—18 years old in most states. These issues are discussed in detail in Chapter 6. Here I only alert you to the most basic ones.

First, who do you want to name as the "personal guardian" for your children—the adult who will be responsible for raising them if both parents die, or the other parent can't or won't accept responsibility for them? While your nomination isn't automatically legally binding, courts normally confirm as the legal guardian the person named by the parent if the other parent isn't available.

Next, how much property do you want to leave for your minor children, and who will supervise it? Finally, there are different legal methods you can use to leave property to your minor children, including establishing a children's trust, which allows you to delay the age your child gets his or her inheritance outright until an age you establish. This is important because many parents worry that age 18 (the age children are normally entitled to obtain outright property left to them) is far too young for the responsibility of handling money and property. The living trust forms discussed in Chapter 9 and set out in the Appendix contain simple children's trusts allowing parents to leave their children property in a trust that ends only when each child becomes the age the parents have chosen.

I. Providing Ready Cash

ANOTHER IMPORTANT GOAL of estate planning is to provide ready cash (also called "liquidity") to pay debts, taxes and for your family, and sometimes also for other inheritors of your estate. Particularly if you are your family's main provider, your survivors will immediately need cash for living expenses. Cash will also be needed for the "costs of dying"—hospitalization and funeral and burial expenses, and to pay other debts and taxes which are due promptly.

If most of your property is to be transferred by will, your family won't get it while probate drags on. Limited amounts for family necessities can normally be obtained by petitioning the probate court, but it's wiser to plan to have sources of money available that don't require going to court and paying attorneys' fees.

If most of your property will be transferred outside of probate, there is usually less reason to worry about arranging for ready cash, since property in a living trust or owned in joint tenancy can often be transferred to inheritors in a few days. However, if most of your assets aren't "liquid"—cannot easily be converted to money—you may still need to provide a source of ready cash. For example, if your worth is in real estate and shares of a private corporation which can't readily be sold, your family might have trouble obtaining cash for daily expenses.

A life insurance policy payable to a survivor or survivors is one traditional means of providing ready cash, but it's by no means the only method available. For example, money held in a joint bank account can often be released immediately, or in a few days, if you plan it properly.[3] Also, most banks offer informal trust accounts (often called "pay-on-death" accounts) which can be used to promptly provide the cash in the account to named beneficiaries free of probate. An advantage of this type of

---

[3]If your state has an inheritance tax (see Chapter 14, Section E), it is wise to check with your bank to learn if joint accounts are "frozen" upon the death of one of the account holders, and if so, how to get the account released. In most states, even if accounts are frozen by state tax authorities, it's only for a short period.

account is that the person named as an account beneficiary can not take any money from the account before the depositor dies. (See Chapter 11.)

J.   Planning for Possible Incapacity

THOROUGH ESTATE PLANNING includes considering what happens if you become incapacitated and are unable to make medical or financial decisions for yourself. There's a simple legal document you can use to appoint whoever you want to have authority to act for you if you become incapacitated. It's called a "Durable Power of Attorney," and preparing one should be part of every estate plan (see Chapter 18).

K.   Funeral and Burial Plans

AS PART OF your estate plan, you may want to decide on, and arrange for, a funeral and burial plan.

There are a number of possible choices, including:

- services offered by commercial funeral homes;
- services offered through no-profit funeral societies;
- cremation; and
- donation of body parts to organ banks for medical transplants.

L.   Do You Need Professional Help?

BY THE TIME you're finished with this book you'll be able to make a sensible evaluation of whether or not you need to hire a lawyer or other expert to help you. Many readers don't need professional help to adequately plan their own estate. This is especially true if the estate is worth $600,000 or less. Others, especially those with larger estates or special needs, such as the responsibility to

provide long-term care for a serious mentally or physically disadvantaged child, will conclude that they need a lawyer or other expert to handle at least some portion of their overall estate plan. In a number of situations, I believe getting formal legal help is essential. These are clearly indicated throughout this book. (Use of lawyers, accountants and other estate planning experts is discussed in Chapter 22).

Even if you do conclude that you need the help of a professional, or decide that you simply feel more comfortable consulting one, you'll be sufficiently informed so you should have a clear general idea of what you want. In addition, you'll be able to evaluate whether the lawyer you talk to is dealing honestly and appropriately with you.[4]

Some members of the legal establishment have tried to frighten the public with horror stories of disasters that befell some benighted person who prepared her own estate plan. A renowned lawyer once remarked sarcastically that anyone who can take out his own appendix can write his own will. This analogy is false. A more accurate one is that if you can understand a standard tax form, doing your own estate planning should present you with no problems, unless yours is an unusual situation.

 This is the symbol you'll see throughout *Plan Your Estate* when I suggest that you consult a lawyer, account or other estate planning expert. It is not likely that most readers will find this necessary, but if you face a more complicated situation, please take seriously my advice that you get expert help.

---

[4]For instance, lawyers have been known to charge hundreds or even thousands of dollars to set up elaborate tax-saving devices for people whose estate is quite likely to be exempt from federal taxation.

PART II

Groundwork

CHAPTERS 3-6

State Property Ownership Laws

CHAPTER 3

State Property Ownership Laws

BEFORE YOU CAN SENSIBLY PLAN your estate, you need to inventory the property you own and estimate how much it is worth. You'll do this in the next chapter. Before you do, however, you need to know the basic rules governing property ownership to be sure you don't include any property in your estate plan that you don't actually own, or overlook property you do own.

What you own is determined by the laws of the state where you live, with one important exception: if you own real estate in another state, the laws of that other state govern its ownership. Property ownership rules are very similar from one state to the next, with this major exception: eight states (mostly in the west) follow a community property ownership system which is substantially different from that of the other 41 states and Washington D.C. (Remember, this book does not cover estate planning for residents of Louisiana.)

Fortunately, many readers, married or single, will find state property ownership laws raise no problems for them. If, as you read Section A of this chapter, you learn that it's clear what you own, you can skip the rest and move on to Chapter 4, "Inventorying Your Property." But if your situation isn't clear, be sure you understand how state property laws affect you before you go ahead.

A. How Marital Status Affects Property Ownership

THE RULES FOR PROPERTY OWNERSHIP vary depending on whether you are single or married.

1. Unmarried People

If you're single and own all your property outright, and don't share ownership with anyone else, your property ownership situation is definitely simple. You should have no estate planning problem with any state ownership law. By "outright," I mean that you don't own property with anyone else, as would be the case, for example, if you

owned property with a friend in "joint tenancy" or a partnership. For these purposes, the fact that an institution has a mortgage on your home or a claim to title to your car for a loan isn't shared ownership, because you're entirely free to give that home or car (subject to the debt, of course) to whomever you choose.

If you do own any property in shared ownership—such as property in joint tenancy,[1] tenancy in common,[2] partnership or a small, closely-held corporation in which there are other owners—you'll need to understand how this shared ownership affects ownership rights to the property and your power to give away your share. Joint tenancy and tenancy in common are discussed in greater detail in Chapter 10; partnership and small business corporate ownership are discussed in Chapter 20.

---

[1]Joint tenancy is a form of property ownership by two or more persons where surviving owners automatically inherit the share of a dead owner.

[2]Tenancy in common is another form of shared ownership; the surviving owners of tenancy-in-common property don't automatically inherit the share of the deceased owner. Each owner is free to give her share—but only her share—by will or living trust to whomever she chooses.

Unmarried Couples

Unless an unmarried couple agrees to share ownership of specified property, each member of the couple owns only his or her own property. Individual or separate ownership must be in writing to be effective. An oral agreement is effective if it can be proved, but that can often be difficult. Obviously, it is always best for unmarried couples to put any property-sharing agreement in writing.

If you're part of an unmarried couple where each person has kept all property separate (a written agreement to do this, listing the property of each person, is a good idea here as well), each of you is free to give your property to whomever you wish. However, if property ownership is shared, either under the terms of a written contract or in a tenancy in common or partnership, you're only free to dispose of your share. Property in joint tenancy goes to the survivor automatically.

For more information on property ownership problems of unmarried couples and sample property-sharing agreements, see either *The Living Together Kit*, a detailed guide designed to help unmarried couples minimize their entanglements with the law, by Ihara & Warner (Nolo Press) or *The Legal Guide for Lesbian and Gay Couples*, Clifford & Curry (Nolo Press).

2. Married People

PROPERTY OWNERSHIP SITUATIONS are often more complex for married people[3] than for singles. This is primarily because spouses often own property together. In the eight community property states, spouses typically share ownership of most property, even if only one spouse's name is on the title slip or deed. [See Sections A(3) and B of this chapter for a list of these states and an explanation of community property.] In these states, each spouse can leave his or her share as desired.

In the other 41 "common law" states and the District of Columbia, the spouse whose name appears in the ownership document is the owner of that property.

---

[3]You are "married" if you are separated or getting a divorce, but haven't received a final decree.

However, unlike the legal situation in the community property states, each spouse has a legal right to inherit a portion of the other's property at death, even if the deceased spouse has left it all to someone else. (See Section C for a list of states and an explanation of common law property rules.)

If you and your spouse plan to leave all, or the lion's share, of your property to each other, it's not of much practical importance to understand who legally owns each item of property. After all, as long as the survivor will get all, or even most, of the property, it's not important how it's labeled. However, if you plan to make substantial gifts of property to someone other than your spouse (especially if your spouse might prefer that you didn't), it's essential that you understand both who owns the property and whether there are any rules in your state which give your spouse the right to a portion of it at your death. Otherwise, your decision to give property to someone other than your spouse may occasion a nasty conflict after your death.

To understand how marital property laws affect your situation, you need to know:

- The property ownership laws of the state where you have your home. The legalese term for where you permanently live is "domicile." You can only have one domicile. The state of your domicile governs your marital property—except real estate in another state or country. If you have homes in two or more states, it can be important which you choose as your legal domicile, both for property ownership and state inheritance tax purposes. Given a choice, it's usually best to opt for a no or low tax state. (See Chapter 14, Section E for information on state tax rates.)

 If you own two or more homes in the U.S. or live both in the U.S. and abroad, see a lawyer to discuss how this affects your estate planning, to determine which state's or county's laws govern your marital property and what, if anything, you can do to change this if you so desire.

- The property ownership laws of any state or country where you own real estate. The marital ownership laws applicable to real estate are the laws of the state or country where the real estate is located, no matter where you live.

Divorce Means a New Estate Plan: If you get divorced, you should always re-examine your estate plan and bring it up to date. One obvious reason for this is that, in some states, divorce doesn't automatically revoke your will as to gifts made to your former spouse. Even in the majority of states, where a divorce invalidates an earlier will as far as the divorced spouse is concerned, you still need to designate who you now want to get that property. Also, divorce doesn't revoke a living trust, even if an ex-spouse benefits from it. The moral is simple: If you get divorced, be sure you revise your estate plan to keep it current.

3. Community Property and Common Law States

As I've mentioned, states can be broadly divided into two types for the purpose of deciding what marital property is in your estate when you die:

- Community property states, and

- Common law property states.

Community Property	Common Law
Arizona	All other states
California	(except Louisiana)
Idaho	and the District
Nevada	of Columbia
New Mexico	
Texas	
Washington	
Wisconsin[4]	

[4] Although the terminology is different, Wisconsin has adopted a marital property law which works much like those found in community property states.

- If you live or own real estate in a community property state, you should read Section B of this chapter.

- If you live or own real estate in a common law state, you should read Section C.

- If you have moved, while married, from a community property state to a common law state, or vice versa, also read Section D.

The discussions in these three sections present the basic rules that apply to marital property in your state. It's impossible, short of a ten-volume treatise, to cover every complexity and nuance of marital property law for every state. If you have a question that isn't answered in these pages, you'll need to research it yourself or see a lawyer.

Varying State Property Ownership Laws By Contract

If you don't like the way your state's law defines how you and your spouse share ownership of property, both spouses can often agree to share (or not share) ownership as they desire. To accomplish this, you need a valid contract between you and your spouse. For example, in most states you can agree to hold all property acquired during a marriage separately or to jointly own property owned by one spouse prior to marriage. A written agreement made before a marriage, where the couple set out the terms by which their property, before and after marriage, shall be owned, is called a "prenuptial contract." Valid agreements can also be made after a couple is married.

 If you have a marital property contract and are in doubt as to how its provisions affect your rights to give that property away at death, or, if you want to explore preparing this kind of contract after marriage, see an attorney.

B. Marital Property in Community Property States

THE BASIC RULE of community property law is simple: During a marriage, all property earned or acquired by either spouse is owned in equal half shares by each spouse—except for property received as "separate property" by one of them through gift or inheritance. This community property concept derives from the ancient marriage laws of some European peoples, including the Visagoths, which passed to Spain and then to many Western states through Spanish explorers and settlers. For estate planning purposes, there are no restrictions on how each spouse can give away his or her half of their community property. Neither is required to give it to the surviving spouse, although, of course, many spouses do.

In community property states, "separate property" is property owned entirely by one person. A married person residing in a community property state can own separate property. Property owned by one spouse before a marriage remains separate property even after the marriage, as long as it's kept separate. Also, property given to one spouse or left to one spouse at someone's death is his or her separate property.

Community Property and Common Sense

For many couples in long-term marriages, characterizing their property is relatively easy: it's all community property. Any property owned by either spouse before marriage is either long gone or totally mixed with community property, and neither spouse has inherited or been given any substantial amount of separate property during the marriage, or if they have, it has long since been merged into the community pot. Still, even if you believe this to be your situation, read the next few pages to be sure.

1. What Is Community Property?

Unless the husband and wife agree to something different, the following is community property:

- All income received by either spouse from employment or by other means (except by gift or inheritance to one spouse) during the marriage;[5]

- All property acquired with community property income during the marriage;

- All separate property that is transformed into community property under state law. This transformation can occur in several ways, including when one spouse makes a gift of separate property to both of them. Generally, this must be done with a written document.

Ned Terrlin owned a home for five years before he married Sally. He then signed a new deed for the house, listing the new owners as "Ned and Sally Terrlin, as community property." Thus, Ned has given one-half ownership of the house to Sally.

Community property can also be transformed into separate property by gifts between spouses. The rules for how to do this differ somewhat from state to state. The trend is to require that this sort of gift be made in writing, and it must be in writing if real estate is given.

---

[5]This generally only refers to the period when the couple is living together as husband and wife. From the time spouses permanently separate, most community property states consider newly-acquired income and property as the separate property of the spouse receiving it.

Another common example of transformation of separate property is when it gets so mixed together with community property that it's no longer possible to tell the difference between the two; lawyers call this "commingling."

When she was married, Felicity had a bank account with $10,000 in it, her separate property. During her marriage, now in its 27th year, she continued this account, depositing money she or her husband earned and making frequent withdrawals. She no longer has a separate property interest in any money in the account. The original $10,000 has long since been "commingled" with community property funds.

Each Spouse Can Keep Income as Separate Property

All community property states except Washington allow spouses to treat income earned after marriage as separate property if they sign a written agreement to do so and then actually keep their income separate (as in separate bank accounts). *California Marriage and Divorce Law,* Warner, Ihara and Elias (Nolo Press) contains instructions for how to do this in California.

2. What Is Separate Property?

The following property qualifies as separate property:

- all property owned by either spouse prior to marriage;
- all property received by one spouse after marriage by gift or inheritance; and
- all property earned or accumulated by one spouse after permanent separation.

As mentioned, separate property keeps its separate property legal status only so long as it is not:

- hopelessly mixed (commingled) with community property, or

- transferred to joint ownership by its separate property owner, in writing.

Note on Income From Separate Property: Community property states have different rules for classifying certain types of income derived from separate property:[6]

California, Arizona, Nevada, New Mexico and Washington: Any income from separate property during a marriage is also separate property.

Texas and Idaho: Income from separate property during a marriage is community property.

3. Pensions

Generally, private pensions (and pensions from the military) are considered community property—at least the proportion of them attributable to earnings during the marriage. However, certain major federal pension programs, including Social Security and Railroad Retirement, aren't community property because federal law classifies them as the separate property of the employee.

4. Distinguishing Community and Separate Property

Most married couples have little difficulty determining what's community property and what is each one's separate property. However, these issues can get complicated. Divorce courts churn out a continual stream of decisions on the fine points of community versus separate property. Here are a couple of potential problem areas in estate planning.

Appreciated Property: In most community property states, when the separate property of one spouse goes up in value, this appreciation is also separate property. However, sometimes one spouse owns separate property before a marriage, but both spouses contribute to the cost

---

[6]Wisconsin's statutes on this point are confusing; if this point matters to you, see a Wisconsin lawyer.

of maintaining or improving that property during the marriage. The result can be that the property is part community, part separate. If the property substantially appreciates in value over the years, it can be difficult to determine what percentage of the current value of the property is separate property and what is community property.

> *The most common example is a house originally owned by one spouse. Then for a length of time, say 10 or 30 years, both spouses pay, from community funds, the costs of maintaining the house (mortgage, insurance, upkeep). Assuming the value of the house grows during the marriage, the couple can determine what portion of the present value is community property by agreeing in writing on any division they decide is fair.*

Businesses: A family-owned business can pose difficult ownership questions, especially if it was owned by one spouse in whole or part before marriage and grew later. As with home ownership, the basic problem is to figure out whether the increased value is community or separate property. Again, a married couple can agree on any division they want to. One sensible approach is if both spouses work in the business, then the increase in value which the business undergoes during that period is community property. However, if only the spouse who originally owned the business as separate property works in it, resolving ownership can be more difficult. If it's likely the business would have grown in value anyway, the increase could more reasonably be regarded as separate property.

Monetary Recovery for Personal Injuries: As a general matter, personal injury awards or settlements are the separate property of the spouse receiving them, but not always. In some community property states, this money is treated one way (community property) while the injured spouse is living and another way (separate property) upon his death. Also, the determination as to whether it's separate or community property can vary when the injury is caused by the other spouse. In short, there's no easy way to characterize this type of property.

5. Resolving Conflicts Over Property Ownership

Remember, it's not crucial to define which spouse owns what property if the spouses plan to leave all or most of their property to each other, or in a way the other approves of. However, if you and your spouse discover any conflict over your property ownership that will significantly affect your estate planning (e.g., you want to leave property to your brother and your spouse doesn't), we highly recommend that you talk it out. It's best, of course, to discuss and resolve any uncertainties between yourselves. But it's far better to get professional help—from a mediator, lawyer, or even a therapist—than to allow confusion to remain unresolved. After death, it may well be a disaster if agreement hasn't been reached, because then other inheritors may dispute the way property is given. After resolving any problems, both spouses should sign a written "Marital Property Agreement" setting forth the determinations.

6. Additional Resources

Good sources of information if you're interested in pursuing this subject further are *Community Property Law in the United States,* by W. S. McClanahan (Bancroft-Whitney) and the *Family Law Dictionary,* Leonard and Elias (Nolo Press). Californians will particularly benefit by reading the very thorough *California Marriage and Divorce Law,* by Warner, Ihara and Elias (Nolo Press).

C. Marital Property in Common Law States

IN COMMON LAW STATES, there's no rule that property acquired during a marriage is owned by both spouses. Common law principles are derived from English law, where in feudal times the husband owned all marital property and a wife had few legal property ownership rights and couldn't even will property. Even today, the spouse who earns money or acquires property owns it,

unless, of course, he or she transfers it into joint
ownership.

Common Law Marital Property States

Alabama	Kentucky	North Dakota
Alaska	Maine	Ohio
Arkansas	Maryland	Oklahoma
Colorado	Massachusetts	Oregon
Connecticut	Michigan	Pennsylvania
Delaware	Minnesota	South Carolina
District of Columbia	Mississippi	South Dakota
Florida	Missouri	Tennessee
Georgia	Montana	Utah
Hawaii	Nebraska	Vermont
Illinois	New Hampshire	Virginia
Indiana	New Jersey	West Virginia
Iowa	New York	Wyoming
Kansas	North Carolina	

In common law states, the property you own for estate
planning purposes, whether you are married or not, consists of:

- everything held separately in your name if it has a title
  slip, deed or other legal ownership docum   and

- everything you have purchased with your
  income.

If you earn or inherit money to buy a ho   se, and tide
is taken in both your name and your spous   , you both
own it. If your spouse earns the money to   it, but you
take title in your name alone, you own it.   If title is   in
your spouse's name, he owns it.

---

[7]Despite the general rule stated here, c   mon law states won't allow a blatant injusti
common law states employ some type of "E
Law" for divorces. Under these laws, the c
distribute marital property fairly (often eq
the ownership documents say. While thos
bution laws haven't been applied to the c
property upon death, in extremely unjust
court could use its "equity powers" (its in
justice). Still, this isn't certain, and wou
it's far wiser to resolve all marital prope
amicably while both spouses are alive.

1. Family Protection in Common Law States

To protect one spouse from being disinherited and
winding up with nothing after the other's death, common
law states give a surviving spouse legal rights to a certain
portion—usually one-third to one-half—of the other's
estate. Suppose, for example, one spouse owns the family
house, the car and bank accounts in his name alone and
attempts to leave it all to a stranger (or, worse, a lover).
Can the stranger kick the surviving spouse out of the
house, empty the bank accounts, and so on? Of course,
this rarely happens, but just in case, all common law
property states have some way of protecting the surviving
spouse from being completely, or even substantially,
disinherited.[8] While many of these protective laws are
similar, they do differ in detail.

2. The Spouse's Minimum Share

These methods of protecting families were developed by
English courts. Hundreds of years ago, confronted with
the problem of a few people disinheriting their spouses,
they developed the fancy concepts called "dower" and
curtesy. "Dower" often   the rights of a surviving wife;
curtesy   received by a surviving husband.
When the United   settled, most states adopted
these concepts. To this day, all common law states still
retain some version of dower and curtesy (although many
dropped the old terminology). No such legal pro-
           are needed in community property states because

                            some common law states and some community property
                            states, additional, relatively minor protection devices
           family allowances   and "probate homesteads." These
                      from state to state   oo much detail to discuss here.
                            Generally,   these devices attempt to assure that your
                            ot totally left out in the cold imme-
                                      y allowing them temporary pro-
                                      : to remain in the family home for a
                                      ost typically while an estate is being
                                      they shouldn't prove unwelcome to any

each spouse owns one-half of all property acquired from the earnings of the other during the marriage.

In most common law property states, a spouse is entitled to one-third of the property left by the other. In a few, it's one-half. The exact amount of the spouse's minimum share often depends on whether the couple has minor children. In some states, the surviving spouse must be left only a certain percentage of the estate transferred by will. In other states, property transferred by means other than a will, such as a living trust, is included when calculating whether a spouse has received his or her minimum legal share of property. (This is called the "augmented estate" and is discussed in subsection 3 below.)

What happens if a person leaves nothing to a spouse or leaves less than the spouse is entitled to under state law? In most states, the surviving spouse has a choice of either taking what the will or other transfer document provides or rejecting the gift and instead taking the minimum share allowed by state law. Taking the share permitted by law is called "taking against the will."

> Leonard's will gives $50,000 to his second wife, June, and leaves the rest of his property, totaling $400,000, to his two children from his first marriage. June can take the $50,000 or elect to take against the will and receive her statutory share of Leonard's estate. Depending on the state, this will normally be from one-third to one-half of Leonard's total estate.

When a spouse decides to take against the will, the property which is taken must come out of one or more of the gifts given to others by the will (or in many states, other transfer documents, such as a living trust, as well). In other words, somebody else is going to get less. In the above example, the children will receive much less than Leonard intended. So, if you don't provide your spouse with at least the statutory share under your state's laws, your gifts to others may be seriously reduced.

 Put bluntly, if you don't wish to leave your spouse at least one-half of your property, and you haven't gotten your spouse's unforced and written consent to your plan, your estate may be heading for a legal mess and you should see a lawyer.

3. The Augmented Estate

As mentioned above, in many common law states, all property of a deceased spouse, not just the property left by will, is considered in determining whether a spouse has been left the statutory share. This is called the "augmented estate." It means that in determining whether a surviving spouse has been adequately provided for, courts in most common law property states look to see the value of the property the spouse has received outside of probate, as well as counting the value of the property that passes through probate. This makes sense because many people devise ways to pass their property to others outside of wills—with living trusts or joint tenancy, for example—to avoid probate fees.

> Alice leaves her husband, Mike, $10,000 and her three daughters $90,000 each in her will. However, Alice also leaves real estate worth $500,000 to Mike by a living trust. The total Mike receives from this augmented estate, $510,000, is more than one-half of Alice's total property, so he has nothing to gain by insisting on his right to make a claim against her estate.

4. Family Law Protection in Common Law States

Note: Most state laws are quite complicated; not all details are included here.

I. Surviving spouse receives right to enjoy one-third of deceased spouse's real property for life

Connecticut	South Carolina
District of Columbia	Vermont
Kentucky	Virginia
Ohio	West Virginia
Rhode Island	

II. Surviving spouse receives percentage of estate

a) Fixed percentage

Alabama	1/3 of augmented estate
Alaska	1/3 of augmented estate
Colorado	1/2 of augmented estate
Florida	30% of estate
Hawaii	1/3 of estate
Indiana	1/3 of estate
Iowa	1/3 of estate
Maine	1/3 of augmented estate
Montana	1/3 of augmented estate
Nebraska	1/3 of augmented estate
New Jersey	1/3 of augmented estate
North Dakota	1/3 of augmented estate
Oregon	1/4 of estate
Pennsylvania	1/3 of estate
South Dakota	1/3 of augmented estate
Tennessee	1/3 of estate
Utah	1/3 of estate

b) Percentage varies if there are children (usually one-half if no children, one-third if children)

Illinois	New York
Maryland	North Carolina
Massachusetts	Ohio
Michigan	Oklahoma
Mississippi	Wyoming
Missouri	Minnesota
New Hampshire	Kansas

c) Other

Delaware
($20,000 or one-third of estate, whichever is less)

III. One year's support

Georgia

D. Moving from State to State

A WILL OR LIVING TRUST validly made in one state is, broadly speaking, valid in all. However, problems can develop when married people move from a community property state to a common law property state or vice versa. This is because the property each spouse owns (and is therefore free to give away) may change. If spouses move from one state to another which follows the same property ownership system (e.g., New York to Florida, or California to Texas), there is no need to worry about property ownership.

Remember, technical property ownership rules are not a worry if spouses plan to leave all (or the lion's share) of their property to each other, or in a way the other spouse approves of.

1. Moving From a Common Law State to a Community Property State

What happens when a husband and wife acquire property in a non-community property state but then move to a community property state? California and Idaho (com munity property states) treat the earlier acquired property as if it had been acquired in a community property state. The legal jargon for this type of property is "quasi-community property." The other community property states don't recognize the quasi-community property concept and instead go by the rules of the state where the property was acquired.[9] Thus, if you and your spouse moved from any non-community property state into California or Idaho, all of your property is treated according to community property rules (see Section C above). However, if you moved into any of the other community property states from a common law state, you'll need to assess your property according to the rules of the state where the property was acquired.

2. Moving From a Community Property State to a Common Law Property State

When spouses move from a community property state to a common law property state, each generally retains one-half interest in the property accumulated during marriage while the couple lived in the community property state. However, the courts have not been entirely consistent in dealing with the problem in situations where the property is in one spouse's name.

 If you have moved from a community property state to a common law state, and you and your spouse have any disagreement or confusion as to who owns what, check with a lawyer.

---

[9]Arizona and Texas recognize quasi-community property for divorce purposes, but not for will or living trust purposes.

Inventorying Your Property

CHAPTER 4

Inventorying Your Property

NOW THAT YOU HAVE AN OVERVIEW of how state property ownership laws affect your estate, it's time to actually tally up what you own. Preparing a written inventory is almost always necessary for thorough estate planning, so you can:

- remind yourself of what you own;
- estimate the value of your estate for tax purposes;
- determine what you owe;
- list any shared ownership of property;
- make a handy list to refer to when making gifts to beneficiaries; and
- get organized in case you later consult an estate planning advisor.

Nevertheless, you may decide you don't need or want to complete a property inventory now. For example, if you have no substantial debts and plan to leave your moderate-sized estate to one person, or divide it equally between two or three, you may not need to prepare a detailed list of all of your property. Similarly, if you plan to make only one, or few, individual gifts and leave all the rest of your property to one person, you may sensibly decide that making a detailed list isn't necessary.

Jane wants to leave all of her woodworking tools and equipment to her friend Alice, her car to her friend Amy, and everything else she owns (which includes stocks, jewelry, money market funds and personal household possessions) to her longtime companion Mary. She knows her estate is worth no more than $400,000, that the state she lives in has no death taxes, and that she has no significant debts. Jane decides there's no need for her to list separately each item of property she's giving to Mary.

Tax Warning: Even if you plan to give all your property to one person, if your estate is large, you should inventory it to estimate whether you are likely to be subject to federal or state death taxes. If you haven't already made any substantial gifts, $600,000 is exempt from federal taxes. (See Chapter 14.) If your net worth (or, if you are married, that of you and your spouse) is more than $600,000, you should consider estate tax planning. (See Chapter 14, Section C and Chapter 16, Section B.)

A. Instructions for the Property Inventory Worksheet

SECTION B OF THIS CHAPTER contains a worksheet to help you inventory your property. As you'll see, the worksheet is designed to permit recording a wide range of property. Take a look at it now to get acquainted with its structure.

It's up to you to decide how extensive and detailed your own listings need to be. The following detailed description of the chart and the suggestions for completing it are for those who want or need to be thorough.

In Section I of the chart, you list your assets—all the property you own. There are four kinds of information to give for each item of property:

- Column 1—A description of the item of property;
- Column 2—If ownership of that item is shared, enter the type of shared ownership;
- Column 3—The percentage of any shared ownership property you own;
- Column 4—The value of each item of property (or share of shared property) you own.

Now let's take a minute to review the information that should be entered in each column.

COLUMN 1

Identify and Describe Your Property

Here you identify your property with sufficient detail so there can be no question what it includes. This worksheet divides your property into four groups:

(A) **Liquid assets,** which include cash, savings, checking and money market accounts, CDs and precious metals;

Examples:

- Certificate of Deposit No. 10235, Lighthouse Savings and Loan Association, Ventura, CA;

- My savings account at Bay Bank (if you have only one savings account);

- My savings account number 18-17411 at Bay Bank (if you have more than one savings account);

(B) **Other personal property,** which includes all your property except liquid assets, business interests, and real estate. This catch-all category includes stocks, mutual fund shares, other securities, bonds, automobiles, jewelry, furs, art works, antiques, tools, life insurance, collectibles, etc.;

Examples:

- 50 shares Transpacific Corporation common stock;

- $10,000 El Dorado Drainage and Water System, District of Alameda, 1980 bond series C, 10.5% due June 1, 2000;

- 1986 Ford automobile, License # 123456;

- All my fishing equipment;

- Gold earrings with the small rubies in them purchased from Charles Shreve and Co. in 1971;

- Daumier print captioned "Les beaux jours de la vie";

- Life insurance policy #A106004, You-Bet-Your-Life Insurance Co.;

- All my carpenter's tools, including my power saws.

Note on Miscellaneous Personal Property: If you are like most people, you have all sorts of minor personal possessions you don't want to bother itemizing. To deal with these, you can group a number of items in one category ("all my tools," "all my dolls," or baseball cards, or records, or machines and equipment or household furniture). Of course, some items without large monetary value have great emotional worth to you and your family: a photo album, an old music box, a treasured chair. These can be separately listed as you desire.

As another alternative, you can conclude your list with one catch-all item such as "all my other personal possessions and furnishings."

(C) **Business personal property,** including all business interests, except any real estate used in that business.[1]

Examples:

- My shares of stock in the Mo-To Corporation;

- My business d/b/a Ace Stationery Store, Boca Raton, Florida;

- My partnership interest in JTL Partnership Enterprises, Main Office, Detroit, Michigan;

- All my copyrights and rights to royalties in the book with the following titles, currently published by Acme Press, Berkeley, California [titles listed];

(D) **Real estate,** including all business real estate, and all home, coop/condominiums, mobile homes attached to land,[2] undeveloped or agricultural land, etc.

To describe real estate, simply list its address or location. This is normally the street address, or condominium number. If there's no post office address, as is the

---

[1]Chapter 20 discusses major estate planning concerns of small business owners, whether sole proprietors or shared owners like partners or shareholders in small closely-held corporations.

[2] The rules on when an attached mobile home becomes "real estate" vary. If this matters to you, see a lawyer.

case if you own undeveloped land, simply describe the real property in normal language (my 120 acres in Lincoln County near the town of Douglas). You don't need to use the legal description from the deed.

Examples:

- 126 Oceanview Terrace, Mendocino, California;

- My lot on Keeler Street, Middletown, Ohio;

- 1001 Main Street (the Fullerton Hardware Building), Moose, New York.

Real property often contains items which are properly classified as personal property. For instance, farms are often sold with tools and animals. If you intend to keep both together (as a gift) generally indicate what this "together" consists of. It's best to specify the large ticket items (tractor, cattle) and refer generally to the rest of the items as "personal property."

Examples:

- My 240-acre truck farm in Whitman County with all tools, animals, machines and other personal property located there;

- My fishing cabin on the Wild River in Maine with all the fishing gear, furniture, tools and other personal property which are found there;

- My ownership of the mobile home located at E-Z motor camp, and all possessions and furnishings contained in it.

COLUMN 2
Type of Shared Ownership

You only need to be concerned with Column 2 if you own one or more items of property listed in Column 1 with someone else. If you are single and own all your property outright, you can skip to the instructions for Column 4. (Column 3 also deals with shared ownership.) However, if you are married or have entered into personal or business shared ownership transactions, please read what

follows carefully. Obviously, before you can sensibly plan your estate, you must clearly understand what you own and therefore have the power to give away.

Most people know whether they own property with others. However, occasionally, you may have to do some investigating to be sure about the ownership status of a particular piece of property, For example, you may have to locate the deed to your house or stock certificates to clarify whether you own property in joint tenancy. You can check real property records at the county real property recorder's office. Never guess. If you're not sure how you own an item of property, take the time to find out.

If you live in a community property state, are married, and you and your spouse own both separate and community property, you may have some difficulty determining exactly what you and your spouse own. (I discuss this in Chapter 3, Section B.) Be sure you resolve who owns what. For example, if you are unsure whether a $10,000 bank account is community property or your separate property, bear in mind that you and your spouse can resolve the confusion by jointly characterizing this account in either ownership category. When you do this, however, put your conclusion in writing, signed by both of you.

Below I give you a summary of the different legal forms possible for shared ownership. Some of these concepts may be new to you. If you don't understand a form of shared ownership now, you needn't worry. They are explained in more depth in the chapters identified. Simply note on your chart that the property is held in some form of shared ownership. Once you understand precisely what the legal form for that shared ownership is, and how it works, come back and complete the "Shared Ownership" category for that property.

Here are the symbols you can use to record the major types of shared ownership on the chart:

- **Joint Tenancy (J.T.):** Property held with a written ownership document identifying the owners either as Joint Tenants or Joint Tenants With Right of Survivorship.[3] Under these forms of ownership, each joint tenant owns an equal share of the property with all other joint tenants. The share of the first tenant to die must go to any survivors, even if there's a will or living trust to the contrary. Joint tenancy is discussed in detail in Chapter 10.

Joint tenancy must be created by a written document. If you own property using the phrase "Joint Tenancy With Right of Survivorship," there is no question what type of shared ownership you have. But what about writings that are less clear? For example, suppose your real estate deed says "Tenancy in Common With Right of Survivorship"? In Oregon, this has the same practical effect as joint tenancy; in other states, it might not. The point is—don't guess. If you're not clear what kind of legal animal you've got, check it out.

Similarly, suppose owners are listed simply with an "and" or an "or"? For example, two people own real estate with the title listed as held by "Smith and Jones." Two others own real estate with title listed as "Smith or Jones." Are either of these joint tenancy? The answer is that it's not clear. Probably, under most states' laws, neither constitute joint tenancy, but if you hold ownership with another person with "and" or "or" in the title document, you need to know the specific rules of your state. If you don't know them, you have to do your own research, either by asking someone who does know (a reliable title company) or by checking out your state's laws yourself. (See Chapter 22, Section A for legal research tips.)

- **Tenancy by the Entirety (T.E.):** This form of ownership is recognized in a minority of states. Its use is limited to a married couple. Basically, it amounts to joint tenancy with right of survivorship between spouses. It must be created in writing. (Discussed in Chapter 10.)

---

[3]In a few states, the words "with right of survivorship" added to "joint tenancy" or "joint tenants" are necessary to create a joint tenancy. In most, the words "joint tenants" or "joint tenancy" do the job. In Oregon, the term "tenancy in common with right of survivorship" means the same thing.

- **Community Property (C.P.):** In the eight community property states (listed in Chapter 3), property spouses earn or acquire during a marriage is community property, with a few exceptions, including property which is given to or inherited by one spouse which is the separate property of that spouse. You can leave your one-half share of community property to whomever you want to have it. The other one-half of the community property already belongs to your spouse and you have no power to give it away in your will (discussed in Chapter 3, Section B).

- **Separate Property:** In the eight community property states, all property that isn't community property is held separately. This usually includes property acquired prior to marriage or after permanent separation or divorce and property given or left to one spouse.

In the other 41 common law property states (listed in Chapter 3), separate property means all property that each spouse owns individually, including all property where one spouse's name appears on the title document, unless there is a written contract to the contrary.

- **Tenancy in Common (T.C.):** Any property held in shared ownership which isn't in another type of ownership—in other words, all shared property not owned in joint tenancy, tenancy by the entirety or community property, partnership or corporation. This includes a great deal of the property spouses own together in the 41 common law property states. You can own any percentage of tenancy in common property (.005%, 95%, etc.)—owners' shares don't have to be equal, as they must be for joint tenancy property. If the ownership deed doesn't specify the type of shared ownership, it's probably tenancy in common, although, as mentioned above, in some states the words "or" or "and" may indicate joint tenancy ownership. You can leave your portion of property held as tenants in common as you choose, unless restricted by a contract. There is no automatic right of survivorship between tenants in common as there is for joint tenancy. (Tenancy in common is discussed in Chapter 10.)

Natalie and Jeremy Engels live in North Carolina, a common law property state. They hold several securities, their house and a piece of land with both their names on the title documents, but no joint tenancy designation. They are presumed to own the property as tenants in common, with each owning a 50% share.

- **Partnership (P.):** Property owned by business partners, regulated by a partnership agreement (including shares in a limited partnership). (Partnership property is discussed in Chapter 20.)

- **Corporate Shares (C.S.):** Shares of a small or closely-held corporation, if your freedom to transfer them is regulated by corporate by-laws or a shareholders' agreement. (Corporate shares are discussed in Chapter 20.)

COLUMN 3

Percentage of Shared Property You Own

In this column, list the percentage of each item of shared property you own. People who own property as tenants in common, or in partnership, should be particularly careful —you can own any percentage of property in this owner-ship form, from 1% to 99%. Especially with a partnership,

you must check your partnership agreement to be sure. With a tenancy in common, co-owners normally own equal shares (33.3% if you are one of three), unless there is a written agreement to the contrary.

Don't overlook the fact that you and your spouse may own partnership interests, corporate shares, or own interest in a tenancy in common as community property if you live in one of the eight community property states. Working all this out can be tricky, but it's necessary—not only to determine what is in your estate, but also for purposes of establishing the net value of your property for tax purposes.

If the property (or a share of property) is owned as community property or a tenancy by the entirety, ownership is shared equally. So, if there are two joint tenants, the ownership is 50-50; if there are three, each owns one-third, and so on.

Johnny Ryan is a one-third partner in Electric City, an electric product distributor in Washington state. Johnny has been married to Maeve for 40 years, and used money he earned while married to her to help start the business. Since Washington is a community property state, Johnny and Maeve each own one-half of his one-third partnership interest, and both can leave their share as they choose.

Assume Johnny and Maeve live in Maine, a common law property state. Johnny owns his one-third partnership share outright. However, as discussed in Chapter 3, under Maine law, Maeve is entitled to inherit a significant part of it (or other valuable property) if Johnny doesn't adequately provide for her.

 While deciding what property you own is a fairly easy task for many people, this is obviously not always the case. If you have trouble or questions, see a lawyer. You don't want to die leaving a property ownership mess.

COLUMN 4

Net Value of Your Ownership

In this column, you estimate the "net value" of each item listed. Net value means your equity in your share of the property—the market value of your share, less your share of any debts on that share, such as a mortgage on a house or the loan amount due on a car. Doing this not only helps you determine the value of the property you have to dispose of, but also tells you whether you're likely to be subject to death taxes, especially federal estate taxes (See Chapter 14, Section A.)

Obviously, listing net values for your property means making estimates. That's fine; there's no need to burden yourself with seeking absolutely precise figures. After all, your death taxes, if any, will be based on the net value of your property when you die, not its current worth. For example, if you think the net worth of your house, after you subtract the mortgage, is about $200,000, your car $5,000, and your stamp collection would fetch $2,000 if you put an ad in a philatelist's journal, use those numbers. (If these items are owned as community property with your spouse or in joint tenancy with someone, divide each of these amounts in half to determine the value of your share.) Only with more complex types of property, in particular business interests, are you likely to need expert help.

Clay owns a house with a market value of $250,000 as a tenant in common with his sister Ava; each owns half. Clay computes the net value of his share by first subtracting the amount of mortgages, deeds of trust, liens and past due taxes from the market value to arrive at the total equity in the property. There's a $100,000 mortgage and a $10,000 lien against the property. The total equity, then, is $250,000 minus $110,000, or $140,000. The net worth of Clay's half of the property is $70,000.

Stacey is sole owner of the Maltese Falcon Restaurant, a successful business she has run for 20 years. She has only a vague notion of its market value since she has never been interested in selling it. To competently plan her estate, she needs a reasonable estimate of the worth of the business. This can be difficult to make, since the market value of her restaurant includes the intangible of "good will." Stacey talks to an accountant or tax lawyer to help her arrive at a sensible estimate of the worth of the restaurant.

The last step in Section I of the Property Worksheet is to add up the net value of all your assets, and list that sum in Part E.

In Section II, Liabilities, list any liabilities—debts—you haven't already taken into account in Section I. For example, in Section II, list any significant personal debts—the $10,000 loan from a friend or $5,000 unsecured advance on a line of credit. Also list all other liabilities, such as tax liens or court judgments. Remember, you have taken account of mortgages on your real estate and payments owed on your motor vehicle in Section I, so don't list them here.

Add up your estimate of all your liabilities and list that sum in Part D of Section II.

Finally, in Section III of the chart, estimate your current net worth. To get this figure, simply subtract your total liabilities listed in Section II from your total assets listed in Section I.

B. Your Property Worksheet

REMEMBER, THIS CHART is purely for your convenience. It can be as messy or as neat as you care to make it. Also, pencil is recommended (unless you're the type who does the *NY Times* crossword puzzle in ink).

PROPERTY WORKSHEET

I. Assets

Column 1
Description of Your Property

A. Liquid Assets

1. cash (dividends, etc.)

2. savings accounts

3. checking accounts

Column 2 Type of Shared Ownership	Column 3 Percentage You Own	Column 4 Net Value of Your Ownership

Column 1 Description of Your Property	Column 2 Type of Shared Ownership	Column 3 Percentage You Own	Column 4 Net Value of Your Ownership
4. money market accounts			
5. certificates of deposit			
6. mutual funds			

Column 1
Description of Your Property

Column 2
Type of
Shared
Ownership

Column 3
Percentage
You
Own

Column 4
Net Value
of Your
Ownership

B. Other Personal Property
(all your property except liquid assets, business interests and real estate houses, buildings, apartments, etc.)

1. listed (private corporation) stocks and bonds

2. unlisted stocks and bonds

3. government bonds

Column 1 Description of Your Property	Column 2 Type of Shared Ownership	Column 3 Percentage You Own	Column 4 Net Value of Your Ownership
4. automobiles and other vehicles, including planes, boats and recreational vehicles			
5. precious metals			
6. household goods			
7. clothing			

Column 1 Description of Your Property	Column 2 Type of Shared Ownership	Column 3 Percentage You Own	Column 4 Net Value of Your Ownership
8. jewelry and furs			
9. art works, collectibles and antiques			
10. tools and equipment			
11. valuable livestock/animals			

Column 1 Description of Your Property	Column 2 Type of Shared Ownership	Column 3 Percentage You Own	Column 4 Net Value of Your Ownership
12. money owed you (personal loans, etc.)			
13. vested interest in profit sharing plan, stock options, etc.			
14. limited partnerships			
15. vested interest in retirement plans, IRAs, death benefits, annuities			

Column 1 Description of Your Property	Column 2 Type of Shared Ownership	Column 3 Percentage You Own	Column 4 Net Value of Your Ownership
16. life insurance			
17. miscellaneous (any personal property not listed above)			

C. Business Personal Property

1. patents, copyrights, trademarks and royalties

Column 1 Description of Your Property	Column 2 Type of Shared Ownership	Column 3 Percentage You Own	Column 4 Net Value of Your Ownership
2. business ownerships (partnerships, sole proprietorships, corporations, etc.; list separately and use a separate sheet of paper if you need to elaborate)			
name and type of business	___	___	___
	___	___	___
	___	___	___
name and type of business	___	___	___
	___	___	___
	___	___	___
3. miscellaneous receivables (mortgages, deeds of trust, or promissory notes held by you; any rents due from income property owned by you; and payments due for professional or personal services or property sold by you that are not fully paid by the purchaser)			
	___	___	___
	___	___	___
	___	___	___

D. Real Estate

Column 1 Description of Your Property	Column 2 Type of Shared Ownership	Column 3 Percentage You Own	Column 4 Net Value of Your Ownership
address			
address			
address			

Column 1 Description of Your Property	Column 2 Type of Shared Ownership	Column 3 Percentage You Own	Column 4 Net Value of Your Ownership
address			
address			

E. TOTAL NET VALUE OF ALL YOUR ASSETS　　$ _____

II. Liabilities (what you owe)

Many of your liabilities will already have been accounted for because you listed the net value of your property in Part I of this chart. For example, to determine the net value of your interest in real estate, you deducted the amount of all mortgages and encumbrances on that real estate. Similarly the value of a small business is the value after business debts and other obligations are subtracted. For this reason, the only liabilities you need list here are those not previously covered. Don't bother with the small stuff (such as the phone bill, or what you owe on your credit card this month), which changes frequently. Just list all major liabilities not previously accounted for, so you can get a clearer picture of your net worth.

Column 1 To Whom Debt Is Owed	Column 2 Net Amount of Debt You Owe

A. Personal Property Debts

1. personal loans (banks, major credit cards, etc.)

2. other personal debts

Column 1	Column 2
To Whom Debt Is Owed	Net Amount of Debt You Owe

B. Taxes (include only taxes past and currently due. Do not include taxes due in the future or estimated estate taxes)

_____

_____

_____

_____

_____

C. Any other liabilities (legal judgments, accrued child support, etc.)

D. TOTAL LIABILITIES [excluding those liabilities already deducted in Section I]

III. NET WORTH   [Total Net Value of All Your Assets (Section I. E.) minus Total Liabilities (Section II. D.)]

Beneficiaries—Deciding Who Gets Your Property

Beneficiaries— Deciding Who Gets Your Property

A. Introduction

DECIDING WHAT PERSONS or organizations you want to receive your property—who will be your beneficiaries—is obviously a principal focus of your estate plan. This chapter raises some important concerns about choosing them and provides a chart where you can list each beneficiary and what property you give him or her.

Even if you believe your beneficiary decisions are cut-and-dried and you are tempted to skip directly to the chart, please read at least Sections A through G before recording your decisions on it. These sections cover important information you should take into account even if you have already decided who will inherit your property. For instance, you may initially think you don't want to bother naming alternate beneficiaries for gifts, to cover the contingency that a primary beneficiary will die before you do. But to make that decision sensibly, you should understand how alternate beneficiaries are used in estate planning, and why people often conclude that it's wise to name them.

After these sections come some optional ones, H through M, which you need read only if the subjects concern you.

Finally, in Section O of this chapter, you'll make a tentative list of your beneficiaries. It's prudent to regard this list as preliminary. You may wish to revise it as you gain more knowledge by reading this book.

B. Some Thoughts About Gift Giving

BEFORE PLUNGING INTO technical concerns about how to name beneficiaries, let's pull back for a moment and consider what gifts are. In our predominantly commercial culture, whether they are made during life or at death, gifts are special. They are free, voluntary transfers of property, made without any requirement of receiving anything in return. The essence of gift giving is generos-

ity, an open spirit. To say one makes gifts "with strings attached" is not a compliment.

Much of the real pleasure of estate planning comes from contemplating the positive effects your gifts will have on those you love. Sometimes, these pleasures are focused—you know how much Judith has always liked your mahogany table, and now she'll get to enjoy it. Others are more general—your son will be able to buy a house with the money you leave him, which will relieve some of the financial pressure that has been weighing on him.

I mention the spirit of giving here because I've learned that it's easy to get entrapped by the details of estate planning and lose sight of your real purpose. So, if technicalities and legalities start to get to you, take a break and remember who you're giving your property to, and why. And if you wish to explore in profound depth what gift giving is, or can mean, read Lewis Hyde's *The Gift* (Vintage/Random House), a brilliant exploration of how gifts work in many cultures.

C. How to Name Beneficiaries

YOU WILL ENTER the names of your beneficiaries and the property they will receive in your formal estate planning documents—your living trust, will, or both. How do you do this? I raise this question now, well before you record your choices, because I've learned that many people worry that some precise, technical language must be used in formal documents to identify their beneficiaries and describe their property, or their gifts won't be legally binding. Fortunately, this isn't true. There are no laws requiring gifts in wills or living trusts to be made in legalese; none that penalize you for stating your intentions in simple plain English. So, when you actually specify your beneficiaries, and what they are to receive, in a formal legal document, you can safely use the same names you have recorded in the Beneficiary Chart. You need only state your desires clearly.

"I give my son, Fred Rubellem, all my stock in International Merger Corporation."

"I give Elizabeth Danford my interest in the house and real estate at 44 White Deer Road, Ardmore, Pennsylvania."

Note on Gifts to a Married Person: When you make a gift to someone who's married, the gift is that person's individual or separate property if you make the gift only in his or her name. For example, suppose your will says: "I give my antique clock to Mary Kestor," or "I give $10,000 to Mary Kestor." This means Mary would be entitled to keep the entire gift if she divorces (assuming the gift had been kept separate, not commingled with other shared marital property so that the gift could no longer be separately identified). If you want to emphasize this intent, you can say: "I give my antique clock [or $10,000] to Mary Kestor, as her separate property."

By contrast, if you wish to make a gift to a married couple, simply make it in both their names. For example: "I give my silver bowl to Edna and Fred Whitman." Again, you can provide clarity by expressly stating your intent: "I give my silver bowl to Edna and Fred Whitman, as husband and wife."

Pets as Beneficiaries

As a part of their estate planning, many pet owners arrange informally for a friend or relative to care for a pet. But what if the person you asked to provide care can't afford to keep an animal, or isn't available when needed? Usually, more formal arrangements are better. These issues are discussed in detail in *Dog Law* (Nolo Press). Here are a few things to keep in mind:

- You can use your will or living trust to leave your pets, and perhaps some money for expenses, to someone you trust to look out for them. Don't make the gift of an animal a surprise—make sure the people you've chosen are really willing and able to care for pets.

- Consider making arrangements for veterinary care for your animals. You can leave money to a vet (working out an amount with the vet in advance) or write out a life care contract with a vet. A vet may agree to pro-

vide lifetime care in exchange for a lump sum, or to use the money as a credit toward services.

- You can't leave money or property to a pet, either through a will or a trust. The law says animals are property, and one piece of property simply can't own another piece. If you do name a pet as a beneficiary in your will, whatever property you tried to leave it will go, instead, to the residuary beneficiary (the person who gets everything not left to the beneficiaries named in the will). If there's no residuary beneficiary, the property will be distributed according to state law. The legal problem is the same if you make a pet the beneficiary of a trust, because a beneficiary is considered the owner of certain interests in the trust property. Courts sometimes allow trust property to be used for an animal's benefit, but don't force the trustee to follow the terms of the trust.

D. Naming Alternate Beneficiaries

NAMING ALTERNATE BENEFICIARIES to receive property if your first choices die before you do can be sensible for a number of reasons. Perhaps you've made some gifts to older people, or ones in poor health. Or you're just a cautious person. Or you don't want the bother of redoing your estate planning if the unlikely occurs and a beneficiary does die before you. Or you're concerned that you might not have time, before your own death, to revise your estate plan after a beneficiary dies.

On the other hand, some people decide they don't want the morbid bother of worrying about their beneficiaries dying before they do. They make their gifts—as many people do—to those considerably younger than they are. If a beneficiary dies before them, they'll normally be able to modify their will, trust or other document to name a new beneficiary.

The beneficiary chart in this chapter provides space for listing alternate beneficiaries for each gift you make.

"I give my Mercury Outboard Motor to Mike McGowan, or, if he fails to survive me, I give that property to his son, Pat McGowan."

It's up to you to decide whether you want to complete these spaces.

Whatever you decide about alternate beneficiaries, you should definitely name a "residuary" beneficiary in your will and living trust who will receive all property you don't specifically give to other beneficiaries. The residuary beneficiary you name in your living trust (assuming you use one) receives all property in the trust which is not given to other named beneficiaries. Similarly, the residuary beneficiary you name in your will receives all property covered by the will (i.e., excluding property in your living trust) not given to other named beneficiaries.

Edward places his house in a living trust and leaves it to Lila. He leaves his car to Alan through his will. Edward does not name alternate beneficiaries and names Monica as the residuary beneficiary of both his living trust and his will. Both Lila and Alan die before Edward does. When Edward dies, Monica inherits both the house and the car.

As this example shows, if you don't name an alternate beneficiary for a specific gift, and that beneficiary dies before you, your residuary beneficiary receives that gift. Thus, you always have one back-up plan for all your gifts. It's a good idea to name an alternate residuary beneficiary as well in both your living trust and will, so you have another back-up in case your choice for residuary beneficiary in either document dies before you. Both the living trust and will forms in this book provide space for you to name a residuary beneficiary and a alternate residuary beneficiary.

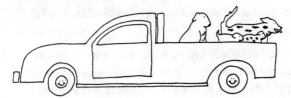

E. Making Shared Gifts

SOMETIMES PEOPLE WANT to make shared gifts, particularly to their children.

Virginia wants to leave her house to her three children—Alan, Patsy and Phillip. That seems simple enough, doesn't it? But even in this simple situation, important questions should be asked and resolved. First, what percentage of ownership does each child receive? Second, who controls what happens to the house? Third, what happens if one child dies before Virginia does?

One obvious way to avoid these problems is to not make shared gifts. At the very least, you should consider any shared gifts carefully, and see if they are really necessary. Often there are other ways to accomplish the same purpose. But in some situations, particularly gifts from parents to children, shared gifts are desired. If you decide on a shared gift, read the rest of this section, on the three major concerns that must be resolved when making a shared gift.

1. Percentage of Ownership

The key here is to say in the estate planning document how ownership is to be divided between the beneficiaries. If you don't specify shares of ownership, it's generally presumed that you intended equal shares, but this rule isn't ironclad, and there's no good reason to be silent on this matter. If you want a gift shared equally, say so.

"I give my house at 1123 Elm St., Centerville to my three children, Anne, Rob and Tony, in equal shares."

"I give my stock accounts equally to my daughters Maxine and Simone."

You can divide ownership any way you want. For example:

"I give my house and real estate known as 111 11th St.,
Muncy, Iowa, as follows:

40% to my spouse Mary,
25% to my son Jon,
25% to my daughter Mildred, and
10% to my brother Tim."

2. Control

Control is the most basic problem with shared ownership. Suppose the people to whom you've given a gift disagree about how to use it. In most states, any co-owner can force a partition and sale, with the net proceeds divided by percentage of ownership. To return to the example of the house given to the three children, suppose two want to sell it, and one doesn't. The house would be sold even if one child wanted to live in it. Do you want to allow this?

You can put provisions governing the issue of what the shared owners can do in the estate planning document (will or living trust) where the gift is made. For instance, "The house cannot be sold unless all three of my children agree on it." But often other problems follow. If two want to sell the house, but one doesn't, who manages the house? Does it have to be rented at market value? Can the child who wants to keep the house live in it? If so, must that child pay the others rent? And what happens if one child dies? The difficulties of dealing with these types of complications is why it seems more sensible not to specify details of long-term control of property you leave your beneficiaries. Let them work it out. If you don't think they can, a shared gift probably isn't appropriate.

 If you are apprehensive about a particular shared gift, discuss it with the proposed beneficiaries. If there's genuine agreement between them, potential problems are less likely to become real ones. If you conclude there's genuinely no risk of conflict, you can simply make the shared gift without any conditions or directions, leaving it up to the beneficiaries to resolve any problems. Otherwise, review this problem with an attorney.

3. Naming Alternate Beneficiaries for a Shared Gift

Things can become quite complicated if you decide to move on to the next level of contingencies—naming alternate beneficiaries for a shared gift. To return once more to the house Virginia wants to give to her children Alan, Patsy and Phillip, what are Virginia's options if she wants to name alternate beneficiaries?

- She can specify that a deceased beneficiary's share is to be divided between the remaining beneficiaries;

- She can provide that a deceased beneficiary's share is to be divided equally between that beneficiary's own children, and, if there are none, then between the remaining beneficiaries;

- She can name another alternate beneficiary (a friend or other relative) to receive the interest of any child who dies before she does;

- She can name three separate alternate beneficiaries, one for each child (for example, each of their spouses).

As you can see, juggling these types of remote contingencies is tricky. Often the wisest solution is to provide that the other beneficiaries of a shared gift divide the interest of a deceased beneficiary.

Mollie Rainey, Allen Rainey and Barbara Rainey Smithson shall be given my house at [address]. If any of them fail to survive me, his or her interest in my house shall be divided equally between the survivors.

The directions for completing a living trust (see Chapter 9, Section D) show you how to name the surviving beneficiaries of a shared gift as alternate beneficiaries for a deceased beneficiary's share.

 If you decide you want another type of alternate beneficiary provision for a shared gift, you'll need to see a lawyer. Before you do this, consider carefully whether you really want to worry about this kind of complexity in naming alternate beneficiaries. After all, once you get started worrying about remote possibilities, where do you stop? For example, you could also worry about what happens if all your alternate beneficiaries, as well as the beneficiaries themselves, die before you, and so on. In other words, there's no total security, no matter how many alternate beneficiaries you name.

Also, as discussed below, you will name a residuary beneficiary in your living trust and will to take any property left by that document but not validly given to a specific beneficiary. So, you always have a back-up if one—or all—beneficiaries of a shared gift dies before you and you didn't name alternate beneficiaries.

F. Naming Your Residuary Beneficiary

AS I'VE SAID EARLIER, in your estate planning documents where you make your gifts—your living trust and will—you should always name a residuary beneficiary— one or more people or organizations to receive all property not specifically given to named beneficiaries. You should also name an alternate residuary beneficiary who will inherit if the residuary beneficiary dies before you.

Your residuary beneficiary under your living trust or will receives:

- All property transferred by that document which wasn't specifically given to an identified beneficiary or alternate beneficiary. This includes both property you didn't mention and property you acquire after the document was prepared (for example, if you win a lottery a week before your death);
- All property given to specific beneficiaries (including alternate beneficiaries) who die before you do.

Peter leaves his interest in a house to his brother Joe, or if Joe dies before him, to Joe's wife Carolyn. He names his sister Julie as residuary beneficiary. Joe and Carolyn are killed in a car crash three days before Peter dies. Peter's interest in the house goes to Julie.

It's possible, and fairly common, to make the residuary beneficiary your main beneficiary. Thus, some people's estate plan consists of a few relatively small gifts to specifically-named beneficiaries, with the bulk of their estate given to the residuary beneficiary.

Jennifer wants to give her two Tiffany lamps to her friend Linda, $5,000 to her niece Martha, and her car to her sister Joan. She wants to leave all the rest of her extensive estate—houses, stocks, limited partnerships—to her long-time living together partner Paul. She can simply name Paul as her residuary beneficiary, after listing her three specific gifts. She names Joan as her alternate residuary beneficiary.

It's also common to split the bulk of your estate among children by making a few specific gifts and then naming the children as residuary beneficiaries. For example, after leaving some cash gifts and heirlooms to other friends and charities, you could name as residuary beneficiaries "my children, Henry and Aaron, in equal shares."

G. Explanations and Commentary Accompanying Gifts

IF YOU WISH, you can provide a brief commentary when making a gift. You can do this whether you use a will or a living trust as as your primary estate planning document.

"I give my business associate, Mildred Parker, who worked honestly and competently with me over the years, and cheerfully put up with my occasional depressions, $40,000.

"I give my best friend, Hank Pike, who I enjoyed fishing with for so many years, all property listed on Schedule A, including my cabin on Lake Serene and boat and outboard motor."

There are times, particularly in family situations, when an explanation of the reasons for your gifts can help avoid hurt feelings or family fights. For example:

"I give my house at 465 Merchant St., Miami, Florida, and all stocks and bonds I own as follows:
  40% to my son Theodore Stein
  40% to my daughter Sandra Stein Smith
  20% to my son Howard Stein

"I love all my children deeply and equally. I give 20% to Howard because he received substantial family funds to go through medical school, so it's fair that my other two children receive more of my property now.

"I give Matt Jackson my bank account #41-6621-9403 at First Maple Bank. I love all my children deeply and equally. I give more of my property to Matt than my other children because Matt is physically disadvantaged, and is likely to need special care and attendants throughout his life."

Another approach is to write a letter stating your view and feelings, and attach the letter to your will or living trust. Your letter isn't part of a legal document, and has no legal effect. It is prudent for you to state in your letter that you understand this, to eliminate any possibility someone could claim you intended the letter to somehow modify the terms of your legal documents. If you have a lot to say, a letter can be a better way to do it than trying to include it all in your will or living trust.

Short of libel,[1] the scope of your remarks is limited only by your imagination. Some writers have expressed, at length and in their own chosen words, their love for a mate, children and friend. By contrast, Benjamin Franklin's will left his son William, who was sympathetic to England during our Revolution, only some land in Nova Scotia, and stated, "The fact he acted against me in the late war, which is of public notoriety, will account for my leaving him no more of an estate that he endeavored to deprive me of." And the German poet Heinrich Heine wrote a will leaving his property to his wife on the condition that she remarry, so that "there will be at least one man to regret my death." William Shakespeare cryptically left his wife his "second best bed," a bequest that has intrigued scholars for centuries.

H. Disinheritance

YOU CAN DISINHERIT most people simply by not making them beneficiaries of your estate. If you don't give someone any of your property, he has no rights to it, period. However, as discussed in the next section, special rules control disinheriting your own children or the children of a deceased child. When it comes to your spouse, no disinheritance is possible except in the eight community property states (see Section 2 below).

1. Disinheriting a Child

The rules for disinheriting a minor child are discussed in detail in Chapter 6, Section E. Here I briefly summarize them. In all states, you have the power to disinherit any or all of your children. However, unlike the situation with

---

[1]If you write something so malicious (and false) that you libel someone in a will or living trust, your estate can be liable for damages.

other people, merely leaving a child (or child of a deceased child) out of your estate plan doesn't "disinherit" that child. Those children who aren't mentioned in your estate planning documents (or in some states, who aren't provided for in your will) have a legal right to claim part of your estate.

If you want to disinherit a child (or children of a deceased child), you have two options:

• You can leave them a minimal amount in your will, which, functionally, serves as a disinheritance.

The will forms in this book require you to name all your children (and children of a deceased child) and give each of them $1, in addition to any other property also given them, by will or otherwise. This is to insure you haven't accidentally failed to legally provide for a child—surely an unlikely possibility, but one I can't ignore. Obviously, mentioning a child and leaving him or her only this one dollar, and no more, effectively disinherits that child;

• You can explicitly disinherit a child in your will.

If you want to explicitly state that a child is totally disinherited, you must do so by a specific clause in your will. You can also include a statement of why you disinherited that child. If you decide you want this approach, you need an express disinheritance clause. This type of clause is not provided in this book, because the will forms here are for a basic will only. Disinheritance clauses can be found in *Nolo's Simple Will Book*.

2. Disinheriting a Spouse

If you live in one of the 41 common law states or the District of Columbia, you cannot disinherit your spouse. As discussed in Chapter 3, Section C, these states allow a spouse to claim a significant portion (often one-third) of your estate despite your wishes. By contrast, in community property states, a spouse has no legal rights to receive any of the other spouse's property. Or, put another way, each spouse has the right to leave their one-half of the

community property and all his or her separate property as he or she sees fit.

Note on Unmarried Couples: Unmarried couples living together have no rights to inherit any of each other's property. In short, each person can leave his or her property to anyone he or she wants to. However, if the couple has created a valid contract which gives the other the specific right to inherit specific property, that contract will normally be enforced.

3. General Disinheritance Clauses

You may have heard that some lawyers recommend leaving $1 to each of your relatives. This is not legally necessary. There's generally no need to mention a relative or anyone else but your children and your spouse in your will. No one else has a legal right to any of your property. If, however, you think a relative might try to contest your estate plan, you might give that relative $1, to make it absolutely clear you did consider that person and wanted to give no more.

4. No Contest Clauses

A "no contest clause" in a will or living trust is a device used to discourage beneficiaries of your estate plan from suing to void the plan and claiming they are entitled to more than you left them. Under a no contest clause, a beneficiary who unsuccessfully challenges a will or living trust forfeits all his inheritance under that document.

> *Pip leaves his daughter Estelle $10,000 in his will, and includes a no contest clause in that document. If Estelle challenges the will and loses, she does not receive the $10,000.*

No contest clauses can be sensible if there's a risk a beneficiary might challenge your estate plan. On the other hand, many people do not like to include a no contest clause in their estate planning documents because it seems to imply a suspicion of their beneficiaries that they don't actually feel. For this reason, the forms in this book don't include no contest clauses. The more complex assemble-it-yourself will clauses found in *Nolo's Simple Will Book* do allow you to include a no contest clause in your will.

 If you think you want a no contest clause because you sense the possibility of a court fight, see a lawyer to discuss how you can best arrange to handle that risk.

I. Forgiving Debts

WHEN YOU'RE THINKING ABOUT who you want to leave gifts to, consider the people who owe you money. One type of gift you can make is to forgive a debt—release the person who owes you the debt from responsibility to pay it. Any debt, written or oral, can be forgiven.

> *Bud loaned his daughter Kathlyn and son-in-law Tyrone $30,000 for a down payment on a house, but doesn't want them to be obligated to his estate for this loan after he dies. So, in his will, Bud includes a provision stating "I forgive the loan of $30,000 I made to Kathlyn and Tyrone Benson in 1988."*

If you're married and forgiving a debt, be sure you have full power to do so. If the debt was incurred while you were married, you may only have the right to forgive half the debt (especially in community property states) unless your spouse agrees in writing to allow you to forgive his or her share of the debt as well.

J. Minors as Beneficiaries

ESTATE PLANNING ISSUES concerning children are discussed in Chapter 6. Here I summarize the options available if you're considering naming a minor child as a beneficiary.

Minor children can only own a small amount of property outright in their own names. This amount, which is set by state law, varies from $2,500 to $5,000. Any property belonging to a minor above this amount must be legally supervised by an adult. Anyone contemplating making a substantial gift to a minor must therefore determine which adult will be responsible for the gift. This decision can be made in different ways:

- If the gift is intended for your own children, it can be made outright to the other parent, who will use the gift for the children's benefit. If spouses—or even ex-spouses—get along, this is usually the simplest way to handle the matter.

- The gift can be expressly given to the child, and you name an adult to be responsible for supervising that gift. That adult can be one of the child's parents, but doesn't always have to be. When you have decided who the adult supervisor will be, your next step is to decide what legal form you want to use to make the gift. Options include establishing a simple children's trust, making a gift under the terms of the Uniform Transfers to Minors Act (if it has been enacted in your state) or naming a property guardian in your will.

K. Restrictions and Controls on Gifts

THERE ARE TWO possible types of restrictions on gifts:

- restrictions you, the giver, want to impose; and
- restrictions imposed by law.

1. Personal Restrictions on Gifts

Most people simply leave their property outright to family, friends or charities. However, occasionally a person wants to make a gift with restrictions on it. Unfortunately, if done thoughtfully, this is usually a complex task.

Cindy wants to give her house to her sister, Karen, to use during her lifetime, then leave it in trust equally to Karen's two young children, until each becomes 40. Then each will receive half the property, unless only one is married and has children, in which case she shall receive 75% ownership of the house. Some of the issues that must be resolved are: Can Cindy's sister sell the house? Who is the trustee of the trust? Can he sell the house if he thinks that's a good business decision?

Imposing restrictions and controls on a gift is sometimes called "dead-hand control." The obvious risk of dead-hand control is that circumstances can change, so you must try to anticipate what is likely—or even possible—to occur in the future, and provide for it. This, at best, is complex work, and helps to enrich estate planning lawyers.

 Aside from simple children's trusts, this book doesn't show you how to impose controls or restrictions on gifts, because the possibilities and contingencies involved are likely to be far too complex to handle here. So, If you want to make one of the following kinds of gifts, you'll need to consult a lawyer:

- Any situation where you want to impose conditions on a gift. If conditions are imposed, someone must be responsible for being sure they are fulfilled. While many conditional gifts create far more problems than they solve, if you're determined to go ahead, the best way to do it is to leave the property in a trust to be managed by a trustee. You'll need a lawyer to help you establish the trust.

Don wants to leave money to a nephew, Ed, if he goes to veterinary school, but, if he doesn't, to his niece Polly. This sounds simple, but here are just a few problems inherent in this approach: How soon must Ed go to veterinary school? What happens if he applies in good faith but fails to get in? Who decides if he's really studying? What happens to the money before Ed goes to veterinary school? What happens if Ed goes to veterinary school but drops out after a year and says he'll go back eventually? What happens if he graduates but doesn't become a vet?

- Any gift involving a "life estate" and a life estate trust. As explained in Chapter 16, Section B, in a "life estate," the life beneficiary normally has the right to use property and receive income from it for life, but does not have outright ownership of it. When the life beneficiary dies, all her ownership interest in the property terminates, and the property goes to the final beneficiaries, as named by the person who originally created the life estate.

- Any gift left in trust for tax savings or property management purposes. Some people need this kind of trust. For example, you want to set up a trust for your eight grandchildren, but only for their college or graduate school expenses. Or you want to provide care for a disadvantaged relative. Unfortunately, the issues which must be resolved and the forms necessary to establish these specialized types of trusts are too complex to explain in this basic self-help book. (See Chapter 16, Section C for a further discussion.)

2. Legal Restrictions on Gifts

With very few limits, you can give your property however you choose. While the few existing legal restrictions rarely apply, let's be cautious and review them briefly.

First, there are a few legal restrictions all states impose on gift-giving:

- Some felons, and anyone who unlawfully caused the death of the person who wrote the will (or living trust) cannot inherit under it;

- You cannot attempt to encourage or restrain some types of conduct of your beneficiaries. For example, you cannot make a gift contingent on the recipient's marriage, divorce, or change of religion;

- You cannot validly leave money for an illegal purpose—for example, to establish the Institute for the Encouragement of Using Psychedelics.

Second, a few states (the District of Columbia, Florida, Georgia, Idaho, Mississippi, Montana and Ohio) have laws restricting your ability to make gifts to charities. These laws, holdovers from centuries past, were enacted primarily to discourage churches and other charitable organizations from using unfair means, such as promising elderly people a place in heaven, to fill their own coffers at the expense of a surviving family.

 If you're in one of these states, you should check with an attorney if you desire to leave a large part of your estate (certainly more than half) to a charitable institution, especially if you believe your spouse or children will object or that you may not have too long to live. However if you're leaving a relatively small percentage of your estate to a charity, you needn't worry about these restrictions no matter where you live.

L. Establishing a Survivorship Period

A SURVIVORSHIP PERIOD requires that a beneficiary must survive you by a specified time period to inherit. The purpose of a survivorship period is to insure that if the beneficiary dies soon after you do, the property will go to the alternate you've selected, rather than to the people the beneficiary chose to inherit his property.

> *"I give my 1955 T-Bird to my best friend, Francois de Croissy, or, if he fails to survive me by 45 days, to my cousin Jacques Marquette."*

Survivorship periods can make sense if most of your property is transferred by will and will be subject to probate. Since probate takes months anyway, you're not tying up your property by imposing a short survivorship period on it.

However, this book emphasizes the value of using a living trust instead of a will to transfer most property. Generally, establishing a survivorship period isn't desirable for property transferred by living trust. As explained in Chapter 9, a principal advantage of a living trust is that property can be transferred quickly to the new owners. A survivorship period means ownership of property is in legal limbo until the period expires. It's wisest to allow your living trust beneficiaries to receive their property as quickly as possible, rather than protect against the remote contingency that a beneficiary may die shortly after you do. For this reason, the living trust forms in this book do not contain survivorship clauses. Neither do the wills, because they are designed primarily to function as back-up wills, to catch any property not included in your living trust, and to make small gifts, and therefore may not be subject to probate.

 If you decide, despite this advice, to impose a survivorship period on gifts you make by living trust or back-up will, you'll need to see a lawyer.

M. Simultaneous Death

MANY COUPLES, MARRIED OR NOT, who give their property to each other wonder what would happen to the property if they were to die at the same time. (Another common concern of couples—what happens to their children if the parents die simultaneously—is discussed in Chapter 6.) If property is left to a spouse by will or trust without a specific clause to cover simultaneous death, and you and your spouse die simultaneously, your property could pass to your spouse or mate, and then immediately to your spouse's inheritors. That might not be the result either of you want.

To prevent this, the marital living trust form (Appendix I, Form II) and the will for a member of a couple (Appendix I, Form VII) contain a "simultaneous death" clause, providing that when it's difficult to tell who died first, the property of each spouse or mate is disposed of as if he or she survived the other.

Under their marital living trust, Edith and Charles leave much of their property to each other. However, Charles wants his property to go to his daughter from his first marriage if Edith dies before he does. Edith wants her property to go to her sister if Charles dies before she does. Edith and Charles are killed in a car crash. Under the simultaneous death clause, Charles' property would go to his daughter, and Edith's to her sister.

You may ask, "How, logically, can simultaneous death clauses work? How can I be presumed to have outlived my spouse for my purposes, but then she's presumed to have outlived me for her purposes?" Yes, it is a paradox, but it does work. Under the law, each estate is handled independently of the other. Thus, each provision in the separate estate plans provides the result each would have intended. As Oliver Wendell Holmes put it, "The life of the law has not been logic, it's been experience."

N. Property You Give Away by Will or Trust That You No Longer Own at Your Death

BEFORE YOUR ESTATE CAN PAY your cash gifts, it must pay all your last debts and taxes, including death taxes. After that, if your estate doesn't have enough money available to pay your cash gifts, there's trouble. For example, suppose in your living trust you give your house to your daughter Anne and $30,000 to your cousin Joan. But when you die, the only property in your living trust is the house. Can Joan force Anne to mortgage or sell the house to pay Joan the $30,000? The answer is that Joan might be able to prevail in this type of lawsuit, depending upon how a court interpreted your "intent" in creating the trust. Even if Anne prevailed, she's had the burden of a lawsuit.

If your will or living trust makes more in money gifts than you have ready cash, this necessitates what's called an "abatement" in legalese. An abatement means a reduction of gifts when there isn't enough to go around. Assuming you haven't taken the somewhat unusual step of specifying how to make an abatement if one is necessary, the abatement is made according to state law.

 If you desire more information about how your property will be distributed if an abatement or reduction of gifts is required because your estate comes up short of cash, consult an attorney knowledgeable in such matters.

What does all this mean to you? Simple. Don't give away more cash than you have. If you make cash gifts by a living trust, be sure the trust itself owns liquid assets sufficient to pay those gifts. So, aside from calculating the amount of your cash gifts, you need to estimate what you owe and what your estate will need to pay for death taxes. Revise your estate plan if you ever don't have enough liquid assets to pay cash gifts.

O. The Beneficiary Chart

IN THE FOLLOWING CHART, list your gifts by describing the property and who it's given to.

Note: If you think you'll need more space than this chart provides, simply photocopy the blank chart before you begin filling it out.

Beneficiary Chart

1. Specific Cash Gifts

_____ to _____
Amount   Beneficiary

                            _____
                            Alternate Beneficiary

_____ to _____
Amount   Beneficiary

                            _____
                            Alternate Beneficiary

_____ to _____
Amount   Beneficiary

                            _____
                            Alternate Beneficiary

_____ to _____
Amount   Beneficiary

                            _____
                            Alternate Beneficiary

_____ to _____
Amount   Beneficiary

                            _____
                            Alternate Beneficiary

_____ to _____
Amount   Beneficiary

                            _____
                            Alternate Beneficiary

2. Gifts of Specific Personal Property

_____ to _____
Item   Beneficiary

                                            _____
                                            Alternate Beneficiary

_____ to _____
Item   Beneficiary

                                            _____
                                            Alternate Beneficiary

_____ to _____
Item   Beneficiary

                                            _____
                                            Alternate Beneficiary

_____ to _____
Item   Beneficiary

                                            _____
                                            Alternate Beneficiary

_____ to _____
Item   Beneficiary

                                            _____
                                            Alternate Beneficiary

_____ to _____
Item   Beneficiary

                                            _____
                                            Alternate Beneficiary

3. Debts Forgiven

_____ to _____
Amount Forgiven   Debtor

_____
Date of Loan

_____ to _____
Amount Forgiven   Debtor

_____
Date of Loan

4. Gifts of Real Estate

_____ to _____
Property Address   Beneficiary

_____
Alternate Beneficiary

_____ to _____
Property Address   Beneficiary

_____
Alternate Beneficiary

_____ to _____
Property Address   Beneficiary

_____
Alternate Beneficiary

5. Residuary Beneficiary or Beneficiaries
(to receive the rest of your estate after all specific gifts are made)

_____
Residuary Beneficiary

_____
Alternate Residuary Beneficiary

CHAPTER 6

Children

CHAPTER 6

Children

THE WORD "CHILDREN" can have two meanings. The first is "minors"—those not legal adults. Basically, minors are under age 18. The second meaning is offspring of any age; parents have "children" who are in their 50's. The primary focus of this chapter is on minor children because of the special problems inherent in planning for people who are not adults.

Most parents of minor children are extremely concerned about what will happen to their children if disaster strikes and the parents die unexpectedly. If both parents are raising the children, the major concern is usually simultaneous death of the parents. If only one parent is involved—because the other parent is deceased, has abandoned the child or is unavailable for some other reason—the single parent wants to arrange for someone else to care for and support the child if that parent dies.

Providing for your minor children if you die involves two distinct concerns:

1. Who will raise the children if you can't (be each child's legal personal guardian)?

2. How can you best provide financial support for your children? (What property will be available? Who will handle and supervise it for the children's benefit? And what legal method is best for leaving it to them?)

These concerns are addressed in depth in the first three sections of this chapter.

This chapter does not deal with adult children with nearly as much detail as minor children. In most instances, adult children can be treated just like any other adult beneficiary—you determine what you want to leave them and use your living trust, will or other estate planning device to accomplish this. However, I do focus on two concerns applicable to children of any age:

- rules for disinheriting a child [see Section E(1)];
- rules affecting adopted or out-of-wedlock children [see Section E(2)].

Other problems involving adult children are discussed elsewhere in this book, including:

- Ongoing trusts for a child with mental or physical disadvantages who will need care for life [discussed in Chapter 16, Section C(1)];
- Potential problems of spouses marrying later in life when one or both have children from a former marriage, whose inheritance expectations they want to protect [discussed in Chapter 16, Section C(4)].

A. Custody of Your Minor Child

IF TWO BIOLOGICAL or adoptive parents are willing and able to care for the child, and one dies, the other normally has the legal right to assume sole custody. If the parents are married, or even if they are divorced, as long as both parents are cooperating to raise their children, this rule normally presents no problem. But what happens if both parents die? Or suppose there's only one parent in the picture, and he dies?

If there's no parent available who is competent and willing to do the job, some other adult must become the child's legal manager, unless she's legally emancipated.[1] This adult is called the child's "personal guardian."

A child's personal guardian must be named in a will. You cannot use other estate planning devices, such as a living trust, for this purpose. A person named as a minor's personal guardian in a will doesn't actually become the legal guardian until approved by a court. The judge has the authority to name someone other than the parent's choice if she is convinced it is in the best interests of the child. In short, children are not property, and naming a personal guardian in a will doesn't have the same automatically-binding effect as a provision giving a lamp

---

[1]An "emancipated minor" is a minor who has achieved legal adult status. The rules for emancipation are governed by your state's laws; normal grounds are marriage, military service, or factual independence validated by court order for children who are within a year or two of becoming a legal adult. Emancipation is uncommon. Most importantly, for this book's purposes, you cannot emancipate your child through estate planning.

to a beneficiary. However, if no one contests the right, or competence, of your choice for your child's personal guardian, a court will almost certainly confirm this person. In practice, a court will only reject an unopposed nominee if there are grave and provable reasons, such as alcoholism, a serious criminal background, or record of marital instability. A responsible parent should not, of course, select a guardian with such problems.

Most people with minor children probably know who they want to name as their child's personal guardian. You should always name an alternate personal guardian as well, just in case your first choice is unable or unwilling to serve.

When choosing a guardian and alternate guardian, remember the obvious: You can't draft someone to parent your kids. Be sure any person you plan to name is ready, willing and able to do the job. Also, if two parents are involved, they should agree on who they want to appoint. And it's best not to name a couple as joint managers, even if they will likely function that way. Doing this raises many potential problems, including what happens if the couple splits up.

 If you're determined to appoint joint personal guardians, see a lawyer.

If you're now confident that you can safely name your child's personal guardian and alternate guardian, proceed to Section A(2) and record your choices. However, if you have any doubts or questions, read the material immediately below before making your choice.

1. Complications in Naming a Personal Guardian

For some parents, appointing a personal guardian for their minor child is unfortunately not cut-and-dried. Here are some fairly common problems:

"I don't want my ex-husband, who I believe is mentally unstable, to get custody of our children if I die. Can I choose another guardian?"

"I have legal custody of the kids and I've remarried. My present wife is a much better mother to my daughter than my ex-wife, who never cared for her properly. What can I do to make sure my present wife gets custody if I die?"

There is no definitive answer to this type of question. Assuming a contested case was presented to a court, a judge's decision would very likely turn on both the facts of each situation and the judge's own belief system (prejudices). Here are a few general rules that usually are followed:

- One parent (whether he has custody or not) cannot usually succeed in appointing someone other than the other natural parent to be guardian, unless the second parent has:
  - abandoned the child,[2] or
  - is unfit as a parent.

It's usually quite difficult to prove that a parent is unfit, absent serious problems such as alcohol abuse or mental illness. The fact that you don't like or respect the other parent is never enough, by itself, to deny custody. If you want to name someone other than the other parent as personal guardian for your children, and that person is fully apprised that this may lead to a custody fight, you should write a letter to accompany your will.

"If my husband and I die simultaneously, his mother is sure to try to get custody. Neither my husband nor I want this to happen. How can we be sure that our good friends

---

[2]This normally means not providing for or visiting the child for an extended period. "Abandonment" must be declared in a court proceeding, where a judge finds that a parent has substantially failed to contact or support a child for an extended period of time, usually (depending on state law) at least a year or two. Abandonment can be declared at a guardianship hearing if, after your death, the other parent, who has not visited or supported for an extended period, contests your choice in your will of someone else as guardian.

Betty and Carl, who know the kids well and would make great substitute parents, get custody instead?"

It shouldn't be a serious problem to handle this one. Name either Betty or Carl as personal guardian (not both, for reasons already discussed) in both wills. A judge will normally follow your recommendation. However, it can be wise to attach a letter to your will explaining why you prefer Carl or Betty to a grandparent.

"If I die, I want my sister to raise my kids, but she isn't sensible with money. Can I have my sister take care of the kids and someone else manage the money I leave?"

You can, but there are obvious risks of conflict in having one person have legal authority to raise a child and another to manage money used to support and educate the child.

Explaining Your Choice of Personal Guardian

If you honestly believe the other natural parent is incapable of properly caring for your children or simply won't assume the responsibility, or if you think that a particular relative or friend will try to be appointed personal guardian against the wishes you have expressed in your will, here is how to proceed:

1. Name the person you want to be your child's personal guardian in your will.

2. Explain why you're making your choice in your will or in a separate letter, and attach it to your will. Here's an example of such a letter:

I have nominated my companion, Peter N., to be the guardian of my daughter, Melissa because I know he would be the best guardian for her. For the past six years, Peter has functioned as Melissa's parent, living with me and her, helping to provide and care for her, and loving her. She loves him and regards him as her father. She hardly knows her actual father, Tom D. She has not seen him for four years. He has rarely contributed to her support or taken any interest in her.

Date: January 15, 1989

Nancy J

It is also possible to explain your choice of guardian in your will. In *Nolo's Simple Will Book,* there are thorough step-by-step instructions as to how to do this. The much more basic will forms in this book don't provide space for you to state the reasons you've chosen the personal guardian.

 Discuss the details of your situation with a lawyer who specializes in family law. If there's a disputed custody proceeding after your death, a judge has wide discretion in deciding how much weight, if any, to give to written statements about your child's custody you made before you died. A knowledgeable lawyer can help you prepare your best case.

"I want to appoint different guardians for different children."

This is unusual, but in some families, where all children don't share the same two biological parents, the need does occur. The basic will forms in this book aren't geared to handle this type of problem. However, you can name separate guardians for each of the children in *Nolo's Simple Will Book*.

2. Name One Personal Guardian and Alternate Personal Guardian for Your Minor Children

Okay, enough background. In the spaces below, record your choice for personal guardian and alternate guardian of your minor children. You'll incorporate these decisions in the will you prepare later (Chapter 17, "Wills").

_____

Personal guardian's name

_____

Address

_____

Alternate personal guardian's name

_____

Address

B. Naming an Adult to Manage Your Minor Children's Property

MINOR CHILDREN CANNOT own property outright, free of supervision, beyond a minimal amount—in the $2,500 to $5,000 range, depending on the state. This means there must be an adult legally responsible for supervising and administering all property owned by a child. Therefore, a vital part of your estate plan is arranging for responsible supervision of property of your minor children. This includes both property you leave for your children's benefit and any other substantial amounts of property they may acquire by gift or inheritance, which does not come with an adult supervisor written in. It also includes any substantial amount of income they earn (e.g., your 12-year-old is a genius computer programmer).

1. Providing Money for Support of Your Minor Children

Parents of minor children want to be sure there will be sufficient funds to properly raise their children if they die. Before they resolve who will be their children's property manager, they want to insure they will leave enough property to take care of their kids. For some families, providing these funds poses no problem. However, many families need every nickel for living in the here and now, and don't have the luxury of putting significant amounts aside. This isn't a book about acquiring an estate, but obviously you need to have some property for your children before you concern yourself with who manages property you leave them.

2. Choosing Your Children's Property Manager

Assuming you have property you want to leave for your minor children's benefit, the next question is who will manage it for them? For now, I'll call the adult you choose to supervise your minor children's property if you die your children's "property manager." After you have chosen this person, you must select the legal form you want to use for that property manager to handle the children's property. These choices are discussed in the next section.

Leaving Property to Your Spouse for the Benefit of Your Children

One alternative for parents of minor children is for each to give property outright to the other spouse to be used for their children's benefit. If you do this, you don't need to worry about appointing someone to manage that property—you've already done it by leaving it to your spouse. This approach makes sense if the parents trust each other, but doesn't work well if the other parent is out of the picture or financially imprudent.

Leaving property to the other parent and not to the children directly obviously does not work if both parents die simultaneously. Also, this method won't handle any property the children acquire from some other source. For this reason, it's always wise to name a children's property manager, even if you don't leave your children any property.

When deciding who to name as your children's property manager, here's a sensible rule: Name the same person you choose to have custody of the children (their personal guardian) unless there are compelling reasons to name someone else—for example, you're concerned that the personal guardian doesn't have sufficient economic or practical experience to manage property prudently. You should also name an alternate property manager in case your first choice can't serve. Again, name the same person you designated as the children's alternate personal guardian unless there are strong reasons to choose someone else.

The duties of the property manager are not onerous, normally: the main responsibility is to act honestly and in the best interests of the children. This means using the money you leave to provide for normal living expenses and health and education needs. If you pick someone with integrity and common sense, your children's property will probably be in good hands. If substantial funds are involved, the property manager can pay for help to handle the more technical aspects of financial management. For instance, where large amounts of property are involved, it's routine for a property manager to turn tax and accounting functions over to an accountant.

Obviously, it's important to name a property manager who is sincerely willing to do a job which may, depending on the ages of your children, last for many years. It's also wise to choose someone the other members of your family respect and accept. You want your children to inherit money, not family arguments.

Except as a last resort, don't name a bank or other financial institution to be property manager. Most banks won't manage accounts they consider too small to be worth the bother; as a rough rule, this means accounts worth less than $250,000. And even for larger estates, they charge hefty fees for every little act. In addition, it's my experience that banks are simply too impersonal to properly meet your own children's needs. Far better, I think, to name a human being you trust than a bureaucracy. But if you can't find any adult who's willing and competent to be your children's property manager, it's normally better to name a financial institution than to make no choice at all, which amounts to leaving the matter up to a court. You'll need to check around with different banks and private trust companies to see which ones will accept the job, and seem most likely to do it for reasonable fees.

Selecting Different Property Managers for Different Children: In some unusual situations, you may want to name different property managers for different minor children. This can't be done using the legal forms provided in this book. You can use the more detailed will forms in *Nolo's Simple Will Book* to achieve this goal.

3. Name a Property Manager and Alternate Property Manager for Your Minor Children

It's time now to record, in the space below, your choice for your minor children's property manager and alternate property manager. To be effective, these names must be listed in your will and living trust. But before you can do that, you must decide, in Section C, the legal method you'll use to leave your children property.

_____

Property manager's name

_____

Address

_____

Alternate property manager's name

_____

Address

C. Choosing the Legal Method to Leave Property to Your Minor Children

ONCE YOU HAVE CHOSEN your children's property manager, your next task is to choose which legal method you want to use to leave property to your minor children. Here I list the choices and then discuss them in more detail. And as you'll see, the legal name used to identify your children's property manager will vary, depending on which form you choose.

a. A Children's Trust

You can leave property to your children through a children's trust. In this situation, the children's property manager is called a "trustee" or "successor trustee."

A children's trust can be established either by will, or as part of a living trust. If it is established as part of a living trust, the property placed in the children's trust avoids probate. If a will is used, the property in the children's trust must go through probate before it's turned over to the trust.

Children's Trust Defined

A trust is a legal entity under which a person called a "trustee" has the responsibility of handling money or property for someone else (in this case, your child), called a "beneficiary." A written document creates the trust and sets out the trustee's responsibilities and the beneficiary's rights.

In a children's trust, you designate property to be used for the children's benefit. You appoint a trustee who manages the property for the benefit of your child after you die. And you specify at what age the trustee is to end the trust and give the trust property to your children outright. When substantial amounts are involved, many parents want the money handled by a more mature person at least through the children's middle 20's and sometimes longer. During the existence of the trust, the trustee can spend any trust income or principal for the minor's benefit, as defined in the trust document. The trustee must also file state and federal tax returns for the trust.

b. The Uniform Transfers to Minors Act

You can make gifts to your child in your will or living trust under what is called "the Uniform Transfers to Minors Act," if it's applicable in your state. Here your children's property manager is called a "custodian." Again, if the gift is made from your living trust, the property doesn't go through probate. If the gift is made from your will, it does go through probate.

c. Life Insurance

You can purchase life insurance to benefit your children. The proceeds can be turned over to your living trust and funnelled through it to your children's trust.

d. The Property Guardian Named in Your Will

In your will, you'll name your children's property manager as the "property guardian" and "alternate property guardian" to supervise all property owned by your minor children which isn't handled by one of the other methods just mentioned.

While you can leave property to your children by your will, to be supervised by the property guardian named in the will, using this method is generally less desirable than leaving your property in a children's trust, or under the terms of the Uniform Transfers to Minors Act. In many states, a property guardian who is supervising a minor's property must make frequent burdensome reports to a court, which usually means paying a lawyer to get the job done.

In addition, your children's property guardian must spend the money you leave as state law dictates. By contrast, a trustee of a children's trust or a custodian under the Uniform Transfers to Minors Act is generally free of court supervision and reporting requirements, and has considerable power to use money for living expenses, health needs and education, under the terms of the trust document. Also, a guardian must turn property over to the minor when she becomes a legal adult at age 18. When you set up a trust, you specify (in the trust document) the age at which the minor gets the property. Property left under the terms of the Uniform Transfers to Minors Act may be retained by the custodian until the child is 18 to 21, depending on the state (25 in California).

Although it's generally not desirable to rely on the property guardian you name in your will to supervise property you leave your minor children, you should still name a property guardian (and alternate property guardian) in your will as a back-up method in case an adult manager is somehow needed for any property of your minor children. (The will forms in the Appendix enable you to do this.) You can't handle these contingencies through a children's trust, because it can only be used for property you actually place in the trust.

Specifically, naming a property guardian in your will provides a supervision mechanism in case:

- Spouses leave property to each other for use for their children and both spouses die simultaneously.

- Your minor children earn substantial money after you die, or receive a large gift or inheritance which doesn't, itself, name a property manager.

- You failed to include in your living trust some property you want your children to inherit. This can occur because of oversight or, more likely, because you didn't yet have ownership of the property when you established the living trust and didn't amend it later.

1. Creating a Children's Trust

If you have substantial assets—more than $25,000 or so—you wish to leave to a minor, a children's trust is usually the best way to do it. As already discussed, a children's trust allows you to name a person you trust to manage property for your children with a minimum of red tape.

The best way to establish a children's trust is to do it as part of a probate avoidance living trust.[3] The living trust forms discussed in Chapter 9 and set out in the Appendix contain simple children's trusts. A separate trust is created for each child. Your successor trustee can spend any of that child's trust income or property for the child's health, education or living needs. When the child reaches the age you've designated, the trustee turns the remaining trust property over to him or her.

You can also establish a children's trust by using a will, but, as you know, this results in the property going through probate before it is turned over to the children's trust. For this reason, the back-up will forms in this book, which are designed with the assumption that you are also creating a living trust, don't include children's trusts.

---

[3]A living trust only works to pass property owned by the trust. As discussed in Chapter 9, some types of property can't be owned by a trust because the settlor herself doesn't yet have title to them (e.g., property which is inherited but still in probate). If you face this sort of situation for valuable property and don't want to wait until you get clear title, the best alternative is to establish a children's trust through your will.

Children's trusts are included in *Nolo's Simple Will Book* and *WillMaker*, Nolo's computer software program.[4]

In this book's forms, children's trusts are technically a "subtrust" established by your living trust. This means that at your death, each child to whom you leave property in the living trust does not receive the property. Instead, it is held in a separate subtrust. All children's trusts are managed by the same person, who winds up the living trust after you die. (This is your "successor trustee," discussed in Chapter 9, Section D). The children's trusts established by your living trust allow the trustee to spend trust property for the beneficiary's "health, support, maintenance and education." The trustee is given broad discretion to interpret these terms.

Each children's trust provides that each child's property is held in trust until that child becomes 30. You can change this age to any age you want to, over 18. However, if you want a child's trust to last beyond age 30, you may want to review your situation with a lawyer; if children aren't able to manage money by then, they may never be, and you'll need a more complicated trust. [See Chapter 16, Section C(2).]

 In some situations, you might want a different type of children's trust than the ones in the living trust forms in the Appendix. Consult a lawyer if you want to:

- Place extensive controls over the use of property in the trust (for example, you place real estate in the trust that you want managed in a specific way);

- Provide for special care for a disadvantaged child [discussed in more detail in Chapter 16, Section D(1)].

- Combine property for different children in the trust (in legalese, called a "family pot" trust).

---

[4]If you want to use a will to establish a children's trust, please take advantage of the discount coupon in the back of this book to order either of these books.

- Create a children's trust for a child—or any beneficiary—who is already over age 18.

2. When a Children's Trust Isn't Desirable

Despite the advantages a children's trust offers, it may not be advisable if the value of the property left to a minor child is small—generally, less than about $25,000. In this situation, the cost of managing the trust, such as charges for preparing and filing tax returns, may eat up an unacceptably large percentage of the property. Also, a trust smaller than this simply won't produce enough annual income to justify tying up the principal. Thus, with very small estates, it often makes sense to leave property to children under the Uniform Transfers to Minors Act, if that can be used in your state [see Section C(3) below], or directly to your spouse or co-parent. If these alternatives are not sensible in your situation, consider, as a last resort, leaving smaller gifts to your children through your will, to be supervised by the property guardian. Also, if you conclude that the amount you can leave each of your children is small, consider buying a term life insurance policy so that the children will inherit enough to justify establishing a children's trust.

Summary: Leaving Property to Your Minor Children

Method	Property Manager's Legal Title	Probate Required?	Ease of Administration
Children's Trust covers only property left to children which is owned by trust)	Trustee (successor trustee)	No	Relatively easy. Created in Living Trust. No court involvement. Trust tax forms must be filed
Children's Trust Created by Will (covers all settlor's property left to children which is not disposed of in other ways)	Trustee (successor trustee)	Yes	Relatively easy . Once estate is probated and property transferred to trust, no further court involvement. Trust tax forms must be filed.
Uniform Transfers to Minors Act (not good in every state) (used in either living trust or will)	Custodian (successor custodian)	Yes, if property left through will. No, if left through living trust.	Relatively easy. No court involvement once trust gets property. No separate tax returns need be filed. Income is reported on minor's personal return
Will	Property Guardian (alternate property guardian)	Yes	Complicated. Most states impose rules on use of funds and require annual accountings.

3. Leaving Property Under the Uniform Transfers to Minors Act

In the majority of states, you can give property to your children in your will or living trust by use of a law called "The Uniform Transfers to Minors Act."[5] The states which have adopted the Uniform Transfers to Minors Act are listed below. If your state isn't on this list, it's not legally possible for you to leave property to your minor children by this method.

Note: The Uniform Transfers to Minors Act (or, in some states, the Uniform Gifts to Minors Act) can also be used to make gifts to minor children, your own or others, while you are alive.

Here's how the Uniform Transfers to Minors Act works for leaving property to your minor children. Under the Act, in either your will or living trust, you make a gift by identifying the property given, the minor it is given to, and appointing a "custodian" to be responsible for supervising the property. You state that the custodian is to act "under the [your state] Uniform Transfers to Minors Act." You can also name a "successor custodian" in case your first choice can't do the job. The "custodian" is the person you've selected as your children's property manager. The "successor custodian" is your children's alternate property manager.

The authority of the custodian to supervise the gift is defined in the Act, and is very broad. Basically, the custodian has complete discretion to control and use the property as she determines is in the children's interest. The custodian is entitled to be paid reasonable compensation from the gift property. No bond is required. And normally, no court supervision of the custodian is required.

[5]Uniform laws, as the name states, are standardized laws created by a legal commission. However, when it adopts a uniform law, a state legislature can make changes in the "uniform" version.

States Which Have Adopted the Uniform Transfers to Minors Act

State	Gift Must be Released When Minor Reaches Age
Alabama	21
Arizona	21
Arkansas	21
California	21 *
Colorado	18
District of Columbia	18
Florida	18
Hawaii	18
Idaho	18
Illinois	21
Iowa	21
Kansas	18
Kentucky	18
Maine	18
Massachusetts	21
Minnesota	18
Missouri	18
Montana	18
Nevada	18
New Hampshire	21
New Jersey	21
North Carolina	21
North Dakota	18
Ohio	21
Oklahoma	18
Oregon	18
Rhode Island	18
South Dakota	18
Virginia	18
West Virginia	18
Wyoming	18

*Can be extended in gift document to 25.

Each gift under the Uniform Transfers to Minors Act can be made to only one minor, with only one person named as custodian. Once the minor reaches the age the Act specifies for termination, the custodian gives the child the remaining balance of the gift, with an accounting of all funds distributed.

If you are leaving a substantial amount of property to your children, it's generally preferable to use a children's trust and have that property supervised by your successor trustee rather than making your gift under the Uniform Transfers to Minors Act. As discussed, gifts made through a children's trust do not have to be turned over to the child until the age you specify. Gifts made under the Uniform Transfers Act must end when the Act specifies. This is age 18 or 21, depending on the state, except California, where the age can be extended at your option, to 25. See the list above.

In some ways, a gift to your minor child in your will or living trust made under the Uniform Transfers Act functions like a children's trust. The custodian is the functional equivalent of a successor trustee, with the legal authority to supervise property owned by the minor, and the terms of the custodian's supervision, while defined by a statute, are quite flexible. But in one very important way, a gift under the Uniform Act isn't a trust: No separate legal or tax-reporting entity is created when the Act is used. Income and expenses are reported on the minor tax return. In contrast, a children's trust becomes, for tax purposes, a distinct entity, and the trustee must keep trust tax records and file trust income tax returns, as well as a minor's return.

Gifts to your children under the Uniform Transfers Act can be particularly sensible if you leave property worth less than $25,000 to your child. Normally, amounts of this size will be fairly rapidly expended for the child's education and living needs, and are simply not large enough to tie up beyond age 21. And if you make the gift under the Act in your living trust, you avoid probate of the property. And even if you choose to make the gift under your will, using the Act does avoid the court supervision problems involved when you leave property to be managed by the property guardian named in your will.

4. Leaving Life Insurance to Benefit Your Minor Children

Life insurance is discussed in depth in Chapter 12. The main point I want to make here is that it doesn't make good sense to name your minor children as beneficiaries of a life insurance policy, or as alternate beneficiaries, should the primary beneficiary (probably your spouse or co-parent) fail to survive you. If you die while the children are minors, the insurance company cannot legally give the proceeds directly to the children. Instead, it will require court proceedings to name and confirm a children's property guardian. Doing this, as I've discussed in this chapter, means this property guardian can become enmeshed in the time-consuming court reporting requirements state laws typically impose. It also means the property guardian can only spend money under the terms of state law, which in some instances can be quite restrictive.

As I noted earlier, one simple way to avoid this problem is to name your spouse, co-parent or other adult as the beneficiary of your life insurance policies and trust him or her to use the proceeds to benefit the children.

But if, for some reason, you don't want to do this, or you and this other adult die simultaneously, the best approach is to establish a living trust and name it as the beneficiary (or alternate beneficiary) of the policy. In the trust document, you make a gift to your children of any insurance proceeds received by the trust. If you die while your children are minors, the proceeds paid to the living trust will be held in the children's trusts. Thus, the proceeds would be paid directly to the trust, outside of probate or other court proceedings. Your successor trustee would manage the proceeds as part of the children's trust property.

Your living trust, itself, does not have to be the formal owner of the policy, because you have the right to designate whomever you choose to be the beneficiary of the policy. Simply naming your living trust as beneficiary works to have the proceeds paid directly to it. Of course, you do have to complete whatever paperwork the insurance company requires to have your living trust named as beneficiary of the policy. This may require sending your insurance company a copy of your living trust.

5. Leaving Property to be Supervised By the Property Guardian Named in Your Will

As discussed, there are serious drawbacks to leaving property to your minor children through your will, to be managed by the property guardian you name in that will. This requires that property to go through probate. Worse, property guardians are often subject to court review, strict rules as to how they can expend funds, and must file frequent accountings with the court and work under other restrictions. For those who engage in serious estate planning, the property guardian and alternate property guardian named in their will should serve solely as a back-up to handle situations such as those discussed previously in Section C, where property falls through the cracks and isn't covered by a more efficient management device.

However, for those who want to postpone estate planning or keep it to the bare minimum, it is far wiser to leave property to minor children to be managed by a property guardian rather than ignore the issue altogether. Having your children's property supervised by a property guardian you name in your will is certainly preferable to having a judge appoint someone to supervise that property. So, for example, a young couple who are both healthy and unlikely to die for decades may not want to deal with establishing a children's trust now. But if they do both die, they don't want a court deciding who'll manage the property they leave for their children. So, they create wills, where each names a property guardian to manage property for their children's benefit if both die simultaneously.

D. Leaving Property to Minor Children Who Are Not Your Own

IF YOU WANT to leave property to minors who aren't your own children, you have the following legal choices:

- Make the gift outright to the child's parent or legal guardian, and rely on the parent to use the gift for the benefit of the child. If the child is under 14 when the gift is received, this may have adverse income tax consequences, as any income received by the child over $1,000 is taxed at whatever tax rate is higher, the children's or the parent's—which almost invariably means the parent's. (If the parents are together but file separate tax returns, the tax rate—naturally—is the parent's with the higher income. If the parents are separated, it's the custodial parent's rate.) If you are interested in this possibility, investigate the various ways to give property that doesn't accrue interest until after the child is 14. Series EE U.S. savings bonds, which are tax-deferred until the bonds are turned in, provide one way to do this; zero-coupon tax-exempt municipal bonds are another. Also, some states sell tax-deferred bonds specifically designed for educational purposes.

- Make the gift through your living trust, by creating a children's trust for that gift. The living trust forms discussed in Chapter 9 and set out in the Appendix allow you to create a children's trust for any beneficiary who is a minor when you create the trust, not simply your own minor children. The successor trustee of your living trust manages all property left to minor beneficiaries in children's trusts. Doing this makes sense for large gifts, more than $25,000. This plan can make good sense for gifts to grandchildren, particularly if your successor trustee is the child's parent and will supervise that child's trust.

- Make the gift in your will or living trust through the Uniform Transfers to Minors Act. (The Act, and the states where it can be used, are discussed in Section C above.) This is usually the best alternative for gifts under roughly $25,000.

John, an elderly widower, wants to make a cash gift to his 12-year old grandniece Sally from his living trust. Her mother Mary will be the custodian. Her husband Fred is the alternate custodian. In his living trust, John makes the following gift: "To Sally Earners...$20,000; Mary Earners is to be custodian under the Minnesota Uniform Transfers to Minors Act. If Mary Earners is unable to serve, or continue serving, as custodian, the successor custodian shall be Fred Earners."

- Make the gift by your will. This may require court proceedings to appoint a property guardian to supervise the gift, and is the least desirable method. And since you are not a parent of the child, you can't appoint a property guardian for him or her in your will.

E.   Children of Any Age

IN TWO AREAS, special rules apply to one's children no matter what their age: disinheritance of children and concerns about adopted children or children born outside marriage.

1.   Disinheriting Children

To an outsider, it may seem sad that a parent would want to disinherit a child, but nevertheless, it happens rather regularly. Whatever the reasons, it's legal for a parent who intends to disinherit a child to do so. At the same time, legal rules protect children, and children of a deceased child, from being accidentally disinherited. The legalese for accidentally overlooked children is "pretermitted heirs." In most states, your children (and the children of deceased children) have a statutory right to inherit from you if you leave them out of your will or fail to make one. Grandchildren do not have any statutory right to inherit if their parent (your child) is still alive, so there is no need to disinherit them if you don't want them to inherit.

It's not that you can't exclude or disinherit a child if you wish. You can. It's simply that laws on the books in most states require you to do it by using specific language in your will. If you don't mention a child (or the children of a deceased child) in your will, the general rule is that the omitted child, or the children of a child who has died before you, are entitled to some of your property anyway. How much they get depends on whether you leave a spouse and how many other children you have. In addition, the laws of most states protect your children who are born after the will is made ("afterborn children") by entitling them to a similar share of your estate.

To disinherit a child, or the children of a deceased child, you must use a will, even if you transfer all your property by a living trust. The reason is simple: some state laws require disinheritance to be accomplished by will. There are two ways to disinherit a child in a will. One is to leave the child a minimal amount, which functionally works as a disinheritance, and insures the child cannot successfully claim to have been overlooked, or omitted. The other way is to expressly disinherit the child in the will, by stating that you aren't leaving him anything.

The will forms in this book allow you to use the first method to disinherit a child (or child of a deceased child). The will accomplishes this by asking you to list all your children, the form then provides that each child receives $1, in addition to any other property you give them by will or in any other method, including your living trust. If you choose not to give the child any other property, you have functionally disinherited that child and need do nothing more.

The will forms in this book do not allow you to expressly disinherit a child. These wills are designed to be basic back-up wills, used as one part of an estate plan where most property is transferred by other probate avoidance methods, such as living trusts or joint tenancy. The back-up wills are not geared for making the types of individual changes involved when you wish to insert an express disinheritance clause for one or more children. Express disinheritances can be accomplished using the more comprehensive will forms provided in *Nolo's Simple Will Book,* or *WillMaker* computer software.

Revise Your Estate Plan When a Child Is Born or Dies

If, after preparing your estate plan, you have an additional child or children, you must revise that plan by providing for (or disinheriting) the new child.

If a child dies, leaving children (your grandchildren), you should revise your estate plan to provide for or disinherit these grandchildren. You should also, of course, make sure that all property left to the deceased child is redirected to other beneficiaries.

You may wonder how it can be that if you provide for your children outside your will—by giving them property from your living trust, for example—but didn't mention them in your will, these children may be able to, at least in theory, successfully claim to be accidentally overlooked heirs and demand additional shares of your estate. The answer is that, in defining whether a child is pretermitted (overlooked), and therefore entitled to receive a share of your estate, some state's laws specifically refer to omitting a child from a "will." Read literally, these statutes don't allow property left to a child by a living trust (or in joint tenancy, or by life insurance proceeds) to be considered to determine if a child has been overlooked. Of course, given the purpose of the pretermitted heir statutes—to protect children from being accidentally disinherited—it's senseless to read the statute so literally. But who says the law can't be senseless?

So, to be absolutely safe, even if you generously provide for your children outside of your will, you should list the names of all your children (and children of a deceased child) in your will and make some provision for them. As I've mentioned, the will forms in the Appendix contain space for you to list all your children and children of a deceased child, and state that you give each child listed $1, aside from any other property you leave them. This may sound a little cumbersome, but it does ensure that your estate won't face a "pretermitted heir" claim.

Note of Sanity: Remember, for the "pretermitted heir" issue to become a real problem, a child must file a lawsuit contesting your will and estate plan. If you trust that your children aren't going to sue, you don't have to worry.

2. Adopted and Out-of-Wedlock Children

For centuries, courts have been confronted with the issue of whether a gift to "my children" includes adopted children and children born out of wedlock. To avoid any confusion in this area, when you make a will from a form in the Appendix, simply name all your children, including any born while you were not married and any you have adopted. (As discussed in the last section, doing this means the child will be left $1 in addition to whatever else you provide. Even if you leave the child nothing else, the fact that you named the child and made a $1 gift protects your estate from challenge on the theory that you overlooked the child. If you want to expressly disinherit any of these children, see *Nolo's Simple Will Book* or the *WillMaker* software package.)

If there is some question about who is included in a gift to "my children," judges attempt to determine what the person making the will intended. Most states automatically consider adopted persons, whether they were minors or adults when adopted, as "children" for the purpose of a gift to "children." This means that if you've legally adopted a child and leave a gift to "my children," the adopted child will take a share.

The rule for children born out of wedlock cannot be so clearly stated. Basically, for inheritance purposes, states recognize an out-of-wedlock child as a child of the mother unless the child was formally released by the mother for adoption. However, an out-of-wedlock child isn't a child of the father for inheritance purposes unless the father has legally acknowledged the child as his. Just what constitutes legal acknowledgment differs from state to state. Generally speaking, if a father signs a paternity statement or later marries the mother, the child is acknowledged for purposes of inheritance in all states and has the same legal standing as a child born to parents who are married.

Also, in some states, a father who welcomes a child into his home, and publicly states that the child is his, also establishes a parent-child relationship for inheritance purposes. Fortunately, it isn't really necessary to understand all of these legal technicalities if you want to disinherit an illegitimate child. Simply name the child in your will. Using the forms in this book, this means the child will inherit $1 and will not have legal standing to claim he or she was overlooked.

PART III

Avoiding Probate

Probate and Why You Want to Avoid It

CHAPTER 7

Probate and Why You Want to Avoid It

MANY PEOPLE AREN'T SURE what probate actually is, except that it involves lawyers in transferring property after death. One thing they do know is they want to avoid it. That's a sound instinct. In most instances, probate is a costly and time-consuming business, providing no benefits except to attorneys.

A. What Is Probate?

PROBATE IS THE LEGAL PROCESS that includes:

- Filing the deceased person's will[1] with a local court;[2]

- Identifying and inventorying the deceased person's property;

- Having that property appraised;

- Paying off legal debts, including death taxes;

- Having the will "proved" valid to the court; and

- Eventually distributing what's left as the will directs.

If the deceased person didn't leave a will, or a will isn't valid, the estate will undergo probate through what is called "intestacy" proceedings, with the property distributed to immediate family members as state law dictates.

People who defend the probate system (mostly lawyers, which is surely no surprise) assert that probate prevents fraud in transferring a deceased person's property. In addition, they claim it protects inheritors by promptly resolving claims creditors have against a deceased person's property. In truth, however, most property is transferred within a close circle of family and friends, and few, if any, estates face creditors' claims. In short, most people have no need of these so-called "benefits," so probate usually amounts to a lot of time-wasting, expensive mumbo-jumbo of aid to no one but the lawyers involved.

The actual probate functions are essentially clerical and administrative. In the vast majority of probate cases, there's no conflict, no contesting parties, none of the normal reasons for court proceedings. Likewise, probate doesn't usually call for legal research, drafting, or lawyers' adversarial skills. Instead, in the normal, uneventful probate proceeding, the family or other inheritors of the dead person provide a copy of the deceased person's will and other needed financial information. The attorney's secretary[3] then fills in a small mound of forms and keeps track of filing deadlines and other procedural technicalities. In some states, the attorney makes a couple of routine court appearances; in others, the whole procedure is normally handled by mail.

Because of the complicated paperwork, a typical probate takes up to a year or more, often much more. I once worked in a law office that was profitably entering its seventh year of handling a probate estate—and a very wealthy estate it was. By contrast, property transfers by other legal means, such as a living trust, can usually be completed in a matter of weeks.

Probate usually requires both an "executor" (called a "personal representative" in some states) and someone familiar with probate procedures, normally a probate attorney. The executor is a person appointed in the will[4] who is responsible for supervising the estate, which means making sure that the will is followed. The executor, who is usually a spouse or friend of the deceased, hires a

---

[1]If there's no will or other valid transfer device, such as a living trust or joint tenancy, the deceased's property is probated under state "intestacy" laws, which provide that specified family members receive your property.

[2]The court can have various names, such as the "probate," "surrogate" or "chancery" court.

[3]There is so much money in the probate business that some lawyers hire probate form preparation companies to do all the real work. In most instances, the existence of these freelance paralegal companies is not disclosed to clients, who assume that lawyers' offices at least do the routine paperwork they are paid so well for.

[4]If the person died without a will, the court appoints an "administrator" (whose main qualification may be that he's a crony of the judge) to serve the same function.

probate lawyer to do the paperwork.[5] Then the executor does little more than sign where the lawyer directs, while wondering why the whole business is taking so long. For these services, the lawyer and the executor are each entitled to a hefty fee from the probate estate. It's common for the executor to waive her fee, especially if she is a substantial inheritor.

Probate sometimes evokes exaggerated images of greedy lawyers consuming most of an estate in fees, while churning out reams of gobbledygook-filled paper as slowly as possible. While there is more truth in these images than lawyers care to admit, the lawyer's fees won't actually devour the whole estate. In many states, the fees are what a court approves as "reasonable." In other states, the fees are based on a percentage of the estate subject to probate. Either way, probate attorney fees for a "routine" estate with a gross[6] value of $400,000 (these days, this may be little more than a home, some savings and a car) can normally amount to $10,000 or more. And, in addition, there are court costs, appraiser's fees and other possible expenses. Moreover, if there are any "extraordinary" services performed for the estate, the attorney or executor can often petition the court for additional fees. Some lawyers even persuade (or dupe) clients into naming them as executors, enabling the lawyers to hire themselves as probate attorneys and collect two fees—one as executor, one as probate attorney.

Marilyn Monroe's estate offers an extreme example of how outrageous probate fees can be. She died in debt in 1962, but over the next 18 years, her estate received income, mostly from movie royalties, in excess of $1,600,000. When her estate was settled in 1980, her executor announced that debts of $372,136 had been paid, and $101,229 was left as the final assets of the

estate, for distribution to inheritors. Well over a million dollars of Monroe's estate was consumed by probate fees.

I HOPE I AVOIDED PROBATE!

B. Avoiding Probate

IN RESPONSE TO the manifest waste perpetrated by the probate system, a number of legal methods have been developed to avoid probate entirely. Because leaving property in a will usually results in probate, probate avoidance methods involve arranging, prior to death, to transfer property by other legal means. The major probate avoidance methods are:

- living trusts (discussed in Chapter 9);

- informal bank account trusts—also called "pay-on-death accounts" (discussed in Chapter 10);

- joint tenancy (discussed in Chapter 11);

- life insurance (discussed in Chapter 12);

- state laws which exempt certain (small) amounts of property left by will from probate (discussed in Chapter 13); and

- gifts (discussed in Chapter 15).

Deciding which method, or combination of methods, is best for you is a major part of estate planning. So please read all the chapters on probate avoidance methods before you decide how to proceed. To assist you in

---

[5]The executor often hires the decedent's lawyer (who may even have possession of the will), but this is not required.

[6]"Gross" probate estate means that debts on property are not deducted to determine value. Thus, if a house has a market value of $200,000 with a mortgage balance of $160,000 (net equity of $40,000), the gross "value" of the house is $200,000.

reaching your decision, Chapter 8 provides a summary chart of the pluses and minuses of each method.

1. Informal Probate Avoidance

Some people ask, "Why not just divide up a deceased relative's or friend's property as the will directs, and ignore the laws requiring probate?" Indeed, some small estates are undoubtedly disposed of this way, directly and informally by family members. The people involved may not think of such an arrangement as avoiding probate, but that's what occurs.

For example, an older man lives his last few years in a nursing home. After his death, his children meet and divide the personal items their father had kept over the years. What little savings he has have long since been put into a joint account with the children anyway, so there's no need for formalities there. If the father owned no other property, the children have, in effect, "probated" his estate.

For this type of informal procedure to work, the family must be able to gain possession of all of the deceased's property, agree on how to distribute it, and pay all the creditors. Gaining possession of property isn't difficult when the estate consists entirely of personal effects and household items. However, if real estate, securities, bank accounts or other property bearing legal title papers, such as cars and boats, are involved, informal family property distribution can't work. Title to a house, for example, can't be changed on the say-so of the next of kin. Someone with legal authority must prepare, sign and record a deed transferring title to the house to the new owners, the inheritors.

One good rule is that whenever outsiders are involved with a deceased's property, do-it-yourself division by inheritors is not feasible. For instance, creditors can be an obstacle to a family disposing of an estate informally. A creditor concerned about being paid can usually file a court action to compel a probate proceeding.

Another stumbling block for an informal family property disposition can be getting family members to agree on how to divide the deceased's possessions. If there's a will, the family will probably follow its provisions. If there is no will, the family may look up and agree to abide by the inheritance rules established by the law of the state where the deceased person lived. Or, in either case, the family may simply adopt their own, mutually agreed on settlement. For example, if, despite a will provision to the contrary, one sibling wants the furniture and the other wants the tools, they can simply trade. All inheritors must agree to the estate distribution if probate procedures are bypassed. Any inheritor who is unhappy with the estate distribution can, like creditors, file for a formal probate.

In sum, informal probate avoidance, even for a small estate, isn't something one can count on. Realistically, probate avoidance must be planned in advance.

2. Planning to Avoid Probate

Because probate has justifiably come to be viewed as an unnecessary device designed to fill lawyers' coffers, some have concluded that probate must be avoided for every last bit of one's property. In my view, this is too rigid. True, most people who take the time to plan their own estate decide they want to avoid probate, at least for the major items of property they own (house, business interests, stocks, money market funds). However, many younger people sensibly elect to put off planning to avoid probate until later. For example, a younger couple may decide that making wills sufficiently accomplishes their principal needs, which are to leave most or all property to the survivor, and to provide money and a guardian for their children if they should die at the same time. They understand that using probate avoidance methods will require some paperwork now, and perhaps some legal fees. Since it's highly unlikely they will die soon, and suddenly (should they become ill, they'll normally have time to plan), and because they haven't yet accumulated a great deal of property, they decide to wait a few decades before engaging in probate avoidance planning.

There are even a couple of circumstances in which probate can be desirable.

- **If your estate owes a lot of debts.** If there's a significant risk that many creditors will make claims against your estate, probate can be advisable, especially if your executor will contest one or more of these claims. For example, if you own a failing business, or are involved in complex financial transactions, probate can provide benefits because it provides a ready-made court procedure for resolving creditors' claims faster than by normal lawsuit. Creditors who are notified of the probate proceeding must file their claims promptly with the probate court, often within four or six months of the filing of petition for probate, or they needn't be paid. This is a much shorter "statute of limitations" than would otherwise apply and can allow beneficiaries to take their property (or their remaining property) free of anxiety about future creditors' claims.

  It's important to note, though, that most estates don't involve complex creditor problems. Most deceased persons leave little more than conventional household debts (mortgages, utilities, magazine subscriptions, auto loans, credit cards).

- **If you believe someone may challenge your estate plan in court.** Any estate planning device, whether it be a will, living trust, or any combination of legal methods, can be attacked by a lawsuit after your death. Fortunately, however, the legal grounds for attack are quite limited. The challenger must prove the estate plan is a result of someone's illegal act, such as fraud, duress or undue influence over the person who signed the documents, or the challenger must establish that the deceased person was mentally incompetent when the estate plan was authorized. Both of these legal theories are as hard to prove as they are easy to allege. If you believe there's a risk that your estate may be subject to legal attack, even by someone who has little chance of success, probate may be advisable as part of your plan to defeat that attack.

Under probate law, only a brief time is allowed for attacking a will, and the people who witnessed the signing of the will should be able to testify to the will maker's competence.

 If you're worried about a lawsuit, you should discuss your estate planning with an attorney, and decide together what your safest course of action is.

C. How to Reduce or Eliminate Probate Fees

ONE WAY TO REDUCE PROBATE FEES is for the executor to appear in court without an attorney ("in pro per") as the representative of the estate. Unfortunately, a few states don't permit the executor to act without a lawyer. And some judges in states which do officially permit executors to act in pro per make it difficult in practice. The only states in which pro per representation is truly accessible for probate proceedings are California, (see *How to Probate an Estate*, California Edition, Nissley, Nolo Press, an excellent self-help book designed for non-lawyers) and Wisconsin, which has an established pro per procedure (see Chapter 13, Section B). In other states where in pro per action is theoretically possible, there are no comprehensive published materials nor is other help available which makes probate accessible to non-lawyers. Consequently, learning to complete the forms, understanding all the intricacies of court petitions, estate inventories, proof-of-service declarations, and so on, is likely to be difficult. The courts and clerks aren't usually sympathetic (to put it mildly), so any mistake is likely to cause delay, as well as embarrassment.

In all states (including California and Wisconsin), rather than trying to save money by considering having your estate probated without an attorney, it generally makes more sense to see if you can avoid probate altogether. As mentioned earlier in this chapter, this means transferring your property by probate avoidance methods. Obviously, if there is no probate, there are no probate fees. At the very least, I recommend that you consider reducing the size of the estate that will be subject to probate in order to reduce probate fees.[7] This approach involves transferring the big ticket items of your property—for example, your house and stock portfolio—outside of probate, leaving only less valuable items to be passed by your will.

Finally, if some of your estate will be subject to probate, you can try to reach an agreement with your future executor and attorney that they'll do your probate for less than the conventional fees. However, you cannot bind your executor, or an attorney, to handle the probate of your estate for a reduced fee. In fact, legally you don't have the power to select the attorney at all. The law gives this authority to the executor. (Indeed, the executor can legally revoke any waiver of fees made while you were alive, and claim full statutory fees.) But, obviously, there's no reason for you to pick an executor you don't completely trust; usually, for moderate estates, an executor is a spouse or a close friend who will be likely to waive the fee, or serve at a reduced fee, if that was the agreement. Similarly, an attorney who agrees to handle the estate at a reduced fee will likely do so. If the probate of your estate is routine, it will be sufficiently profitable even at a fee lower than the conventional rate. There's nothing illegal or unethical about bargaining with an attorney to reduce fees. If you do arrange with an attorney to handle your estate at a reduced fee, you should be able to rely on your executor to designate that person as the probate attorney. Be definite on the terms of the fee, and put something in writing, even if it's only a letter confirming this arrangement.

---

[7]In some states, probate fees are strictly based on the value of the estate. And even in states where a judge has discretion to award probate fees, they normally follow guidelines which gear fees to the size of the estate.

D. Debts, Taxes and Probate

WHAT ABOUT DEBTS? If an estate is probated, debts and taxes are paid before property is distributed to inheritors. If duly notified creditors don't make their claims within the allotted time, they're simply cut off. This raises the question of how the deceased's debts, including death taxes, get paid if there's no probate. Obviously, a probate court can't ensure that debts get paid if property is transferred outside of probate. However, there's no indication any judicial policing is needed. Many people leave no significant debts, and even if some do, they normally leave sufficient assets to pay them. It's important to realize here that the primary financial obligations most people do have—mortgages on real estate, or loans on cars—aren't debts which must be paid off promptly after the owner dies. Normally, these kinds of assets are transferred to an inheritor who becomes liable for the mortgage or loan. In other words, mortgages or car loans pass with the property and don't need to be paid off separately.

If no probate occurs to cut off creditors' claims, all the deceased's property remains liable for his debts, including any death taxes. This is true even after the property is transferred to inheritors. If only one person will inherit from you, that person will be responsible for paying your debts and any death taxes from the inherited property. If there are several inheritors, the responsibility for paying debts and taxes can theoretically become more confusing, but this confusion can be eliminated in advance by earmarking money in your estate plan to pay debts. One way to do this is to allocate, in a living trust, specific assets (a bank account, or a particular stock) to pay debts and taxes. If you don't have a suitable asset available to do this, consider purchasing insurance to accomplish it.

Tax Note: In Chapter 14, I show you how to estimate whether any federal or state death taxes will be due at your death. If the answer is "no," this is one less thing to worry about. If the answer is "yes," plan to leave adequate cash or property that can easily be sold, to cover your estate's likely tax obligation.

E. Probate Reform

WHY IS PROBATE SO TIME-CONSUMING and expensive? Why is probate court approval required for so many routine actions when there's normally no conflict whatsoever? Aside from the mystique of professionalism and good old greed, the history of probate supplies most of the answer. Probate became legal business through a quirk of English history. In medieval England, wealth and power resided almost exclusively in the ownership of land. It passed, by feudal law, to the eldest son. Inheritance of land was a political matter of direct concern to the king, so land transfers after a death were done through the king's courts.

The proceedings were technical, formal and costly. Personal property (everything except real estate) was transferred by much simpler ways. When the United States became independent, it accepted and followed the traditional British legal system for land inheritance. But instead of distinguishing between land and personal property, we tossed everything into the new "probate" court. Thus, in post-revolutionary America, all property could be transferred at death only through formal judicial proceedings. Our current probate system evolved (or rather, like Topsy, it "just grow'd"). Because a compli-

cated, formal probate system means substantial fees for lawyers, naturally the legal profession fiercely defends it.

Lawyers' assurances that probate is necessary sound increasingly hollow. Even the British eliminated tedious, expensive probate proceedings over half a century ago. In 1926, England reformed its probate system to provide that the person named in the will as the executor (normally a non-lawyer) simply files an accounting of the estate's assets and liabilities with the tax authorities, who appraise the inventory and assess any death tax due. If the papers are in order (as they should be in all routine probates), a "grant of probate" is issued in as little as seven days. Without any further court proceedings, the executor then handles all the estate's problems—paying the bills, collecting assets and distributing gifts to inheritors. Only if there's a problem, such as a will contest or a contested debt claim, is the matter referred to the Principal Registry, the functional equivalent of our probate courts.

In most civil law countries (including those in Western Europe and Central America), probate is even simpler. Wills are presented to a notary when signed. A notary, under civil law, is a quasi-judicial official who's responsible for ensuring the validity of documents. Upon death, the deceased person's successor named in the will performs the probate functions without any judicial supervision. If there are disputes such as contests of the will or disputed creditors' claims, they are handled like any other legal conflict.

Will our probate system be reformed soon? Not likely, in my opinion. True, most people favor probate reform, in a vague way. And there's some real pressure on a number of state legislatures to adopt genuine probate reform, on the order of the simplified estate distribution system used in England or civil law countries. HALT (Help Abolish Legal Tyranny), an excellent Washington D.C.-based law reform organization, is a leader in this movement. Unfortunately, though, probate reform isn't a hot, glamorous issue; without lots more public pressure, politicians (many of whom are lawyers, or sensitive to the lobbying of lawyer groups) are unlikely to become seriously interested in it. Much of what passes currently for probate reform merely simplifies probate procedures for the lawyers, but keeps the overall system, particularly the fees, intact.

Some of the forces deterring real reform are obvious: inertia, public confusion about what probate is, and lawyers' greed. (After all, what did lawyers go to law school for, if not to be able to live like aristocrats?)

There's more at work here, though. Ours is a society professing devotion to equality, but also to freedom, and that leaves us a little confused about money, especially inherited wealth. We don't have any blood aristocracy, but the grandchildren of capitalists like Rockefeller, Vanderbilt or Kennedy inherit money taxed at a much lower rate than any English lord or French duke can. Lawyers are the priests of money. So corporate lawyers dress in dull, priest-like garb, display grave demeanors and occupy somber offices. Part of the law's function in the U.S.—quite a large part indeed—is to legitimize wealth. Wherever those millions come from—whether hard, honest toil or robber baron's thievery—after a couple of generations of lawyers get through with that money, it becomes respectable, clean and almost holy. Probate has been an essential part of this sanctification process. If you make the legal process surrounding the transfer of money on death complex and formal, it seems to help keep attention off more basic issues, like who decides what the rules are about inherited wealth.

Probate is obviously not designed for the efficient, economic handling of the average moderate estate where there are almost never any contests, frauds or conflicts. The only real incentive to probate reform is the fact that many people are learning to avoid the system. Americans are as good at avoiding rules as they are at inventing them. It may start to occur to lawyers that something's wrong when more and more people adopt probate avoidance devices rather than using their overpriced, over-complicated, time-consuming probate dinosaur.

Chart:
Probate Avoidance Methods

THIS CHART SUMMARIZES the advantages and disadvantages of each of the major methods for transferring property after one's death. Each probate avoidance method is explained in depth in the following five chapters. You can use the chart now to gain a rough understanding of the basics of probate avoidance methods. And, if you wish, you can refer to it later to remind yourself of the pluses and minuses of one, or several, methods.

Transfer Device	Avoids Probate?	Major Drawbacks	Major Advantages
Will	No, except in limited circumstances defined by state law (see Chapter 11).	Normally puts property in probate where inheritors face attorneys' fees and other costs and time delays	Generally simplest transfer method to prepare; can serve other purpose, such as naming guardian for minor children.
Living Trust	Yes	Initial effort to establish; can be initial attorney's fees.	Complete control over property while alive; flexibility in providing for beneficiaries
Joint Tenancy	Yes	Each joint tenant can normally sell their interest; may be gift taxes involved in creating joint tenancy; may mean partial loss of stepped up tax basis	Can be simplest probate avoidance device to create
Pay on Death Bank Accounts (Totten Trust)	Yes	Limited to bank accounts only	Very easy to create; no additional costs.
Naming beneficiary to Pension Plan, IRA, etc.	Yes	Can be limits imposed by specific policy, program, plan.	Generally easy to do.
State law exemptions to normal probate	Yes	Only relatively small amounts of property qualify. Rules vary for each state (see Chapter 11). You have to understand your state's laws; research or hiring an attorney may be required.	Can work well if state allows this method to be combined with other probate avoidance methods.
Life insurance	Yes	Do you really need it? Investment considerations	Can provide considerable bang per buck.
Dying intestate, without creating any property transfer method	No	Property distributed according to state law, executor appointed by judge. Guardian for your minor children selected by a judge.	No effort required

Revocable Living Trusts

Revocable Living Trusts

LIVING TRUSTS are an efficient and effective way to transfer property at your death. Essentially, a living trust is simply a legal document controlling the transfer of property in the trust when you die. Unlike wills, living trusts avoid probate and allow property to be transferred promptly to your beneficiaries. And they are extremely flexible: You can transfer all your property by living trust, or, if appropriate, use a living trust to transfer only some assets, transferring the rest by other methods. Also, living trusts normally are not made public. Wills are routinely made public as part of the probate process.

These trusts are called "living" or sometimes "inter vivos" (Latin for "among the living") because they're created while you're alive. They're called "revocable" because you can revoke or change them at any time, for any reason, before you die. In other words, while you live, you still effectively own all property transferred to your living trust and can do what you want with it, including selling it, spending it, or giving it away. Basically, a revocable living trust is simply a piece of paper which becomes operational at your death to transfer your property privately and outside of probate to the people or organizations named in the trust.

Aside from some paperwork necessary to establish a probate avoidance living trust and transfer property to it, there are no serious drawbacks or risks involved in creating or maintaining the trust. You don't even need to maintain separate trust tax records; all transactions which are technically made by the trust are reported on your personal income tax return.

As with a will, creating a probate avoidance living trust requires the use of some tried and true "legalese." The living trust forms in the Appendix contain the necessary legal language. Most people with modest-sized estates (roughly, under $600,000) and fairly straight-forward desires for transferring their property can create an effective living trust from these forms without the assistance of a lawyer. In addition to creating a probate avoidance living trust, the living trust forms in the Appendix enable you to leave property to minor beneficiaries in simple children's trusts designed to delay the age at which the children inherit until the ages you designate. [See Section D(3) of this chapter and Chapter 6, Section C.] In other words, one component of a living trust drafted from this book can be a trust for children who are under 18 when you prepare your living trust; this simple children's trust remains operative until the child reaches the age to receive her property outright.

 It's important to realize that the basic probate avoidance living trusts set out in this book can also be combined with other types of trusts. For example, you can create a living trust which first avoids probate and then continues for years after your death to serve such purposes as saving on death taxes or imposing controls on property, as is commonly done for gifts to people with special needs, or to spouses in second marriages. While these more complicated ongoing trusts are discussed in some detail in Chapter 16, this book does not show you how to establish them. If you conclude, after reading this book, that you want your living trust to also establish an ongoing trust, you will need to see a lawyer.

For most people, the job is simply to avoid probate; let's examine how a living trust works to accomplish that.

Creating and Maintaining a Living Trust

To create a living trust using *Plan Your Estate*, complete the following steps:

1. Read the entire book, including the information in this chapter.

2. Select the appropriate living trust form from the Appendix. There are two: Form I for one person, and Form II for a couple with shared property.

3. Complete the living trust form, following the instructions provided in this chapter. In the trust document, you:

- list the property transferred to the trust;

- appoint yourself as trustee to manage property during your life;

• name a "successor trustee" to take over after you die (or if you become incapacitated) who will transfer property to the beneficiaries you name; and

• name the beneficiaries who are to receive trust property at your death.

4. Have the trust document typed and then sign it before a notary.

5. Transfer title to property listed in the trust into the trust's name.

6. Make a simple back-up will to deal with a few matters that can't be covered by the living trust, such as appointing a personal guardian for your minor children and providing for any property not transferred to the trust. (Chapter 17 shows you how to prepare a back-up will.)

7. Keep the trust up to date by amending or redoing it as necessary.

Caution: Please don't begin to draft your own trust until you've studied the entire book with care. It can be safe and sensible to draft your own living trust if you are equipped to make informed decisions and your estate planning needs are relatively straightforward. But you really do need to understand all your options, including other possible probate avoidance methods, and the possible effects of death taxes on your estate planning, before you begin to prepare a living trust. And you also should take the time to understand the situations in which you'll need a lawyer's help to achieve your objectives.

A. Does Everyone Need a Living Trust?

GIVEN THE ADVANTAGES of avoiding probate that a living trust confers, shouldn't every prudent person use one for all their property? Despite my enthusiasm for living trusts, my answer is "not necessarily." The reason for saying this is twofold. First, some people don't really need to plan to avoid probate now and, second, there are

other probate avoidance methods which may fit a particular estate planning situation better.

Good estate planning isn't mechanical. To make sensible decisions about using a living trust, you need to understand what it can and cannot accomplish, and how it can be used with other estate planning methods in devising your overall plan. Norman Dacey, in his pioneering work *How to Avoid Probate* (Crown), essentially asserts that living trusts should be used by all people in all situations. A number of lawyers now make the same claim in advertisements and seminars. These sweeping claims are too extreme. Generally, there are a number of categories of people who may conclude that creating a living trust is not their best estate planning strategy, at least not right now:

• People who are young, healthy and unlikely to die for a long time. These people's primary goals usually are to be sure their property will be distributed as they want, and to provide financial resources and a person to care for any minor children. A will (perhaps coupled with the purchase of life insurance) often achieves these goals easier than a living trust. Here's why: A will is simpler to prepare than a living trust. While using a will usually means property goes through probate, this only occurs after death. As long as a person is alive, the fact that probate will be avoided is of no benefit. Because very few younger, healthy people die without any warning (and because they often don't yet own enough property that probate fees would amount to that much anyway), it can make good sense now to use a will for a number of years. Later in life, when the prospect of death is more imminent, and the person has accumulated more property, a revocable living trust can be established to avoid probate.

• People who can more sensibly transfer their assets by other probate avoidance devices, including joint tenancy, informal bank trusts ("pay-on-death" accounts), life insurance and gifts. In addition, the laws in some states allow certain amounts or types of property (and occasionally property left to certain classes of beneficiaries, such as a surviving spouse) to be transferred without probate even if a will is used.

None of these devices has the overall breadth of a living trust, which can be used to transfer virtually all types of assets. However, each can be easier to use, and equally efficient, in particular circumstances. In short, it's best to understand all probate avoidance methods and then to decide which ones will work best for you.

- People who have complex debt problems. For instance, if you have a business that has many creditors, probate provides an absolute cut-off time for notified creditors to file claims. If they don't do so in the time permitted, your inheritors can take your property free of concern that these creditors will surface later and claim a share. A living trust doesn't create any such cut-off period, which means your property could be subject to creditors' claims for a much longer time.

- People who don't currently have title to property but expect to receive it. A living trust only works to transfer property you currently own. If you've been left property by someone's will that is still in probate, or you expect to get money from a lawsuit settlement, only a will can be securely used to transfer that property. Of course, no one knows what property they might receive shortly before death, which is one reason it is always wise to back up a living trust with a will.

- People whose primary goal is to name a personal guardian to care for their minor children. A living trust can't be used for this; a will can. Of course, if you have a great deal of valuable property, you may want to create a living trust (or other probate avoidance device) to transfer it and name a personal guardian for your minor children in a "back-up" will.

- People who own little property, so there isn't much point in bothering with a living trust and probate avoidance. Often parents in this situation will provide financial resources for their children by purchasing life insurance. The proceeds of insurance do not go through probate, so there is no need to plan to avoid it. However, if the policy is fairly large, you will want to establish a children's trust (as part of a will or living

trust) and name it as beneficiary of the policy, not the children. See Chapter 6, Section C for more on this.

Despite these exceptions, the fact remains that for all those who want to arrange to avoid probate now, including the elderly, the seriously ill, and anyone who is cautious and doesn't want any risk of subjecting property to probate, living trusts are usually the best probate avoidance device. Most people who plan their estates ultimately choose a living trust as the best device to transfer their property.

B. Living Trusts Explained

DON'T LET THE WORD "TRUST" scare you. True, the word can have an impressive, slightly ominous sound. Historically, monopolists used trusts to dominate entire industries (for example, the Standard Oil Trust in the era of Teddy Roosevelt's "trust-busting"). Some legal authors do wax ecstatic over trusts—e.g., "The trust has been called the crowning achievement of Anglo-American law."[1]

While many people don't know exactly how a trust works, they do know, vaguely, that trusts have traditionally been used by the very wealthy to preserve their riches from generation to generation. (Indeed, isn't one version of the American dream to be the beneficiary of your very own trust fund?) Trusts may even appear to some as a particularly obnoxious form of lawyers' black magic, somehow enabling people to escape taxes or other financial obligations. The reality is more mundane, as it often is.

---

[1]Denhardt, *Everyone's Guide to Estate Planning* (Contemporary Books). Surely it's odd for anyone, even a lawyer, to rate trusts higher than the Constitution or Bill of Rights.

1. What Is a Living Trust?

Living trusts are, in basic concept, simple. Here's a valid bare-bones living trust:

> "I, Cynthia Sims, hereby place my diamond necklace in trust for my niece, Sara Sims. The necklace shall be given tĺo her outright when she is 35. I retain all rights in the necklace until I die. I appoint myself as trustee of this trust, and Sara's mother, Nancy Sims, to be successor trustee after I die."

Here is how this trust operates: The person who establishes the trust (Cynthia Sims) is called, in legalese, the "settlor"[2] or "grantor" or "creator." She puts something of value (in this case, the diamond necklace) in a legal entity ("legal fiction" might be a better term) called a "living trust." This trust entity is simply a written document which states that it's a trust and specifies:

1. The "trustee," who manages the trust property. This is normally you, the person who establishes the trust;

2. Your "successor trustee," who takes over after you die and turns the trust property over to your beneficiaries;

---

[2]I use the term "settlor" to define the person who creates a trust, because that term is widely accepted in the financial and legal worlds.

3. Your beneficiaries (or "beneficiary") of the trust, who are entitled to receive the trust property at your death;

4. Your property that is subject to the trust; and

5. The terms of the trust, including the fact that you can amend or revoke it at any time.

2. How a Living Trust Works

The key to a living trust established to avoid probate is that the settlor (remember, that's the person who sets up the trust) isn't locked into anything. She can revise, amend or revoke the trust for any (or no) reason, any time before her death, as long as she's legally competent. The settlor appoints herself as the initial trustee, to control and use the trust property as she sees fit.

And now for the legal magic of the living trust device. Although a living trust is really only a legal fiction during the settlor's life, it assumes a very real presence for a brief period after death. When the settlor dies, the living trust can no longer be revoked, or altered by a will. The trust really does own the property now. And since property held in living trust does not need to be probated, the successor trustee can immediately transfer all property owned by the trust to the trust beneficiaries. So one crucial element to have a living trust work effectively is that you have someone you fully trust to be your successor trustee. There is no court or any governmental supervision to be sure your successor trustee complies with the terms of your living trust. So, if there's no one you believe in sufficiently to name as successor trustee, a living trust isn't for you.

Practically speaking, after the trust settlor dies, there is some paperwork necessary to complete transfer of the trust property to the beneficiaries, such as preparing new ownership documents, and paying any death taxes assessed against the estate. Still, these matters can normally be handled without a lawyer in no more than a few weeks. Once the trust property is legally received by the beneficiaries, the trust ceases to exist.

Travis intends to leave his painting collection and his house to his daughter, Bianca, but he wants to have complete control over the house and the collection until he dies, including the right to sell any painting in the collection if he chooses. At the same time, he doesn't want the $300,000 value of this house and the $250,000 value of the collection to be subject to probate. (Travis reasons that it's pretty silly to pay a thousands of dollars in probate fees just to have his own house and paintings turned over to his daughter.) So Travis establishes a revocable living trust, with the house and paintings as the trust's assets. He names himself as trustee, with full power to control the trust property. Bianca is named as the successor trustee, to take over after he dies. He also names Bianca as the trust beneficiary. When Travis dies, Bianca, acting as successor trustee, turns the paintings over to the beneficiary, herself, as directed by the terms of the trust. And, as trustee, she prepares and records a deed transferring the house from the trust to herself. The trust then ceases to exist. All probate proceedings, delays and costs are avoided. Because the estate is worth less than $600,000, no federal estate taxes are assessed (see Chapter 14).

3. Living Trusts and Your Income Taxes

Fortunately, once a living trust has been created, and property is placed in it, maintaining the trust is easy. During the settlor's life, the trust doesn't exist for income tax purposes. The IRS treats the trust property as it does any other property owned by the settlor; all transactions which are technically made by the trust are included as part of the settlor's regular income tax return. So, you don't have to maintain separate books, records or bank accounts for your living trust. While you live, the trust isn't functionally distinct from you, which means it can't be used to lower your income taxes. But, when you die, the trust is, as I've stated, treated as a separate legal entity for probate avoidance purposes. So, for once, you can have your cake and eat it too.

4. Living Trusts and Death Taxes

Let me say it loud, clear and in big type: REVOCABLE LIVING TRUSTS DESIGNED TO AVOID PROBATE DON'T SAVE ON DEATH TAXES. I emphasize this because when some people hear the word "trust," they feel it must mean "tax savings." However, to make matters more complicated, there are other types of trusts which can be used to reduce death taxes. And, in some situations, a revocable living trust designed to avoid probate can be combined with a second trust designed to save on death taxes. A common example of this is when a spouse uses a living trust to avoid probate and then establish a "marital life estate" trust to pay income to the surviving spouse for his or her life, with the property in the trust going to the children or grandchildren when that spouse dies.[3]

5. Living Trusts and Your Debts

Property in a revocable living trust is not immune from attack by the settlor's creditors while he's alive. Some "authorities" have inaccurately stated that property in a revocable living trust can't be grabbed by the settlor's creditors to pay his debts during his life. These authorities argue that for collection purposes a revocable living trust is legally distinct from its creator. I know of no law or case that supports this position. It's most unlikely that any judge would accept it, since during his life the settlor has complete and exclusive power over the trust property. On

---

[3]If the combined estate of you and your spouse exceeds $600,000 (the federal estate tax threshold), please read Chapter 14, Section B and Chapter 16, Section B(1) for a better idea of how this type of trust can be used to save on estate taxes. Basically, a marital life estate trust allows spouses to avoid piling up all their property in the estate of the surviving spouse and therefore having a substantial tax liability when the second spouse dies, by making the surviving spouse the life beneficiary of the property of the first spouse to die, with the principal eventually going to their children or other trust beneficiaries.

the other hand, if property is put in an irrevocable trust,[4] it's a different legal matter (ongoing irrevocable trusts are discussed in Chapter 16). Property transferred to a bona fide irrevocable trust is immune from the settlor's creditors. The key words here are "bona fide." If an irrevocable trust is set up to defraud creditors, it's not bona fide.

 If you're concerned about protecting your assets from creditors, see a lawyer. The materials in this book aren't designed for you.

6. Living Trusts for Couples

A living trust can work as effectively for a couple as for a single person. And any couple, married or not, can use one living trust for their shared ownership property. Because most couples who use living trusts are married, the discussion which follows is cast in terms of "spouses" and "marital property." However, the concepts discussed apply equally to unmarried couples. I neither restate this point in every sentence, nor sprinkle the text with terms

such as "mates," "significant others," or "lovers"; both devices are too cumbersome. So please, if you are a member of an unmarried couple, make the necessary semantical substitutions for yourself.

If each spouse owns property separately, each can establish an individual living trust for the property. But if spouses share ownership of much or all of their property, as is usually the case, it's generally preferable that they use one revocable living trust for their shared property.

Shared ownership is almost always the situation in the eight states which follow the community property ownership system, under which spouses equally own most property acquired after marriage. Even in the other (common law) states, where one spouse may legally be the sole owner of much property, spouses who have been married for many years typically regard most or all property as owned by both. (See Chapter 3 for a list of common law and community property states and an explanation of both systems of property ownership.)

Why is setting up two separate living trusts for shared property owned by a couple generally undesirable? Because each owner can transfer only his or her share of the property to his or her separate trust. To accomplish this, ownership of the shared property must be divided. Why go to the trouble of doing this? Worse, dividing shared marital property in half could lead to unfair and undesired imbalances—for example, one spouse's stocks might go up in value while the other's declines.

Fortunately, there is no need for spouses to divide property ownership as long as one trust is created to handle both spouses' shared property. This can be done using the marital living trust form in Appendix I (Form II). In it, each spouse has full authority to designate the beneficiaries of his or her portion of the property put in trust. When the first spouse dies, the shared marital property is then divided. The deceased spouse's portion of the property is transferred to the beneficiaries he or she named in the trust document. One beneficiary is commonly the surviving spouse, but children, friends and charities may also receive property. If the surviving spouse inherits property from the deceased spouse, he or she

---

[4]An irrevocable trust is very different from the revocable living trust discussed in this chapter, the main difference being that once property is transferred to an irrevocable trust, it can't be taken back by the settlor.

normally transfers it to her living trust, which continues in effect in its revocable form.

The diagram below shows how this type of marital living trust works. In this example, the husband and wife transfer their shared ownership property into one living trust. The husband is the first spouse to die, the "deceased spouse." The wife is the "surviving spouse."

HOW A MARITAL LIVING TRUST WORKS

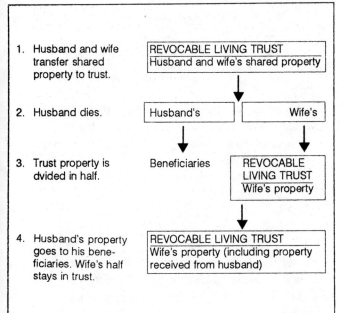

1. Husband and wife transfer shared property to trust.

   REVOCABLE LIVING TRUST
   Husband and wife's shared property

2. Husband dies.

   Husband's   Wife's

3. Trust property is dvided in half.

   Beneficiaries   REVOCABLE LIVING TRUST
                     Wife's property

4. Husband's property goes to his beneficiaries. Wife's half stays in trust.

   REVOCABLE LIVING TRUST
   Wife's property (including property received from husband)

Separately-Owned Property

If a spouse owns some property separately, she or he has a choice as to whether to place this property in a separate living trust (Form I in Appendix I) or in a marital living trust (Form II). If they choose this latter option, they clearly identify the separate property as the sole property of the spouse who owned it.

7. When Couples May Need a More Complex Living Trust

 In a few situations, couples may want a more complex living trust than the one provided in this book and will need to see a lawyer. For example:

- If the total combined estate of both spouses is worth more than $600,000 and the spouses are elderly it may be advisable to establish a marital life estate trust for the surviving spouse.

- If spouses want to use their living trusts to put conditions or limitations on their gifts. Let's say one spouse wants to bind the other to leave property in trust for their mentally-disturbed son, or simply to leave property to a designated list of beneficiaries. In both of these situations, you will need the help of a lawyer.

Claudia and John want to give their summer home in Lake Placid, New York to their two children, but they want them to keep the home in the family for at least one generation. They also want to leave $200,000 in trust for a mentally-ill nephew. Finally, they want to leave a large amount of money to several charities, but don't want to give all these funds outright; rather, they want to have someone monitor the charities they've selected, to be sure these charities continue to adhere to their principles. Because in all these instances, Claudia and John want to place conditions or limitations on their gifts, they'll need to see a lawyer to prepare their trust.

- The marital living trust form in the Appendix cannot be used to impose controls on property left by the deceased spouse to the surviving spouse. Property left to the surviving spouse is received with no strings attached; he can do whatever he wants to with it. If spouses want the surviving spouse to get the benefit of the other spouse's property during life, but also want that property to ultimately go to other beneficiaries (chosen by the deceased spouse), additional controls must be imposed. Usually a marital life estate trust is used. While many couples don't feel the need to impose such controls, it is not unusual to want them in second or subsequent marriages, particularly if the spouses have married later in life and one or both has children from a prior relationship.

When Alfred Wilcalder and Georgette Heflin marry, each has adult children from an earlier marriage. Using both their savings, the couple buys a house. Each wants the other spouse to be able to continue living in the house after the first spouse dies. But each wants his or her interest in the house to go to his or her children after both spouses die. So, with the help of a lawyer, they create a revocable living trust by which each leaves a "life estate" interest in the house to the other, with the children of each being the ultimate beneficiaries of each share. As long as both spouses are alive, the living trust may be revoked by either. But when the first spouse dies (let's say it's Georgette), then her half of the trust becomes irrevocable, and her property is distributed, outside of probate, as the trust directs. This means her half of the house goes to her husband for his life and then to her children when he dies. Under the terms of the living trust, Alfred's portion of the trust remains revocable until he dies. If he subsequently decides he does not want to give his property to his children, he is free to revise his trust and name new beneficiaries.

 If you decide you want to explore imposing controls such as these on property left by one spouse to another, please read Chapter 16, Sections B(1) and C(4), where I discuss marital life estate trusts in more detail. I do not provide "how to" instructions in this book, however. There are simply too many options and possibilities involved to be dealt with in detail here. To draw up such a trust, you will need to see a lawyer.

8. Trusts for Minor Children

If your living trust property is given to a beneficiary who's a minor when you die, an adult must manage that property for the minor. Minors cannot own any substantial amount of property outright.

In Chapter 6, Section C, I discuss the various legal devices which can be used to leave property to minors. In some circumstances, where an estate is relatively modest and there is a trusted person to care for the child (usually the other parent), it's easiest simply to leave property directly to the adult who will care for them. But for larger estates, the best way to leave property to minor children is in a children's trust, which allows you to designate the age at which the child will receive the property, and name a trusted person to manage the trust for the children's benefit.

A children's trust may be created as a part of a revocable living trust. If you die before a child beneficiary has reached the age you designated, the children's trust becomes irrevocable, and continues until the child does reach that age. (If the child has reached that age when you die, she receives her property outright, and no children's trust is created for her.)

One of Edward's beneficiaries of his living trust is Abigail, age 17. Edward establishes a children's trust for her, in his living trust. She is to receive her trust property when she becomes 35. Edward dies when Abigail is 26. Her property is maintained in her children's trust until she becomes 35.

The living trust forms in the Appendix allow you to create simple children's trusts for all beneficiaries who are under 18 when you create the living trust. If you die before any minor beneficiary has reached the age you've specified for them to receive their trust property outright (the form makes it 30 unless you specify another age), that child's property is retained in a separate children's trust managed by the successor trustee of your living trust. When the child reaches the age you specified, the successor trustee turns his trust property over to him. While a children's trust is operational, the trustee has broad powers to spend any of that trust's income or principle for the child's health, support, maintenance or education.

 Other types of children's trusts are possible. For example, a "family pot trust" keeps all trust property for minors in one combined trust. Establishing this sort of trust is usually not a good idea, for several reasons. Among them is the fact that it's harder (and therefore more expensive) to prepare tax returns, the trust doesn't end until the youngest child reaches the designated age (the older ones can't get their share outright before this) and it allows the trustee to prefer one child's needs over another's, thereby setting up the the possibility of conflict. On the other hand, precisely because the trustee is empowered to expend any amount of the pot for any beneficiary, this sort of trust may be a good idea if one child is likely to need a lot more financial help than others.

 Note on Establishing Trusts for Children Over 18: The living trust forms in the Appendix do not allow you to create an ongoing trust for your adult children. Thus, if you have a child who is already 19, or 42 for that matter, you cannot use these forms to delay the age at which your child gets the property you give her. If you want to do that, you will need to see a lawyer.

C. Common Questions About Living Trusts

NOW, LET ME CHANGE GEARS and answer some common questions about living trusts I've been asked over the years.

1. Real Estate

Will real estate be reappraised for property tax purposes if I transfer it to a living trust?

Generally, no. In some states, some real estate transfers, such as sales to new owners who aren't family members, can result in property being immediately reappraised for property tax purposes. By contrast, if the property is not transferred to new owners, it usually won't be reappraised for a set period of years, or (in a few states) at all. In states that don't reappraise property until it's transferred to a new owner, placing title to property in a living trust doesn't usually trigger a property tax reappraisal. Because you and your living trust are considered the same basic entity while you're alive, no taxable transfer is seen to have occurred. But to be absolutely sure that this is true in your state if you're transferring real estate that's risen substantially in value since you bought it into a living trust, check with your local property tax collector to make sure you know exactly what reappraisal rules apply. Also, there may be special local forms that must be completed for the transfer to be recorded. For example, in California, every transfer of real estate must be reported on a "Preliminary Change of Ownership" form, available at County Recorders offices.

If I'm over 55, do I keep my one-time federal tax benefits if I sell the home I live in after I've placed it in a living trust?

Yes. If you're over 55, you have the right, under Internal Revenue Code § 121, to sell your principal home once and exclude $125,000 of receipts from income taxation, even if you have transferred that home to a living trust. And you also retain your rights to defer or "roll over" profits from the sale of one home by using that gain to purchase another within 18 months of the sale.

Will I lose the homestead on my home if I transfer it to a living trust?[5]

Generally, no. State homestead protections, which typically protect a homeowner's equity interest in a home from creditors up to a designated amount, should not be lost because real estate is transferred to a living trust. However, if you're in debt and concerned that a creditor may try to force a sale of your house, check your state's homestead rules carefully. If you are not seriously in debt, there is no need to worry about this one.

2. Moving

Does my living trust remain legal and valid if I move to a different state after establishing it?

Yes. Revocable living trusts are valid and used in every state. However, as discussed in Chapter 3, Section D, if you're married, and you move from a community property state to a common law state, or vice versa, you may want to check the marital property ownership laws of your new

---

[5]A "homestead" is a legal device, available under the laws of most states, to protect your equity in your home, up to a statutorily specified amount, from creditors. In some states that allow homesteads, you record a Declaration of Homestead with the County Recorder; in others, the protection is automatic. In either case, if you qualify for a homestead, your home is protected against forced sale by creditors (other than mortgage holders) if your equity is below the statutory limit. If your equity is larger than the amount protected by the homestead laws, the house can be sold, but in many states you get that protected amount to invest in another house.

state to make sure that the property you believe is yours really is.

3. Gift Taxes

Do I make a legal gift, possibly subject to a gift tax, when I transfer my property to my living trust?

No. Since your living trust can be revoked at any time before you die, you don't make a gift simply by transferring property to the trust. Therefore, no gift tax can be assessed. (See Chapter 15 for a discussion of gift taxes.)

4. Selling Property That Is in a Living Trust

Will it be difficult for me to sell or transfer property that I have transferred to my living trust?

No. If you decide to sell property owned by your trust, you can either:

• sell the property directly from the trust, acting in your capacity as trustee to sign the title document or otherwise authorize the sale by completing a bill of sale, sales contract or other document, or

• in your capacity as trustee of the living trust, first transfer title of the particular item listed as trust property back to yourself as an individual, and then sell the property in your own name.

Whichever way is most convenient is the one to use. When selling real estate owned by a trust, what is most convenient is generally what the title company involved requests. As far as marketable securities are concerned, most brokers have a convenient procedure to deal with selling assets held in a living trust.

Of course, you'll need to amend your revocable living trust if property given to a particular trust beneficiary is no longer owned by the trust. Obviously no document can give away what you don't own. (Amending living trusts is discussed in Section H.)

D. Major Decisions in Creating a Living Trust

OKAY, ENOUGH GENERAL INFORMATION. Now let's focus on the key decisions you need to make to establish a revocable living trust to avoid probate. Once you do that, you will be prepared to actually create your trust document, as explained in the next section.

Initially, you (the settlor) must make four major decisions:

What property will be in the trust?

Who will be the successor trustee(s), with the authority to transfer the property in the trust to your beneficiaries after your death? (You'll be the initial trustee.)

Who will be your beneficiaries?

How will any debts and taxes outstanding at your death be paid?

1. Choosing Property to Put in the Living Trust

You can place all your property in your living trust, or transfer some, or even most, of your property by other means, such as a will or joint tenancy. But in general, if you decide to use a living trust to avoid probate, it's sensible to transfer all your "big-ticket" items to it, unless they are subject to another probate avoidance technique. For example, if you and your spouse already own your house in joint tenancy, you've already arranged to avoid probate of the house.

Mr. and Mrs. Tramsey share ownership of a house with an equity of $150,000, held in joint tenancy, personal possessions worth $20,000, U.S. Government bonds worth $40,000, stock worth $100,000, two cars worth $20,000 each, and a joint savings account with $20,000 in it. Each wants to leave his or her half of the house, personal possessions, cars and stocks and bonds to the other. As the house is already in joint tenancy, the survivor will become the sole owner free of probate. To take care of the personal possessions, stock, bonds and cars, the Tramseys decide to create a revocable living trust. However, when it comes to their savings account, they both decide that, at death, each will leave his or her half directly to their son, not to the surviving spouse. They learn that the simplest way to transfer bank accounts outside of probate is by using what's called an informal bank trust account, or "pay-on-death account." (I discuss this device in Chapter 11, Section C.) So, the Tramseys divide the money in their joint savings account in half, and each spouse then creates a separate pay-on-death account for half, naming their son as beneficiary, to receive the money in that account when he or she dies.

Violet McKensie, who lives in California, owns a house worth $200,000, a stock account, a car worth $12,000 and personal possessions worth $15,000. After reading Chapter 13, Section D, she learns that, under California law, she can transfer personal property worth up to $60,000 (with no need to count amounts transferred by probate avoidance devices) by her will free of probate.[6] Violet decides to transfer her house and stock account by a living trust, thus avoiding probate on these items. Violet also understands that it is wise to have a back-up will (she plays the lottery once in a while, and who knows?). Since she plans to prepare a will anyway, she decides to use it for her car and personal possessions. One reason why Violet decides it makes sense to transfer her car by her will rather than by her living trust is that transferring title of the car to the living trust would require a trip to the Department of Motor Vehicles, something that past experience in seemingly endless lines has taught is best avoided if possible. Also, she'd have to check with her insurance company to be sure it would continue her insurance if her car were technically owned by her trust—another hassle she'd prefer to avoid.

2. Choosing the Trustees of Your Living Trust

You must make two choices when it comes to naming a trustee to manage the trust property: who will be the initial trustee, and who will take over as the successor trustee when the first trustee dies or becomes incapacitated.

a. Your Initial Trustee

As discussed, the initial trustee of your living trust is almost always you, the person (or, in a marital trust, the people) who set it up. Grasping this point is, of course,

---

6Exemptions to probate are substantially lower in most other states. See Chapter 13, Section C.

essential to understanding what a living trust is—a device by which you continue to absolutely control your own property while you are alive, and at the same time you arrange to avoid probate of the property after you die.

With a marital trust for shared property, both spouses (or members of the couple) are normally co-trustees. The marital trust in the Appendix calls for this arrangement. When one spouse dies, the other spouse continues as sole trustee.

 One Spouse as Trustee: If you want only one spouse to be the original trustee of a marital living trust, there's an unusual—and unequal—distribution of authority over shared property, and you should see a lawyer.

 Naming Someone Else as Initial Trustee: If you want to name someone besides yourself to be your initial trustee because you don't want to, or cannot, continue to manage your own assets, see a lawyer. When you make somebody else your initial trustee, you create a more complicated trust, often necessitating much more detailed controls on the trustee's powers to act. In addition, under IRS rules, if you aren't the trustee of your own living trust, separate trust records must be maintained, and a trust tax return filed.

b. Your Successor Trustee

In addition to naming yourself as initial trustee, it's essential that you name at least one successor trustee. Your successor is the person who makes your trust work after you die, by distributing its assets to your beneficiaries. Also, under the terms of the trust forms in the Appendix, the successor trustee takes over management of the trust if you (or you and your spouse, with a marital trust) become incapacitated. This is a standard provision to avoid the need for court proceedings in this situation. (Chapter 18 discusses how you can create a durable power of attorney to choose someone to be responsible to handle property not held in your living trust should you become incapacitated.)

With a marital trust, the successor trustee takes over after both spouses die.

When you decide on your successor trustee, your job isn't done. You should also name an alternate successor trustee, in case the successor trustee dies before you do or for any other reason can't serve.

The Job of the Successor Trustee. To sensibly choose your successor trustee, you should understand what he or she will need to do under a living trust prepared from this book. The primary job of the successor trustee is to turn trust property over to the beneficiaries you have named. This is normally not difficult if the property and beneficiaries are clearly identified. Still, some effort is required.

Normally, the successor trustee obtains several certified copies of the death certificate of the settlor. Then she presents a copy of the death certificate and a copy of the living trust document, along with proof of her own identity, to financial institutions, brokers and other organizations having possession of the trust assets. If any documents of title must be prepared to transfer trust property to the beneficiaries, the successor trustee prepares them. For example, real estate owned by a living trust is transferred to the beneficiaries, after the death of the settlor, by the successor trustee preparing, signing and recording (in the County Recorder's office) a deed from herself, as trustee of the living trust, to the specified beneficiaries. No court or other administrative action is required.

What happens if an institution won't cooperate with the successor trustee? Happily, this is unlikely to happen. Institutions that deal with financial assets—from title companies to recorder's offices to stock brokers—are familiar with living trusts and how they work.

In addition to dealing with property subject to formal ownership (title) documents, the trustee supervises the distribution of all trust assets without documents of title—household furnishings, jewelry, heirlooms, collectibles—to the appropriate beneficiaries. The distribution process ends when all beneficiaries have

actually received the trust property given to them in the trust document.

In some situations, additional tasks may be required of the successor trustee:

Preparing and filing death tax returns. If a death tax return (state, federal or both) must be filed, and death taxes paid, the successor trustee is responsible for these tasks. (See Chapter 14 for a discussion of federal and state death taxes.) If you also prepare a back-up will, the executor you name in the will shares legal responsibility for filing these tax returns. Of course, usually, the same person is appointed as the successor trustee and executor.

Managing children's trusts (if they are established). The trust forms in the Appendix allow you to leave trust property to beneficiaries who are minors when the trust is created in simple children's trusts [see Section B(8) above]. If you die before any minor reaches the age you've specified in the trust document, your successor trustee will manage trust property left for the benefit of that minor until she reaches that age. The forms do not permit you to name one person to be successor trustee of your trust and another to be trustee of children's trusts. Thus, the successor trustee can have ongoing management responsibilities for a children's trust. Annual trust income tax returns are required for each operational children's trust, and are the responsibility of the successor trustee.

If you have minor beneficiaries, you should consider, when selecting your successor trustee:

- The fact that a trustee of a children's trust may have ongoing trust management responsibilities for an extended period of time.
- Whether you want the trustee of the children's trust(s) to be paid. The trust form provides that they are entitled to "reasonable compensation."

The duties and burdens of a successor trustee who manages a children's trust can be substantial. The trust can last for decades and entail extensive financial responsibilities. If you have more than one minor beneficiary, the job can become even more demanding, as each minor's property is managed in a separate trust.

Particularly if you have several minor beneficiaries, consider reviewing your situation with a lawyer to see what type(s) of children's trusts and successor trustee arrangements will work best for you.

Who Should You Choose to Be Your Successor Trustee? Your successor trustee should be whomever you feel is most trustworthy to do the job, who's willing to do it, and can actually do it. Often a principal beneficiary, such as a spouse or adult child, is named as successor trustee. However, you aren't compelled to name a beneficiary as trustee. If you believe the beneficiary (much as you love him or her) will be troubled by having to handle the practical details and paperwork, it is preferable to name someone else, often another family member, to be successor trustee.

If your minor children are beneficiaries of your living trust, they'll receive their property in the form of ongoing children's trusts that won't terminate until they reach a set age; your successor trustee will manage these children's trusts as well. So, if you have already chosen the person you want to be your children's property manager (see Chapter 6), you should name that person as successor trustee.

When you prepare a back-up will, the person you name as executor should be the same as your successor trustee. (See Chapter 17 for more on back-up wills.) This eliminates any possible conflict that might arise if a different person fulfills each function.

 If for some reason you want to name a person to be your successor trustee and another to be your executor, see a lawyer.

What about the idea of naming two successor trustees to serve together? Legally, you can name as many successor co-trustees as you want, with power divided between them as you specify. However, as a general rule, because of coordination and possible conflict problems between multiple trustees, it's generally best to name a single successor trustee. This isn't invariably true, however. For example, a parent may not want to be seen as

favoring one child over others, and to avoid this could name two or more children as successor co-trustees. This can be especially appropriate if the children are equal beneficiaries of the trust. And if the children all get along, doing this rarely causes a problem. However, if the children are prone to conflict, you risk creating a serious problem (and doing none of them a favor) by having them share power as trustees. It's better just to name the most qualified and let the chips fall as they will.

 Methods for Handling Potential Conflicts Between Co-Successors: If you're naming successor co-trustees, and have any fear of potential conflicts, see a lawyer. Such situations are too touchy to resolve without careful individual analysis. For this reason, the trust forms in the Appendix don't contain clauses for resolving conflicts between successor co-trustees. Methods a lawyer may recommend include compulsory arbitration, or a provision that if there is a dispute, one identified trustee shall prevail.

 Naming Someone Other than Your Spouse as Successor Trustee of a Marital Living Trust: With a marital living trust, you choose a successor trustee to take over after both spouses die. If you want someone other than a surviving spouse to be trustee for a deceased spouse's portion of a marital living trust, see a lawyer, because this raises many complexities and possible coordination problems between the surviving spouse and other trustee.

Naming a Bank as Successor Trustee. In my experience, it is almost always a bad idea to name a bank as successor trustee. I've heard some horror stories involving the indifference or downright rapaciousness of banks acting as trustees of family living trusts. Your successor trustee is your link with the ongoing life of your loved ones. You want that link to be a human being you trust, not a corporation dedicated to the enhancement of its bottom line. However, if there is no human being you believe will act honestly and competently as your successor trustee, you'll need to select some financial institution to do the job. Probably the best choice here is a private trust company. These companies generally offer more humane and personal attention to a trust than a bank or other large financial institution. Also, they can be more reasonable about fees charged to wind up a living trust than a bank is.

Should the Successor Trustee Be Paid? Usually the successor trustee of a living trust isn't paid when the only purpose of the trust is probate avoidance, especially if the successor trustee is also a primary beneficiary. After all, the task of transferring assets to beneficiaries is not arduous. For this reason, the trust forms set out in the Appendix provide that no compensation is paid to the successor trustee, except for services rendered managing a children's trust.

 Compensating a Successor Trustee: If you decide that you do want your successor trustee compensated for tasks entailed in transferring trust property to adult beneficiaries, see a lawyer. Compensation might be appropriate if your estate is a large one which will require federal tax returns to be filed.

If the successor trustee will have to manage property held in a children's trust for minor beneficiaries, it seems fair to provide "reasonable compensation" for the trustee for doing this job, because it entails ongoing management responsibilities. So the trust forms in the Appendix provide that the successor trustee is entitled to reasonable compensation for managing a children's trust; the successor trustee decides what is a reasonable fee for these services.

 If you're uneasy at this kind of open-ended provision for compensation, and want more precise and limiting terms, discuss this with a lawyer.

The Powers of the Successor Trustee. A trustee of a trust must have a written authority defining what he can do. The legalese for this is "trust powers." The living trust forms in the Appendix contain a broad general grant of powers to the successor trustees to transfer property to adult beneficiaries or institutions. A simple probate avoidance trust has no need for more than this.

 If you're worried about such a broad grant of powers, and want for some reason to limit what the successor trustee can do, you will need to see an attorney. Such a concern normally indicates potential serious problems of mistrust, which require careful professional attention.

The Powers of a Trustee of a Children's Trust. Aside from the general powers of the successor trustee, the living trust forms state that he or she has broad authority to manage any children's trust, including the power to spend any amount of each children's trust income or principal for that child's "health, support, maintenance or education." As long as you trust your successor trustee, defining her power to manage minor beneficiaries' trust property in this broad way is the best approach.

 If you want to restrict the authority of your successor trustee over the children's trusts, see an attorney.

3. Naming the Beneficiaries of Your Living Trust

Beneficiaries, of course, are simply the people or organizations you've chosen to receive your property after you die. You've already decided who these people and organizations are in Chapter 5, Section O. Now you simply plug the names of those beneficiaries into the right blanks on the living trust forms.[7] The probate avoidance

---

[7] If you want to explain your estate plan, intentions or feelings to your beneficiaries, as is discussed in Chapter 5, you can also prepare a letter to accompany your living trust. Remember, this letter is not a valid legal document, and cannot be used to transfer any property. But to convey your thoughts and feelings, a letter works fine.

living trusts in the Appendix allow you to name the following beneficiaries.

a. Direct Beneficiaries

Direct beneficiaries are those people you name to be given trust property.

The adult beneficiaries you name receive their trust property promptly after your death.

Minor beneficiaries have their property retained in a children's trust until they reach the age you've specified for them to receive it [see (d) below].

Some people ask whether it's permissible to name only one beneficiary who also is the successor trustee. The answer is yes.

Nikki, a widow, establishes a living trust to give her house and personal possessions to her adult daughter, Christine. Christine is named as successor trustee. After her mother dies, Christine puts on her successor trustee hat and executes a deed transferring the house to herself, wearing her beneficiary hat.

---

b. Alternate Beneficiaries

For each item of property your living trust gives to a beneficiary, you can name an alternate beneficiary to receive that gift if the beneficiary dies before you do.

c. Residuary Beneficiary

You can name a person (or people) or organizations to receive all trust property not specifically given to a direct beneficiary or alternate beneficiary alive at your death. You can also name an alternate residuary beneficiary.

d. Minor Beneficiaries

After you've named all (direct) beneficiaries, alternate beneficiaries, and residuary beneficiaries of your living trust, the form requires that you list each beneficiary who is a minor when you create your trust, except those you made gifts to using the Uniform Transfers to Minors Act [see Section E(2), Step 7, and Chapter 6, Section C]. The trust document provides that the property you leave to each listed minor beneficiary is, at your death, retained in a separate children's "subtrust" until that child reaches the age specified for that subtrust to end. A subtrust, as the name indicates, is simply a trust that is part of a larger trust. In this instance, the subtrust is a children's trust established by the living trust. If, at your death, a child has already reached the age you designated in your living trust for the children's subtrust to end, the children's trust is never activated and your successor trustee will simply turn her property over to that beneficiary.

If you don't specify an age for a children's subtrust to end, the trust form specifies that it ends when that sub-trust's beneficiary becomes 30 years old. Remember, since you establish a separate children's trust for each minor, you have the ability, when listing each minor beneficiary, to select the age at which you want that particular child to inherit. Thus you can specify that different subtrusts end when different minor beneficiaries reach different ages.

Esmerelda, a single parent, has two children, Jackie, 17 and impractical, and Vicki, 15 and sensible. Esmerelda creates a living trust, dividing her property equally between her two children. In the trust document, Esmerelda specifies that Vicki is to receive her trust property when she's 25, but Jackie not until she's 35. By that age, Esmerelda hopes Jackie will have matured enough to handle money prudently. Esmerelda dies when Vicki is 27 and Jackie 29. Vicki gets the property left to her outright, while Jackie's will be held in trust for six years.

e. Beneficiaries of a Marital Living Trust

In the marital living trust (Form II in Appendix I), each spouse can name her or his own beneficiaries, alternate beneficiaries, residuary beneficiary, and minor beneficiaries. Often, each spouse names the other as the sole beneficiary, with their children as alternate beneficiaries. In other situations, people may wish to divide their property between their spouse and children. Particularly, in second or subsequent marriages, each spouse may want to name his or her own children from prior marriages as beneficiaries for some or all of their property. And of course, no matter how many times married, a spouse may want to make at least some gifts to people other than the other spouse and children—e.g., him to his cousins, her to her sisters. Accomplishing any of these goals using the marital living trust form is easy. Spouses can name as many beneficiaries as they want.

4. Arranging for Your Debts and Taxes to Be Paid

Many people won't leave any significant debts or have any substantial income or death tax obligations when they die. If you fit into this category, you can go on to other concerns. However, if you will likely leave debts, including death tax obligations, and don't make provision to pay them, any of your property may be taken to pay for them.

As a general rule, if your debts are likely to be small, little planning is required. When you die, your successor trustee will pay whatever bills you have, and your estate accumulates, either from property you specified in your trust for this purpose, or from trust property generally. In either case, as debts are small, no beneficiary will suffer a substantial loss. If you have larger debts, including estate tax obligations, more planning is required.

Let's look at how this works and whether you need to do any planning to deal with this eventuality.

a. Assessing Your Debts

When estimating your debts, don't include the kinds of obligations that are directly tied to specific items of property, such as the mortgage on a house or money owed on a car.[8] When you make a gift of these items, the debt on them goes right along. So, if you leave your house, which is subject to a mortgage, to your son, he gets both the house and the mortgage. These kinds of debts do not have to be paid off by your estate at death, unless you create a specific provision to do so in your living trust or will, and identify assets to be used for paying them.

Your estate is liable for all other (unsecured) debts, which include such things as personal bank loans, court judgments, unpaid credit card balances and taxes—both income and death. In adding up your debts, also consider funeral expenses and the possibility that you will incur expenses of a last illness. Many people prepay the former, and have insurance which covers the latter, but if any of these expenses aren't taken care of in other ways, your living trust property can be liable for these debts.

b. Do Death Taxes Have to Be Paid?

Before you worry about how your death taxes will be paid, you need to learn whether you're likely to owe any. If the

---

[8]These are usually called "secured debts" in legal parlance, and typically exist in situations when a creditor would have the right to repossess (foreclose on) the property if the debt isn't paid.

net worth of your estate is less than $600,000 when you die, there will be no federal estate tax (unless you've made taxable gifts during your life. (See Chapters 14 and 15.) Also, transfers to a surviving spouse are free of federal estate tax.

A number of states, including California and Florida, impose no death taxes. Other states do impose death taxes; the minimum amount taxed and the tax rates vary substantially from state to state. In some states, whether a tax is imposed depends not only on the value of the estate, but who it is given to. I provide state tax information in Chapter 14.

c.   Choosing Assets to Pay Debts and Taxes

Unless you plan to leave all, or the great bulk of, your estate to one person (say your spouse), in which case that person will be responsible to pay any debts or taxes as they see fit, you will probably want to designate specific assets to be used to pay them. Fortunately, there is an easy way to handle this matter. The living trust forms in the Appendix contain a clause where you can specify which trust property (such as a bank account) you want used to pay any debts and death taxes. The clause provides further that if this specified property isn't sufficient to pay all debts and death taxes, your successor trustee has the authority to decide which other trust property shall be used.

If you have substantial debts, it's often a good idea to list several assets which should be used for their payment. Otherwise, someone you wanted to give a particular gift to may have a portion of it taken to help pay your debts. Also, you can list the order in which you want these assets used to pay debts and taxes. And finally, make sure that together they're worth more than what's likely to be required, or your other gifts will have to be used to pay a portion of your debts and taxes.

When she prepares her estate plan, Ms. de Soirée has several large debts totalling, roughly, $50,000. She also has substantial assets. Her living trust provides that her debts are to be paid from an identified trust stock account (presently worth $70,000). If that account proves to be insufficient, the remaining debts are to be paid from an identified trust savings account, with a current balance of $20,000. When Ms. de Soirée dies, her debts total $96,000. The stock account is liquidated for $54,000. The savings account holds $29,000. The total amount in the specified property is $83,000, which is $13,000 less than her debts. Ms. de Soirée's successor trustee can use any trust property she wants to pay this additional $13,000.

Assuming you wish to designate specific assets to pay your debts, the best general rule is to select liquid assets over non-liquid ones. Liquid assets are those that are easily converted into cash. For instance, bank and deposit accounts, money market accounts and stocks and bonds can normally be converted to cash easily and at full value. On the other hand, tangible assets such as cars, planes, jewelry, stamp and coin collections, electronic items and musical instruments must be sold to raise the necessary cash to pay debts and taxes. Forced sales (often called "fire sales" or "distress sales") seldom bring in anywhere near the full value of the items sold; it's common to only receive 30%-50% of the item's full value. In short, if your successor trustee will have to sell tangible assets to pay your debts and expenses, the overall value of your estate will be reduced both by the costs of sale and the fact that full value will not likely be received.

When designating property to use to pay debts and taxes, review your specific gifts. Obviously, if property you select to pay debts and taxes is also earmarked for a specific beneficiary, that beneficiary is likely to feel slighted. For this reason, it is usually advisable to designate property that hasn't been left as a specific gift to pay debts and expenses. Or, if you do designate property that has been left to a specific person, make sure you have left them enough other property so that their entire inheritance isn't wiped out.

E. How to Create Your Living Trust Document

NOW IT'S TIME for some "hands on" work. This section explains, step-by-step, how to prepare your own living trust document. You'll remove the form you need from the Appendix and complete it by following the instructions. Read this entire section carefully so you understand the choices you will make. Take your time and reread as much as you need to.

1. Select the Trust Form You Want

The Appendix contains two living trust forms:

- Form I: Living trust for one person.
- Form II: Living trust for a married couple with shared ownership property.

Select the form which fits your situation. It's generally best to use one trust form for all your property you wish to include in the trust, simply designating in it different beneficiaries for different items of property. However, there are some special situations where it may be preferable to use more than one living trust, including:

- When you want to keep different types of property clearly separate, particularly when they will be handled differently after you die. For example, although the same goal could be achieved in one trust, a person in a second marriage may prefer to create one trust for property that's solely owned by her, which she wants to go to children from the first marriage, and another for property held in shared ownership with her husband, which will go to him.

- When you want different successor trustees to serve different purposes. For example, if you are establishing an ongoing children's trust for a minor child, it's conceivable that one person might be best to serve as trustee for the minor child's trust, and someone else might better serve as successor trustee to distribute the rest of the property. To do this using the forms in the Appendix, you'd need two living trusts—each with different successor trustees and different trust property.

- If one living trust becomes so unwieldy that coherence seems to demand additional trusts. This is a subjective decision. If you have many different types of property and many different beneficiaries, and find that trying to handle it all in one trust is becoming unmanageable, try using more than one.

Reminder: A married person can use either Form I or II for separately owned property.

2. Drafting Your Living Trust

Once you've selected the appropriate trust form:

- Read the form carefully to understand what it says and how it works.

- Photocopy it so you have several clean copies to work on if it turns out you need to prepare more than one draft.

- Use a pencil to make corrections easier, fill in all needed information, including listing your property, naming beneficiaries, and designating your successor trustee. To help you do this, follow each numbered step set out below. The numbers are keyed to the form. Thus, you'll see a ① on each living trust form whenever you insert the information called for by Step 1. The steps are set out in the most logical order. However, the circled numbers on the forms do not always proceed sequentially (e.g., number 1, the name of your trust, appears at the beginning of the form and then later, after other circled numbers). The result is that occasionally a later portion of the form must be completed before an earlier portion.

- Be sure you go through the form slowly and carefully, filling in all blanks with information needed. Some simple, clear information you must fill in is not keyed to a circled number because no explanation seems necessary. Where you see a blank and a "he/she" printed underneath, put in either "he" or "she," depending on whether the person referred to (which will be clear in the context) is male or female. Similarly, where you see a blank with "your state" printed underneath, you fill in the state where you live.

- When you have satisfactorily completed the form, proofread it carefully. Then proceed as explained below in Sections E(3), E(4) and E(5) to finish your trust.

Note on Form II, the Marital Living Trust: For the most part, the same decisions must be made whether you're preparing a living trust for one person or for a couple. Thus the same numbers for each step appear in the marital trust as the trust for one person. However, some additional concerns apply only to marital living trusts. These instructions are identified by the symbol

Step 1: Name Your Living Trust

A living trust document must be given an identifying name. Normally, you simply use your own name—for example, The Denis Clifford Trust. It's legal to use more

inventive names, for reasons ranging from a desire for privacy to nostalgia. (I once had a client who created the "Rue de Rivoli Trust.") Also, if you create more than one trust, you will want to distinguish them. One way to do this is to use numbers (e.g., The Denis Clifford Trust #1, The Denis Clifford Trust #2, and so on).

A married couple normally uses both their names to identify their trust: "The Kay and Ornette Lewison Trust"; or "The Cynthia Duffy and Mike O'Mally Trust."

If you use your name(s) for your trust, insert your name(s) every time there is a 1 on the living trust form. This includes naming yourself(s) as the initial trustee(s) of your trust.

If your trust doesn't have your own name, you'll need to distinguish, each time you see a 1, whether your own name or the trust's name is required.

Step 2: Decide How Many Property Schedules Your Trust Needs

By this time, you should have decided which items of your property you will place in your living trust and which you will transfer by other means. To create your trust, you define which of your property you've given to it. You do this by listing all property that is owned by the trust on a sheet (or sheets) of paper (called a "schedule(s)") attached to the trust document, as explained in Step 3. Here you decide how many trust schedules you want to use. Normally, if you're creating a trust for one person (Form I), you will only use one schedule— "Schedule A," even if there are several different types of property transferred to the trust.

Mrs. Johnson wants to transfer her house, two cars, stock accounts and jewelry to her living trust. She can list all this property on one trust schedule, "A."

The trust form for a married couple states that the trust has three schedules, A, B and C. Schedule A is for their shared ownership property, B is for the husband's separate property, and C is for the wife's separate property. If all the couple's property is shared ownership property, they should simply delete the reference to Schedules B and C and use only Schedule A. If both (or either) have separate property, they will want to use Schedule B and/or C to list that separate property, assuming they want to handle everything in one trust.

Mrs. and Mr. Andrezly, in their 60's, have been married for 15 years. Each has children from a former marriage. When they got married, each owned property which they agreed would remain each's separate property. Since they have been married, they have acquired shared property, including a home. Each wants his or her separate property to go to their children from the first marriage; their shared property goes to the surviving spouse. One simple way to list their property in the marital living trust is by using three schedules: Schedule A for the shared property, Schedule B for Mrs. Andrezly's separate property, and Schedule C for Mr. Andrezly's separate property. Another approach is to create three separate trusts, the marital living trust for the shared marital property and two living trusts for each spouse's separate property. If the Andrezlys did this, they would use only a Schedule A in the marital trust for their shared marital property. You can use whichever method works best for you.

Step 3: List Your Living Trust Property on the Trust Schedule(s)

When you've decided how many schedules you want to use, you list the trust property on them. As you can see by looking at the trust forms in the Appendix, a trust schedule is nothing more than a sheet of paper identified at the top by a capital letter—"Schedule A" or "Schedule B," etc.

Listing the trust property on a schedule is not making a gift of it to beneficiaries. You list the property to be clear what property you have transferred to the trust. Then, in the trust document itself (as described in Step 7), you specify to whom this trust property will be given after your death.

To complete the transfer of property to the trust, you also must re-register title to that property in the trust name. This essential process is explained in detail in Section F.

To list property on a schedule, you need to identify each item of property in a way that your successor trustee and beneficiaries unambiguously know what's referred to. There are no legal rules which require property to be listed in any particular form. The whole point is to be clear as to exactly what property you transfer to the trust. General descriptions of property transferred to the trust are sufficient for listing it on a schedule. Thus, you can list:

"The house, furnishings, and personal possessions at 1000 Eccles St., Burnfield, Michigan;

Bank account #88-124406 at First Savings, Burnfield."

When you name the beneficiaries for the trust property, your gifts must, of course, be consistent with the property listed on the schedule. But the schedule listing does not automatically have to be as detailed as your gifts. For example, as just stated, you list "The house, furnishings and personal possessions at…[street address]" on the schedule. You can give all this property to one beneficiary, or you could divide it, naming one beneficiary for the house and another for the furnishings and possessions.

If you need to refer to yourself or your property in a trust schedule, do so in the third person, by calling yourself "the settlor" rather than using "I" or "my." Living trusts traditionally use the term "settlor," and it's prudent to use the traditional form. Sometimes, to clarify what property is owned by the trust, it helps to state on the schedule that identified property was "formerly" or "previously" owned by the settlor.

On a trust schedule, you list: *"The three-quarter carat diamond bracelet formerly owned by the settlor."*

A variation of this is to identify and list property "in possession of the settlor," e.g., *"All C.D.'s and videos in possession of the settlor."*

Here are some examples of how typical types of property can be listed on your trust schedule(s).

a. Real Estate

A house can be listed by the common street address: *"The house and real estate at 10001 Lakeway Drive, Seaview, Florida."* A full legal description isn't required. Similarly, unimproved property can be listed by its common name: *"The lots previously owned by the settlor on Alligator Road, Seaview, Florida."*

b. Furnishings

Household furnishings can also be generally listed: *"The house and real estate at 12 High St., Chicago, Illinois, and all household furnishings and personal possessions in it."* Or, if you rent (or own and want to leave your household goods to someone different from the person to whom you leave the real property): *"All the settlor's household goods and personal possessions located at 82 West Ave., Chicago Ill."*

c. Bank Accounts

You can list bank accounts by any means sufficient to identify them. Generally, it makes sense to list the account number: *"Bank account # 78-144212-8068 at Oceanside Savings, Market St. Branch."*

d. Cash

You cannot transfer cash to a living trust simply by stating a dollar figure on the schedule. For example, if you list "$25,000" on Schedule A, this doesn't transfer that amount of cash to the trust, because no source for these funds is given. Effective transfers would be:

"$25,000 from bank account #33-931007-6214 at Bonanza Thrift, Miami, Florida" (assuming title to that bank account is transferred to the trust's name—see Section F).

"$25,000 from the settlor's stash in his desk." This is obviously risky. If the money is moved from the desk, it technically is no longer owned by the trust.

e. Valuable Personal Possessions

Valuable personal property, whether it be a fur coat, computer, antiques, collectibles, set of tools or whatever else, should be listed in a way that is easy to identify:

"The collection of 19th century American coins previously owned by the settlor."

f. Stock Accounts and Money Market Accounts

These need to be listed clearly enough so there is no question what property is referred to.

"The money market account #6D-32 2240001, at International Monetary Inc."

"All stock and any other assets in account #144-16-4124, at Smith Barney & Co."

"100 shares of General Motor common stock."

g. Business Interests

Solely-owned businesses can be listed simply by name:

"The Funjimaya Restaurant";

"The King of Hearts Bakery."

Your ownership of a shared business can be listed as:

"All the settlor's interests in the Ben-Dee partnership";

"All shares of X Corporation formerly owned by the settlor."

Step 4: Identify the Nature of Shared Marital Trust Property (Marital Trust Only)

When preparing a marital living trust, the spouses should state in the trust document that all shared property transferred to the trust retains the legal character it had before. So, in addition to listing shared property in Schedule A, the spouses should include a provision, in the text of the trust, that this property was community property,[9] or common law property with equal ownership,[10] and that this legal type of ownership is retained when the property is placed in the trust.

To accomplish this, insert one of the following clauses in the marital living trust form, where you see a ④:

---

[9]Community property is jointly owned marital property of spouses residing in the eight community property states. See Chapter 3, Section B.

[10]Common law property with equally shared ownership by spouses is property held in both spouses' names (or otherwise owned by both spouses) in the 41 common law property states. See Chapter 3, Section C.

- **If you live in a common law state.** For marital property with title held in shared ownership by spouses of a common law state and listed on Schedule A, state in the living trust document, where you see ④:

    "(All trust property listed on Schedule A) was co-owned equally by the settlors and shall retain that character after being transferred to this trust. Any power reserved to the settlors to alter, amend, modify or revoke this trust, as to the property listed in Schedule A, must be exercised by both settlors, in writing, to be effective. If the trust is revoked as to any property listed in Schedule A, this property shall be returned to the settlors as co-owned equally by them."

- **If you live in a community property state.** For community property owned by spouses of a community property state and listed on Schedule A, state in the living trust document, where you see a ④:

    "(All property listed in Schedule A) is community property of the settlors, and shall retain that character after being transferred to this trust. Any power reserved to settlors to alter, amend, modify, or revoke this trust, as to the property listed in Schedule A is held by the settlors during their joint lifetimes as managers of the community property. If the trust is revoked, any property listed in Schedule A shall be returned to settlors as their community property and not as the separate property of either or both."

Step 5: Arrange for Management of Trust Property If You Become Incapacitated

Living trust Form I states, in Section III(C), where ⑤ appears, that if the settlor becomes incapacitated, the successor trustee will manage the trust property for the benefit of the settlor until he becomes able to manage his own affairs. These provisions eliminate any need for court proceedings to appoint a guardian or custodian for trust property if you, as settlor, become incapacitated.

The form for a married couple provides, in Sections VI(E) and VI(F), where 5 appears, that if both spouses become incapacitated, or if the survivor becomes incapacitated after one spouse dies, the trust property shall be managed by the successor trustee for the settlor's benefit. (If both spouses are alive and one becomes incapacitated, the other spouse has the right to manage all the trust property as a trustee, so no provision for incapacity is needed in this situation.)

The term "incapacitated" is not defined in the trust document. It doesn't really need to be; the trust states that physical or mental incapacity must be determined by a doctor, in writing, and that is normally sufficient.

If for some reason you want to specifically limit the successor trustee's powers to handle the trust if you become incapacitated, see a lawyer. Relatively few people, in my opinion, need to worry about this. You've chosen someone you trust as your successor trustee. However, if there are certain limits or restrictions you want to bind that person to (e.g., not to sell your house), you will need a custom-tailored document.

Durable Power of Attorney Note: Another way to provide in advance for someone to mange your affairs if you become incapacitated is the Durable Power of Attorney. I discuss this important document in Chapter 18. However, you should understand that a Durable Power of Attorney does not control property transferred to a living trust. As stated above, with a living trust created from this book your successor trustee has the power to manage property transferred to your living trust if you are unable to do so. However, if you own some property not transferred to your living trust (e.g., your house is in joint tenancy, you leave some property by will, or you receive new income from a pension plan), your successor trustee has no power to manage this property. For this reason (and because you may receive other property or income in the future), I strongly suggest that you also create a Durable Power of Attorney. (See Chapter 18.) If you don't, and you become incapacitated, property not trans-

ferred to your living trust will need to be managed by a court-appointed conservator or guardian.

Step 6: Name Your Successor Trustees

In the blank with the ⑥ on the trust forms, you name your successor trustee and your alternate successor trustee. Choosing the successor trustee was discussed in Section D. You've already named yourself as the initial trustee.

The trustee clauses provide that no trustee has to post a bond.[11] In most all situations, there's no requirement of a bond, but just in case the question is somehow raised by lawsuit or otherwise, it's sensible to have waived any bond requirement. The cost of a bond would have to be paid for by your estate, and your beneficiaries would then receive less. If you select a trustworthy successor trustee, there's no reason for a bond.

If you do want to require a bond, see a lawyer.

Step 7: Name the Trust Beneficiaries

Now you enter the names of your beneficiaries, alternate beneficiaries, and residuary beneficiaries for trust property by inserting their names, and descriptions of property given them, in the appropriate blanks, where you see ⑦ on the form. Be sure to read this entire step before you begin filling in the names of your beneficiaries.

The living trust forms contain five clauses for listing specific beneficiaries—people or institutions you want to get identified trust property—and alternate beneficiaries, in case your first choice dies before you do. The

---

[11]A bond is basically an insurance policy guaranteeing that a person will honestly carry out their duties and paying off up to a stated amount if they don't.

instructions on the form read "[Beneficiary] shall be give [property identified]." If you want to name more than one beneficiary for a gift, you can, of course, do so. The form itself doesn't state "[Beneficiary or beneficiaries]" because that's too ungainly.

You list each specific beneficiary in a separate clause. If you have more than five specific beneficiaries and need more clauses than are provided in the forms, simply copy the blank form clauses and insert the additional beneficiaries.

After the specific beneficiary clauses, there's a clause for naming your residuary beneficiary (and alternate residuary beneficiary), who will receive any property transferred to the trust for which no specific beneficiary is listed and any property given to a specific beneficiary and alternate beneficiary if both die before you do.

There are three basic approaches to identifying property given in a beneficiary clause.

1. Identify the item in exactly the same words you used on your schedule. Thus, if you listed "Money Market Account #60-32 2240001 at International Money Inc." on your schedule, use exactly the same words in the beneficiary clause. If you listed property on more than one schedule, be sure you indicate which schedule each item of property is listed on.

2. If you listed and specifically identified a number of similar items on a schedule (e.g., five different bank accounts, ten valuable paintings, four automobiles) and you wish to leave all items in a particular group to the same beneficiary, it's sufficient to say "all bank accounts listed on Schedule A," or "all paintings listed on Schedule A."

3. The gifts you made can be more specific than the general listing of your trust property on a schedule. For example, suppose on your Schedule A you listed "all books in possession of the settlor," to indicate that ownership of all your books is transferred to your living trust. However, you don't wish to give all these books to one beneficiary. When making gifts, you could state:

"Beth Ruveen shall be given all books by F. Scott Fitzgerald owned in the trust."

"John Advale shall be given all books in French owned by the trust."

"Jim Horton shall be given all books owned by the trust, except those given to Beth Ruveen and John Advale."

Obviously, if you do divide property listed generally on a trust schedule between different beneficiaries, it's crucially important to be clear who is given what.

As you know, shared marital property is listed on Schedule A. Each spouse can only give away his or her half interest in this shared property, not all of it. So, when making a gift from property listed on Schedule A of the marital living trust, a spouse should be clear that it is only his or her share of the property that's given.

"All [husband's name] interest in the house listed on Schedule A shall go to [wife's name.]"

"All [wife's name] interest in the stock accounts listed on Schedule A shall be given in equal shares to [her two children's names]."

If both spouses want to give their interest in shared marital property listed on Schedule A to the same beneficiary, each spouse must make a separate gift of his or her interest.

Fay and Herb Feinberg want to give their limited partnership shares, and a stock account, to their daughter Elizabeth. When completing their trust, they provide:

"Elizabeth Feinberg shall be given all Herb Feinberg's interest in [limited partnership shares and stock account] listed on Schedule A."

"Elizabeth Feinberg shall be given all Fay Feinberg's interest in [limited partnership shares and stock account] listed on Schedule A."

 Reminder: You cannot make life estate gifts using this living trust form. If, for example, you want to give your interest in your house to your spouse for her life, and then, when she dies, to your children, you'll need to see a lawyer.

Simple Beneficiary Situations

In many situations in which you plan to leave all of your property to one person, or divided between several, you can accomplish your goal using one beneficiary clause. Here are some examples:

When one spouse wants to leave all property to the other: *"John Andrews shall be given all Mary Andrews' interest in the property listed on Schedules A, and all property listed on Schedule B."*

When a person wants to divide property equally among her children: *" Steve, Elizabeth and Roarke Cronin shall be given all property on Schedule A in equal shares."*

Making Divided Gifts

Sometimes, people want to divide an item of trust property between several beneficiaries. This is fine, as long as you use language that clearly identifies what proportion or amount of property each beneficiary is to receive.

From a money market fund transferred to his living trust, Jim Denniston wants to give $10,000 to each of his four nieces and nephews, Melinda, Mike, Roger and Margo Denniston, with the balance in the account going to his friend Cerrita Gibbs, and her son, Timothy Gibbs, as alternate beneficiary for the balance. In his trust, Jim provides:

"Melina Denniston shall be given $10,000 from the money market fund [identified] listed on Schedule A."

"Mike Denniston shall be given $10,000 from the money market fund [identified] listed on Schedule A."

"Roger Denniston shall be given $10,000 from the money market fund [identified] listed on Schedule A."

"Margot Denniston shall be given $10,000 from the money market fund [identified] listed on Schedule A."

"All money remaining in the money market fund [identified] listed on Schedule A, after the gifts to Melinda Denniston, Mike Denniston, Roger Denniston and Margot Denniston have been made, shall be given to Cerrita Gibbs, or, if Cerrita Gibbs doesn't survive the settlor, that property shall be given to Timothy Gibbs."

 Sometimes, making a divided gift can become quite complex. If you have any doubts at all that the language you use to make a divided gift isn't clear, review those gift clauses with a lawyer.

Shared Beneficiaries

If you decide you want to name shared beneficiaries for a gift, be sure you review the discussion in Chapter 5, Section E.

Naming Minor Children as Beneficiaries

You name a minor child as a beneficiary exactly as you do an adult beneficiary, listing the child's name and identifying the trust property given him or her. Then, in Step 8, you complete the provision which creates a minor's trust for property left to each minor beneficiary (except for gifts made under the Uniform Transfers to Minors Act).

Use Uniform Transfers to Minors Act for Smaller Gifts to Minor Beneficiaries

As discussed in Chapter 6, Section C, for smaller gifts to minors—roughly, gifts worth less than $25,000—creating a minor's trust can be more trouble than it's worth. An alternative for smaller gifts to minors is to make them using the Uniform Transfers to Minors Act, rather than having them turned over to a children's trust. To see if this approach can work for you:

First, check the list in Chapter 6, Section C to see if the Uniform Transfers to Minors Act applies in your state, or if real property is involved, the state where it is located.

Second, if it does, and you want to make a smaller gift to a minor, in the beneficiary clause where you make the gift, where you see 7, add the language necessary to make a gift under the Uniform Transfers to Minors Act. As explained in Chapter 6, Section C, this consists of identifying the minor's name, the property given, the state where you live (or where real property is located), using the words "Uniform Transfers to Minors Act" and identifying the custodian.

"Flora Lederman shall be given $10,000 under the California Uniform Transfers to Minors Act, Michelle Lederman, custodian."

Making Life Insurance Policies Payable to Your Trust

How can you ensure that your minor children benefit from your life insurance policy without the necessity of going to court to have a property guardian appointed? The first step, as discussed in Chapter 6, Section C, is to name your living trust (which contains children's subtrusts) as the beneficiary of the life insurance policy. Do this by calling your agent or broker and completing the necessary paperwork. (You don't need to list the policy on a trust schedule, because the trust never owns the policy; it is simply the beneficiary of it.) Then you name your children as the beneficiaries of any life insurance proceeds paid to the trust, as follows:

"The settlor's children, Zack Philson and Zelda Philson, shall be given, in equal shares, all life insurance proceeds on the settlor's life paid to the trust."

Under the children's trusts provision of the living trust, these proceeds would be managed by the successor trustee until each child reached the age specified for receiving his or her trust property outright.

Alternate Beneficiaries: There is no legal requirement that you name an alternate beneficiary for each gift, but it's commonly done and is usually a sensible idea.

Here's an example of a completed clause naming a specific beneficiary and alternate beneficiary:

"1. Timothy Plant shall be given the collection of American stamps listed on Schedule A. If Timothy Plant doesn't survive the settlor, the property shall be given to Joan Plant."

Alternate Beneficiaries for Shared Gifts

As discussed in Chapter 5, Section E(3), naming alternate beneficiaries for a shared gift can become quite complex. As stated earlier, this book recommends you name the other surviving beneficiaries to receive a deceased beneficiary's share. You can accomplish this by using, or adapting, the following language:

"[Beneficiaries' names] shall be given [property identified] in equal shares. If any of these beneficiaries do not survive the settlor, the surviving beneficiaries for this gift shall divide the deceased beneficiaries' interest in the gift in equal shares."

 If you decide you want another type of alternate beneficiary clause for a shared gift, review that matter with a lawyer.

If you don't name an alternate beneficiary, you should follow both of these other approaches to handle the problem of a beneficiary who dies before you:

1. Revise your trust when a beneficiary dies. This should be done whether you name an alternate or not. The problem with relying on this approach is, of course, that you may not have time to do it, or get around to doing it.

2. Name a person or persons as residuary beneficiary who you want to have any property given to a specific beneficiary who dies before you. Under the living trust forms in this book, all property left to a specific beneficiary will go to the residuary beneficiary if the specific beneficiary doesn't survive you and you haven't named an alternate. Thus, it's common for settlors with three major beneficiaries (e.g., children) to leave much of their estate between each and then also name all three children as residuary beneficiaries.

Step 8: List Minor Beneficiaries and Specify When Property Will Be Turned Over to Each

In the blank with the ⑧ on the trust forms, you establish children's trusts by listing each trust beneficiary who is under 18 years old, except those minor beneficiaries you made gifts to using the Uniform Transfers to Minors Act. You cannot leave a gift to a minor by both the Uniform Transfers Act and a children's trust. Here you are listing only each minor who will be left property through a children's trust.

For each minor beneficiary you list where you see the ⑧, you then specify at what age you want that beneficiary to receive his or her trust property. If you die before the beneficiary reaches the age you specify, the beneficiary's property is retained in a children's trust until the age is reached, as explained in Section D(3) of this chapter, and Chapter 6. Section C. If you don't specify an age, each listed beneficiary will receive his or her property outright on becoming 30 years old.

Step 9: Provide for Payment of Your Debts and Taxes

If, after reviewing the discussion in Section D(4), you decide you want to make provision for the payment of

your debts and taxes, insert the provision you decide upon in the blank 9 on the trust forms. For example:

"The settlor's debts and death taxes shall be paid by the trustee from the following property:

First, the bank account #99-8062144, Wells Fargo, Berkeley, California.

Second, the stock account #82-304, Smith Barney & Co., San Francisco, California."

In a marital living trust, each spouse can specify the property to be used to pay his or her debts and death taxes.

Sid and Ellen Wall want each's debts and taxes paid from a shared stock account. In their living trust, they provide:

"Any debts or death taxes of Sid Wall shall be paid from his interest in stock account #0014463, Smith Barney & Co., as listed on Schedule A."

"Any debts or death taxes of Ellen Wall shall be paid from her interest in stock account #0014463 Smith Barney & Co., as listed on Schedule B."

Remember that any property you specify to pay your debts and taxes must be owned by your trust. That means you must list it on a schedule, and transfer title into the trust's name, as explained in Section F.

3. Proofread Your Draft Living Trust and Have It Typed

When you have completed all the steps necessary to draft your living trust, proofread it carefully. Have you included everything and everyone you wish to? Assuming the answer is yes, the next step is to have the final version typed from your draft. It should be typed on 8 1/2" by 11" typing paper. Although not required by law, it obviously makes sense to use high quality (bond) non-erasable paper.

Eliminate the following material on the form so that it isn't typed:

- Underlined instructions
- Circled numbers
- Any printed material in the draft that doesn't apply to you. These can include:

  - beneficiary clauses, if you don't have as many beneficiaries as the forms provide space for.

  - alternate beneficiary provision of each beneficiary clause, if you've decided not to name alternates for specific gifts.

  - all material relating to a trust for minor beneficiaries if none of your beneficiaries are minors or if you make all gifts to minors using the Uniform Transfers to Minors Act.

I find it handy to cross out all material I want to eliminate before typing.

For example, The trust for one person, Form I, begins:

The ___ *[Your Name]* ___ Trust

As you know, you give your trust a name by writing your name in the blank. To prepare the trust for final typing, cross out the line, circled number, and the bracketed directions:

The Denis Clifford Trust

So, after it has been typed, the final trust document reads:

The Denis Clifford Trust

4. Consider Having Your Work Checked By a Lawyer

After the final trust document has been typed, carefully proofread it again. Once you are sure it is clear and correct, consider whether, in your circumstances, it makes sense to have your living trust (or your entire estate plan) checked by a lawyer. If you have any questions or doubts about your trust, it can be wise to have a lawyer review it. If your estate is good-sized (more than $600,000), this can be a particularly good idea. Also, if you have a long list of property and a number of beneficiaries and alternate beneficiaries, you may wish to have an experienced person review it. On the other hand, if your desires are clear and straightforward, and you're confident your trust unambiguously transfers your property to your named beneficiaries, a lawyer's review is unlikely to be necessary. (I discuss using lawyers in Chapter 22, Section B.)

5. Sign Your Living Trust in Front of a Notary

As a practical matter, it is essential to have your trust notarized by a Notary Public in your state. There are normally no witnesses to a living trust, nor any requirement that it be filed with any state agency. Because of this, it's always possible that after your death someone could claim that the signature wasn't genuine. As you won't be around to verify it then, you should do it now. The best way to remove any question of whether the signature on the document is authentic is to sign it in front of a notary.

A notarization form is included with each living trust form in the Appendix. If your notary prefers to use a different form, fine—the important thing is to get the notarization done.

 Both spouses must sign a marital trust, and both must appear before a notary.

equipment, antiques, electronic and computer equipment, art works, bearer bonds, cash, precious metals, and collectibles. You transfer these items to the trust simply by listing them on a trust schedule. No other action is needed.

Ms. Rotzinski lists on Schedule A: "All household goods and furnishings previously owned by the settlor." On the same schedule, she also lists her jewelry: "The gold bracelet, two star-sapphire pendants, and gold Huntingcase watch in possession of the settlor." She doesn't need to do anything else to legally transfer her household possessions, furnishings, and jewelry to the trust. Of course, she will need to use one or more beneficiary clauses to actually give these items to a beneficiary.

F. How to Transfer Title of Trust Property into the Trust's Name

YOUR LIVING TRUST can't transfer property it doesn't own. So, an essential step in making your trust effective is to transfer ownership (title) of property to the trust's name. Some lawyers recommend you transfer title into the name of the trustee. It's better to transfer title into the trust's name because trustees may change but the trust name remains the same throughout the trust's existence. So, when the trustees change, no new transfer of title is needed. I mention this point, which may seem minute, because I've heard from people who've become worried about their living trust when someone warned them, "Oh, that's not the way to do it. Title has to be held in the trustee's name." It does not.

For the purposes of transferring title into the trust's name, there are two types of property—those with ownership (title) documents and those without. Each type of property is treated differently when it comes to transferring it to your living trust.

1. Property Without Ownership (Title) Documents

Many types of property don't have title documents, including all kinds of household possessions and furnishings, clothing, jewelry, furs, tools, most farm

2. Property With Ownership (Title) Documents

After the trust document has been signed and notarized, it is vital that you formally re-register ownership of all items of trust property which have ownership documents (title papers) into the trust's name.

The types of property owned by the trust which must have title documents re-registered in the trust's name include:

- Real estate, including condominiums and cooperatives
- Bank accounts
- Stocks and stock accounts
- Most bonds, including U.S. Government Securities
- Corporations/limited partnerships/partnerships
- Money market accounts
- Mutual funds
- Safety deposit boxes
- Vehicles, including cars, most boats, motor homes, and planes

Insurance, IRAs, Keoghs and Other Property Naming a Living Trust as Beneficiary Don't Have to Be Re-registered

You do not have to re-register title for the types of property where you name the trust itself as beneficiary, to receive specified property after you die. For example, if you want your living trust to receive your life insurance policy, IRA, and Keogh plan, you do, of course, have to be sure the trust has been properly designated as the beneficiary. But you do not have to transfer ownership of the policy, IRA or Keogh accounts into the trust's name. While you live, the trust is not the legal owner of these types of property; you remain the legal owner. The trust is simply who you've named to receive benefits payable on your death—life insurance proceeds, or the balance in your IRA or Keogh accounts. (Since the trust never owned the insurance policy, IRA and Keogh, these assets were, of course, not listed on a trust schedule.

Important: You must re-register property in the name of your living trust promptly. Your living trust won't be effective for any property with an ownership document which is not re-registered in the trust's name. The new document of title must show that the trust—not you, the settlor—is the legal owner of the property. If the trust isn't the legal owner of the property, the successor trustee has no legal authority to transfer that property to the beneficiaries.

If title to property listed on the trust schedules remains in your name (you fail to re-register it), that property will pass under the terms of your back-up will. Since it's not actually listed in the will, it will go to the residuary beneficiary, who, of course, may not be the person who you intended to receive it. If you have no will, property not transferred to the trust will be left under the terms of your state's intestate succession law. In either case, it will be subject to all the expense and delay of probate—the very things you are trying to avoid.

Ms. Kaloia creates a living trust and lists her stock brokerage account on Schedule A, as trust property. In the trust document, she gives this stock accounts to her daughter. However, she never notifies her stock broker to re-register ownership of the account in the name of "The Kaloia Trust." When she dies, her successor trustee will be unable to successfully transfer the account to the daughter. The brokerage company will say to the successor trustee "We don't show that account owned by any living trust. It's owned by a Ms. Kaloia, and you have no legal authority to collect her assets." Thus, the account must pass by her will (assuming she has one) and go through probate, or pass to an inheritor designated by state law, which also requires probate.

Okay, I'll assume you are convinced. How do you get this transfer job done? For each of your assets with a document of title which you have listed on a trust schedule, you must prepare a new title document, transferring ownership of that property from your own name to the trust's name. For example, the deed of a house listing "Mary Jones" as owner must be redone to show the new owner as "The Mary Jones Trust." I discuss how to actually transfer title to real estate immediately below and outline how to re-register other types of property in the sections that follow.

3. Real Estate (Real Property)

The term "real estate" includes land, houses, condominiums, cooperatives and any other interest in what lawyers call "real property." To transfer title of a piece of real estate to a living trust, you prepare and sign a deed listing the trust as the new owner of the property. Then you have that deed notarized and recorded. This isn't difficult, although it does involve some leg work. (This process is set out in far more depth in *The Deeds Book*, Randolph, Nolo Press. This book specifically applies to California deeds, but much of the information it contains applies in any state.)

Here are the basics:

- Locate your existing deed.
- Purchase a blank quitclaim or grant deed form[12] (either will do) at an office supply store in the state where the property is located;[13]
- Deed the property from yourself to your living trust. Be sure to use exactly the same form of your name for yourself on the new deed that you used on the old one. Your trust is listed in its own name.

Janice Kingsley locates her old deed, which lists her as "Janice P. Kingsley." She would deed her property as "Janice P. Kingsley to…The Janice Kingsley Trust."

Mary and Paul Jones's old deed identifies them as "Mary Meg Jones and Paul Mellon Jones, Tenants in Common." They list themselves in exactly these words on the new deed, transferring the real estate to "The Mary and Paul Jones Trust."

Transferring Partial Ownership

If you share ownership of real estate with anyone except a spouse, it's wise to check with a title company to learn how it recommends you transfer title of your interest into a living trust. While you could simply deed "all [your] interest…" to the trust, some title companies prefer a transfer approved by all owners.

---

[12]A quitclaim deed is a simple deed form, where you transfer whatever ownership you have in real estate, without making any promises or guarantees of ownership. Since you are transferring your property from yourself to your trust, you're not worried about guarantees. Other types of deeds where guarantees are made are called "warranty" or "grant" deeds. These can safely be used as well.

[13]Required deed language can vary slightly from one state to the next. If possible, it's best to use a form in general use in the state where the real property is located.

- Delete (cross out) any language on the deed form that relates to a sale—your transfer is not a sale;
- Type all technical information (such as the legal description of the property) on the new deed exactly as it appears on the old one;
- Sign the deed in front of a notary;
- Record the deed with the County Recorder of Deeds for the county in which the real estate is located. Before you actually take the deed in, call and ask:
  - How many copies you need;
  - If there are any local or state transfer taxes applicable to transfers to living trusts—usually there aren't, but it pays to check;
  - Will your transfer trigger a tax reappraisal. As previously discussed, it shouldn't, but it's wise to check;
  - Do any special transfer forms have to be completed? A few states require additional paperwork.

Jane and Gordon McCann want to transfer their home to their living trust. Here's their completed quitclaim deed. As you'll see, this deed contains bunches of legalese (e.g., "…appurtenances thereunto belonging or appertaining.") I use this deed as an example because it's typical of a deed you're likely to get at a stationary store, and to show you that you can make use of this type of form. Obviously, I'm no fan of the legalese it uses.

Quitclaim Deed

This Indenture made the ......twenty-first................................day of ......April....................one thousand nine hundred and ....eighty-eight................

Between ....Jane and Gordon McCann..
....the part...ies of the first part,
and .....The Jane and Gordon McCann Trust.......................................
....the part..y... of the second part,

Witnesseth: That the said part...ies.... of the first part XX XXXXXXXXXXXXXXXX XX XXXX ofXXXXXXXXXXXXXXXXXXXXXXXXXXXXXXXXXXXXXXXXXXXXXXXXXXXXXXXXXXdollars, lawful moneyxof the United Statesxof Americax XoXXXXXXXXXXXXXXXXX XXXbxxxbpartbyxXbe partXXXXXX ofXthexsecond partxthexreceiptx whereofxisxherebyxacknowledged, do ....hereby release and foreverxQUITCLAIM unto the part y........ of the second part, anXdXX XXXXX XXXxx xothxxxssignxxall that........certain lot.........., piece.........or parcel.........of land situate in the ...City..of.Chicago........................County of ......Cook...................... State of ......Illinois................................., and bounded and described as follows, to-wit:

Commonly known as 47 Greene Street, and more particularly described as:

(Legal description, exactly as given in previous deed)

Together with the tenements, hereditaments, and appurtenances thereunto belonging or appertaining, and the reversion and reversions, remainder and remainders, rents, issues, and profits thereof.

To have and to hold the said premises, together with the appurtenances, unto the part .y........ of the second part, XxxXxxXXXXXXXXXXX XeXXxxandxassignsxforever

In Witness Whereof the part...ies.... of the first part have........ executed this conveyance the day and year first above written.

Signed and Delivered in the Presence of

[*Notarized*] *Jane McCann*
Gordon McCann

4. Stock Market or Mutual Fund Accounts

To register stocks, bonds, or mutual fund accounts in your trust's name, ask your broker or money fund officer what is required. Usually, they require a copy of the trust with your notarized signature for their files, and a letter instructing them to register the account in the trust name. They should then confirm in writing to you that this has been done.

If you have personal possession of the stock certificates or bonds (most people don't), you will need to get new certificates issued, listing the trust as owner. Your broker may be willing to do it for you. If your broker won't help, get another who will, or deal directly with the "transfer agent" of the corporation. Your broker (or the corporation) can tell you who this is. Ask the transfer agent for instructions, which will likely involve sending in your share certificates or bonds, a stock power, and a copy of the trust, and asking that new certificates or bonds be issued in the trust's name.

Mutual Funds Note: Mutual funds should be re-registered in the name of your living trust by communicating with the company and meeting its requirements. These normally consist of sending a letter of instructions (or form which they provide) and a copy of the trust. To re-register T-Bills and other government corporate and U.S. bonds, notes, bills and securities in the trust name, contact the appropriate government office directly or have your broker do it.

5. Bank Accounts

Title to bank accounts can be readily transferred to the trust's name simply by completing the appropriate bank form. Before you decide to transfer bank accounts into your trust's name, be sure you've checked out whether you'd rather use an informal bank trust account, described in Chapter 11, Section C. With this type of account, you name a beneficiary (who can be anyone you choose, including your living trust) on the account form, to receive the funds in the account after you die; the account itself remains in your name. This can be particularly desirable for your personal checking account used to pay normal bills, because most people don't want to hold that account—and its checks—in the name of a living trust.

6. Limited Partnerships

Limited partnerships are a form of investment, governed by securities laws. To re-register a limited partnership interest in a trust name, contact the general partner's office and see what documentation is needed.

7. Business Interests

A living trust can be a good way to transfer business interests to beneficiaries, since the hassles and delays of probate can be extremely damaging to a business. Transferring title to a business depends on the form of ownership.

- An unincorporated, solely-owned business is easiest to transfer. Since there is no title document for the business itself, all that needs be done is list the business on a trust schedule. Then, any ancillary title documents of property owned by the business, such as real estate, must be re-registered in the trust's name.

- A solely-owned corporation can be transferred by preparing the appropriate corporate records, transferring ownership to the trust, and then re-registering the share certificates in the trust's name.

- An owner's interest in a shared business partnership or corporation is the most complicated to re-register in the trust's name. First, the partnership agreement or corporate by-laws must be checked to be sure they permit transfer of an owner's interest to a living trust. Then, the appropriate records authorizing the transfer must be prepared, and signed by all required to approve the transfer. Finally, the title document—

corporate shares or partnership certificate (if there is one)—must be re-registered in the trust's name.

Often the complicated part of a living trust for a business is arranging for continuity and management of the business after the owner's death. (This is discussed in Chapter 20.)

 If you plan to transfer your interest in a shared business to a living trust, you should discuss and review your trust with an expert. Often the trusts should be designed to continue for some time after the death of the settlor. Also, you have to be sure the trust is coordinated with the partnership agreement or corporate bylaws. And, of course, before you prepare any living trust, or see an expert, you should discuss your plans with your other partners or co-owners.

8. Motor Vehicles

Before you decide to transfer your vehicle by trust, check out your state's special probate avoidance transfer laws to see if you can use your will to transfer your car outside of normal probate (see Chapter 13). This will save you from having to deal now with the Department of Motor Vehicles, and the hassles that inevitably entails. Also, check with your insurance company to be sure they'll continue your insurance if the car is technically owned by your trust. If you decide you do want to transfer your motor vehicles by your living trust, you'll need to contact your state Department of Motor Vehicles and see what form it requires to accomplish this.

9. Other Property with Documents of Title

As stated above, all other property with documents of title which is transferred to a living trust must be re-registered in the trust's name. For example, if you want to

transfer a promissory note to your living trust, you must complete a "Notice of Assignment," formally placing title to the note in the name of the trust. "Notice of Assignment" forms can be obtained from some stationery stores or title companies. (And, of course, you'd also list the promissory note on a trust schedule.) Other types of property which can be assigned to a living trust include patents and copyrights.

G. After Your Trust is Completed

AFTER YOUR LIVING TRUST has been completed and all property with documents of title re-registered in the trust's name, it still requires some attention. Obviously, you need to store it securely. You may want to make copies. In addition, you obviously need to keep it up to date by making necessary changes as you acquire and dispose of major items of property or find that, for one reason or another, your beneficiaries have changed. Let's now look at these issues individually.

1. Storing Your Living Trust

It's usually best to store your living trust document with your other important papers. Some people use a safe deposit box jointly owned with their successor trustee for this purpose. (See Chapter 11, Section B.) Others use a secure place in their home, such as a home safe, fireproof metal box or file cabinet. The important thing is that the successor trustee knows where the trust document is and has fast access to it. Whether you reveal the contents of your living trust to your successor trustee is a personal decision. As you know from reading Chapter 1, I am generally in favor of openness and suggest that you let your successor trustee know what's in the trust. After all, he'll find out eventually.

2. Making Copies of Your Living Trust

As discussed in Section F, you will need to provide photocopies of your trust to organizations that keep property with ownership (title) documents in order to successfully transfer title to trust property. This includes banks, brokers, mutual funds, and limited partnerships. Also, you may decide you want copies for other reasons, such as to give to your successor trustee or beneficiaries. And if you store your original trust document in a safe deposit box, you may want to keep a copy at home. It's fine to make as many copies as you need, as long as there is only one original—that is, one living trust document you have actually signed. Don't sign or notarize any copies. Doing this creates a duplicate original which can raise serious legal problems, especially if you decide to amend or revoke your trust. Photocopying the page of your original living trust with your signature and notary seal is okay and does not create a duplicate original.

H. Amending or Revoking Your Living Trust

THE LIVING TRUST FORMS in the Appendix give you the power to amend your living trust while you live.

The marital living trust can only be amended by both spouses while both live. This is to guard against one spouse being able to pull a fast one with trust property in the event of a dispute or divorce. When one spouse dies, his or her portion of the trust becomes binding and irrevocable and the property is distributed according to its terms by the successor trustee. The surviving spouse can now amend his or her own portion of the trust, like any other single person.

1. How to Change Trust Property, Beneficiaries or Successors Trustees

You must amend your living trust by a written document. Form III in the Appendix can be used to amend a living trust for one person. Form IV can be used to amend a living trust for a married couple.

These forms should be used for simple, clear amendments only—such as adding a new beneficiary, deleting a beneficiary, changing a successor trustee, or deleting or adding property. These forms are not appropriate for making major revisions or wholesale changes in your living trust. Attempting major revisions by amendment creates risks of confusion or inconsistency. To achieve major changes, you need to revoke your trust and prepare a new trust document (revocation is discussed in Subsection 3 below).

Mr. Howard decides he will give his golf clubs to his (new) friend Ron Kolbert, not to William Boyd. Using Form III, he amends his trust as follows:

"1. The following language is added to the trust:

[in V(A)(3)] Ron Kolbert shall be given the golf clubs listed on Schedule A, or if Ron Kolbert doesn't survive the settlor, the property shall be given to Mario Martinelli."

"2. The following is deleted from the trust:

[in V(A)(3)] William Boyd shall be given the golf clubs listed on Schedule A, or, if William Boyd fails to survive the settlor, that property shall be given to Mario Martinelli."

Mr. Howard then completes Form III, proofreads it carefully, has it typed and signs and dates it before a notary.

If you decide to amend your trust, you must have the amendment form notarized. You can give a copy of the amendment to anyone who has a copy of your trust, but this isn't always mandatory. For example, there's usually no reason to give an amendment to a bank or brokerage company which required a copy of your trust to transfer title of an account into the trust's name.

Some people wonder why they can't make amendments to a trust simply by retyping a page on the original document. For example, suppose you want to name a new beneficiary for property listed on your property schedule and eliminate one beneficiary currently listed. Why can't you simply detach the page where the beneficiaries and gifts are listed, have the new information typed on a replacement page and reassemble the pages? The answer is that, as a practical matter, you might very well be able to do this without your trust encountering subsequent legal trouble. But this approach does risk the possibility that someone could challenge the trust on grounds it was improperly altered by making changes after it had been notarized. This is particularly true if an excluded beneficiary is resentful about losing a gift and makes an issue of how the trust was changed. In sum, making "informal" changes is not legally proper, and is unwise.

2. Adding Property to Your Trust

It isn't necessary to formally amend your trust just to add additional property to it. The living trust forms in the Appendix specifically give you the right to add "after-acquired" property to your trust. You can add property to

your trust simply by listing it on the appropriate schedule and transferring title to it (if it has a title document) to the trust's name. (Either detach the old schedule—unstaple it—and type in the new property on it, or type up a replacement schedule. Then simply re-staple the schedule to the trust document.)

If you've left all property on the new trust schedule to one beneficiary, or divided it between several, you don't need to amend your trust to state who receives the newly-listed property. Likewise, if you want the property to go to the residuary beneficiary, you don't need to amend the trust. But if you want the newly-listed property to go to a specific beneficiary who isn't your residuary beneficiary or doesn't receive any of the property on the schedule, you'll need to amend your trust to identify this beneficiary for the newly-listed property.

Property added to the trust can be one of two types: property you owned before the trust was created but didn't transfer to the trust, or property you acquired after the trust's creation. In both instances, you need to be sure that if the property has a title document, it appears in the trust's name. With newly-acquired property, you can simply take title in the trust's name when you get that property; it will automatically become part of the trust. For example, real estate purchased in the name of "The Denis Clifford Trust," would go directly into the trust. Property you previously owned must have title re-registered in the name of the trust.

3. Revoking Your Living Trust

As long as the settlor lives, she can revoke her living trust at any time, for any reason.

A marital trust can be revoked by either spouse any time. The reason either spouse can revoke the marital trust, but it takes both to amend it, is that revocation simply returns both spouses to the status quo. By contrast, in event of divorce or (other) bitter conflict, it's risky to permit one spouse to amend a trust that governs both spouse's property.

 You will need to see a lawyer if one spouse wants control over marital property, and doesn't want the other to have authority to revoke the living trust.

A revocation form (Form V) is contained in the Appendix.

A living trust can be revoked:

- Because the settlor wishes to end the trust entirely, and transfer her property at death by other methods; or

- Because the settlor desires such extensive changes in her existing trust that amending it will be too unwieldy, so a new trust document must be prepared.

It's rare that a living trust is entirely ended. After all, the reason it was established—to avoid probate—hasn't gone away. If a trust is revoked to end it entirely, it ceases to have any legal existence, and property cannot be transferred by it. When a trust is revoked for this reason, you must be sure that you've transferred title to all former trust property back into your own name.

If a new trust document is prepared to reflect the settlor's current desires and situation, the previous trust must, obviously, be revoked. The new trust can be given the same name as the old one. The old one is identified, in the revocation form, by name and date of signature. Because the new trust has the same name as the old one, title to trust property doesn't have to be re-registered again. That property will continue to be owned by your (new) living trust. It's prudent to track down and destroy all copies of your old trust, to diminish the possibility someone could claim you didn't really intend to revoke it (an unlikely possibility in any case).

Joint Tenancy

CHAPTER 10

Joint Tenancy

THIS CHAPTER EXPLAINS what joint tenancy is, how it works, and explores the advantages and drawbacks of using joint tenancy to avoid probate.

A. What Is Joint Tenancy?

JOINT TENANCY is a way for co-owners (called "joint tenants") to own property together. It is a useful probate avoidance tool because property held in joint tenancy carries with it the "right of survivorship." This means that when one joint tenant dies, his or her ownership share of the joint tenancy property is "automatically" transferred to, and becomes owned by, the surviving joint tenant(s), without the need for probate.

> *Ron and Linda own their house in joint tenancy. At Ron's death, ownership of his share automatically goes to Linda, without probate.*

The automatic right of a surviving joint tenant or tenants to inherit is basic to this form of ownership. You can't leave your interest in joint tenancy property to anyone but the other joint tenants.[1] Property owned in joint tenancy passes automatically to the surviving joint tenants even if a deceased joint tenant provided to the contrary in a will or living trust. By contrast, other forms of shared ownership, such as tenancy in common or community property, don't create a right of survivorship, and an owner's share of such property can be transferred by will (and become subject to probate) or living trust.

Any number of people can own property together in joint tenancy, but they must all own equal shares. All joint tenant owners share equally in all income, profits and losses from their property. If an ownership document specifies different percentages or shares of ownership, it's a tenancy in common, not a joint tenancy, and there's no right of survivorship for the co-owners.

---

[1]In most states, any joint tenant may first sever (terminate) the joint tenancy and create tenancy in common ownership. If this is done, each tenant in common may leave his share of the property to anyone he chooses.

Unequal Ownership of Property

If you want to own property in unequal shares, you must do it as tenants in common. For example, two people living together may decide to own property in unequal shares because one person initially has more money to invest in the property than does the other. (Contracts and forms to create a tenancy in common and to switch to joint tenancy ownership should ownership shares become equal are contained in the *Living Together Kit* and the *Legal Guide for Lesbian and Gay Couples,* both published by Nolo Press.)

Property held in tenancy in common does not avoid probate automatically. However, this can be accomplished by each owner putting his or her interest in the property in a living trust. (See Chapter 9.)

It's common that real estate, or land, is owned in joint tenancy, but any type of property can be owned in this manner and avoid probate. Bank accounts, automobiles, boats and mobile homes are all routinely held in joint tenancy for just this reason.

B. Joint Tenancy in Community Property States

THIS SECTION IS OF INTEREST to people who live in or own real property in a community property state: Arizona, California, Idaho, Nevada, New Mexico, Texas,

Washington or Wisconsin. If you don't live in one of these states, go on to Section C.

Most property accumulated by either spouse during a marriage is the community property of both. (See Chapter 3, Section B for a discussion of the rules.) Spouses can, and commonly do, hold their community property in joint tenancy with each other to avoid probate when the first spouse dies. Doing this can make good sense. However, for certain important income tax reasons [explained in Section D(2) of this chapter], it's important to be able to show the IRS that community property held in joint tenancy for probate avoidance purposes is still community property. One simple and effective way to do this is to state right on the ownership document that the property is "community property held in joint tenancy."

One spouse may consider placing property into joint tenancy with someone other than the other spouse. If the property is the separate property of the transferring spouse, there's no problem. However, if the property is community property, serious problems can develop between the surviving spouse and the surviving joint tenant. The reason for this is simple: The surviving spouse automatically owns one-half of all community property, whether or not his or her name appears on property ownership documents. The surviving spouse can successfully contend that the deceased spouse only had authority to transfer half of the community property into joint tenancy with someone else. This point may seem a little confusing. If so, this example should help.

> Mrs. Abruzzi, who has one daughter, owns a house as her separate property. She remarries Mr. Mykenas. For several years, they use their community property income to pay mortgage payments on the house. Mrs. Abruzzi decides to transfer the house into joint tenancy with her daughter to avoid probate at her death. When Mrs. Abruzzi dies, Mr. Mykenas could claim that part of the house was community property because community funds were used for mortgage payments. Half of the community property portion of the house is his. Mrs. Abruzzi has no legal right to transfer his portion to her daughter.

 The moral: If you're married and want to transfer community property into joint tenancy with someone other than your spouse, be sure that the property is 100% your separate property (as explained in Chapter 3, Section B). If you have any doubts, have your spouse agree (in writing) that this property is your separate property before you create the joint tenancy with someone else. Doing this can be tricky, so see a lawyer.

C. Simultaneous Death of Joint Tenants

MANY JOINT TENANTS, especially spouses and mates, wonder what happens to joint tenancy property if they die simultaneously. After all, if there's no surviving owner, the right of survivorship that's central to joint tenancy has no meaning. The answer is that in case of simultaneous death, the interest of each joint tenant passes under his or her will, if there is one, or under intestate succession laws if there's no will. Thus, only if all joint tenants die simultaneously does each joint tenant have the legal power to transfer his or her share to someone besides the other joint tenants. To deal with this highly unlikely but still potentially worrisome possibility, your will serves as your back-up device, to transfer your interest in joint tenancy property if all joint tenants die simultaneously. Most people, however, don't need to specifically mention joint tenancy property in their wills; the residuary clause, which passes all property not specifically given to other beneficiaries to the residuary beneficiary, takes care of the problem.

> Tom and Mary Jones, owners of a house in joint tenancy, die together in a plane crash. One-half of the joint tenancy property is included in Tom's estate and is transferred by his will to his residuary beneficiary, his son by a prior marriage. The other half is included in Mary's estate and is transferred by her will to her residuary beneficiary, her sister. If either Tom or Mary had no will, the property would be distributed to his or her legal heirs. If Tom and Mary had named each other as residuary beneficiaries in their wills, the property would go to their alternate residuary beneficiaries.

The back-up will set out in Chapter 17 will transfer your property in joint tenancy should a simultaneous death occur. Indeed, this is a good example of why you need such a will, even if you leave the bulk of your property by a living trust. A living trust only works to dispose of property transferred to trust ownership. This can't be done for property you decide to keep in joint tenancy (because if the trust owned the property, it would no longer be jointly owned by the former co-owners), so your living trust cannot dispose of joint tenancy property if the owners die simultaneously.

D. Tax Concerns Affecting Joint Tenancy

BEFORE DECIDING WHETHER you want to use joint tenancy in your estate planning, you should understand the potential tax implications of holding property as joint tenants. The major tax concerns are estate taxes, income tax "basis" rules, and property tax reappraisals. I know wading through this probably sounds dreary, but hang in there—it matters.

1. Federal Estate Taxes

Owning property as a joint tenant doesn't reduce your taxable estate for federal estate tax purposes. The federal government includes the value of the deceased's jointly-owned property in the taxable estate. The amount of that interest is based on how much was contributed when the jointly-owned property was bought. If the deceased put up all the money to purchase a piece of joint property, the full market value of the property (at death) is included in the taxable estate. With the exception of married couples, the IRS *presumes* that the first joint tenant to die contributed all of the money for the purchase (and capital improvements, if additional costs were required for that) of jointly-owned property. The burden of proof is on the surviving tenant(s) to overturn this presumption by

establishing that the survivors made cash or other contributions toward buying or maintaining the property. To the extent the surviving tenants can prove that they put up part of the purchase price, or expenses, the value of the joint tenancy property interest included in the deceased's taxable estate will be reduced proportionately. Therefore, one risk of holding property in joint tenancy is that, unless good records are kept, the full value of the jointly-owned property will be subject to death taxes twice.

Years ago, Phil and his sister Patsy bought a house as joint tenants. They each contributed half the purchase price, but any records that can prove that have long since vanished. Patsy dies in 1990. The full 1990 market value of the house is included in her taxable estate, since it's presumed she contributed all the purchase price. Phil, the surviving joint tenant, owns the entire house until he dies in 1992. The full 1992 market value of the house is included in his taxable estate, because he now owns all the property. Had Phil and Patsy kept records, only half the value of the house would have been included in Patsy's taxable estate.

Marital Joint Tenancies Note: When a husband and wife are joint tenants, only one-half of the value of the joint tenancy property is included in the federal taxable estate of the first spouse to die, no matter who put up the money to buy the property.

2. Federal Income Tax Basis Rules

Note: This section doesn't apply to people who buy joint tenancy property together. People who buy property together and leave it to one another face the same income tax liabilities whether or not they take title as joint tenants. This section is for people who take property they already own and make someone else a joint tenant.

Transferring solely-owned property into joint tenancy in order to avoid probate can result in adverse tax consequences for inheritors (the surviving joint tenants). Sorry, but to grasp this important point, you must take a moment to understand the tax concept called "basis." Put simply, the basis of property is the essential figure used to determine taxable profit on subsequent sale. Usually, the basis of real estate is its purchase price, plus the cost of any capital improvements. Once you know the basis, you subtract it from what you sell the property for. The result is your taxable profit.

Ardmore buys a house for $100,000 and puts $20,000 into capital improvements. The property's basis is $120,000. If Ardmore sells the house for $350,000, his taxable profit (Sales Price minus Basis) is $230,000.

This is simple enough. Unfortunately, now things gets a bit more complicated. Enter the concept of "stepped-up basis." Under federal law, the basis of inherited property is increased, or "stepped up," to its market value as of the date that the deceased owner dies. In other words, if B inherits property from A, B's basis in the property is its market value when A died, *not* its cost when A bought it.

In the previous example, Ardmore's basis in his house was $120,000. Now suppose that instead of selling the house, Ardmore died and the house was given to Serena under Ardmore's will. The market value of the house when Ardmore died was $350,000. When Serena inherits the house, her tax basis for it is stepped up to that market value of $350,000. If Serena sells the house for that amount, she has no taxable gain.

Okay, now to relate all of this to joint tenancy and to zero in on the reason why transferring solely-owned property into joint tenancy can be a poor estate planning choice. A surviving joint tenant only gets a stepped-up basis for one-half the value of the property, the half owned by the deceased owner. The half owned all along by the surviving joint tenant retains its original tax basis.

Ellen transfers her property into joint tenancy with her daughter Julie. Ellen's basis in the house was $50,000. The basis of Julie's, and Ellen's, half interest in the joint tenancy property becomes $25,000 each. When Ellen dies, the market value of the house is $250,000. The basis of Ellen's share of the joint tenancy ownership is "stepped up" to $125,000 (half the market value of the property). But Julie's basis remains at $25,000—which means she'll pay a lot more income tax when she sells the house than she would have if she'd inherited all (not just half) of the house from Ellen.

The stepped-up basis rules mean it's usually unwise for a sole owner to transfer property into joint tenancy if it has gone up in value or is likely to go up in value. Probate is avoided, but if property has gone up in value when an owner dies, more may well have to be eventually paid out by the surviving joint tenant in income taxes than was saved in probate fees.

Using a living trust for appreciated property offers a way to avoid probate and get a stepped-up tax basis as well.

Mary buys a house for $15,000 in 1956. What's the difference in its basis if Mary transfers the house into joint tenancy with her daughter Eileen or leaves it to her by a living trust?

If the house is transferred by living trust, the basis of the whole house will be stepped-up to its fair market value when Mary dies. If the house is worth $500,000 when Mary dies, that's the basis Eileen receives. If Eileen then sells the house for $500,000, she receives no taxable gain. And if she waits a year and sells it for $525,000, her taxable gain is only $25,000.

However, if Mary transfers the house into joint tenancy to avoid probate and then dies, Eileen gets a stepped-up basis only for Mary's half, but not on the half that was already hers. Eileen takes her half with Mary's original basis (1/2 of $15,000 = $7,500). If the house is owned in joint tenancy, here's the basis situation when Mary dies:

Mary's 1/2 ownership:
   Stepped up to $250,000

Eileen's 1/2 ownership:
   Retains original basis 7,500

Total basis 257,500

If the house is sold for $525,000
   Eileen's taxable gain is.................. $267,500

On a more positive note, only half the value of the house is included in Mary's taxable estate, because she only owned half at her death. However, the half Mary gave Eileen was subject to a gift tax[2] at its value when it was transferred into joint tenancy [see Section E(3) below].

---

[2]Tax valuation of property given as gifts is discussed in Chapter 15.

If this seems confusing, that's because it is. Basis questions can get complicated fast. My rule here is: Don't transfer substantially appreciated property, or property which may substantially appreciate, into joint tenancy. Remember, you can transfer appreciated property by living trust, in which case the entire property receives a stepped-up basis and avoids probate, too.

Note on Community Property Held in Joint Tenancy: Tax basis rules are different for married couples who live in the eight community property states. Both shares of community property held in joint tenancy are entitled to a stepped-up basis upon the death of a spouse. Thus, if a husband and wife own community property real estate located in a community property state in joint tenancy worth $2,000,000 at the husband's death, the basis of *both* the husband's and wife's share of that real estate is stepped-up to $1,000,000 (no matter what they paid for it originally). But to get the stepped-up basis, you must prove to the IRS that the joint tenancy property is community property. Otherwise, only the half of the deceased spouse gets the stepped-up basis. So if you're married and hold *any* community property in joint tenancy, be sure you can prove it retained its character as community property. As mentioned in Section B above, it's sensible to hold title as "community property held in joint tenancy." It's also a good idea to keep records showing that community property was used to purchase or make capital improvements to the property.

3. State Income Tax Basis Rules

State tax basis rules can be quite complicated, too. However, in general, there's little need to worry about state basis rules. State income taxes take small enough bites that, in my opinion, they aren't worth bothering about when you're doing estate planning.

 If you have a large estate and want to be extremely cautious and review the impact of your state's basis rules on your estate plan, see a tax lawyer or other tax expert.

4. Local Property Taxes

In many areas of the country, real property is reassessed for local property tax purposes every time it changes hands. This usually means that taxes go up, sometimes a lot if your property hasn't been reassessed recently.

In general, creating a joint tenancy interest in real property isn't a "change of ownership" if the original owner is one of the new joint tenants. In California, for example, there is no property tax reappraisal if you transfer your property into joint tenancy with yourself and others. However, as a general rule, if the original owner isn't one of the new joint tenants, then any "creation, transfer or termination" of a joint tenancy interest is a change of ownership, and the property will be reassessed. Before relying on this advice, however, contact your local property tax assessor and determine the specific rules for what types of transfers trigger the reassessment of property.

Example 1: Mrs. Jefferson owns two pieces of real estate. She transfers title to the first lot to herself and her husband, Raymond, as "joint tenants with right of survivorship." She transfers title to the second lot to herself and her daughter, Lila, as "joint tenants with right of survivorship." There has been no change of ownership for reassessment purposes in most states. However, when Mrs. Jefferson dies, there may be a reappraisal, depending on state property tax rules.

Example 2: Mrs. Jefferson transfers (by gift or sale) a third lot to her son and his wife "Raymond Jefferson and Lila Jefferson, as joint tenants with right of survivorship." There has been a "change of ownership," since the original owner, Mrs. Jefferson, isn't one of the new joint tenants. Depending on state tax rules, this may trigger a property tax reassessment.

E. Drawbacks of Joint Tenancy

I'VE ALREADY DISCUSSED the advantageous fact that joint tenancy property avoids probate, and the disadvantageous one that federal income tax basis rules make it unwise to transfer into joint tenancy solely-owned property if it has gone up in value since you bought it, or is likely to do. However, as part of deciding whether to use joint tenancy, there are several other possible risks you should consider.

1. Any Joint Tenant Can End the Joint Tenancy

Generally, as long as joint tenants are alive, any of them can terminate the joint tenancy, whether or not the other owners consent to it.[3] Some states require a formal court partition of the property before an owner can end the joint tenancy. In other states, any joint tenant has the power to end it, and sell his interest in the jointly-owned property, at any time. In either case, if there's a sale to a new owner, he takes his interest as a tenant in common with the remaining original owners. If the remaining (original) owner, and the new (tenant in common) owner conflict, either can ask a court to partition the property into two equal halves. If that isn't feasible, the court will order a sale with the proceeds divided in equal shares.

The risk that a co-owner may sell her share of the property may not be serious for couples or close friends who purchase property together with money they each contribute. In this situation, if a divorce, separation or other reason to end the joint tenancy occurs, each joint tenant simply gets her fair share. However, if solely-owned property is transferred into joint tenancy by an older person, the situation is quite different. The older person has given up ownership of half her property. And unlike putting property into a living trust, he can't change his mind later and take it back.

---

[3]As with so many legal rules, there are curious exceptions to this one. For example, in California, a joint tenancy in personal property can only be ended with consent of other joint tenants.

Sid transfers his house into joint tenancy with his nephew Joe. Then the two have a bitter fight. Sid wants to regain sole ownership of the house. Joe says, "Nothing doing. I'm half owner, legally, and there's nothing you can do about it." Worse, Joe can then try to sell his half-interest in the house. If he does, Sid will share ownership with a stranger.

In short, one question to answer before you transfer property into joint tenancy is: Do you absolutely trust that your joint-tenant-to-be won't sell the property, or do anything with the ownership interest that's adverse to you? If you have any doubts, joint tenancy isn't for you. To deal with this potential problem, I advise people in Sid's situation to create a revocable living trust naming Joe as beneficiary. Then, if Joe and Sid have a falling out, Sid can simply amend the trust and change beneficiaries.

2. Creditors and Joint Tenancy

Creditors of any joint tenant may go after (legally "attach") that tenant's individual interest, but not the other joint tenants' interests. If there is an attachment, a court may order the whole property sold to reach the debtor's share.

Generally, upon the death of one owner, the surviving owner takes the property free of any responsibility for the deceased's debts. But, in a number of states, a creditor of the deceased owner can go after the property if:

- the deceased person had pledged his interest in the property as security for a loan;

- the creditor sued, got a judgment and initiated legal steps to collect the money before the deceased died; or

- the creditor can show that the joint tenancy arrangement was a scheme set up solely to defraud creditors.

3. Joint Tenancy as a Taxable Gift

Creating a joint tenancy (except between married couples) may involve making a taxable gift. To understand the basics of how gift taxes can affect joint tenancy, all you need to know is that the federal government assesses taxes against any gift over $10,000 made to any person in a calendar year. (Gift taxes are explained in Chapter 15.)

Gift taxes affect joint tenancy because the IRS takes the position that, except for joint bank accounts (discussed below), a taxable gift is made when joint tenancy is created, and the owners don't pay equally for the property. Thus, if one person puts up all the money to purchase property, but another is listed as a joint tenant, the person who puts up the money makes a legal gift of half-ownership of the property. If the value of that gift exceeds $10,000, the giver must file a gift tax return and gift taxes are assessed. Likewise, if a sole owner of property (worth more than $20,000) transfers ownership into joint tenancy with another person, a taxable gift has been made.

Martha transfers her house, worth $300,000 (all equity), into joint tenancy with her son Richard solely to avoid probate. The IRS position is that she has made a taxable gift of one-half the value of the house (less the $10,000 exempt amount). In other words, the IRS doesn't recognize the concept of "joint tenancy for convenience only."

If the taxable value of the gift is less than $600,000, no gift taxes must actually be paid. Instead, any tax assessed is deducted from the estate/gift tax credit (see Chapter 14, Section A). So, the problem here is not that money will have to be spent, out-of-pocket, to pay gift tax, but that a gift tax return must be prepared and filed, a hassle to many people.

There are some limited exceptions to the IRS rule that a gift is made whenever a sole owner places property in joint tenancy:

- If a bank account is opened in joint tenancy, with one person actually paying all or most of the deposit, there's no taxable gift. The same rule applies for buying a savings bond in joint tenancy. Only when a person who didn't contribute half the original deposit or cost takes possession of more than his original contribution (by withdrawing money from the bank account, or selling an interest in the bond) can there be a taxable gift.

- No gift taxes are assessed against any gift made between husband and wife. Either spouse may transfer any separately-owned property into joint tenancy with the other spouse without concern over gift taxes.

4. Incapacity

Any form of shared ownership can become difficult if one owner becomes incapacitated. The other owner(s) may need someone with legal authority to act for the incapacitated owner, particularly to sell the property or refinance it. The best way to authorize someone to act for you if you become incapacitated is by use of a durable power of attorney (discussed in Chapter 18). To be secure about possible incapacity, owners of joint tenancy property should be sure each has prepared a durable power of attorney. Otherwise, there's a risk a court proceeding will be required if one owner becomes incapacitated.

F. When Joint Tenancy Makes Sense

BY NOW, SOME OF YOU may have read my negative comments about the risks of joint tenancy as a damning indictment against it. Please don't. In some situations, owning property in joint tenancy certainly does make sense. For people who value simplicity (joint tenancy is easy to create), and whose situations don't involve the drawbacks and risks I've discussed, joint tenancy can work fine.

Mr. Berg, who is old and in rapidly-declining health, lives in a coop apartment he very recently purchased in Manhattan. Mr. Berg wants the apartment to go to his daughter, Molly, who he trusts totally—and he wants to avoid probate. He also loathes paperwork and wants the transfer accomplished as simply as possible. His wisest plan is to transfer ownership of the property into joint tenancy. It requires less paperwork than a living trust. And since he recently purchased the apartment and isn't expected to live for a long time, neither Mr. Berg nor Molly is concerned with stepped-up basis problems. Joint tenancy gets the apartment to Molly outside of probate, with the least bother to Mr. Berg.

Isadore and Randall plan to buy a house together. If either dies, they want the other to receive his or her share, outside of probate. Each fully trusts the other. If they take title in joint tenancy, they achieve their estate planning goal with a minimum of bother. Since each owns half the house, there's no stepped-up basis problem; only the deceased owner's half-interest in the house will receive a "stepped-up" basis, no matter how they hold title to the house.

G. Creating a Joint Tenancy for Property with Documents of Title

THERE ARE TWO WAYS property with documents of title can be placed in joint tenancy:

- Two or more people buy or acquire property and take title in joint tenancy; or

- A person who owns property can transfer title into joint tenancy with another person or people.

Joint tenancy is commonly used for many types of property with documents of title, including real estate and bank accounts or safe deposit boxes. (Joint bank accounts and safe deposit boxes are discussed in Chapter 11, with "pay-on-death" bank accounts, because these kinds of accounts are similar in many ways.)

1. The Language Required

To own property in joint tenancy, the title document must contain words that clearly demonstrate the owners' intention. In most states, joint tenancy may be created by using the phrase "in joint tenancy" or "as joint tenants" in the ownership document. In some states, it's traditional or required to use the phrase "joint tenants, with right of survivorship," or "in joint tenancy with right of survivorship." This is sometimes abbreviated "JTWROS." Simply listing the owners' names joined by "and" or "or" is not normally adequate to create a joint tenancy, although a few states allow it.

You may not remember how you took title to a piece of real estate, or your car, or your bank account. To see if shared ownership property is held in joint tenancy, look on the deed (for real estate) or the title slip (for other kinds of property, such as cars). If it doesn't say the co-owners own the property "as joint tenants" or "with right of survivorship" or similar language, the property isn't held in joint tenancy.

If you decide to transfer some of your existing property into joint tenancy, double-check your state's law to learn the wording needed. If you're transferring real estate, any reliable title company or lawyer can tell you.[4] You'll find that a few states have special requirements governing how a joint tenancy is created. For example, in Florida, a joint tenancy can be created only in an instrument of transfer—a deed made when property is sold. And in Oregon, the functional equivalent of joint tenancy is created by using the phrase "tenancy in common with right of survivorship."

2. Real Estate

To demonstrate how simple joint tenancy can be, here is a deed used to transfer solely-owned real estate into joint tenant. In this deed, Alfred Smyth has created a joint tenancy in real property between himself and his son Anthony, by giving Anthony a "joint ownership" interest in the real property. Again, however, remember that if the property has gone up substantially in value since you bought it, or is likely to before you die, the tax basis rules discussed in Section D(2) above usually militate against transferring that property into joint tenancy.

H. Creating Joint Tenancy for Personal Property Without Documents of Title

YOU CAN CREATE JOINT TENANCIES for personal property without documents of title, such as valuable paintings, jewelry or even for your shoes. (To remind you, "personal property" is all property except real estate.) To create a joint tenancy for personal property that doesn't have a formal document of title, all you have to do is declare in a written document that you and the co-owners own the property "in joint tenancy" or "as joint tenants." The document doesn't need to be filed with the County Recorder, unlike deeds putting real property in joint

---

[4]Nolo Press publishes *The Deeds Book*, by Randolph, which contains all the forms (deeds) and instructions necessary to transfer real property into joint tenancy in California.

RECORDING REQUESTED BY

AND WHEN RECORDED MAIL TO

NAME **Alfred Smythe**
ADDRESS **Easy Street**
CITY & STATE **El Dorado Hills, Ca.**

Title Order No._____ Escrow No._____

——— SPACE ABOVE THIS LINE FOR RECORDER'S USE ———

MAIL TAX STATEMENTS TO

NAME **Alfred Smythe**
ADDRESS **Easy Street**
CITY & STATE **El Dorado Hills, Ca.**

Individual Grant Deed

~~FOR A VALUABLE CONSIDERATION~~

Alfred Smythe
GRANTS to

Anthony Smythe and Alfred Smythe, as Joint Tenants

all that real property situate in the **City of El Dorado Hills**

County of **Dreams** , State of California, described as follows

(property described and identified)

**Said property to be owned in joint tenancy by Alfred Smythe
and Anthony Smythe**

Dated **July 1, 1980** XXXXXX

_____ /s/ Alfred Smythe _____

_____ /s/ Anthony Smythe _____

STATE OF CALIFORNIA
_____County of _____ } ss.
On_____ 19___ before me, the undersigned,
a Notary Public, in and for said State, personally appeared_____

known to me to be the person whose name _____
subscribed to the within instrument, and acknowledged to me that
__he__ executed the same.

_____
Notary Public

FOR NOTARY SEAL OR STAMP

MAIL TAX STATEMENTS AS DIRECTED ABOVE

tenancy. However, you should have the document notarized.

Guy and Danielle have been together for years. They have acquired a considerable amount of household furnishings, including appliances, furniture and glassware. Each wants the other to receive all their property when one of them dies. They want to avoid probate and the possibility that a member of either's family could claim any of their property. So, Guy and Danielle execute a joint ownership document, reciting that all the household furnishings listed in it are their joint tenancy property.

The following forms can be used to create joint tenancy ownership of personal property for items that have no formal deed of title. The first form is used when you're making a gift of ownership to the new joint tenants. The second form is for the less common occurrence of actually selling one half or a greater interest to others. The third form is for newly acquired property, to document that it was bought in joint tenancy.

Form #1
Joint Tenancy Ownership Document

The personal property identified below, previously owned by [your name], is transferred to [your name] and [joint tenant's name] as joint tenants. This joint tenancy property is described as:

[list and clearly identify the property]

Dated:_____
_____(your signature)_____
Dated:_____
_____(joint tenant's signature)_____

[notarized]

Form #2
Joint Tenancy Ownership Document

The personal property identified below, previously owned by [your name], is transferred to [your name] and [joint tenant's name] as joint tenants, for [purchase price] paid by [joint tenant's name] to [your name]. This joint tenancy property is described as:

[list and clearly identify the property].

Dated:_____
_____(your signature)_____
Dated:_____
_____(joint tenant's signature)_____

[notarized]

Form #3
Joint Tenancy Ownership Document

The personal property identified below is held by [your name] and [other joint tenant's name] as joint tenants.

This joint tenancy property is described as:

[list and clearly identify the property].

This joint tenancy property was purchased on _____, 19__ for a purchase price of $_____, of which _____ contributed $_____ and _____ contributed $_____ .

Dated:_____
_____(your signature)_____
Dated:_____
_____(joint tenant's signature)_____

[notarized]

I. Obtaining Title to Joint Tenancy Property After One Owner Dies

The major benefit of joint tenancy is the "automatic right of survivorship." To evaluate joint tenancy, it can be helpful to know how this right of survivorship actually works. Obviously, the words on a deed to real property or certificate of title to a car don't magically change the day a joint tenant takes that last breath. Until someone acts, the legal title remains recorded in all the joint tenants' names. What "automatic right of survivorship" really means in this context is that compared to most legal tasks it's possible to transfer title to the surviving owner fairly easily, quickly and cheaply, without probate. This is true for all joint tenancies, whether of real estate or personal property. Of course, though, there is some paperwork involved.

To get the deceased owner's name off the ownership document, so that the surviving joint tenants can fully function as legal owners, they must:

- establish with the appropriate government official or recorder of title that the joint tenant has died by filing a copy of the death certificate; and

- file a document establishing that the surviving owners are sole owners to the property.

A lawyer can be hired to do this, but is normally unnecessary, as the procedures are routine. If a lawyer is hired, however, be sure the fee charged is a reasonable hourly one. An unhappy practice I'm familiar with is for a lawyer to propose charging one-third of what the probate fee would be for property of the same value. Usually, this is far too high a fee; the work is neither complicated or time-consuming.

For example, to terminate a joint tenancy in real estate, you need to file a certified copy of the deceased's death certificate and a form called "Affidavit of Death of Joint Tenant," or something similar, with the county office of property records where the property is located (called the "County Recorder" in many states). The affidavit is a standard legal form, available in many office supply stores. On this form, the surviving joint tenant states that a joint tenant has died. In some states, such as

California,[5] a new deed doesn't need to be completed. After the affidavit and death certificate have been recorded, title to the property can be transferred or sold by the survivor by signing a deed "as surviving joint tenant."

Tax Liens. In some states which have state death taxes, tax liens (legal claims) may be imposed on all of a deceased person's property, and title cannot be transferred until the lien is removed. Removing the lien may involve posting a bond, filing a final inheritance tax return, or otherwise satisfying the tax authorities that taxes will be paid. In those states, a major hassle for the surviving joint tenant can be obtaining a release of the tax lien. You'll need to locate the governmental agency that imposes and releases these tax liens, and see what is required to release them.

Federal Estate Taxes. Joint tenancy property can also be liable for a proportionate share of a deceased's federal estate taxes, if the estate is large enough to be subject to them. To simplify, federal taxes are assessed if the net estate is over $600,000. (See Chapter 14, Section A.) The taxes due will depend on the size of the overall taxable estate, which probably won't be determined for some time. But if the surviving owner must wait until the full amount of estate taxes are known (or even worse, paid) before obtaining clear title to the joint tenancy property, the practical advantages of the right of survivorship are severely diminished. After all, one purpose of a right of survivorship is to obtain clear title fast. Fortunately, the IRS will usually allow clear transfer of joint tenancy property if there's an estimate of the value of the property in the estate and clear indication that there are enough other assets to pay off all estate taxes. The proof required that all taxes due can be paid from the remaining taxable estate will vary depending on the size, complexity and liquidity of the estate.

---

[5]Detailed how-to information as to all the steps required to transfer any kind of joint tenancy property in California is contained in Nissley, *How to Probate an Estate*, California edition (Nolo Press).

Bank Accounts as Estate Planning Devices

CHAPTER 11

Bank Accounts as Estate Planning Devices

BANK ACCOUNTS can play a useful part in your estate plan. You can use certain types of bank accounts to:

- avoid probate,
- provide cash quickly to your family or other inheritors, and
- make gifts.

In addition, a bank safe deposit box can be a convenient place to store valuable papers.

If you have substantial amounts of cash, you may wonder if bank accounts are a sensible investment, whatever their estate planning benefits. Some people who consider themselves sophisticated investors disparage bank accounts, claiming that you can get a better return on your money by being more aggressive—making more speculative investments, in stocks, bonds, real estate, precious metals, or commodities. Investing aggressively in these ways means taking risks. People can be badly burned in such gambles; for many readers, putting at least a significant amount of money in a federally-insured bank can make excellent sense. W.C. Fields' investment strategy was "All my money's tied up in currency." Generally, bank accounts, especially certificates of deposit for six months or longer, aren't bad investments. On the average, they yield in interest at least twice as much as the average stock pays in dividends, which means the stock price must increase a fair percentage before people who buy it do as well as they would if they made a safe and secure bank deposit.

A. Joint Tenancy Bank Accounts

JOINT TENANCY BANK ACCOUNTS can be a useful means of avoiding probate, especially when two people are already a family unit and are sharing income and expenses. Most banks have standard joint tenancy account forms, and most types of bank accounts may be owned in joint tenancy, including checking, savings and certificates of deposit. To open such an account, all people involved sign the account papers as "joint tenants with right of survivorship." (Some banks abbreviate this

"JTWROS.") When one joint tenant dies, the other can (within the limits on the account and by the procedures described below) obtain all the money in the account, with no need to go through probate.

In most joint tenancy bank accounts, either person can withdraw any or all of the money in the account at any time. If the purpose of the account is for shared expenses—as the family account of a husband and wife—this isn't normally a problem. If it is, inquire if a bank will let you require two signatures for withdrawals on a joint tenancy account. Many will.

A joint tenancy account is generally not a good idea if your purpose is to transfer your own money at death to someone else, who you list as a joint owner of your account. A joint tenancy account exposes you to the risk that the other person can remove the money while you're alive—unless, as just mentioned, two signatures are required to withdraw money. But this means you'll have to get someone else's signature each time you want to withdraw your own money from the account. Fortunately, there is a better alternative. If your main goal is to avoid probate for money in your own account, an "informal bank trust account" (often called a "pay-on-death" bank account), which I discuss in Section C, allows you to retain full and exclusive control over your money while you live and still have the account avoid probate.

One question that commonly arises is whether creating a joint bank account by adding someone's name to your account means you've made a gift, and so have to concern yourself with gift taxes. Legally, there's no gift made by creating a joint bank account or depositing money in it. However, a gift is made if the other person takes money out. (The legal rules for gifts and gift taxes are discussed in Chapter 15.)

B. Joint Tenancy Safe Deposit Boxes

A JOINT TENANCY safe deposit box can be a sensible place to keep important papers—wills, funeral instructions, burial or body donation, veteran, union death benefits or pension documents. This is true because either joint tenant can normally obtain instant access to the documents when they are needed.

If you decide to get a joint tenancy safe deposit box, be sure to specify on the bank account cards whether the co-owners share ownership of all contents of the box. This can be particularly important if you keep valuable objects, such as jewelry, in the box. In some states, joint tenancy rental of a safe deposit box gives both joint tenants access to the box, but doesn't necessarily create ownership rights in that box's contents unless it's clearly spelled out. Of course, if you don't want the other person with access to the box to own certain property in it, be sure it's clear that the joint tenancy in the safe deposit box is for access purposes only. And of course, you would also want to leave the property in the box by your living trust or will.

Caution: In some states with state death taxes, safe deposit boxes are sealed by a bank as soon as it is notified of the death of an owner. The contents cannot be released until the box is inventoried by a government official. So if your state has death taxes (see Chapter 14, Section E) check with your bank's officials to see whether the safe deposit box will be sealed upon death of a joint tenant, and how one gets the box unsealed. Usually this can be done reasonably quickly and easily. If not, however, a safe deposit box isn't a good place to store documents that you want to be readily available at your death, including your living trust and will.

C. Informal Bank Trust Accounts

THERE'S A CONVENIENT type of bank account that avoids probate, allows you to keep absolute control of your money while you're alive, and allows you to name the person you want to inherit the contents of the account when you die. This type of account completely eliminates the risk of a joint tenancy bank account—that the other joint tenant can withdraw your money before you die. Curiously, this type of account is called by various names by different banks in different parts of the country. Common names include "informal trust," "pay-on-death" account, "bank trust account," and a "Totten trust" (after a Mr. Totten, who apparently came up with the concept.)

Whatever it's called, it works the same way. You open an account in your name, as depositor, and as "trustee for the benefit of [your beneficiary, whoever you name to receive the money when you die]." As long as you live, the beneficiary has no rights to any money in the account. After your death, the beneficiary can promptly obtain the money in the account simply by presenting the bank with proof of identity and a certified copy of the death certificate.

Ray Jones wants to leave cash, probate-free, to his two daughters. He simply opens a Totten Trust savings account as "Ray Jones, depositor, as trustee for Michelle and Mary Jones, equal beneficiaries." After he dies, his daughters go to the bank, present a death certificate and proof of their identities to bank officials, and then remove and divide equally all money in the account.

---

1. Advantages of Informal Bank Trust Accounts

There are normally no risks in creating an informal bank trust or pay-on-death bank account. As noted, unlike joint tenancy bank accounts, the beneficiary cannot withdraw any money from the account while the depositor is alive. In addition, the depositor can close the account any time, and can change the beneficiary at any time.[1] Also, the depositor can withdraw, or deposit, any amount desired. Because the depositor retains complete control over the account until death, establishing a pay-on-death account isn't a gift, and therefore doesn't

---

[1] If the beneficiary dies before the depositor, and no new beneficiary is named, the money would be transferred under the residuary clause of the depositor's will, if there is one.

involve gift tax concerns. (See Chapter 15.) Only when the beneficiary gets the money at the depositor's death does legal ownership of that money change.

2. Opening an Informal Bank Trust Account

An appealing aspect of an informal bank trust account is that it's so easy to open. Most banks, including most credit unions, and savings-industrial loan companies, have standard forms for opening this kind of account; they will do the paperwork for you. A pay-on-death or informal bank trust account may either be a newly-opened account or an existing account to which you add a trust designation. Banks don't normally charge extra fees for holding your money in an informal bank trust account.

Generally, any regular bank account, including checking, savings, or certificates of deposit accounts, may be used as informal bank trust accounts. In practice, these accounts are usually savings accounts, since it's more likely there will be substantial funds in the account on the depositor's death. Not only do checking account balances fluctuate, but many don't pay interest, so aren't suitable places to keep substantial sums.

3. Estate Taxes

The money in an informal bank trust account is included in the taxable estate of the depositor (see Chapter 14). So this type of trust only works as a probate avoidance device, and will not save on federal or state death taxes, assuming your estate is large enough to pay them.

4. Before You Open an Informal Bank Trust Account

If you decide to open an informal bank trust account, there are a few concerns you should be aware of and ask about at your bank:

- **Notice to beneficiaries.** In a few states, an informal bank trust account is created only if the beneficiary is notified of the deposit. In the majority of states, simply opening the account is sufficient. Your bank will know your state's rules for what kind of notice, if any, must be provided.

- **Early withdrawal penalties.** If the type of bank account you choose for an informal bank trust account requires holding a deposit for a set term, or paying a substantial penalty for early withdrawal—as would be the case, for example, for a six-month certificate of deposit—the penalty is usually waived if the depositor dies before that term expires.

- **Spouse's share of estate.** In many states, funds deposited in an informal bank trust account are included in the assets against which a surviving spouse who hasn't received from one-third to one-half of the total estate is given a "statutory right of election." (See Chapter 3, Section C.) In other words, the person who you name as trust beneficiary may not get the money if you have tried to disinherit your spouse.

- **State death taxes.** If your state has state death taxes (see Chapter 14, Section E), immediate death tax liens (legal claims) may be imposed on informal trust bank accounts, and the liens must be removed before the funds can be transferred to the beneficiaries. This is normally done by demonstrating to the tax authority that the estate has ample funds to pay taxes and is routine for most estates.

5. Informal Trusts for Assets Other than Bank Accounts

An informal trust or a pay-on-death account generally cannot be used for certain other types of cash assets (aside from bank accounts) such as mutual funds, capital funds, stocks, bonds, or other securities. Most brokerage companies, and other non-bank money holders won't allow you to own cash assets, mutual funds, capital funds, stocks, bonds and securities in an informal trust or "pay-on-death" form. If you want to avoid probate of these kinds of assets, you have to use some other form acceptable to the institution. This can be joint tenancy if you and the other joint tenant own the property together, as is common for couples. However, if you want to transfer your solely-owned securities or mutual funds, etc. to someone else, probate free, it's usually better to use a living trust rather than joint tenancy, for several reasons. (Living trusts are discussed in Chapter 9.) These include the facts that:

- the beneficiary of the living trust has no right to the property while you live;

- you can change the beneficiary or end the living trust if you wish; and

- with a living trust, you inheritor gets a stepped-up tax basis on the entire property instead of only on one-

half of the property transferred to joint tenancy [see Chapter 10, Section D(2) for an explanation of these tax basis rules].

D. Using a Living Trust to Avoid Probate of Bank Accounts

IF YOU HAVE BANK ACCOUNTS which are solely owned, and held as informal bank trust accounts, consider transferring these accounts into your living trust (as described in Chapter 9, Sections E and F) and naming beneficiaries for those accounts in the trust. Using a living trust will allow the money to pass to your beneficiaries without probate. If you leave these accounts by your will, probate is normally required before the money is turned over to the beneficiaries you named for them in your will. However, accounts likely to have a small balance, such as personal checking accounts, may be able to be transferred by will and still avoid probate (see Chapter 13). Also, many people don't want their personal checking account in a trust name, rather than their own, even if this does eventually require probate of that account.

Life Insurance

CHAPTER 12

Life Insurance

LIFE INSURANCE has long been a basic part of much estate planning in the United States. Indeed, one fear many people have of the phrase "estate planning" is that it's a cover for hard sell visits by life insurance agents. Still, life insurance can be very useful, especially for parents of young children and those who support a non-working spouse or a disadvantaged or incapacitated adult.

A. An Overview

LIFE INSURANCE is, of course, a relatively inexpensive means of providing cash for survivors should the purchaser die unexpectedly; in addition, there are several other common estate problems for which life insurance can be part of a sensible solution. These include:

- **Probate Avoidance:** Normally, the proceeds of a life insurance policy avoid probate because you name your beneficiary in the policy instead of by a will. This means that money can be transferred quickly to survivors with little red tape, cost or delay (see Section C below).

- **Death Tax Reduction:** When a policy is not legally owned by the person who is the insured (as explained in Section E), the proceeds are excluded from the insured's taxable estate. This can significantly reduce death tax liability of the insured's estate. Obviously, though, this is only a benefit for people whose estates are large enough to face death tax liability in the first place.

- **Providing Immediate Cash at Death:** Insurance proceeds are a handy source of cash to pay the deceased's debts, funeral expenses, and income or death taxes.[1] Lawyers and financial advisors call cash and assets that can quickly be converted to cash "liquid." If your estate has almost all "non-liquid" assets (real estate, collectibles, a share in a small business), there may be a substantial loss if these assets

must be sold quickly to raise cash to pay bills, as opposed to what they could be sold for if there was enough ready money to meet all pressing bills.

Ms. Perez's estate consists of several valuable pieces of real estate and a one-half interest in a profitable antiques store, but includes very little cash and no life insurance. When she dies, she owes debts of $40,000 (aside from mortgages) and death taxes totaling $120,000. To raise this money, her inheritors must sell some of her real estate or her interest in the store. Unfortunately, the country is suffering a mild recession, and the market value of both antiques and real estate is down. To make matters worse, canny real estate people spread the word that this is a "distress sale" to raise money for estate obligations. As a result, the price the inheritors receive when they sell one of the pieces of real estate is far below what they would receive if they had the flexibility to choose when to sell the property. Had Ms. Perez purchased an insurance policy with a pay-off at death of $40,000 or more, the need to sell other assets would have been avoided.

Having indicated some of the reasons life insurance can be desirable, let me again emphasize that simply buying some is not an adequate way to plan an estate. Indeed, many people simply don't need life insurance. Those who decide to purchase insurance should know exactly why they are buying it, the best type of policy for their needs, and of course, should buy no more than they need. (As a group, Americans certainly believe in life insurance, holding over two trillion dollars worth, far more, per capita, than any other country.)

Here are some questions to ask yourself to help evaluate your life insurance needs.

1. Long-Term Needs

First, consider whether it makes sense for you to purchase insurance to provide financial help for family members over the long term.

---

[1]Federal estate taxes are due nine months after death, so cash to pay them doesn't have to be raised immediately.

- How many people are really dependent on your earning capacity over the long term? If the answer is "no one," it's doubtful that you need life insurance.

- How much money would your dependents really need, and for how long, if you died suddenly? Don't accept life insurance salesperson hype on this one. Very few people need to be supported for the rest of their lives.

- When you determine how much money your dependents will need, subtract the amounts that will be available from public and any private insurance plans that already provide coverage. Social security and dependents' benefits will almost surely be available, and you may also be covered by union or management pensions or a group life insurance plan.

- Have you subtracted any other likely sources of income, such as the help reasonably affluent grandparents would assuredly provide for your children in case of disaster? Also, remember that bright kids often get scholarships, and dependent spouses can usually return to work at some point.

2. Short-Term Needs

Now you should assess whether you need life insurance for short-term needs.

- How long is it likely to be, after you die, before your property is turned over to your inheritors? If your property will avoid probate, there's usually little need for insurance for short-term expenses. By contrast, if the bulk of your property is transferred by will, and therefore will be tied up in probate for months, your family and other inheritors may need the ready cash insurance can provide.

- What assets would be available to take care of immediate financial needs? Aside from insurance, there are other ways of providing ready cash, such as leaving some money in joint or pay-on-death bank accounts, or placing marketable stocks and other securities in joint tenancy.

- If you own a business, how much cash would it need on your death? To answer this, you have to estimate the cash flow necessary to maintain your business, and how your death is likely to affect it.

Note on Buying Insurance:

If you don't own life insurance and think you want it, you need to talk to an insurance salesperson or broker. Normally, a salesperson sells for one company only, while a broker can place your policy with one of several. In theory, this would seem to be a reason to prefer a broker, but in practice, the integrity of the person you are dealing with is more important than is the legal relationship to an insurance company or companies.

If you do contact an insurance salesperson, look for a person who will function as an ally, offering additional information and proposing alternatives—not forcing you. If you get too much quick-sell pressure, contact someone else. And here's one more tip: some salespeople don't recommend that you buy term insurance, or try to talk you out of it, for no other reason than they get a much higher commission from selling you whole life or universal.

Before you contact anyone who sells insurance, you should have a good idea of what kind of policy you need and how much it should cost. As the cost of the same insurance can vary considerably from company to company (often, relatively small mutual companies charge lower rates than some of the giants of TV advertising), I also recommend that you take a look at the book *Life Insurance: How to Buy the Right Policy From the Right Company at the Right Price* (Consumer Reports Books) which contains an indepth, company-by-company price comparison for all standard types of insurance. The book separates the good from the bad when it comes to policy features and sales practices, and provides helpful charts rating all leading insurers and disclosing how much they charge for similar policies.

B. Types of Life Insurance

IF YOU ARE INTERESTED in life insurance, any salesperson will be delighted to explain the bewildering array of policies available to you. But unless you educate yourself first, it's all too easy to get mesmerized by insurance policy lingo and end up paying too much for a policy that may not even meet your needs. Basically, for estate planning purposes, there are three main types of life insurance—term, whole life, universal life. Also, any of these types of life insurance can be purchased with one lump sum, called a "single-premium payment," which can be a useful estate planning device in some circumstances. And finally, annuity policies which aren't really life insurance at all can be very useful in planning certain types of estates. I explain each in the sections which follow.

1. Term Insurance

Term insurance provides a pre-set amount of cash if the insured dies while the policy is in force. For example, a five-year $130,000 term policy pays off if you die within five years—and that's it. If you live beyond the end of the term, you get nothing (except, of course, the continued joys and sorrows of life itself). Term insurance is the cheapest form of coverage. As a candid life insurance man once told me, "It provides the most bang for the buck, no

question." There are many types of term insurance, but these options don't change the basic fact that term insurance pays off if you die during the policy time period and doesn't pay anything if you live beyond that period.

Term life insurance is particularly suitable for younger people with families, who want substantial insurance coverage at low cost. Since the risks of dying in your twenties, thirties, or forties are quite low, the cost of term insurance during these years is as reasonable as life insurance prices get. Also, if you only need insurance for a short time, say to qualify for a business loan, term is your best bet. However, the older you are, the more expensive term insurance becomes when you compare how much you have to pay in premiums to the pay-off value of the policy. This, of course, is understandable, as the older you are, the greater the chance you will die during the policy term.

As mentioned above, term policies offered by different companies have all sorts of differences, some fairly significant. For example, some policies are automatically renewable at the end of the term, often for higher premiums, and some are not. Some can also be converted from a term to whole life or "universal" policy. But no term insurance has cash surrender value; unlike whole life or universal insurance, term doesn't build up any recoverable cash value that you can borrow against or collect when the policy ends.

2. Whole Life Insurance

Whole life (sometimes called "straight life") insurance provides a set dollar amount of coverage, for fixed, uniform payments, but in addition has a savings feature. If you keep the policy in force long enough, it builds up a "cash reserve," which you can borrow against or cash in.

The premiums for whole life, especially in the early years of a younger person's policy, are much greater than needed to cover the actuarial risk of death. In other words, insurance companies take in substantially more money on whole life policies during their first few years than they pay out for proceeds for insureds who die. The insurance company invests the surplus. Some of the surplus becomes the insured's cash reserve, which grows over time. Like savings held in a bank, the cash reserve earns interest, paid by the insurance company. After a set time, usually several years, the policyholder has the right to cash in the policy and obtain the cash reserves. The amount is sometimes called the "cash surrender value" of the policy. A policyholder who cashes in a policy gets a lump sum, but, of course, is no longer insured. Another way to get money back on the policy, but to keep the insurance in force, is to borrow against the policy. Funds borrowed from the cash or surrender value of an insurance policy are deducted from the proceeds paid at death, if the insured dies without having paid off the loan. When the policy ends, the insured can cash it in or renew it.

Whole life is almost always more expensive than term life insurance, especially in the early years of the policy. Buying insurance and savings is obviously more costly than only buying insurance. It will typically cost you several times more money to obtain the same amount of coverage if you choose whole life rather than term. However, term premiums do increase in cost as you get older, but traditionally, whole life premiums stay roughly the same.

On the other hand, whole life is usually automatically renewable, unlike many term policies; with whole life, the insurance period can be extended without a new physical examination of the insured.

In my view, whole life is not a particularly sensible way to invest money (as opposed to buying term insurance, which, as you know by now, has no savings feature), because other safe investments, like bank money market funds, normally yield higher returns. However, I should note that some investment advisors are more favorable to whole life than I am. They argue that the interest paid on many whole life policies is now (unlike the past), reasonably competitive. And they point out that if you buy whole life and keep up your policy, you are forced to save—a boon if you have trouble saving in other ways.

3. Universal Life Insurance

Universal life, a relatively new and increasingly popular insurance industry creature, combines some of the desirable features of both term and whole life insurance, and offers other advantages. Over time, the net cost often isn't much more than term insurance. With universal life, you build up a surplus, or cash reserve, as with whole life. Insurance companies invest this surplus in fixed-income assets, such as corporate bonds or mortgages. Therefore, a universal cash reserve pays interest at market-competitive rates, a higher rate of return than traditionally paid by whole life. In practice, the interest paid on universal life varies significantly from company to company, so you need to investigate carefully what rates of interest are being paid by different companies. Also, be warned that interest payments aren't permanently fixed, and can be affected by market conditions if there's a crash. Your rate of return could drop significantly.

Aside from higher interest rates, the main advantage of universal life over whole life is that universal is far more open and flexible. With universal, you are told how much of your policy payments goes for company overhead expenses, reserves and policy proceed payments, and how much is retained for your savings. With whole life, all you do is make a payment. You are told only the interest rate paid on your cash reserve. Universal also allows you to vary your policy payments, or amount of coverage, or both, from year to year. Again, in contrast, whole life creates set payments for a set amount of proceeds, which cannot be varied during the period of the policy.

Universal life can also act as a kind of tax shelter. The interest the company pays on the cash (surrender) value of the policy is not taxed as it is earned and accumulates. Only if the insured withdraws any interest is it subject to tax. Certain partial interest withdrawals can even be made without paying tax if the insured has owned a universal policy at least 15 years. By contrast, the interest on bank accounts is subject to tax in the year it is paid, even if left untouched in the account.

There can be other significant advantages to universal life; an insurance agent will be glad to explain them to you.

Note on Variable Life Insurance: Variable life, sometimes called "variable universal life insurance," refers to policies in which cash reserves are invested in securities, stocks and bonds. These policies are basically a form of mutual funds, and can offer unpleasant surprises when financial markets decline.

4. Single-Premium Life Insurance

With single-premium life, you pay, up-front, all premiums due for the full duration of the policy. Normally, any cash reserve policy can be purchased with a single premium. Obviously, this requires the expenditure of a large amount of cash—$5,000, $10,000 or more. A reason to commit so much cash to buying an insurance policy is that it enables the purchaser to give the fully-paid-for policy to new owners. As explained in Section E of this chapter, there can be significant estate tax savings if someone other than the insured owns the policy. And because there are no more payments to make, a gift of a single-premium policy doesn't involve risks that the new owners will fail to make payments and cause the policy to be cancelled.

5. Annuities

Basically, an annuity is a policy in which an insurance company contracts to pay the policy beneficiary a certain cash amount each year, or month, instead of one lump sum upon death. Some people name themselves as beneficiary of their own annuity policies, thus providing themselves with a set income for life, beginning at a specified age.

There are all sorts of annuity policies and combinations of annuity payment plans with whole life and even term policies. An estate planning advantage of an annuity is that you can buy one that will provide periodic payments to someone you believe is unable (too young, or too much of a wastrel) to handle one large lump sum insurance payment. In this sense, annuities work somewhat like a trust.

However, even if you want to arrange for periodic payments to a beneficiary, you should consider other alternatives, including establishing an ongoing trust, before choosing an annuity policy. Why? Because, in most instances, annuity policies are a relatively expensive way to meet your objective. Also, they are not flexible. For example, if special needs of the beneficiary arise, such as an extended illness, the payments normally cannot be increased, as they often can be with a well-designed trust. In short, buying a more prosaic type of insurance and having the benefits put in trust should you die, administered by a trusted friend or family member (see Section G), is usually a wiser choice, providing the control over disbursements you need but also allowing the trustee to vary the payments in certain cases.

C. Life Insurance and Probate

THE PROCEEDS OF A LIFE INSURANCE POLICY are not subject to probate unless the deceased's estate is named the beneficiary of the policy. If anyone else, including a trust, is the beneficiary of the policy, the proceeds are not included in the probate estate, and the proceeds are paid directly to the beneficiary without the cost or delay of probate. Except when your estate will have no ready cash to pay anticipated debts and taxes, there is no sound reason for naming your estate, rather than a person or trust for another person, as the beneficiary of an insurance policy.

In my experience, the problem of substantial debts and no liquid assets is fairly rare. In most instances, estates contain enough cash, or other assets that can be sold for cash, to pay debts and taxes. Unless life insurance proceeds are used for estate costs, they will be distributed to someone, eventually. So it seems foolhardy to reduce the amount inheritors receive from your life insurance because of probate costs—or add to the time your inheritors must wait before they get this money.

D. Choosing Life Insurance Beneficiaries

AS YOU KNOW, when you buy life insurance, you name the policy's beneficiaries—those who receive the proceeds when you die. As long as you are the owner of a life insurance policy, you can change beneficiaries. You can't, however, change a beneficiary of an insurance policy simply by naming a new beneficiary in a will or living trust. If one person is named as a beneficiary of a life insurance policy, but another person is named as the beneficiary of the policy in the insured's will or living trust, the first person remains the legal beneficiary.

1. Community Property States

If you live in a community property state and buy a policy with community property funds, one-half of the proceeds are owned by the surviving spouse, no matter what the policy says about the beneficiary. This result can be varied by a written agreement between the spouses, in which one spouse transfers all interest in a particular insurance policy to the other spouse.

2. Minor Children as Beneficiaries

If you want your minor children to be the beneficiaries of your policy, you must arrange some legal means for the proceeds to be managed and supervised by a competent adult. If you don't, the insurance company would likely require that a court appoint a property guardian for the children before releasing the proceeds. There are several ways to prevent this:

- Rethinking your plan to name minor beneficiaries, and instead, naming a trusted adult beneficiary such as a spouse, who you are confident will use the money for the children's benefit.

- Naming your living trust as the beneficiary of the policy, if your minor children are beneficiaries of the trust. In the living trust, you define how the proceeds are to be used for your children. The proceeds are managed as part of a children's trust created in the living trust. (Basic children's trusts are contained in the living trust forms in the Appendix.)

- Naming a property guardian for your minor children in your will. You can do this in your back-up will (see Chapter 17).

Using a living trust is generally the best strategy. As discussed in Chapter 6, the advantage of using a living trust over a property guardian is that a guardianship must end when the minor becomes a legal adult. Trusts can be continued until each child reaches whatever age you've decided is best for the child to receive property outright. Also, guardianships normally require court supervision, while children's trusts do not.

E. Transferring Ownership of Life Insurance Policies to Reduce Estate Taxes

THIS SECTION IS IMPORTANT ONLY if your estate will face federal estate taxes. An estate must be worth $600,000 (unless you have made substantial gifts during your life) before this occurs.

1. Estate Taxes and Life Insurance Proceeds

One way federal estate taxes can be reduced is by transferring ownership of a life insurance policy. Whether or not life insurance proceeds are included in the deceased's taxable estate, and so subject to federal death taxes, depends on who owns the policy when the insured dies. If the deceased owned the policy, the proceeds are included in the federal taxable estate; if someone else owned the policy, the proceeds are not included.

Melissa owns an insurance policy covering her life, with a face value of $200,000, payable to her son, Jeff, as beneficiary. Melissa's business partner, Juanita, owns a second policy, covering Melissa's life, for $400,000, also payable to Jeff. Melissa dies. All the proceeds of Melissa's policy, $200,000, are included in her federal taxable estate. However, none of the $400,000 payable to Jeff from the policy Juanita owns is part of Melissa's federal taxable estate, because Melissa did not own the policy.

An owner of life insurance has the right to assign or give ownership of the policy to any other adult, including the policy beneficiary. The only exceptions are some group policies, which many people participate in through work, and which don't allow you to transfer ownership. The value of the policy when it is given will always be substantially less than the amount it pays off on death.

When considering whether you want to transfer ownership of your life insurance policies, you need to read and understand Chapter 14, Estate Taxes, and resolve some important questions.

1. What is the estimated net value of your estate?

2. What is the amount of your life insurance proceeds?

3. Will including the proceeds of your insurance policies in your taxable estate affect your federal estate tax liability?

If your estate is larger than $600,000 (or it is less but you made large gifts during your life), there will be tax savings if you transfer ownership of the policy. The question then becomes whether these tax savings are worth losing control over your insurance policy. Once the policy is transferred, you've lost all your power over it, forever. You cannot cancel it or change the beneficiary. To make this point bluntly, suppose you transfer ownership of your policy to your spouse, and later get divorced. You cannot cancel the policy or recover it from your now ex-spouse.

The IRS has some special rules about determining who owns a life insurance policy when the insured dies:

- Gifts of life insurance policies made within three years of death are disallowed for federal estate tax purposes

(and often for state death tax purposes, too). This means that the giver would still own the policy, since the gift was not effective as a matter of law.

Louise gives her term life insurance to her friend, Leon, in 1990. She dies two years later. For federal estate tax purposes, the gift is disallowed, and the proceeds, $200,000, are included in Louise's taxable estate. If Louise had transferred the life insurance policy more than three years before her death, none of the proceeds would have been included in her taxable estate.

The message here is clear: If you want to give away a life insurance policy to reduce estate taxes, give the policy away as soon as feasible. (And don't die for at least three years.)

- Under IRS regulations, a deceased person who retained any "incidents of ownership" of a life insurance policy is considered the owner. Incidents of ownership include any significant powers over an insurance policy. If the deceased has the legal right to do any one of the following, the proceeds of the policy will be included in his taxable estate for tax purposes:

    1. change, or name, beneficiaries of the policy;

    2. borrow against the policy, pledge any cash reserve it has or cash it in;

    3. surrender, convert or cancel the policy;

    4. select a payment option—decide if payments to the beneficiary can be a lump sum or in installments; or

    5. make payments on the policy. (This doesn't mean the policy must be fully paid up, but simply that the original owners cannot retain any legal right to pay any of the premiums as they become due.)

- If the life insurance policy is transferred to someone, the transaction is regarded as a gift by the tax authorities, unless, of course, that person paid for it—which, of course, rarely occurs. So, if a long-standing policy with a present value of more than $10,000[2] is transferred to one person, gift taxes will be assessed. Even so, the amount of gift tax assessed will be far less than the tax cost of leaving the policy in your estate. This is because the proceeds payable under a policy when the insured dies are always considerably more than the worth of the policy while the insured lives.

Eugene transfers ownership of his universal life insurance policy to his son, David. The cash surrender value of the policy when he transfers it is $22,000.[3] Eugene dies four years after giving his son the insurance policy, which pays $300,000. None of this $300,000 is included in Eugene's federal taxable estate. (Nor are the proceeds considered income to David, for federal income tax purposes.)

2. How to Transfer Ownership of Your Policy

You can give away ownership of your life insurance policy by signing a simple document, called an "assignment" or a "transfer." You should notify the insurance company, and use its assignment or transfer forms if it requests you do so. There's normally no charge to make the change. Also, the policy will usually have to be changed to specify that the insured is no longer the owner.

After the policy is transferred, the new owner should make all premium payments. If the previous owner makes payments, the IRS might contend that the previous owner was keeping an "incident of ownership," so the proceeds of the policy must be included in the deceased owner's federally taxable estate—precisely what you're trying to avoid. If the new owner doesn't have sufficient

---

[2]Gifts of $10,000 or less to one person in a calendar year are gift tax free. Even if the policy is larger than this and gift taxes are assessed, they don't have to be paid. The amount of the gift tax is simply subtracted from the amount of the $600,000 federal estate and gift tax credit. For more on gift taxes, see Chapter 15.

[3]Gift taxes are assessed on $12,000, the value of the gift exceeding $10,000.

---

funds to make the payments, the previous owner could give her money to be used for these payments. In other words, it's okay for the previous owners to make payments indirectly by giving money to the new owner, but it's a no-no for the previous owner to make payments directly to the insurance company.

If you give a paid-for single-premium policy to a new owner, there's no question about who makes future payments. There aren't any. Because it's paid for in full once it's purchased, single-premium life can be a particularly convenient type of policy to give to a new owner in order to reduce the giver's estate taxes.

If your insurance company doesn't have a transfer form, here's one you can use or adapt.

Assignment of Life Insurance

__(Original owner)__ and __(new owner)__ agree that the following insurance policy issued to __(original owner)__ on __(his/her)__ life is assigned to __(new owner)__ as __(his/her)__ sole property, and that __(original owner)__ releases and waives all rights to or incidents of ownership in this policy, including:

a) the right to change or name beneficiaries under the policy;

b) the right to borrow against the policy, or pledge any cash reserve it has, or cash it in;

c) the right to surrender, convert or cancel the policy;

d) the right to select a payment option; and

e) the right to make payments on the policy.

This policy is described as __(identify policy by numbers, etc., Life Insurance Company)__

Dated this ____ day of ____, 19 ____.

_____(Signature of old owner)_____

_____(Signature of new owner)_____

[Notarized]

F. Life Insurance Trusts

AN IRREVOCABLE LIFE INSURANCE TRUST is a legal entity you create for the purpose of owning life insurance you previously owned. As explained in Chapter 16, an irrevocable trust is, like a corporation, simply a legal entity, distinct from any human being.

Creating an irrevocable life insurance trust is a means of transferring ownership of life insurance from the insured to a new owner—the trust. As with transferring life insurance policies to another person, one purpose of creating an irrevocable life insurance trust is to reduce death taxes, especially federal estate taxes, by removing the proceeds of an insurance policy from your taxable estate. In other words, the trust owns the policy, not you.

Why create a life insurance trust, rather than simply transfer a life insurance policy to someone else? One reason is that there's no one you want to give your policy to. In other words, you want to get the proceeds out of your taxable estate, but you don't want the risks of having an insurance policy on your life owned by someone else. You want the legal control over the policy that a trust imposes. For example, the trust could specify that the policy must be kept in effect while you live, eliminating the risk that a new owner of the policy could decide to cash it in.

Mrs. Brandt is the divorced mother of two children, in their 20's, who will be her beneficiaries. Neither are sensible with money. Mrs. Brandt has an estate of $500,000, plus universal life insurance which will pay $300,000 at her death. She wants to remove the proceeds of the policy from her estate. If she doesn't, $200,000 of her estate will be subject to federal estate tax. However, there's no one Mrs. Brandt trusts enough to give her policy to outright. With the controls she can impose through a trust, however, she decides it's safe to allow her sister, the person she's closest to, to be the trustee of a life insurance trust for the policy. She creates a formal trust, and transfers ownership of the life insurance policy to that trust.

There are strict requirements governing life insurance trusts. If you want to gain the estate tax savings:

- The life insurance trust must be irrevocable. If you retain the right to revoke the trust, you will be considered the owner of the policy and the proceeds will be taxed in your estate upon death.

- You cannot be the trustee. You must name either an independent adult or an institution to serve as trustee.

- You must establish the trust at least three years before your death. If the trust has not existed for at least three years when the person who set it up dies, the trust is disregarded, for estate tax purposes, and the proceeds are included in the settlor's taxable estate.

 If you decide you want to create or explore using a life insurance trust, you'll need to see a lawyer. Tax complexities must be considered: How will future premium payments be made? If the person establishing the trust makes the payments directly, or even indirectly, how will that affect estate taxes? Personal concerns also have to be carefully evaluated. For example, what happens if the settlor has a child after the trust becomes operational? Or gets divorced? Marries or remarries? There aren't any standard answers to these questions.

G. Taxation of Insurance Proceeds

CASH POLICY PROCEEDS payable to a beneficiary after an insured's death are exempt from *all* federal income taxes. However, if the proceeds are paid in installments, any interest paid on the principal is taxable income to the recipient. Likewise, the proceeds of an insurance policy are exempt from state income tax in most states.

H. Collecting the Proceeds of a Life Insurance Policy

ALTHOUGH COLLECTING INSURANCE proceeds is not technically part of estate planning, some people want to be sure their beneficiaries know how to get these proceeds. Normally, they can be collected soon after the insured's death. The insurance company claim form and a certified copy of the insured's death certificate are submitted to the company. The beneficiary may also have to file a copy of the policy, and proof of identify as the named beneficiary, if the insurance company requires it.

It's normally simple and fast, but there can be several flies in the ointment. In some states with state death taxes, insurance proceeds above a set dollar amount cannot be released until the tax officials approve. If the insurance proceeds will be part of the deceased's taxable estate, the tax officials must first be satisfied that the estate has other sufficient assets to pay state death taxes. In other instances, some companies have been known to delay payments for months, so that they can collect interest on the money for a longer time. If this happens to you, a letter to the insurance commissioner of both your state and of the one where the company is headquartered (with copies to the offending company) will normally pry the money loose pronto.

State Law Exemptions from Normal Probate

CHAPTER 13

State Law Exemptions from Normal Probate

NORMALLY PROPERTY LEFT in a will must go through probate. However, a number of states laws allow a certain amount of property to be left by will either free of probate or subject only to a very simplified probate process. These states typically permit a small amounts of property, usually in the $5,000 to $60,000 range, to be transferred by will probate-free. In addition, a few states exempt larger transfers to a certain class of people, such as a surviving spouse, from probate.[1]

There are two basic types of state law exemptions to normal probate. Some states have adopted one type, some the other, some both, and some neither. A summary of each state's laws is provided in Section C.

The first type eliminates probate altogether in certain circumstances. An inheritor under a will can collect property given him by completing an affidavit (a statement signed under oath), and presenting the person or institution holding the property with whatever additional proof state law requires—such as a copy of the will, a certified copy of the death certificate, or personal identification. The property is then simply turned over to the inheritor.

The second type of state law exemption to probate provides a summary court procedure far simpler—and normally faster and cheaper—than conventional probate. How simplified the procedure is varies by state. Some summary procedures are easy enough to do without a lawyer. Others still require a lawyer, so they result in at least some attorney's fees, court costs and delays.

A. Using Your State Laws in Estate Planning

HOW CAN YOU use your state's probate exemption laws in your estate planning? Generally, by combining a will that qualifies for probate exemption under state law with other probate avoidance techniques for the rest of your property.

Few, if any, readers of this book will be able to totally avoid probate solely by using their state's probate exemptions laws. Most estates are worth far more than the maximum amount that can be transferred under these laws. Unfortunately, in many states, probate lawyer-influenced legislatures have restricted this amount to the $5,000-$10,000 range.

Fortunately, in California, New York and in some other states, the probate-exemption law can still be valuable, even if you have a larger estate than the exempted amount. This is because you can combine this method with other probate avoidance devices, such as living trusts and joint tenancy. For instance, in California, property worth up to $60,000 can be transferred by affidavit probate-free, with the rest of a larger estate transferred by other probate avoidance devices, such as a living trust.[2] Similarly, in New York, property worth up to $10,000 can be left probate-free by will, and the rest of the estate transferred by other probate avoidance devices.[3]

Unfortunately, many states probate exemption laws don't allow this method to be combined with other probate avoidance devices. In these states, it is the total amount of property in the entire estate, not just the property subject to the will, which determines if the dollar limits of the probate exemption law has been exceeded.

---

[1]Aside from the laws discussed in this chapter, some states have very specialized methods for specific circumstances, such as property owned by a military veteran who dies in a state veterans' home, or permitting payment of wages up to $50, etc. Since these statutes aren't germane to estate planning, they're not covered.

[2]I discuss how this works in California in detail in Section D of this chapter.

[3]I discuss how this works in New York in Section E of this chapter.

B. State Law Probate Exemption Rules

EACH STATE'S PROBATE EXEMPTION LAW is different. Section C contains a chart summarizing each state's law. This chart provides three categories of information for each state:

1. The amount of property that can be transferred by will free of probate;

2. The amount of property that can be transferred by will through summary (simplified) probate;

3. The citation to the state's probate exemption law.

The summary chart is designed to give you sufficient information to decide whether you want to investigate the usefulness of your state law for your estate planning. The chart does not set forth the operational details of your state's laws, which would require a book in itself.

The chart does not tell you whether you can combine your state law's exemptions from normal probate (if any) with other probate avoidance methods. Commonly, state laws don't address this issue explicitly, and what is permitted is determined by accepted custom and practice in the legal community. If you learn from the chart that your state has a probate exemption law you might want to use in your state planning by preparing a will that qualifies for the exemptions, you should take one or more of the following steps to determine your state's precise requirements and accepted legal practice:

• Read the statute yourself. In Chapter 22, Section A, you'll find a discussion of how to research legal statutes.

• Contact the clerk of the court which handles probate matters to see if they will provide any information;

• Consult a lawyer who knows about the accepted practices. Since you're asking for limited and specific information, the fee should be reasonable.

The probate exemption rules and legal customs of the four largest states—California, New York, Texas and Florida—are examined in detail in Sections D, E, F, and G. In California and New York, the accepted legal practice is that you can combine a will qualifying for

probate exemption laws with other probate avoidance methods.

The chart in Section C also does not define how state law calculates the dollar limits for exempt transfers by will—i.e., whether they apply to your gross estate (the market value of everything you own with no deduction for debts), net estate (market value less debts and encumbrances), or net probate estate (net value only of property left by will). The statutes are normally not clear on this matter. Again, what works in each state is usually a matter of custom in the legal community, so you will need to check further if this is relevant to your situation.

1. Note for California and Wisconsin Readers

Residents of these two states are fortunate. In California, Nolo Press publishes a detailed book, *How to Probate an Estate*, Nissley, which explains step-by-step how California's probate exemption law works and provides all forms necessary to handle a probate proceeding without a lawyer.

In Wisconsin, there's a state-mandated procedure for probating a deceased's solely-owned property informally without an attorney. An interested person applies to the Probate Registrar, who will assist with the informal probate.

2. Reading the State Law Probate Exemption Chart

As an example of how to read the probate exemption law chart in Section C, let's look at Illinois. The chart provides:

Illinois

Category 1: Affidavit Procedure Instead of Probate: $25,000, personal property; also, if all beneficiaries agree, and are Illinois residents, and no state inheritance or federal estate taxes due.

Category 2: Summary Probate: $50,000

Category 3: Statutes: Illinois Annotated Statutes, Ch. 110 1/2, Sections 9-8+, 6-8+, 25-1+

Category 1: Affidavit Procedure Instead of Probate

This category tells you whether the state has a law allowing any property left by a will to be transferred by affidavit, free of all probate. If there's a "no" in this category, the state doesn't have this kind of law.

"Free of normal probate" means that no actual court proceedings (notice of hearings, hearings before a judge, formal pleadings) are required. Some states still require a relatively simple affidavit to be filed with a court or court clerk. Others don't require any judicial filing at all.

If there's a dollar figure in this first category, it means the state has a law allowing property up to the dollar figure listed to be transferred by this method. Next, any restrictions on the type of property that can be transferred are listed; many states allow only personal property, not real estate, to be transferred. In any case, real estate is normally so valuable these days that it's unlikely that an interest in real estate would fall below the dollar limits, unless that ownership is a small percentage of the property. Finally, any restrictions on who the beneficiaries can be are summarized ("only to spouse and children").

The chart doesn't set forth the precise information which must be in an affidavit if one is required. To determine this, you'll need to research your state's law.

To return to our Illinois example, Category 1 states "$25,000, personal property...." This means personal property worth up to $25,000 can be transferred by affidavit, free of probate, in Illinois. Then this category states "also, if all beneficiaries agree, and are Illinois residents, and no state inheritance or federal estate taxes are due...." This means there is another type of affidavit transfer, free of from normal probate, in Illinois, if the specified requirements are met—all beneficiaries must be Illinois residents, agree to the transfer outside of probate, and no death taxes can be owed.

Category 2: Summary Probate

This category provides the same kind of information as given in Category 1 for those state laws which do require probate, but offer a simplified version. Again, the actual operation of these laws varies widely from state to state. Most importantly, the statutes themselves usually don't specify that probate attorney fees must be reduced from those charged for normal probate.

In our Illinois example, Category 2 reads: "$50,000." This means property worth up to $50,000—either personal property or real estate—can be transferred by summary probate.

Category 3: Statutes

This category gives you the legal citation to your state's probate exemption statute.

If your state has two statutes, one for an affidavit procedure and another for simplified probate, both citations are given. In such cases, the first citation given is to the affidavit procedure statute. The citations are to the first section of the relevant statute. The + symbol after the statutory cite means that other pertinent sections follow the first section that's noted.

The Illinois example states: "Illinois Annotated Statutes, Ch. 110-1/2, Section 9-8+, 6-8+, 25-1+." This means the statute for the $25,000 affidavit procedure is found in Section 9-8 and those immediately following of Chapter 110-1/2 of the Illinois Statutes. (In Chapter 22, Section A you'll find a discussion of how to find and read a statute.) Similarly, the statute for the "all beneficiaries agree, etc." affidavit procedure is found in Section 6-8 and those immediately following of Chapter 110-1/2, and the statute for the $50,000 summary probate procedure is found in Section 25-1 and those immediately following of Chapter 110-1/2.

C. Summary Chart of State Law Exceptions to Normal Probate

Alabama

Affidavit Procedure Instead of Probate: No
Summary Probate: $3,000, personal property only
Statute: Code of Alabama, Title 43, Ch. 2, Section 690+

Alaska

Affidavit Procedure Instead of Probate: No
Summary Probate: No dollar limit
Statute: Alaska Statutes Title 13, Ch. 6, Sections
13.16.08

Arizona

Affidavit Procedure Instead of Probate: $30,000, personal
property only
Summary Probate: No (except for certain types of family
property)
Statutes: Arizona Revised Statute, Sections 14-3971+;
14-1973+

Arkansas:

Affidavit Procedure Instead of Probate: $25,000
Summary Probate: No
Statute: Arkansas Statutes Annotated, Sections
G2.2127+

California

Affidavit Procedure Instead of Probate: $60,000, personal
property, and real property interest, $10,000
Summary Probate: To surviving spouse, community
property petition, no dollar limit
Statutes: California Probate Code, Sections 13,200+,
13500+

Colorado

Affidavit Procedure Instead of Probate: Net estate, $20,000
Summary Probate: No (except for certain types of exempt
family property, etc.)
Statute: Colorado Revised Statute Sections 15-12-1201+

Connecticut

Affidavit Procedure Instead of Probate: No
Summary Probate: $10,000; to spouse, next of kin, or
creditor
Statute: Connecticut General Statutes Annotated Title
45, Sections 266+

Delaware

Affidavit Procedure Instead of Probate: $12,500, personal
property only. Beneficiaries can only be spouse,
grandparents, children or other specified relations
Summary Probate: No
Statute: Delaware Code Annotated, Title 12, Sections
2306+

District of Columbia

Affidavit Procedure Instead of Probate: No (except if entire
estate is no more than two cars, and all debts and
taxes are paid)
Summary Probate: $10,000, personal property only
Statute: District of Columbia Code, Title 20, Section
2101+

Florida

Affidavit Procedure Instead of Probate: No (except for very
small estates with less than specified exceptions)
Summary Probate: $25,000, property in Florida subject to
probate; $60,000 for estate left primarily to family
members)
Statute: Florida Statutes Annotated, Sections 735.301+;
735.201+, 735.103+

Georgia

Affidavit Procedure Instead of Probate: No
Summary Probate: No
[No applicable statute]

Hawaii

Affidavit Procedure Instead of Probate: $2,000
Summary Probate: $20,000 property in Hawaii
Statutes: Hawaii Revised Statutes, Sections 560: 3-1205+;
560: 3-1213

Idaho

Affidavit Procedure Instead of Probate: No
Summary Probate: No dollar limit
Statute: Idaho Code, Sections 15-3-301+

Illinois

Affidavit Procedure Instead of Probate: $25,000, personal property; also, if all beneficiaries agree, and are Illinois residents, and no state inheritance of federal estate taxes due
Summary Probate: $50,000
Statutes: Illinois Annotated Statutes, Ch. 110 1/2, Sections 9-8+, 6-8+, 25-1+

Indiana

Affidavit Procedure Instead of Probate: $8,500, personal property only
Summary Probate: No dollar limit
Statute: Indiana Statutes Annotated Sections 29-1-8-2+; 29-1-7.5-5+

Iowa

Affidavit Procedure Instead of Probate: No
Summary Probate: $15,000 total value of probate and non-probate Iowa property; only surviving spouse, minor children, parents
Statute: Iowa Code Annotated: Section 635+

Kansas

Affidavit Procedure Instead of Probate: No
Summary Probate: No dollar limit
Statute: Kansas Statutes Annotated, Sections 59-3201+; 3301+

Kentucky

Affidavit Procedure Instead of Probate: No
Summary Probate: By agreement of all beneficiaries; when spouse receives probate estate under $7,500
Statutes: Kentucky Revised Statutes: Sections 391.030+, 395.450+

Louisiana

Affidavit Procedure Instead of Probate: No
Summary Probate: No (except Louisiana resident who dies intestate with estate worth less than $50,000)
[No applicable statute]

Maine

Affidavit Procedure Instead of Probate: No
Summary Probate: No dollar limit
Statute: Maine Revised Statues Annotated, Title 18A, Sections 1-101

Maryland

Affidavit Procedure Instead of Probate: No (except if entire estate is no more than two cars, or a boat worth less than $5,000)
Summary Probate: $20,000
Statute: Annotated Code of Maryland, Sections 5-601+

Massachusetts

Affidavit Procedure Instead of Probate: No (except wages less than $100, or bank accounts of $2,000 to $3,000, depending on type)
Summary Probate: $15,000, personal property
Statute: Massachusetts General Laws Annotated, Ch. 195, Section 16+

Michigan

Affidavit Procedure Instead of Probate: No
Summary Probate: $5,000; (and car worth less than $10,000 given to surviving spouse, if no other property)
Statutes: Michigan Compiled Laws Annotated, Sections 27.5101+; 257.236; and 9.1936.

Minnesota

Affidavit Procedure Instead of Probate: No
Summary Probate: $30,000
Statute: Minnesota Statutes Annotated, Section 525.51+

Mississippi

Affidavit Procedure Instead of Probate: No
Summary Probate: $500
Statute: Mississippi Annotated Code, Sections 91-7-147

Missouri

Affidavit Procedure Instead of Probate: No
Summary Probate: $15,000
Statute: Annotated Missouri Statutes, Section 5 473.097

Montana

Affidavit Procedure Instead of Probate: No
Summary Probate: No dollar limit
Statute: Montana Code Annotated, Title 72, Section 3-201+

Nebraska

Affidavit Procedure Instead of Probate: No
Summary Probate: No dollar limit
Statute: Revised Statutes of Nebraska, Sections 30-2414+

Nevada

Affidavit Procedure Instead of Probate: $25,000 (court petition must be filed)
Summary Probate: $100,000
Statutes: Nevada Revised Statutes, Section 145.070+, 146.010+

New Hampshire

Affidavit Procedure Instead of Probate: No (except $500 to surviving spouse)
Summary Probate: $5,000
Statute: New Hampshire Revised Statutes Annotated, Ch. 553,331+

New Jersey

Affidavit Procedure Instead of Probate: No (only if die intestate, then $10,000 to spouse, or $5,000 to others)
Summary Probate: No
[No applicable statute]

New Mexico

Affidavit Procedure Instead of Probate: $5,000
Summary Probate: $10,000 plus certain statutory allowance
Statutes: New Mexico Statutes, 45-3-1202, 45-3-1204

New York

Affidavit Procedure Instead of Probate: $10,000 (plus certain types of exempt property, to specified dollar limits)
Summary Probate: No
Statutes: Consolidated Laws of New York Annotated, Estates Powers and Trusts Law, Section 1301+

North Carolina

Affidavit Procedure Instead of Probate: $10,000, personal property only
Summary Probate: No
Statute: General Statues of North Carolina, Ch. 28A, Section 25-1.1

North Dakota

Affidavit Procedure Instead of Probate: No
Summary Probate: No dollar limit
Statute: North Dakota Code, Title 30.1-14+

Ohio

Affidavit Procedure Instead of Probate: No
Summary Probate: $15,000
Statute: Ohio Revised Code Annotated, Section 2113.03

Oklahoma

Affidavit Procedure Instead of Probate: No
Summary Probate: $60,000
Statute: Oklahoma Statutes Annotated, Title 58, Sections 241+

Oregon

Affidavit Procedure Instead of Probate: $15,000 personal property; $35,000 real estate
Summary Probate: No
Statute: Oregon Revised Statutes, Section 114.515+

Pennsylvania

Affidavit Procedure Instead of Probate: No
Summary Probate: $10,000 personal property
Statute: Pennsylvania Statutes Annotated, Title 20, Sections 3102+

Rhode Island

Affidavit Procedure Instead of Probate: No (except person(s) who paid funeral costs, last bills, etc., up to $7,500)
Summary Probate: No
[No applicable statute]

South Carolina

Affidavit Procedure Instead of Probate: $10,000
Summary Probate: $10,000
Statutes: Code of Laws of South Carolina, Title 62, Ch. 3, Sections 1201, 1203+

South Dakota

Affidavit Procedure Instead of Probate: $5,000
Summary Probate: $60,000
Statutes: South Dakota Codified Laws, Sections 30-11A+, 30-11-1

Tennessee

Affidavit Procedure Instead of Probate: No (except $1,000 wages to widow, bank accounts less than $1,000)
Summary Probate: $10,000 real estate only
Statute: Tennessee Code Annotated, Title 30, Ch. 4, Section 101+

Texas

Affidavit Procedure Instead of Probate: $50,000
Summary Probate: No dollar limit
Statute: Texas Probate Code, Sections 137+, 145+

Utah

Affidavit Procedure Instead of Probate: No
Summary Probate: No dollar limit
Statute: Utah Code, Title 75, Section 3-301

Vermont

Affidavit Procedure Instead of Probate: No
Summary Probate: $10,000 personal property
Statute: Vermont Statutes Annotated, Title 14, Section 1901+

Virginia

Affidavit Procedure Instead of Probate: $5,000 personal property, and $5,000 owed deceased from bank or employment
Summary Probate: No
Statute: Code of Virginia, Sections 64.1-132+

Washington

Affidavit Procedure Instead of Probate: $10,000 personal property
Summary Probate: No
Statute: Revised Code of Washington Annotated, Title 11, Section 62.010+

West Virginia

Affidavit Procedure Instead of Probate: No
Summary Probate: $50,000
Statute: West Virginia Code, Ch. 24, Art. 2, Section 1

Wisconsin

Affidavit Procedure Instead of Probate: $5,000, personal property
Summary Probate: $10,000. Also Wisconsin has an "informal" probate procedure that doesn't require a lawyer and has no dollar limit
Statute: Wisconsin Statues Annotated: Sections 867.03+, 867.045+

Wyoming

Affidavit Procedure Instead of Probate: $30,000
Summary Probate: No
Statute: Wyoming Statutes Annotated, Section 2-1-201.

D. California Exemptions from Normal Probate

CALIFORNIA HAS TWO simplified probate procedures:

1. The "community property petition" allowing all property left to a surviving spouse to be transferred by summary probate.

2. What is commonly called the "Affidavit of Right"[4] allowing property worth less than $60,000 (with no interest in real estate in excess of $10,000) to be transferred by affidavit entirely outside of probate.

1. The Community Property Petition

By using a community property petition, a surviving spouse can readily obtain the portion of the deceased's community and separate property left to him or her. There's no dollar limit either on the total amount of the estate or the amount of the property that can be transferred to the surviving spouse by this method. Even if some of the deceased's share of the community property is left to others, the spouse can still obtain his or her portion of it left through a will, without the expense of probate.

The community property petition is a simple one-page, two-sided form that can be prepared by a surviving spouse who is entitled to property of a deceased spouse, either from a will (or by intestate succession if there was no will). The petition is filed with the local probate court, which sets a hearing date. Notice of the hearing must be given to certain people, including all beneficiaries named in the will. Then the hearing is held, and the property ordered transferred to the surviving spouse unless someone contests the petition, which is very rare. Most surviving spouses should be able to handle the process without a lawyer. The steps needed to file a community property petition, and to get court-approval, are

explained in detail, including sample forms, in Nissley, *How to Probate an Estate* (Nolo Press).

2. The Affidavit of Right

If a deceased left, by will or intestate, property worth less than $60,000 (net), and no interest in real estate worth more than $10,000, the inheritors can obtain that estate by filing a simple form, called an "Affidavit of Right," with the people or organizations holding the deceased's property.[5] The basic purpose of the affidavit of right is to enable beneficiaries of a deceased who left a small estate to obtain the cash and other assets they inherit immediately without a lot of red tape. The affidavit can be prepared and filed by the inheritors who are entitled to the deceased's estate, either by will, or if there's no will, by the laws of intestate inheritance. If there's more than one beneficiary under a will (or the intestacy laws if there's no will), all the beneficiaries must sign the affidavit of right. A copy of the affidavit is then presented to persons or organizations holding the property left by the will; they must promptly release the assets to the beneficiaries. Sample forms and instructions are contained in *How to Probate an Estate*, Nissley (Nolo Press).

An affidavit of right doesn't have to be filed with any state agency. No court or other probate proceeding is required. There's no procedure to verify the inheritor's declaration that the deceased's net estate in California is worth less than $60,000. In this one instance, the law appears to go by the honor system.

---

[4]Technically, this may also be called "Affidavit under California Probate Code Section 13100."

[5]Except for any interest in real estate worth less than $10,000, which still must be transferred through a regular probate proceeding.

Harry Billings dies in Los Angeles, California. Under Harry's will, his sole beneficiary is his adult daughter, Myra. Harry owned no real estate, and his estate totals $37,000. Of the $37,000, $5,000 is owed to him by his friend, Charley; $27,000 is in a certificate of deposit and savings account; and $5,000 is personal property, including a 12-year-old Plymouth. Myra simply completes the Affidavit of Right and attaches one copy each of the will and death certificate. She then gives one set of documents to Charley, another to Harry's bank, and the third to the holder of the personal property—in this case, Harry's landlord. Charley then owes the $5,000 to Myra, on the same terms as he owed it to Harry. The bank and the holder of Harry's personal property must release it to her promptly. The Department of Motor Vehicles will re-register the Plymouth in Myra's name.

The affidavit must state, under oath, that the total value of the deceased's estate in California is less than $60,000. However, certain important items of property can legally be excluded from the $60,000 total. Assets which can be excluded for determining if the $60,000 limit is exceeded are:

1. Any motor vehicle the deceased owned;

2. Any amounts due the deceased for service in the U.S. Armed Forces;

3. Any salary due the deceased, including compensation for an unused vacation, up to $5,000; and

4. All joint tenancy property or property transferred to a surviving spouse. In other words, in California, as long as property, including real property, is held in joint tenancy, you can ignore its value when it comes to deciding whether the affidavit of right procedure will work.

What about property transferred by a living trust or informal bank trust account? The California statute isn't clear, but as previously mentioned, standard California legal practice has long assumed that property in a living trust or informal bank trust account isn't counted toward the $60,000 limit. Thus, savvy Californians with good-sized estates can use other probate avoidance methods to pass their valuable items of property and rely on the Affidavit of Right Procedure to avoid probate on the rest, which they leave by will.

Teresa has an estate consisting of a house in Los Angeles, equity of $620,000; a summer cottage at Stinson Beach, equity $220,000; the furnishings of her two houses (worth $40,000); a bank account of $60,000; lots of life insurance (proceeds of $300,000); and various heirlooms worth a total of $45,000. At her death, she wants her children to receive all her property, except for the heirlooms, which she intends to give to cousins and other relatives. Teresa doesn't think of herself as wealthy; she acquired her houses years ago, when "a dollar was a dollar" and prices low. But, in fact, her taxable estate now amounts to $1,285,000. Rather than have all this property subject to regular probate:

1. She transfers the houses and furnishings into a living trust, naming her children as beneficiaries;

2. She creates an informal bank trust account for her savings (see Chapter 11), naming her children as beneficiaries;

3. She assigns ownership of her life insurance policies outright to their beneficiaries, and gives up all ownership of them (see Chapter 12).

Only the heirlooms, worth less than the $60,000 limit, remain in Teresa's probate estate. She can distribute these by her will, and her inheritors can claim them simply and speedily by using an affidavit of right.

E. New York Exemptions from Normal Probate

NEW YORK LAW provides a simple affidavit procedure for estates of personal property (no real estate) worth less than $10,000. Also, New York exempts *entirely* certain property of a deceased spouse which is set aside for the surviving spouse, or the deceased's minor children if there is no spouse. The total amount of property that can be set aside for family use is $26,150. All property set aside for family use isn't counted as part of the $10,000 that can be exempted from probate. Thus, in theory, an estate totaling $36,150 could be eligible for New York's affidavit procedure if the maximum amount of exempt property was left to a surviving spouse or minor children.

Under the affidavit procedure, the deceased's executor acts as a "voluntary administrator," preparing an affidavit listing the property and beneficiaries and filing it with the probate court (called "surrogate court") clerk. The executor then has authority to collect the deceased's personal property and distribute it to the beneficiaries according to the will or the intestacy laws.

Although the statute isn't clear about whether the affidavit procedure can be combined with other probate avoidance devices, accepted New York legal practice is that it can be. Thus, if someone transfers big-ticket items like houses and stocks by living trust, she could then transfer small personal gifts, with a total value less than $10,000, by her will free from normal probate.

F. Texas Exemptions from Normal Probate

TEXAS HAS TWO simplified probate procedures:

1. An affidavit allowing summary transfer of estates worth less than $50,000; and

2. A summary probate with no dollar limit.

Let's look at each.

1. The Affidavit

Under Texas law, certain small estates can be transformed by use of an affidavit filed with the clerk of the county court. The affidavit procedure is available only if the estate has a value, *excluding* homestead and exempt property, of less than $50,000. Exempt property is community property which can be "set aside" for the deceased's family—including an automobile, household furnishings, clothing, food and last wages. Homestead property is community real estate protected under Texas law.

All people receiving part of the estate must sign and swear to the affidavit. The affidavit can be filed by any beneficiaries only if 30 days have passed since the deceased has died and no one has filed for formal probate. The affidavit must list the estate's assets and liabilities, the names and addresses of all people receiving part of the estate, and whether they take that property under a will or by intestacy. If there's a will, it usually is filed with the affidavit, although this isn't required by statute.

After the affidavit is filed with the county court clerk, the clerk issues a certified copy of the affidavit to the beneficiaries. The affidavit entitles them to collect debts owed the deceased, collect and receive estate property, and to have title to automobiles, bank accounts, stocks, or real estate transferred. Anyone releasing or transferring property to someone on the authority of such an affidavit is discharged from any further liability on that property. The responsibility for properly disposing of the property falls on the person collecting the property with the affidavit.

A creditor can prevent collection by affidavit by filing for formal probate within 30 days of the deceased's death. And, even if collection by affidavit occurs, those who collect the deceased's property remain liable to the estate creditors.

Since all those with rights to an estate must sign it, the affidavit is practical only if there are no disputes about who should receive what property. Although title can be transferred under the authority of the affidavit, others can dispute it later. (Where title may be disputed, the summary probate procedure described in Section 2 below may be more desirable.)

The $50,000 ceiling on the value of estates collectable by affidavit limits the use of the process. Most estates containing real property will exceed that limit. However, since the value of homestead property is excluded from the $50,000 calculation, the statute may have broader use with small estates where a spouse survives the deceased. The family home, often the principal estate asset, would be excluded from the calculation. Therefore, where there's a surviving spouse, a moderate-sized estate, including the family house, might be collected and distributed by the affidavit process. However, where there's no surviving spouse, the affidavit process will be limited to small estates.

2. Summary Probate

The Texas summary probate has no dollar limitations. Under this procedure, the executor files an application to probate the will, exactly as in traditional probate. A hearing is then held on the validity of the will. If the will is proved valid, and it's shown that the estate has no outstanding debts or other problems, the court orders summary probate, dispensing with many of the tedious steps of normal probate. (The Texas statute is silent, however, on whether summary probate means reduced attorney's fees, which means that it's up to your inheritors to negotiate.)

The court order admitting the will to probate serves the same function as the small estate's affidavit: it authorizes transfer of the deceased's property to those entitled to it under the will. Furthermore, since the will has been proved in court, title to the property transferred in this way isn't open to challenge. This avoids a problem that sometimes occurs with the small estates affidavit.

However, Texas summary probate does normally require an attorney, so the major drawback of normal probate is still involved and it isn't therefore a satisfactory alternative to probate avoidance techniques.

G. Florida Exemptions from Normal Probate

FLORIDA LAW PROVIDES three different types of simplified probate. However, all three are quite restrictive, and therefore of no use to most Florida readers who wish to plan their estate to avoid probate.

1. Simplified Family Probate

Family members can petition a probate court for a simplified form of probate (called "Family administration") if there's a will and:

- The primary beneficiaries are the surviving spouse and/or "lineal descendants" (children, grandchildren) and/or "lineal ascendants" (parents, grandparents, etc.) and any specific or general gift to others is a minor part of the estate; and

- The value of the gross estate, for federal estate tax purposes, is less than $60,000; and

- The entire estate consists of personal property.

Thus a family, or any member, can petition for simplified probate only if the total net value of the estate is less than $60,000, and none of it is real estate. This net value includes all property transferred by a living trust or joint tenancy, since the worth of this property is included in the federal taxable estate. Most Florida readers' estates will be well in excess of the relatively modest amount of $60,000.

PART IV

Tax Planning and Controls on Property

Estate Taxes

Estate Taxes

ALL U.S. CITIZENS (and anyone owning property in the U.S.) are subject to federal death taxes, called "estate taxes," which can take a large bite of a good-sized estate.[1] The tax rate is determined by the size of the taxable estate, with the general rule being that the more you own, the higher the rate. Also, a number of states impose death taxes on property of a deceased who lived or owned real estate in that state.

Fortunately, several exemptions allow you to transfer substantial amounts of property free of federal estate taxes. The most important ones are:

- $600,000 worth of property in an estate;[2] and

- All property left to a surviving spouse; and

- All property left to a tax-exempt charity.

Avoiding death taxes has nothing to do with avoiding probate. All property owned by the deceased, whatever the form of ownership, and whether it's transferred to inheritors through probate or by other means, is subject to federal estate taxes.

If you have an estate that's clearly worth less than the $600,000 exempt amount, you don't need to worry about federal estate taxes and therefore can skip or skim most of this chapter (though you should still check Section E to see if your estate will be liable for state death taxes). However, if you have an estate larger than $600,000, or if you are married and plan to leave your property to your spouse, who will then have an estate exceeding $600,000, please read on.

---

[1]If you also own property in another country, or earn income in that country, your estate may be subject to death taxes in that country.

International estate death tax planning is a complex field. If you may be subject to death taxes by the U.S. and some other country, you'll need to see a lawyer.

[2]Assuming none of your federal "tax credit" has been previously used because you have made large taxable gifts. Generally, gifts worth up to $10,000 to one person in a calendar year are tax exempt. Taxes due on gifts over $10,000 are deducted from your estate "tax credit." See Section B(1) of this chapter and Chapter 15, Gifts and Gift Taxes, for more on the interrelationship of estate and gift taxes.

If your estate is likely to be taxed, it's essential that you resolve several important questions, including:

- What are the tax consequences of leaving your estate the way you want to?

- Do these taxes add up to enough to justify changing your estate plan?

- Are there ways to change your estate plan which will save on taxes and still reasonably achieve your other estate planning goals?

- If it's likely that there will be death taxes due, what source of funds will be used to pay them?

By the time you finish this chapter, you should be able to answer these questions. Now let's start by examining federal estate taxes, by far the most substantial taxes imposed on larger estates.

A. Federal Estate Taxes

TO ESTIMATE YOUR federal estate tax liability, you need to do the following:

1. Estimate the value of your taxable estate.

2. Deduct allowable estate tax exemptions to arrive at the amount subject to tax, if any.

3. Check the applicable tax rate to determine the amount of any tax due.

Now let's look at how to do each one.

Some Thoughts on Death Taxes and Avoiding Them

The decision to tax property a person owns at death is a decision society makes regarding inherited wealth. For example, in the days of "survival of the fittest" capitalism in 19th century America, there were no federal estate taxes. By contrast, in some European countries today, death taxes take a very significant portion of larger estates. Today's United States is somewhere in between.

Trying to reduce death taxes to a minimum through estate planning is sometimes thought of as a form of lawyer's magic, by which taxes can be avoided completely no matter how large the estate. It's true there is some gimmickry in some schemes of the very rich to avoid death taxes, although not as much is allowed as there used to be. But there's no magic way to escape death taxes completely. The best good estate planning can do is use lawful means to reduce death taxes as much as possible.

The process of planning to avoid taxation at death has been criticized by many. They suggest this is a game for the rich, and that society would be better off if people couldn't pass large sums from one generation to the next. Perhaps, although I've noticed that even most socialists seem to prefer to have whatever wealth they've acquired be given to family, friends, or worthy causes rather than turned over to government. Certainly, given present law, I believe that it makes good sense to try to preserve as much of your estate as possible for your inheritors.

1. Estimate the Value of Your Taxable Estate

You estimated the net worth (assets minus liabilities) of your property on the Property Worksheet you prepared in Chapter 4, Section B. Now, use this figure to see if your estate is likely to exceed the $600,000 federal tax threshold. Remember that to *plan* your estate competently, you don't need to know precisely how much your assets are worth. After all, the net worth of your property will surely change by the time of your death. What you need are rough estimates, so you can determine if it seems likely you'll be liable for federal, or (if applicable) state death taxes.

2. Federal Estate Tax Exemptions

As stated, federal law exempts certain property from estate tax. To know if your estate will likely have to pay any tax, you need to know how these exemptions work, so let's examine each one.

a. The $600,000 Exemption

As I stated earlier, property worth up to $600,000 is exempt from federal estate tax, no matter who the property is left to.[3]

Jane leaves her entire estate, which has a net worth of $600,000, to her children. All this property is exempt.

Fred leaves his entire estate of $600,000 divided between two good friends. All this property is estate tax-exempt.

Mike leaves his estate of $700,000 to his son. $100,000 is subject to federal estate tax.

There's one important qualification to this $600,000 exemption—it's reduced by taxable gifts made during one's life. As discussed in depth in Chapter 15, gifts worth more than $10,000 per year per person are subject to federal tax (to the extent they are larger than $10,000) at the same rate as estates. (Indeed, officially the tax is called the "Unified Estate and Gift Tax.") Thus, if you give $70,000 to your son in a single year, $60,000 is subject to tax. However, the gift tax assessed isn't paid in the year you make the gift. Instead, the total amount of the taxable gift is deducted from your $600,000 estate/gift tax exemption.

---

[3]Technically, the $600,000 exemption actually works by means of an estate "tax credit," which exempts the first $192,800 of tax due (the amount due on $600,000). The mechanics of how this tax credit works can be important, and are a little tricky. They're discussed more thoroughly below, in Section A(4).

Annalies gives $50,000 to her son Jean-Paul in one calendar year. The gift tax exemption of $10,000 per person per year means $10,000 is not taxed. The remaining $40,000 is subject to gift tax. This $40,000 is deducted from Annalies' $600,000 exemption, leaving a remaining exemption of $560,000. Thus, if Annalies dies owning property with a net worth of $580,000, $20,000 will be subject to federal estate tax.

Who Appraises Your Estate After You Die?

Having the value of an estate determined is the responsibility of the person the deceased appointed to supervise his property. This is the successor trustee if the property is left by living trust, or the executor if the property is left by will. If all property is left by joint tenancy, the surviving joint tenant has the responsibility to see if an estate tax return must be filed or taxes paid.

The federal government isn't involved in appraising property in an estate. Obviously, though, the IRS can challenge and audit estate tax returns, just as it can income tax returns. In some states which impose death taxes, official appraisals are done as part of the death tax system. However, in the many states without official appraisals, it's the exclusive responsibility of the person supervising the estate to make a bona fide appraisal of the estate's property in order to determine if a federal estate tax return need be filed.

It may often be difficult for an executor or trustee, or a probate attorney, to establish the market value of many items—works of art, closely held businesses, stock in small corporations, for example. Saving cost receipts, bookkeeping records and other documents containing the actual cost of items of property can be very useful and can save time and money later.[4] For large estates which have many assets (appreciated real estate, art, interests in small businesses, to name but a few), determination of the dollar amount of the net estate, for federal tax purposes, can be tricky. Estates in this category can, and usually should, afford to hire an experienced tax accountant to handle this work.

---

[4]To help you keep track of these records, Nolo publishes *For the Record*, a computer software program designed specifically to record the location of all important business and personal records.

b. The Marital Deduction

All property left to a surviving spouse is exempt from federal estate tax. This exemption is called the "marital deduction" in tax lingo.

Warning on Old Wills and Trusts: The 1981 Tax Act provided that the old tax law continues to apply to a will or trust written before September 13, 1981, if what is called a "formula" provision was used. Specifically, if your will or living trust (written before September 13, 1981) provides your spouse is to receive "whatever she/he can free of estate taxes," that surviving spouse will receive only the exempt amounts under the previous marital deduction, which was far more restrictive than current law. The current law, as I have said, allows all of your property to be transferred to a surviving spouse free of estate tax. In this situation you need to revise and update your will or trusts.

It makes no difference how much money or property is left to the surviving spouse; whether it's $10,000 in emeralds or $10,000,000 in cash, it's all exempt from estate tax and is excluded from the value of the federal taxable estate. Likewise, it makes no difference what legal form of property is left to the surviving spouse—whether it's community property, joint tenancy property, "quasi-community" property or separate property. And the marital deduction is in addition to all other exemptions.

Sue has an estate valued at $6,600,000. She leaves $600,000 to her children and $6,000,000 to her husband. All Sue's property is estate tax-exempt.

The marital deduction, however, can be a tax trap. For larger estates (totalling over $600,000 for both spouses) the fact that no federal estate tax is assessed when property is left to the surviving spouse can mislead people into thinking that leaving everything to a spouse is the best thing to do. It may not be. Increasing the size of the surviving spouse's estate is likely to result in a corresponding increase in tax liability (remember, all property over $600,000 is taxed) when the survivor dies. This is a particular danger when both spouses are elderly and the survivor isn't likely to live long enough to really benefit from the money. The alternative of having the first spouse to die leave property directly to children or other beneficiaries or establish a marital life estate trust, under which income from the first spouse's estate can be used to support the survivor is often advantageous from a tax point of view. This is discussed in more detail in Section C of this chapter.

Note on Unmarried Couples: There are no exemptions similar to the marital deduction for lovers or "significant others." Quite simply, the estate tax laws are written to encourage and reward traditional relationships.[5] However, the marital deduction is available for couples who entered into a common law marriage in one of the 13 states and the District of Columbia that recognize this type of marriage.[6] Also, if either spouse has been divorced (from a prior marriage), the divorce must be valid or a subsequent marriage won't be recognized and no marital deduction allowed.

c. Gifts to Charities

All gifts made to tax-exempt charitable organizations are exempt from federal estate taxes. If you plan to make large charitable gifts, be sure you've checked out whether the organizations you're giving money to are in fact tax-exempt. The normal way an organization establishes it's a tax-exempt charity is by a ruling from the IRS, under Internal Revenue Code Section 501(c)(3). [These organizations are referred to, in tax lingo, as "501(c)(3) corporations."] Organizations which are active politically are often not tax-exempt.

 From a tax standpoint, charitable gift-giving can become quite sophisticated, and includes devices such as "split-interest" trusts or "charitable remainder trusts" to maximize use of the estate tax exemption. If you're considering making major donations, review your options with a tax expert. Also, many charitable organizations, particularly colleges and universities, provide extensive information about tax-exempt gift-giving to that group and offer a variety of gift plans.

d. Other Estate Tax Exemptions

The other main exemptions from federal estate tax are:

- expenses of last illness, burial costs, and probate fees and expenses; and

- credits for state death taxes, and death taxes imposed by foreign countries on property the deceased owned there.

3. Must a Federal Estate Tax Return Be Filed?

An estate tax return must be filed for all estates with a gross value worth over $600,000. That's gross, not net. This means that, for purposes of deciding whether a return must be filed, you don't subtract the amount a deceased owed from what he owned. Thus, there can be instances where an estate tax return must be filed even though no taxes are due.

---

[5]Perhaps there is a certain fairness in this, as unmarried couples normally receive significant income tax benefits if both have income. For a thorough discussion of the legal rights and responsibilities of unmarried couples, see *The Living Together Kit*, Warner and Ihara (Nolo Press), and *A Legal Guide for Lesbian and Gay Couples*, Curry and Clifford (Nolo Press).

[6]Alabama, Colorado, District of Columbia, Georgia, Idaho, Iowa, Kansas, Montana, Ohio, Oklahoma, Pennsylvania, Rhode Island, South Carolina, and Texas.

Doug's estate consists of money market funds of $100,000 and two houses. One has a market value of $400,000 and $300,000 owing on a mortgage; the other has a market value of $200,000 and $100,000 owing on a mortgage.

Gross Estate	Net Estate
$100,000 cash	*$100,000 cash*
$400,000 house	*$100,000 equity in house*
$200,000 house	*$100,000 equity in house*
$700,000 total	*$300,000*

Because Doug's gross estate is more than $600,000, an estate tax return must be filed. But because his net estate is well under the $600,000 exemption, no tax will be due.

If an estate tax return must be filed, it's due within nine months of the death of the deceased, but extensions can be granted.

4. How to Calculate Federal Estate Taxes

Once you've estimated the amount of your taxable estate, you can fairly easily calculate how much tax will be due. Tax rates are shown in the schedule below.

Unified Federal Estate and Gift Tax Rates

Column A	Column B	Column C	Column D
net taxable estate over	net taxable estate not over	tax on amount in column A	rate of tax on excess over amount in column A
$ 0	$ 10,000	$ 0	18%
10,000	20,000	1,800	20
20,000	40,000	3,800	22
40,000	60,000	8,200	24
60,000	80,000	13,000	26
80,000	100,000	18,200	28
100,000	150,000	23,800	30
150,000	250,000	38,800	32
250,000	500,000	70,800	34
500,000	750,000	155,800	37
750,000	1,000,000	248,300	39
1,000,000	1,250,000	345,800	41
1,250,000	1,500,000	448,300	43
1,500,000	2,000,000	555,800	45
2,000,000	2,500,000	780,800	49
2,500,000	3,000,000	1,025,800	53
3,000,000	infinity		55

First let's look at a simple example to see how to read the schedule. Bernie's anticipated net estate, after subtracting liabilities from assets and then subtracting exempt amounts, including charitable gifts and funeral costs, totals about $4 million. He plans to leave $3 million to his wife and $1 million to his children. All the property he leaves to his wife is exempt from federal estate tax because of the marital deduction. His net estate subject to tax is thus $1 million. Column C on the Estate Tax Chart reveals that the tax assessed on a $1 million estate is $345,800. From $345,800 Bernie deducts the $192,800 tax credit (again, the tax assessed against a

$600,000 estate.) Thus, Bernie determines that his estate will have to pay federal taxes of $153,000.[7]

Now let's determine the tax due on a "net taxable estate" of $700,000. Net taxable estate means that after you subtract liabilities from assets, you then also subtract all tax-exempt amounts—property left to a spouse, or charitable gifts, or used for expenses of last illnesses, burial costs, probate fees. However, at this point the $600,000 exemption has *not* been deducted.

1. Locate the numbers in Column A and B between which the anticipated value of your estate falls

   Column A = $500,000
   Column B = 750,000

2. Subtract the amount in Column A from the anticipated value of your estate

   700,000
   - 500,000
   200,000

3. Multiply this remainder by the percentage in Column D

   200,000
   x   .37
   74,000

4. Add the result to the tax for $500,000 listed in Column C

   74,000
   + 155,000
   229,800

5. Subtract the federal estate tax credit ($192,900 is the tax assessed on a $600,000 estate, the exempt amount); the difference is your estate tax liability

   229,800
   - 192,800
   Tax due = $ 37,000

What's the practical significance of the "tax credit" mechanism rather than an outright exemption of the first $600,000 on an estate from federal estate tax? None whatsoever, if your estate turns out to be exempt from tax. However, if your estate is subject to tax, it's impor-

[7]Incidentally, Bernie is an excellent candidate to give money to his kids while he is still alive. By doing this, he can reduce the size of his estate and therefore the tax. See Chapter 15, Section F for a further discussion of how gifts can be used to reduce estate taxes.

tant, because the tax rate is based on the worth of the total estate, not just how much is over the exempt sum.

Willie's net estate amounts to $660,000. Practically, $60,000 of this estate is subject to federal tax. The tax rate applied, however, isn't the rate the tax schedule has for $60,000, which is 26%. The tax rate is the tax applied to an estate worth $660,000, which is 37%. Thus, after the $600,000 which is exempt is subtracted, Willie's estate will owe 37% of $60,000, or $22,200 in tax.

What this means is that if your estate is subject to federal estate tax at all, the minimum tax rate starts at hefty 37%, increasing to a maximum of 55% for estates over $2,500,000. Clearly this is a tax worth avoiding or minimizing if you can do so legally.

More Information on Federal Estate Taxes

More detailed information about federal estate and gift taxes can be found in the publication "Federal and Estate Gift Taxes," IRS publication no. 448. It's available at many IRS offices or by mail. Send a request for it with $.75 to Superintendent of Documents, U.S. Government Printing Office, Washington, D.C. 20402. Other research sources for information about federal estate taxes are listed in Chapter 22, Section A.

B. How to Reduce Federal Estate Taxes

WHAT CAN YOU DO to reduce federal estate taxes if you think your estate will be liable for them? Not as much as you might think. Aside from making use of the estate tax exemptions discussed above, including leaving property to your spouse or to charity, the following are the major ways you can lower estate taxes.

1. Give Away Property

While you're alive, you can give away property in amounts of $10,000 or less per person per year tax-free. A couple can give $20,000 a year tax-free to one person (see Chapter 15) and $40,000 to another couple. Tax-exempt gift-giving works well for people who can afford it, and can be particularly advantageous for those who have several children, grandchildren or other objects of their affection. For example, a couple can give each of their three children $20,000 per year tax-free, a total of $60,000 per year. If these children are married and the couple wishes to include spouses in their gift-giving program, these amounts can be doubled.

One good gift is life insurance you own on your own life, if you give it away at least three years before your death. This works because the present value of the insurance policy, which is subject to gift tax, is far less than the proceeds amount the policy will pay off at death. If the insured owned the policy, the proceeds are included in her taxable estate. If someone else owns the policy, the proceeds are not included in the insured's taxable estate. (See Chapter 12.)

2. Create a Trust for Your Grandchildren

Create a "generation-skipping" trust for the benefit of your grandchildren [discussed in Chapter 16, Section B(3)]. This type of trust won't reduce your own estate taxes; it can, however, exempt up to $1 million from tax in the next generation. A generation-skipping trust, as the name indicates, leaves property in trust for beneficiaries two generations removed from the trust creator, i.e., normally the creator's grandchildren. The creator's children can receive the trust income, but are not entitled to the principal. So, if you leave $1 million in trust for your grandchildren, with the income from the trust available to your children, that $1 million is excluded from your children's taxable estate when they die. However, it *is* included in your taxable estate.

3. Create a Marital Life Estate Trust

Create a "marital life estate" trust [discussed in detail in Section C below, and in Chapter 16, Section B(1)]. This can be appropriate where you and your spouse have a combined estate of more than $600,000 and are both elderly. It allows you and your spouse to each leave property in trust, with the income going to the survivor during his or her life. Once that spouse dies, the principal goes to your children or other named beneficiaries. This kind of trust allows you to avoid increasing the size of your spouse's estate above $600,000, or, if it's already over $600,000, further increasing it.

 Large Estate Note: If your estate is worth $1 million or more, see a tax expert to learn what new schemes tax lawyers and accountants have come up with to minimize estate taxes. They're always trying.

C. Federal Estate Tax Planning for Couples: The Marital Life Estate Trust

USING A MARITAL LIFE ESTATE TRUST is a vital part of the estate plan of many married couples whose combined assets exceed $600,000. Because this type of trust can be so important, let's examine how it works to provide estate tax savings [these trusts are also discussed in Chapter 16, Section B(1)].

Married people who plan to leave their property to their spouse are often reassured when they learn that all property left by one spouse to the other is exempt from federal estate tax. But is it enough to rely on that tax exemption? That depends, in large part, on the size of the couple's combined estates, their ages, and their health. If they are young and healthy, they may conclude they don't want to bother with estate tax planning now. If each leaves the other the bulk of his or her property, the survivor will take it, estate tax-free, and have plenty of years left to enjoy it. But if they have a combined net estate exceeding $600,000, and they are old or not in good health, or merely cautious, they may want more extensive planning, to focus on the tax consequences following the death of the second spouse. Assume both spouses are elderly, and want their children to ultimately inherit their estate, after both spouses die. If the first spouse leaves his or her share to the survivor, the second spouse will own a net estate in excess of $600,000; a substantial portion of the excess will go to pay the federal estate tax, at tax rates starting at 37% when the second spouse dies.

Those "second death" taxes can be reduced in two ways:

1. Each spouse simply leaves his or her property directly to the children. As each spouse gets a $600,000 estate tax exemption, this means $1,200,000 can be transferred estate tax-free.

2. Spouses use a marital life estate trust (also sometimes called a "marital trust" or "A-B" trust). Each spouse leaves all or a good part of his or her assets in trust, with the surviving spouse receiving, for life, the income from the deceased spouse's trust. The final beneficiaries of the trust (often the couple's children or, in cases of second or subsequent marriages, the deceased spouse's children from an earlier marriage) get the principal when the surviving spouse dies. The great benefit of a marital life estate trust is that assets placed in trust by the first spouse to die are subject to estate tax only when that spouse dies. They aren't included in the taxable estate of the surviving spouse (the "life beneficiary"). The only assets taxed when the survivor dies are the ones he or she owned in the first place. In short, the marital life estate trust allows each spouse to get the advantage of their individual $600,000 tax exemption, just as if they had left the property directly to their children or other beneficiaries.

The main drawback is that marital life estate trusts significantly restrict the right of the surviving spouse to spend or consume the assets placed in the trust. Obviously, for a spouse who already owns more than enough property, this isn't much of a problem. However, the surviving spouse can, at the option of the trust creator, be given the right to spend ("invade," in legalese) trust principal for medical needs and other basic necessities. Still, the fact that principal in the trust is not freely available for all purposes is one reason that marital life estate trusts are generally not desirable for younger couples, who normally don't want to tie up their money in this way.

To clarify how a marital life estate works, let's look at how using one affects Nick and Patricia, who have two grown children. They want to leave all of their shared assets first for the use of the surviving spouse, and then, on the death of that spouse, equally to their children.

Nick and Patricia plan their estate without a marital life estate trust. Nick dies first, in 1990. He leaves his estate of $909,000 (one half of their combined marital property) outright to Patricia. She owns an equal share of their property, another $909,000. The cost of Nick's last illness, funeral and burial expenses is $9,000. Patricia receives the balance of his estate, $900,000, free of estate taxes because of the marital deduction. The value of her estate is now $1,809,000. Patricia dies in 1991, leaving her estate to her children. The estate tax due is $498,000, as shown in the diagram below.

**Tax Consequences on Patricia's Death:
No Marital Life Estate Trust**

Total Net Estate	$1,809,000
Last illness, funeral, burial costs	- 9,000
Taxable Estate	$1,800,000
Estate Tax	690,800
Less Tax Credit	- 192,800 [8]
Estate Tax Payable	$ 498,000
Net amount received by children	$1,302,000

Now let's have Nick and Patricia do some estate tax planning, using a marital life estate trust. They create a marital living trust to avoid probate, which then becomes a marital life estate trust for the property of the first spouse to die, the "deceased spouse." The surviving spouse receives a "life interest" in the deceased spouse's trust property. The children are the ultimate beneficiaries of the trust. As you'll see, using a life estate trust makes a big difference in the total amount of estate taxes paid by Nick and and Patricia's property.[9]

**Tax Consequences on Nick's Death (1990)
With Marital Life Estate Trust**

Estate Left in Trust for Children, with life estate for Patricia

Total Estate	$ 909,000
Burial, probate costs, etc.	- 9,000
Taxable Estate	$ 900,000
Estate Tax	306,800
Less Tax Credit	- 192,800 [10]
Estate Tax Payable	$ 114,000
Net amount left in trust	$ 786,000

Patricia's Death (1991)

Total Estate	$ 909,000
Burial, probate costs, etc.	- 9,000
Taxable Estate	$ 900,000
Estate Tax	306,800
Less Tax Credit	- 192,800
Estate Tax Payable	$ 114,000
Net amount transferred to children from Patricia's estate	$ 786,000
Total amount transferred to children from trust =	$1,572,000
Net estate tax savings by using marital life estate trusts =	$ 270,000

---

[8]This is the amount of tax that would be assessed on $600,000, which is exempt from federal estate tax.

[9]Whether it's socially desirable to allow such a variance in estate taxes, depending mainly on the forms of transfer, is debatable, surely. The author would undoubtedly be more favorable if he were likely to inherit large sums of money.

---

[10]To repeat, this is the amount of tax that would be assesed on the $600,000 that is exempt from federal estate tax.

D. Specifying Assets to Be Used to Pay Estate Taxes

UNLESS A WILL or living trust directs otherwise, IRS rules pro-rate estate taxes between all persons and non-charitable organizations inheriting the estate. This means that those receiving a larger proportion of the estate pay a larger proportion of the taxes. If you want to vary this by having certain assets used to pay your estate taxes, you'll need to state that specifically in your will or living trust. [See Chapter 9, Section D(4) for a discussion of how to do this in a living trust. *Nolo's Simple Will Book* and *WillMaker* show you how to do this in a will.]

E. State Death Taxes

TWENTY-FOUR STATES and the District of Columbia have, effectively, abolished state death taxes. The rest impose death taxes on:

- All real estate owned in the state, no matter where the deceased lived; and

- The personal property (to repeat, everything but real estate) of residents of the state.

1. Where Do You Live for State Death Tax Purposes?

Technically, states that impose death taxes on residents do so on all persons "domiciled in the state." "Domicile" is a legal term of art. It means the state where you have your permanent residence, where you "intend" to make your home. Generally, it's clear where a person's domicile is. It's the state where they live most of the time, work, own a home, and vote. However, in some instances, where a person has two (or more) homes in different states, there may be no clear evidence which state is a person's domicile. For example, several states claimed that Howard Hughes was domiciled there. A less dramatic and more common example can be a person who owns two homes. In some circumstances, it's quite possible that more than one state would assert the person was domiciled there.

Mrs. Green retired and moved from Michigan to North Carolina. However, she returns often to Michigan to visit her children, and never bothers to register to vote in North Carolina. Michigan might claim, on her death, that Mrs. Green remained domiciled there and never transferred her domicile to North Carolina.

If you do divide your residence between two or more states, make sure it is clear which state you are domiciled in. Normally, this means being sure that you maintain your major personal business contacts and vote in the state you claim as your domicile. Obviously, if your state doesn't have death taxes (or has very low ones) and the other is a high death tax state, you might want to establish your domicile in the lower tax state.

2. Estate Planning for State Death Taxes

If you live or own real estate in a state that has death taxes, it's sensible to consider what the impact of those taxes on your gifts will be. In many instances, the bite taken from estates by state death taxes is annoying, but relatively minor. However, in some states, larger bites can be taken, especially for property given to non-relatives. For example, Nebraska imposes a 15% death tax rate if $25,000 is given to a friend, but only 1% if it's given to a spouse. It's probably rare that someone would change the amount of property left to a beneficiary because of state death taxes, but you should at least evaluate the issue if it applies.

If your state has death taxes, it may have other laws that affect your estate planning. For example, some states with death taxes require a deceased's bank accounts or safe-deposit boxes to be "sealed" until a release is obtained from tax officials. It's normally fairly quick and easy to do this, as long as the officials are convinced the estate has enough assets to pay the taxes.

As mentioned, if you have connections with more than one state, it can be sensible to have the state of your domicile be the one with lower, or no, death taxes. For example, a couple divides their time roughly equally between Florida and New York. Florida effectively has no death taxes. New York imposes comparatively stiff estate taxes, with rates ranging from 2% for $50,000 or less to 21% for $10,100,000 or more. Other things being equal, it makes sense to the couple to be domiciled in Florida.

3. Summary of State Death Tax Rules

Following is a summary of each state's tax rules, which will enable you to learn if the state where you live imposes death taxes. If it does, you can learn the specifics of those death tax rules from the charts in Appendix II.

a. States That Have No Death Taxes

Nevada is the only state that has no death taxes at all.

b. States That Effectively Impose No Death Taxes

In many states, there's no reason to concern yourself with state death taxes. These states do, technically, impose death taxes on estates subject to federal estate tax, those over $600,000. However, the maximum amount of state death tax is exactly equal to the maximum credit for state death taxes allowed under the Federal Estate Tax Law. So

your estate pays, overall, no more in taxes than it would if the state imposed no death taxes. In other words, part of the money which would otherwise be included with the federal estate tax return is paid to state tax authorities instead. This is commonly called a "pick-up" death tax. To repeat, the important point is that in these states, state death taxes are matters for accountants only, and have no real impact on your estate.

c. States That Impose Inheritance Taxes

Inheritance taxes are imposed on the receiver of inherited property, not the estate. Typically, state inheritance tax statutes divide receivers into different classes, such as "Class A, Husband or Wife," "Class B, immediate family—children, parents, etc.," "Class C, brothers, sisters, cousins, etc." "Class D, all others." Each class receives different death tax exemptions and is taxed at a different rate. The general rule is that the highest exemption and lowest rate applies to spouses, or "Class A."

Each of these state's inheritance tax rules are set out in Appendix II, Chart I.

d. States That Impose Estate Taxes

Some states impose a tax, like the federal government's, on the taxable estate itself, without regard to who the beneficiaries are. For state estate tax purposes, the taxable estate is all real estate in the state, and all personal property of a person who was domiciled in the state, except personal property having a specific, real location in another state. These state's estate tax rules are set out in Appendix II, Chart 2.

State	Inheritance Taxes?	Estate Taxes?
Alabama	effectively, no	effectively, no
Alaska	effectively, no	effectively, no
Arizona	effectively, no	effectively, no
Arkansas	effectively, no	effectively, no
California	effectively, no	effectively, no
Colorado	effectively, no	effectively, no
Connecticut	yes	no
Delaware	yes	no
District of Columbia	effectively, no	effectively, no
Florida	effectively, no	effectively, no
Georgia	effectively, no	effectively, no
Hawaii	effectively, no	effectively, no
Idaho	yes	no
Illinois	effectively, no	effectively, no
Indiana	yes	no
Iowa	yes	no
Kansas	yes	no
Kentucky	yes	no
Louisiana	yes	no
Maine	effectively, no	effectively, no
Maryland	yes	no
Massachusetts	no	yes
Michigan	yes	no
Minnesota	effectively, no	effectively, no
Mississippi	no	yes
Missouri	effectively, no	effectively, no
Montana	yes	no
Nebraska	yes	no
Nevada	no	no
New Hampshire	yes	no
New Jersey	yes	no
New Mexico	effectively, no	effectively, no
New York	no	yes
North Carolina	yes	no
North Dakota	effectively, no	effectively, no
Ohio	no	yes
Oklahoma	yes	no
Pennsylvania	yes	no
Oregon	effectively, no	effectively, no
Rhode Island	no	yes
South Carolina	no	yes
South Dakota	yes	no
Tennessee	yes	no
Texas	effectively, no	effectively, no
Utah	effectively, no	effectively, no
Vermont	effectively, no	effectively, no
Virginia	effectively, no	effectively, no
West Virginia	effectively, no	effectively, no
Washington	effectively, no	effectively, no
Wisconsin	yes	no
Wyoming	effectively, no	effectively, no

CHAPTER 15

Gifts

CHAPTER 15

Gifts

WE'RE USED TO THINKING of gifts as a personal matter, not as an aspect of financial or estate planning. Birthday, Christmas or anniversary presents don't normally have tax consequences. However, if a gift is worth more than $10,000, the rules change and gift taxes become involved. And making non-taxable gifts while you are alive can be one of the most effective ways to reduce tax liability for those with estates over $600,000, the federal tax threshold.

A. The Federal Gift and Estate Tax: An Overview

FEDERAL LAW TAXES the *giver* of gifts over $10,000 per year given to any one person or institution. (Similarly, some states which impose death taxes levy substantial gift taxes, too.) The recipient of a gift is not liable for either gift tax or income tax on that gift. If you give someone a gift worth over $10,000—say $25,000—the first $10,000 of that gift is exempt from gift taxes. The remaining $15,000 is subject to gift taxes.

The federal tax rate on gifts is the same as the estate tax rate levied on property transferred at death. And gifts count toward the $600,000 estate tax exemption. Thus, if you make taxable gifts totalling $400,000 while you are alive, only $200,000 worth of your property can be transferred free of federal estate tax when you die.[1]

In the last 10 years of her life, Sheila gives her two children a total of $300,000 over and above the $10,000 per child per year that is tax-exempt. These non-exempt gifts are counted against the $600,000 exemption, but no tax is due when the gifts are made. Sheila dies with an estate valued at $500,000. Since $300,000 of her total $600,000 unified gift and estate tax exemption has been used up, her estate must pay federal tax on $200,000. ($500,000 estate less $300,000 exemption remaining = $200,000.)

---

[1]Gift taxes aren't actually paid until the credit is used up (that is, you've given away $600,000 of non-exempt gifts) or until estate taxes are assessed after death.

As mentioned, federal law exempts from gift tax gifts up to $10,000 per year given to any person or non-charitable institution (lawyers and accountants call this "the $10,000 annual exclusion"). Thus, if you give $8,000 to a cousin, there are no federal gift tax consequences at all, but if you give $16,000 to the cousin, $6,000 is subject to gift tax. If, by contrast, you give $8,000 each to two cousins, a total of $16,000, none of it is subject to gift tax. With a married couple, each spouse has a separate $10,000 tax exemption, so the maximum the two of them can give, tax-free, to any person is $20,000 per year.

Gifts to minors can qualify for the $10,000 annual exclusion, even though the minor isn't given full present access or control to the gift. IRS regulations provide that in order to make a valid gift to a minor, the property of, and income from, the gift:

1. must be used for the minor's benefit until he or she reaches majority;

2. the remainder (if any) will be legally his once he reaches majority; and

3. if the minor dies before reaching majority, the remainder is payable into his estate.

Aside from the $10,000 annual exemption, the following types of gifts are exempt from gift tax:

- gifts between spouses;

- gifts for medical bills or for school tuition;

- gifts to tax-exempt charitable organizations. (The normal way an organization establishes its tax-exempt status is by ruling from the IRS, under Internal Revenue Code Section 501(c)(3).)

Victor gives $6,000 to his son, $50,000 to his wife, $20,000 to CARE (a tax-exempt organization), $12,000 for his grandson's tuition at college and $60,000 for a granddaughter's medical bills. All these gifts are exempt from gift tax.

B.   What is a Gift?

BEFORE EXPLORING MORE about gifts and estate planning, let's define what a gift is.[2]

A gift is defined by federal law as a voluntary transfer of property made without receiving anything in exchange.[3] In other words, a gift is any transfer of property that isn't commercial in spirit. The crucial element in determining whether a gift was made is the giver's intent, a concept which can become murky in a hurry. For example, you obtain a valuable painting from Frank. Did Frank intend to give you that painting, loan it to you, or was he hoping to sell it to you and wanted you to have it for a while before he mentioned the price? If someone's intent may not be obvious (now or in the future), it is an excellent idea to accompany a gift with some written statement stating it's a gift so that the status of the transaction is clear.

Unless there is such evidence, the IRS doesn't know, when you transfer something for less than its market value, whether you intend to make a gift or you're just a poor businessperson. So, it does the only thing it can do—it looks at the "objective evidence" and demands gift taxes if the transaction doesn't appear reasonable from an economic point of view.

---

[2]For a fascinating discussion of the meaning of giving, see *The Gift: Imagination and the Erotic Life of Property*, by Lewis Hyde (Random House). The book brilliantly explores the spirit involved in giving and receiving a gift, from a Christmas present to creating a work of art, and how the giving spirit interacts with commercial culture.

[3]In legalese, called "consideration," meaning anything of value given in exchange. Consideration does not require that you exchange items of equivalent dollar worth—that would eliminate bargaining and *caveat emptor*.

Linda exchanged $15,000 for an ordinary office lamp and deducted the $15,000 as a business expense. If the tax authorities question this transaction in an audit, and Linda doesn't want it to be treated as a gift, she must somehow convince them it was a bona fide commercial transaction (for example, that the lamp was a valuable antique), not a gift disguised as a sale to avoid assessment of gift taxes. If Linda's antique story is accepted, and the IRS says there's no gift tax liability, the recipient of the $15,000 would have to report $15,000 as ordinary income. If Linda isn't believed, she's liable for gift tax (plus whatever penalties are assessed against her for trying to dupe the tax authorities—a practice they frown upon).

Here are some circumstances that, usually, create gifts:

- Making an interest-free loan. Really? Yes. The Supreme Court has ruled that interest-free or artificially low interest loans are a gift of the interest not charged. So, if you loan a friend $30,000 interest-free, you are making a taxable gift of the interest you didn't charge. An "artificially low" interest rate is any rate significantly below market interest rates when the loan was made. For most people, however, the gift of interest is far below the $10,000 yearly gift tax exclusion. For example, even at a 10% simple interest, a single person can make an interest-free loan of $100,000 without gift tax liability, and a married couple could loan "interest-free" of up to $200,000 before the interest would exceed $20,000, the couple's annual exemption.

 If you're considering making a large (more than $100,000) interest-free loan, consult your tax advisor.

- Creating an irrevocable trust for another person (an irrevocable trust means you can't change your mind and terminate the trust once it is created).

- Withdrawing funds someone else deposited in a joint (not community property) bank account.

- Irrevocably assigning a life insurance policy to another.

- Forgiving a debt.
- Assigning a mortgage or judgment to someone without receiving fair compensation in return.
- Making a non-commercial transfer of your property into joint tenancy with another person. (Except for joint bank accounts; in that case, the rule is that a gift is made only when one depositor withdraws money deposited by the other one.)

Note on Living Trusts: Property placed in a living trust isn't a gift, because the beneficiaries have no present right to the trust property and you can revoke the trust if you wish.

Suppose Roger puts money in a trust for baby Olivia. If the trustee can alter or take back this gift, and Roger has retained the right to substitute a new trustee, there hasn't been a full loss of control, because Roger can make changes if he wants to. If the present trustee won't do what Roger wants, Roger can fire her and install a compliant one.

Likewise, if a person establishes a trust and retains the power to change who will benefit from it, even if he himself is specifically excluded as a possible beneficiary, there's no gift.

For a transaction to be a legal gift, the property must normally be delivered to and accepted by the recipient, and the giver must release all control over the property.

If Matt puts $10,000 into a drawer for Nina, there's no legal gift until she removes the money.

When a tangible item is given (cash, heirloom, picture), the relinquishment of control necessary to establish a gift is usually easy to ascertain, or prove—the recipient gains unrestricted possession over the property. In other situations, the question of control may be more difficult to ascertain. If a gift made by will or living trust is contingent on a future event, for instance, that event must be determinable by some objective standard. "To Desiree, when she becomes 21," or "when she travels to Paris" is objective; "when she's happily married" isn't.

C. How Federal Gift Taxes Work

BEFORE YOU START making gifts to reduce your eventual estate taxes, it's useful to understand how federal gift taxes actually work in more detail. Here are the basics.

1. The Estate/Gift Tax Credit

If you give a non-exempt gift worth more than $10,000, the gift tax assessed must be deducted from your estate/gift tax credit (equal to the tax on property worth $600,000). A gift giver cannot choose to pay any gift tax assessed now and "save" all her $600,000 estate/gift tax credit for later use. In short, gift taxes are actually paid by the giver at the time the gift is paid only if she has already given more than $600,000 in taxable gifts.

Charlene gives her niece Lucy $20,000. As we've learned, $10,000 of this gift is exempt from tax, under the annual gift tax exclusion. The remaining $10,000 of the gift is subject to gift tax.[4] The tax assessed on Charlene's $20,000 gift is $1,800. Under IRS rules, Charlene cannot pay this amount and satisfy the tax. She must use $1,800 of her estate/gift tax credit to satisfy this tax liability. When Charlene later dies, her remaining tax credit (assuming she has made no other taxable gifts) will let her transfer $590,000 free from federal estate tax.

---

[4]Had Charlene given Lucy $10,000 and then waited until January 1 of the next year and given her a second $10,000, there would be no tax assessed.

2. Gift Tax Rates

The gift tax rate, which increases with the size of the estate's gifts, is cumulative. In determining the gift tax rate, the value of all taxable gifts given since January 1, 1977 must be included. The reason for this is that otherwise, large estates could be transferred at a lower tax rate by piecemeal giving.

Carol gives her niece $20,000 two years in a row. Each year $10,000 of the gift is exempt from tax. Here are the gift taxes assessed:

	Amount given	Amount taxed	Tax rate based on	Tax estate	Tax assessed
Year 1	$20,000	$10,000	$10,000	18%	$1,800
Year 2	$20,000	$10,000	$20,000	20%	$2,000

3. Gifts Made Near Death

Some gifts made within three years of death are disallowed for estate tax purposes. The IRS acts as if the gifts weren't made, and includes the value of the gifts in the decedent's gross estate.[5] This is for estate tax purposes only; it doesn't affect ownership of the property.

A gift of a life insurance policy is the most significant type of gift that is disallowed if ownership is transferred within three years of death. This can result in a substantial increase in the size of the taxable estate, as life insurance proceeds are much more than the gift tax value of the policy before the insured dies. [Gifts of life insurance are discussed in more detail in Section F(4) below.] Other types of gifts which are disallowed if made within three years of death are rarely of concern to average folks—e.g., "reversionary interests," and "powers of appointment."

---

[5]If gift taxes have already been assessed, that amount will be credited towards any estate taxes due.

4. The Federal Gift Tax Return

An IRS gift tax return must be filed when a regular income tax return is filed (normally, April 15) if the taxpayer:

- has made non-exempt gifts over $10,000 to any person or organization during the previous taxable year;

- has made gifts to a tax-exempt organization over $10,000 during the previous taxable year. Although no tax is assessed for this type of gift, the IRS still requires a return to be filed. Who knows why?

The IRS does not require a gift tax return to be filed for gifts between spouses, or gifts for educational or medical expenses, no matter how large the gift.

D. State Gift Tax Rules

ONLY A FEW STATES have state gift taxes:

Delaware	South Carolina
Louisiana	Tennessee
New York	Wisconsin
North Carolina	

Generally, state gift tax rules and rates are the same as that state's death tax rules and rates.

For most people, state gift taxes are minor matters and don't enter into their estate planning. An exception can be those whose estate is large enough that they consider whether it's worthwhile to move their home from a state which imposes death taxes to one that doesn't. This can be sensible for those who own homes in two states, one of which doesn't have death (or gift) taxes. See Chapter 14, Section E.

 If you live in or own real estate in a state that imposes gift taxes and want to learn exactly what the taxes are and how they might affect you, you'll need to do your own research or consult a lawyer. (See Chapter 22.)

E.   Gifts and Tax Basis Rules

IT'S USUALLY UNWISE to give away an asset that had substantially appreciated in value since you purchased it. There is considerable income tax savings to the inheritor if that asset is transferred to her after your death. To understand why this is true, you need to understand federal income tax "basis" rules. First let's define what we're talking about. "Basis" is a word used to describe the value put on property you acquire, to determine your taxable profit, or loss, when you later sell that property. Normally, the "basis" of property is the price you paid for it, plus the cost of any major (capital) improvements.[6] Thus, if Jane bought a house for $50,000, and paid $25,000 for capital improvements, her federal tax basis in the house is $75,000. If Jane sold the house for $200,000 (over and above her costs of sale), her profit is $200,000 minus $75,000, or $125,000.

1.   The Value of a Gift

For the donor's gift tax purposes, the value of a gift is its fair market value on the date the gift is made. If Sara gives her house to Megan instead of selling it, the value of her gift is $200,000 for gift tax purposes. However, and this is crucial, Megan's (the recipient's) basis in the house when she obtains it from Sara is Sara's original basis—called the "carryover" basis. Thus, Megan's basis in the house is $75,000.

---

[6]To simplify what can become very complicated tax issues, capital improvements are additions and improvements to property that increase its value, that you cannot remove, that have a useful life of more than one year, and that are more than normal maintenance.

2.   Federal Tax Basis Rules for Inherited Property

There are special tax basis rules applicable to inherited property. You should take these rules into account when doing your planning for appreciated property.

The federal tax basis for property a person inherits from the estate of a deceased is the fair market value at the date of death. This means the tax basis is increased (accountants say "stepped up") from the deceased's original cost (plus capital improvements) to the value of the property at her death. Thus, to continue the previous example, if Sara died and left her house to Megan, Megan's basis in the house would be increased to its market value when Sara died, or $200,000.

The fact that an inheritor has a tax basis in inherited property equal to its current value isn't a windfall. After all, for estate tax purposes, the house is valued at its current market value, not at its original cost plus improvements. So it's only fair that the tax basis the inheritor takes the property at be the same as the value used for death tax purposes. However, this stepped-up basis rule does mean there are major tax savings if an asset that has gone up in value is transferred at death, not sold beforehand.

Edward owns two Redon paintings he bought decades ago, as a poor but astute art student, for a total of $4,000. Sixty years later, an appraiser informs him they're worth $704,000. If Edward were to sell the paintings, his taxable gain would be $704,000 less his "basis" of $4,000, or $700,000. Assuming Edward was in the 28% bracket, he would owe $196,000 in federal income tax. When Edward dies, what remains of this $700,000 (after income taxes and whatever he's spent) will be subject to death taxes. In contrast, if Edward transfers the paintings after he dies, his beneficiary's basis in the painting is $704,000. So, if the beneficiary promptly sells the paintings, there's no taxable gain.

The Tax Basis of Joint Tenancy Property

For joint tenancy property (except community property held
in joint tenancy), only the share of the property owned by the
deceased joint tenant gets a stepped-up basis. The portions
owned by the surviving joint tenant retain their original basis
[see Chapter 10, Section D(2))]

3. Tax Basis Rules and Community Property

If you're married and own community property (see
Chapter 3, Section B for a discussion of community
property and a list of community property states) there's
an additional federal tax basis rule that can be significant
for your estate planning. On the death of one spouse, the
basis of the community property interests of *both* spouses
is "stepped up" (increased) to the property's market value
at time of death, rather than retaining the basis of its
original cost, for federal tax purposes.

*Alicia and Rex are residents of the state of Washington, a
community property state. They own a house they bought
for $50,000. The basis of each spouse's interest is
$25,000, one-half the purchase price. When Alicia dies in
1991, the current market value of the house is $400,000.
Because of the stepped-up basis applicable to community
property, the federal tax basis of each spouse's one-half
interest in the house becomes $200,000. Thus if the house
is sold for $400,000 shortly after Alicia's death, neither
Rex nor Alicia's inheritors have made any federal taxable
gain, because the sale price equals the stepped-up basis of
the house. In contrast, if the house had been sold before
Alicia died, the total federal taxable gain to Alicia and Rex
would have been $350,000. (If Alicia and Rex were over
55, they would have the right to a one-time tax deduction
of $125,000, so their taxable gain would be $225,000.)*

Again, what all this means is that there's a considerable federal tax advantage for inheritors if an elderly
couple retains community property that has substantially
increased in value since they purchased it until one of
them dies, rather than selling that property late in their
lives.

*Suppose Mildred and Harold, residents of California (a
community property state), have been married for 35
years. During that time, they've acquired the following
valuable community property:*

- *a home, purchased for $30,000 in 1955, worth
  $300,000 in 1990;*
- *a summer home, purchased for $50,000 in 1964, worth
  $200,000 in 1990;*
- *two oil paintings, purchased for $3,000 each in 1960,
  worth $100,000 each in 1990.*

*Harold dies in 1990. He leaves his half of the community
property he owns with Alicia to their children. This means
they receive $150,000 worth of the home, $100,000
worth of the summer home, and a painting worth
$100,000.*

*Mildred, of course, owns property of the same value
because it represents her one-half of the community
property. All of this property, both the half received by the
children and the half that Mildred obtains as her share of
the former community property, is entitled to a stepped-up
basis. In other words, if Mildred decided to sell her oil
painting a week after her husband's death for $100,000,
she would owe no tax on the income. Similarly, if Mildred
and the children decided to sell the summer home for
$200,000, no tax would be owed by anyone.*

4. State Basis Rules

In general, the impact of state basis rules on inherited
property is minor, because the tax rates involved are
relatively low in those states which impose inheritance
taxes at all. It's a very rare case when estate planning
decisions are at all affected by state basis rules. State tax
rules regarding the basis of inherited property vary
considerably. If you want to explore your state's rules, you
can either research that issue yourself (see Chapter 22) or
consult an accountant or tax attorney.

Stepped-Up Basis for Community Property Held in Joint Tenancy

A problem with community property and the stepped-up basis rules concerns how title to the property is held. Sometimes title to community property is held in joint tenancy for probate avoidance purposes. Normally, only one-half of separate joint tenancy property is entitled to a stepped-up tax basis. However, as long as community property is involved, both halves of that property are entitled to a stepped-up basis upon the death of a spouse, whether it's held in joint tenancy or not.

Unfortunately, the IRS presumes that joint tenancy property isn't community property, unless the taxpayer can prove that it is. In addition, IRS rules are far from clear concerning what proof suffices to establish the community property status.

As a result, some estate planners advise married couples not to hold community property, especially appreciated property, in joint tenancy to be absolutely sure they obtain a stepped-up basis for both halves of their property. Using a living trust (instead of joint tenancy) allows couples to both avoid probate and eliminate worry that both halves of their community property will not qualify for a stepped-up tax basis.

Another way to avoid this problem is to hold title as "community property held in joint tenancy."

F. Using Gifts to Reduce Estate Taxes

USING GIFTS to reduce eventual estate taxes can be quite sensible if:

- Your estimated estate will exceed $600,000; and

- The property you want to give has not greatly appreciated in value since you acquired it; and

- You don't need all of your assets and income to live on.

This last concern, of course, requires a determination of how much money and property you need (or want) now and in the future, as well as what your resources are, including income from retirement, pensions, social security, savings and investments. Some people, who may not want to use up any of their principal for gifts, may decide to use some of their income for gifts.

Mr. and Mrs. Tureba, in their 70's, have a net estate totalling $1,140,000: a house worth $275,000 (all equity), stocks currently valued at $120,000, savings of $340,000, and business investments of $405,000. The Turebas don't feel comfortable with the thought of giving away any of this property. However, their incomes are substantially more than they need to live on. The figures are:

Retirement Pensions	*$ 32,000*
Social Security	*12,000*
Mrs. Turebas' part-time job	*8,000*
Stocks, savings and investments	*56,000*
Total Annual Income	*$108,000*

The Turebas spend about $35,000 a year, and taxes claim another $30,000. They're saving over $40,000 per year. They decide to give away $10,000 a year to each of their four children. (Because they are giving away cash, they avoid any problem of appreciated assets.)

Some Thoughts on Gift Giving

Estate planners have developed a number of ways gifts can be used to reduce or even eliminate, estate taxes for many people whose estate is in excess of $600,000. Before plunging into this subject (game might be a better word), take stock of what you feel about gifts. Does it detract from the spirit of making a gift to use it for reducing taxes?

Making a gift, under common understanding and the law, means you've given away ownership of some property; you no longer control it. This loss of ownership is precisely why many people don't make substantial gifts. Sometimes this makes good sense; they need, or may need, the money. Often, however, with larger estates, the refusal to make gifts makes little economic sense. Some people, it seems, want to hang on to every nickel they've got while they're alive, whether they will ever need it or not. The pleasure of keeping all their property outweighs any possible tax benefits.

Certainly, I wouldn't encourage a person to give away money if it meant risking sacrifices in lifestyle or the possibility of money fears or anxieties. However, those with more than adequate wealth for their foreseeable needs should seriously consider the giving of tax-exempt gifts while alive. Aside from any tax savings, the giver can feel pleasure and satisfaction in making a gift while living and seeing the help it brings.

1. Using the $10,000 Annual Exclusion

The $10,000 annual gift tax exclusion can, for some people, be used to achieve substantial estate tax savings. The key here is using this $10,000 exclusion as fully as possible. It's a simple matter of multiplication. If you use the $10,000 annual exemption for gifts to one person for, say, five years, you've given away five times as much ($50,000) tax-free as you would if you gave the same $50,000 to the same person in one year and only qualified for one $10,000 exemption. If you make $10,000 gifts to five recipients in one year, you've also given away $50,000 tax-free. And obviously, it follows that if you make five $10,000 gifts to five people for five years, you've given $250,000 away tax-free.

Patti owns a successful small business, with an estimated net worth of $810,000. Her other assets are worth roughly $175,000. Patti intends to leave her business to her four children. To reduce the value of her eventual estate, she incorporates her business. She can give each of her four children stock worth[7] $10,000 per year gift tax-free—a yearly total of $40,000. She wants to retain a minimum of 51% of the stock, so that she takes no risk of losing control of her business. So, for ten years she gives each child $10,000 worth of stock, transferring a total of $400,000 worth. She has retained $410,000 worth slightly more than half of the stock.[8] By giving away the stock, Patti has reduced the net value of her estate to less than $600,000, eliminating estate taxes.

Since spouses can each make $10,000 gifts, giving as a couple multiplies your gift tax exemption by two.

---

[7]Determining the worth of privately-held stock can be tricky, and a good accountant should be consulted.

[8]This example assumes the worth of the company remained the same for 10 years, unlikely in the real world. In practice, Patti would have to review the worth of her company yearly with her accountant to determine how much stock she could give.

A wife and husband, the Zellys, buy (for cash) a summer home worth $160,000. They will leave it, after both die, to their son. Their estate is well over $600,000. Naturally, they want to reduce the tax bite as much as is legally possible. They consider giving the house outright to their son, but this seems like a bad idea, as $140,000 of the gift would be subject to gift tax (the $160,000 value less the $20,000 annual exclusion available to a couple). The couples' $600,000 estate/gift tax credit exemption would be reduced by $140,000. But suppose the Zellys transfer the house to their son in exchange for a "loan" of $160,000 and "reasonable" interest totalling $40,000. The couple records the deed and a mortgage for $200,000 in their names, with the son to make payments of $20,000 a year, for 10 years. As each year's payment comes due, the couple forgives it—that is, makes a gift of that amount to the son. Each year's gift is within the amount exempt from tax. In ten years, the house has been fully transferred to their son and its worth will be excluded from the couple's' taxable estate. If the son is married, the Zellys could shorten the time for the transfer to five years, by making the gift jointly to their son and his spouse. That way, the Zellys would give $40,000 a year tax-free.

Obviously, to engage in this kind of estate tax planning, you must have confidence and trust in the person you're giving the property to. If the Zellys didn't trust their son, and were concerned that he might sell the vacation house while they were alive, their gift-giving would be risky.

2. Gifts of Property Likely to Appreciate

If you're wealthy and your estate will be subject to tax, it can make sense to give away property that you believe will appreciate substantially in the future, especially if it hasn't appreciated much already.

Brook, in her 60's, owns (free of any mortgage) real estate valued at $150,000 which she recently purchased for that amount. She intends to give this land to her niece Laura. Brook is wealthy and doesn't need any income from this land (or from any sale of it). She believes the land will rise greatly in price in a few years, to perhaps two, three or more times its current value. If she waits to transfer the property until her death, then the market value of the property when she dies will be included in her taxable estate. But if she gives the property to Laura now, then all appreciation in value won't be included in her taxable estate. The gift will be subject to gift tax. $10,000 of the gift is tax-exempt, but $140,000 isn't. The tax will be much lower than if the value of the property after it has appreciated is taxed at Brook's death.

Now assume the same facts as the previous example, except this time the $150,000 piece of land was purchased by Brook years ago for $10,000. It's not desirable, from a tax viewpoint, for Brook to give the land to Laura. As discussed in Section E, since the land has already appreciated greatly in value, Laura would take the land with the "carryover" basis of Brook's original purchase price. So, if Laura sold the land, she'd have to pay a hefty tax income. In this situation, it's probably better, from a tax standpoint, for Brook to hold onto the property and give it to Laura in her will.

3. The Timing of Gifts

For those who engage in extensive tax-saving gift giving, the timing of making gifts can be important. To summarize what can become quite involved, non-charitable gifts (above the $10,000 exemption) are often given near the close of the taxable year. The gift taxes are the same, no matter when the gift is made during the year, and you can retain the asset longer. Charitable gifts are often given at the beginning of the tax year, so the income that asset produces won't be taxed as the giver's income.

4. Gifts of Life Insurance

In some situations, making a gift of life insurance can substantially reduce or eliminate federal estate taxes. When the insured dies, the proceeds paid by the policy are part of the insured's taxable estate, if the insured owned the policy. However, if someone else owned the policy, the proceeds aren't part of the decedent's estate. Simply naming a beneficiary of a life insurance policy isn't a gift. The policy itself must be given to a new owner for a gift to occur. Ownership of a life insurance policy is given to someone else by a written document transferring ownership. An example of a written transfer of life insurance is contained in Chapter 12, Section E(2). Also, many insurance companies provide preprinted forms to make gifts of life insurance, so check with your insurance agent.

To qualify as a gift, a life insurance policy must, under IRS rules, be given away at least three years before death.

Kate gave a life insurance policy to her daughter, Ava, in 1989. Its value then was $4,000. When Kate dies in 1991, the policy pays $200,000. Aside from life insurance, Kate's estate totals $560,000. There were no gift taxes assessed when the gift was made, as the gift was exempt because it was worth less than $10,000. However, all the $200,000 must be included in Kate's taxable estate because she died within the three-year period. Thus, Kate's total estate is $760,000, and $160,000 is subject to estate tax. If Kate had given away the insurance policy at least three years before her death, her estate would have been under the $600,000 exemption limit.

If someone gives away an insurance policy more than three years before his death, he can make tax-exempt gifts (up to $10,000 per year) to the new owner, who can use that money to pay the premiums on the policy. These gifts won't be disallowed under the federal life-insurance-must-be-transferred-three-years-before-death rule, so the proceeds of the insurance policy won't be included in the giver's estate.

Under IRS rules, the value of a gift of a new life insurance policy (for gift tax purposes) is its cost. For a policy which has been in force for a while but is paid-up, the value is its replacement cost (what it would cost to buy a similar policy) at the time of the gift, not its cash surrender value. In the case of a cash reserve policy, the value of the gift is the "interpolated terminated reserve as of the date of the gift, plus any prepaid premiums."[9] Other special types of insurance policies also have a gift tax value based on their present worth. Most insurance companies will provide, on request, an informal approximation of the gift tax value of a policy before you make the actual gift. They will also provide the appropriate forms (usually Treasury Department Form 938) for submission with the gift tax return, if any.

However, the value of the gift of an insurance policy is calculated, it will be much lower than the proceeds paid in the event of the insured's death.

G. Using Gifts to Reduce Income Taxes

THERE'S NO LONGER much incentive to give away property while you're alive to reduce income taxes. In the past, a when prosperous person's income was taxed at a 50% or higher rate, considerable tax savings could be achieved by transferring an income-producing asset to someone in the lowest tax brackets. In particular, people made gifts to their children or grandchildren, whose tax bracket was a fraction of the giver's. The 1986 Federal Income Tax Act largely put a stop to this. First, tax brackets have been simplified, with the top bracket reduced to 28% or 33%, depending on your situation. Second, all income over $1,000 received by minors, 14 years of age or younger, from any gift (whether from their parents or otherwise) is taxed at their parents' rate.

---

[9]Yes, these words are bizarre. All you need do with them, however, is repeat them slowly to your insurance company. They will then give you the dollar value, for gift tax purposes, of your policy.

Note on Charitable Gifts: Like anything involving money and taxes in America, income tax saving gifts can get quite complicated. For the very wealthy, charitable giving is a field in itself, involving "charitable lead" trusts, transfers to charitable pools and other sophisticated methods. These abstruse devices aren't normally helpful for people with estates of less than several million dollars, and so aren't covered here. If you're considering making a large charitable gift, be sure you've checked out the technicalities with a tax expert.

Ongong Trusts for Tax Savings and Property management

Ongoing Trusts for Tax Savings and Property Management

THIS CHAPTER EXPLAINS the basics of how trusts can be used to save money on estate or income taxes or for long-term management of property. As discussed in Chapter 9, a trust is simply a legal device created by a person owning property ("the settlor") providing that property be managed by a person or organization (the "trustee"), for the benefit of another (the "beneficiary") under terms the settlor defines in the document that creates the trust. I often refer to trusts established for tax savings and the long-term management of property as "ongoing" trusts, because each typically exists as a functioning entity, legally separate from the settlor for a considerable time. This is in contrast to a revocable living trust, established as a probate avoidance device, which functions as an independent legal entity only for a brief time after the settlor's death.

Because ongoing trusts are inherently complicated, I don't show you how to create one yourself. True, in some relatively straightforward situations, creating one of these trusts yourself can be relatively risk-free. However, fully explaining the "how-to" details would take a hefty book in itself. Instead, this chapter is designed to give you an overview of the basic uses and goals of ongoing trusts. With this information, you should be able to decide if one (or more) of these trusts may be a good idea for you, and if you want to explore them further.

A. How Ongoing Trusts Work

LET'S TAKE A MINUTE to further distinguish ongoing tax savings and management trusts from revocable living trusts used to avoid probate. There are two big differences. First, tax savings and managerial trusts are designed to be fully operational, as distinct legal entities, over extended periods of time. Living trusts become truly functional only at the settlor's death, and then only for the purpose of transferring trust property to beneficiaries. In contrast, an ongoing trust is created by parents to manage property for the benefit of their disadvantaged child after they die. The trustee may administer this trust for years, or decades, and the trust document has to be drafted to encompass this possibility. By contrast, a probate avoidance living trust is actually operational for a short time, normally no more than a few weeks.

Second, once an ongoing trust becomes effective, it's irrevocable. The trust terms are fixed and can't be altered. Again, in contrast, a probate avoidance living trust is revocable for most of its existence; it becomes irrevocable only for the brief time it functions after the settlor's death to transfer property to the beneficiaries.

1. Creating Ongoing Trusts

The fact that an ongoing trust and a probate avoidance living trust are different animals doesn't mean they can't drink at the same pond. In fact, an ongoing trust can be combined with a living trust. In other words, a trust can be created that first avoids probate and then becomes operational as an ongoing trust. For example, suppose you want to establish a trust to manage property left to a disadvantaged child after your death. That trust is an ongoing one and will take effect after you die. If you create this trust in your will, all property that goes into the trust will have to go through probate first. However, you can just as easily establish the same ongoing trust for a disadvantaged child by creating a revocable living trust, first which avoids first probate, and then continues as an ongoing trust.

An ongoing trust can be established to take effect immediately, or to take effect when you die. If the trust takes effect while you are alive, the property placed in the trust is a gift, subject to gift tax rules (see Chapter 15). If the trust takes effect when you die, the property in the trust is subject to estate tax rules (see Chapter 14).

2. The Trustee's Responsibilities

Ongoing trusts have legal lives of their own, fully distinct from any person. This means that each operational ongoing trust must obtain a taxpayer ID number (by filing

IRS Form 4), and the trustee must maintain records of all trust financial transactions. If the trust has a gross annual income of $600 or more, the trustee must file a trust income tax return (IRS Form 1041).

The trustee of an ongoing trust must supervise and manage the trust property according to the terms of the trust, and is responsible for the paperwork, including filing tax returns. And, of course, the trustee must distribute trust income (or principal) to the beneficiaries, as the trust directs. For these services, trustees of ongoing trusts are commonly paid. Often the trust document provides that the trustees can pay themselves "reasonable compensation" from trust property.

Legally, the trustee is a "fiduciary," which means she is held to the standard of highest good faith and scrupulous honesty when handling trust business (unless the trust document itself provides a lesser legal standard). With ongoing trusts, consideration should be given to whether the services of a professional trustee, particularly one from a private trust company, are warranted, or if the duties can be better handled by a trusted family member or friend. Because, by its very nature, an ongoing trust will be functional for a while, the trustee will most likely interact at various times with legal or financial institutions, such as the IRS and banks. A trustee has authority to handle these transactions and prepare trust paperwork.

3. What Ongoing Trusts Can't Do

Before exploring what ongoing trusts *can* do, let's look for a moment at what they *can't* do. Those who believe trusts are truly lawyers' magic may seek what I call the "day-dream" trust. In a day-dream trust, the settlor wants to:

1. Avoid income taxes;

2. Shield her property from all creditors; and

3. Retain complete control over property put in the trust or, at the very least, have full access to it in times of need or adversity.

It should come as no surprise that the day-dream trust is just that—a fantasy. Tax rules prevent a settlor from accomplishing all the purposes listed above. For example, it's obviously not societally desirable to allow people to escape financial liabilities and obligations simply by use of a trust. As a result, you can't use a trust to escape responsibility for legal debts and obligations, including child support, alimony, court-ordered judgments, or, for that matter, any other legal debt. Likewise, if the settlor retains any control over the trust or benefits from it, the IRS will not allow the trust to be used to lower the settlor's income taxes.

B. Tax-Saving Trusts

ONGOING TRUSTS are primarily used for estate tax savings, when your estate is over $600,000. Also, ongoing trusts can sometimes be used for income tax savings.

1. The Marital Life Estate Trust

Couples with large estates can achieve significant estate tax savings by use of what I call a "marital life estate trust," because it's primarily used by married couples. However, this type of trust can be used by any couple, whether married or unmarried. This trust can go by different names, including a "spousal life estate," "bypass" or "A-B" trust. However it's labeled, it can be particularly useful for elderly couples with estates that, combined, total more than $600,000. Since spouses often want to leave their property for the other's benefit, if each spouse establishes a marital life estate trust, the ultimate death tax liability of the surviving spouse's estate will be significantly lower than if each spouse leaves property outright to the other.

A marital life estate trust saves on estate taxes because it allows each member of the couple to use the $600,000 estate tax exemption. It prevents the surviving spouse from ending up with all the property belonging to both spouses and assuming this is more than $600,000, having a hefty estate liability.

In a marital life estate trust, property is left for the use of the surviving spouse or mate during his lifetime, but—and this is the key—he never becomes the legal owner of that property. Since legal ownership "bypasses" the surviving spouse, the obligation of that spouse's estate to pay estate tax on the money received from the first spouse to die is also bypassed.

A husband and wife own $2,100,000 of community property. (This example also applies in non-community property states, assuming the husband and wife own their property equally.) The wife dies in 1990, the husband dies in 1991.

Without Marital Life Estate Trust

If the wife leaves her estate ($1,050,000) to her husband, who then leaves all the estate to their children, here are the estate tax consequences:

On Wife's death, 1990:

Gross estate (1/2 of community)	$1,050,000
Final bills, burial costs, etc.	- 50,000
Net estate	$1,000,000
Estate tax assess	$ 0
	(because of marital deduction)

On Husband's death, 1991: *(assuming, to make the writer's life easier and the example clearer, that none of the net estate has been spent, nor has it appreciated)*

Gross estate	$2,050,000
Final bills, burial costs, etc.	- 50,000
Net estate	$2,000,000
Estimated estate tax	$ 780,800
Estate tax credit	- 192,800
Estate tax payable	$ 588,000

With Marital Life Estate Trust

Now assume the wife leaves her estate to her children in a marital life estate or bypass trust, with her husband to receive the income from her trust for his life. When he dies, the principal of her trust is turned over to the children. Note that the income to the husband can be quite substantial; the wife's $1 million estate should earn healthy interest. Assume the husband has spent all his trust income before he dies. Here are the estate tax consequences of using a marital life estate trust:

On Wife's death, 1990:

Gross estate (1/2 of community)	$1,050,000
Final bills, burial costs, etc.	- 50,000
Net estate	$1,000,000
Estimated estate tax	$ 345,800
Estate tax credit	- 192,800
Estate tax payable	$ 153,000

On Husband's death, 1991:

Gross estate	$1,050,000
Final bills, burial costs, etc.	- 50,000
Net estate	$1,000,000
Estimated estate tax	$ 345,800
Estate tax credit	- 92,800
Estate tax payable	$ 153,000
Total estate taxes paid using a marital life estate trust	$ 306,000
Total estate taxes paid without trusts	- 588,000
Tax savings from using trusts	$ 282,000

---

a.   Drawbacks of a Marital Life Estate Trust

Before deciding to use marital life estate trusts, both spouses (or members of a couple) should understand what they're getting into. Once one spouse or mate dies, a marital life estate trust does impose significant limits and a few burdens on the survivor. And then it's too late for the survivor to decide the trust isn't worth the trouble.

Once one spouse dies, the trust is irrevocable, as to that deceased spouse's (or mate's) property.

Specifically, the drawbacks of a marital life estate trust once a spouse dies can include:

- The surviving spouse doesn't have outright ownership of the trust property. He cannot spend that property freely on a new condominium, a Hopper painting, a stay in Tahiti, or whatever else appeals to him. This is why this sort of trust is usually not recommended unless both spouses are elderly. If both spouses are in their 50's, even if one dies unexpectedly the other will likely live 20-30 years or more. Spouses usually feel that having property tied up, and limited by, a marital life estate trust for so long isn't a good idea, even if some estate taxes are saved in the long run. Similarly, these trusts normally aren't desired if one spouse is considerably younger than the other and presumably will live much longer than the older spouse.

- The surviving spouse, or his financial manager, must keep two sets of books and records. That's because property in the deceased spouse's trust is legally separate from property of the surviving spouse. That trust property must be formally identified. A taxpayer ID number must be obtained for the trust, separate trust records maintained, and a trust tax return filed.

- Any estate taxes assessed when the first spouse dies must be paid within nine months after death. For instance, in the example given in the beginning of this section, if a marital life estate trust were used, estate taxes of $153,000 would be assessed on the death of the wife (the first spouse to die). This means that $153,000 cash must be raised within nine months. If the estate doesn't have substantial liquid assets, such as cash or publicly-traded stocks, gathering this cash may impose hardships on the husband, the surviving spouse, forcing him to sell assets, such as real estate, under pressure. There are ways to avoid this problem. For instance, in some circumstances spouses or couples can use what's called a "Q-Tip" trust [explained in Section B(2) below], or a "disclaimer" [see Section B(4) below], but these devices have, as I discuss, their own limits and problems.

Main Features of a Marital Life Estate Trust

The surviving spouse gets only a "life estate" interest in the trust property. Normally, this means she receives all income from the trust property, and is entitled to use of the property—or example, she can live in a house that's owned by the trust

The first successor trustee of a marital life estate trust normally is the surviving spouse. In other words, after one spouse dies, the other spouse becomes the sole trustee for the life estate trust established by the first spouse. This successor trustee can be given limited power to invade the trust principal for the benefit of the surviving spouse (himself). Still, the legal owner of the trust property remains the trust itself, not the surviving spouse.

After the death of the life beneficiary—to repeat, that's the surviving spouse—the trust property is distributed however the trust document directs. Often the property is given outright to the couple's children. The surviving spouse has no power to decide who receives the property in the marital life estate trust.

b. Complexities of Marital Life Estate Trusts

Preparing a marital life estate trust always involves some complexity. In the absence of any first-rate self-help materials, you'll need the assistance of a knowledgeable expert to prepare one. Technical IRS requirements must be met if the trust is to obtain the desired estate tax savings.

Among the complexities that can arise when preparing a marital life estate trust are:

- Does either spouse want to impose managerial controls on property given to the surviving spouse? This concern may arise if one spouse worries that the other can't sensibly manage money. And in second marriage situations, spouses commonly wish to impose stricter than normal limits on how the property in the life estate can be used to benefit the surviving spouse. For example, a surviving spouse might be given the right to live in a house for life but not the right to rent it out. Or, the surviving spouse might not be named as sole trustee of the marital life estate trust. Instead, a child of the deceased spouse could be named as co-trustee, or even sole trustee.

- Should the trustee be given the right to be able to spend the trust principal for the surviving spouse in case of emergency? IRS rules permit it, but you may not want to do this.

- Should the surviving spouse be given what estate planners call the "5 and 5" power? Under IRS rules, the surviving spouse of a marital life estate trust can be given the right to obtain annually, for any reason whatsoever, up to a maximum of 5% of the trust principal, or $5,000, whichever is greater. There can be drawbacks to including this "5 and 5" power in the trust, however. First, a spouse may not want the other spouse to be able to invade the principal at all. Also, there can be adverse tax consequences if the money isn't taken by the surviving spouse.

- What marital property should be placed in the trust when the first spouse dies? Because tax is assessed on property placed in the trust at the death of the first spouse, and not again when the second spouse dies and that property is turned over to the final beneficiary, it's usually desirable to place property which is likely to appreciate significantly in value in the trust. Doing this means none of the appreciation will be subject to estate tax when the surviving spouse dies.

- How much property should be placed in the marital life estate trust when it's established? This can be a very complicated matter. Your individual situation and needs must be carefully discussed with a knowledgeable expert. For example, suppose each spouse's estate is worth $1,000,000. If $600,000 is placed in each spouse's marital life estate trust, and $400,000 given outright to the surviving spouse, no estate taxes will be assessed when the first spouse dies. The $600,000 is exempt under the estate tax credit, and the $400,000 except because of the marital deduction. But in the long run would it be better to put $1,000,000 in the marital life estate trust, and pay tax on $400,000, rather than combine $400,000 with the surviving spouse's estate of $1,000,000? The answer is that there's no general answer. What is best depends on a variety of interrelated factors, including the surviving spouse's needs and finances, estate tax rules, and income flows.

- What legal phrasing will be used to define what property will be put into the marital life estate trust? There are a number of variations, each of which can have differing consequences.

- How will the couple find a lawyer who's knowledgeable, humane, and doesn't charge a fortune? (Chapter 22, Section B has some suggestions.)

2. Q-Tip Trusts

"Q-Tip" is IRS jargon for "Qualified Terminal Interest Property" (that clears it all up, right?). A "Q-Tip" trust is a specific type of a marital life estate trust used to postpone payment of estate taxes otherwise due when the first spouse dies. It can be used only by a surviving spouse, not a mate in an unmarried couple. The advantage of a Q-tip trust is that it enables the surviving spouse to postpone payment of any estate taxes assessed on the property of the first spouse to die until the death of the second spouse. One drawback to a Q-Tip trust is that the federal estate taxes eventually paid on the property of the first spouse to die are assessed against what the property is worth when the surviving spouse dies, not what the property was worth when the first spouse died.

Mary Edna, a widow, marries Roberto. Mary Edna has three grown children from her first marriage. Her estate, comprised primarily of her house and summer cottage, has a net value of $900,000. Roberto has little property beyond his monthly social security check. Mary Edna wants Roberto to be able to continue to live in both her houses if she predeceases him. After his death, she wants all her property to go to her children. If Mary Edna creates a marital life estate trust, with Roberto having the life estate, all of her property will be subject to estate tax when she dies. This means tax will have to be paid on $300,000. Since neither her estate nor Roberto has much cash, this will necessitate sale of one of her houses. So she creates a Q-Tip trust. No estate taxes will be assessed against her property until Roberto dies. However, suppose the worth of the property has risen to $1,300,000 when Roberto dies. Estate taxes will be based on this value, so $700,000 ($1,300,000 minus the $600,000 exemption), is subject to estate tax.

3. Generation-Skipping Trusts

One of the legal tax savings devices traditionally used by the very wealthy to minimize estate taxes has been to leave the bulk of their property in trust for their grandchildren, with the income from the trusts (but not the principal) available to their children. The advantage of this strategy was that death taxes were avoided several times. Without a trust, taxes would typically be paid when the first grandparent died, then again when the second grandparent died, and then when each of their children died.

Current laws impose a tax on all "generation-skipping transfers" in excess of $1 million.[1] For a generation-skipping trust of $4 million, this means estate taxes are levied on the middle generation for $3 million as if the trust didn't exist.

---

[1] For transfers where the grantor dies before 1990, the exemption is $2 million.

Val leaves $4 million in trust for his grandchildren, with Val's son Tom as a life beneficiary. When Val dies, the property in the trust (less the $600,000 exempt amount) is subject to estate tax. When Tom dies, all property in the trust is subject to estate tax, except for $1 million, the amount that can be passed tax-free in a generation-skipping trust.

Even if you have a spare million dollars for a generation-skipping trust, it may not be advisable to establish one. This type of trust means your children cannot obtain outright the property in the trust. They can only receive the interest or profits from the trust principal. This is all well and good if you'll leave other property to your children, or if they earn plenty on their own, but may be a mistake if there are no other resources. On the other hand, if you do have an estate of several million or more, it may well be advisable to establish a generation-skipping trust; you'll save substantially on eventual estate taxes, and the rest of your estate should suffice for your children and other inheritors.

Generation-skipping trusts should be prepared by someone knowledgeable in estate planning. These trusts are designed to have effect for at least two generations after the settlor's life, normally over 50 years, and there are many contingencies that should be considered. Also, there are IRS requirements regarding the age of the trustee and the time the estate taxes will be assessed.

4. Trusts With Disclaimers

A disclaimer is another legal device to save money on estate taxes. Basically, a disclaimer authorizes someone who's been given a gift to decline to accept it. The gift is then given to an alternate beneficiary originally named by the gift giver. The person who disclaims the gift does so to make the overall estate tax picture better. Of course, this means she should have enough other property so that she doesn't need the gift she disclaimed to live on.

Jim and Hester, in their 40's, have a shared marital estate worth $800,000. Thus each has an estate worth $400,000. In their estate plan, each gives their property outright to the other. However, they worry about what will happen in future years if they acquire considerably more valuable property but don't get around to revising their plan. Suppose their net estate becomes worth, say, $2 million? Then, there will be substantial federal estate taxes when the surviving spouse dies. On the other hand, maybe the surviving spouse will need or want the entire estate. How can Jim and Hester decide now what's wisest? The answer is, they don't have to. They can create a trust with a disclaimer, authorizing the surviving spouse to decline to accept all or any portion of the deceased spouse's property. All disclaimed property goes to a marital life estate trust, with the couple's children the final beneficiaries. Thus, suppose the total estate is worth $2 million when Hester dies. Hester leaves her $1 million to Jim, subject to his right to disclaim. Jim could disclaim $600,000 of that gift and accept $400,000 of it. In other words, Jim could decide that his own estate of $1,000,000, plus $400,000 from Hester, is enough for him to own outright. And by using the disclaimer, Hester's estate and Jim's estate each make use of the $600,000 exemption. If Jim accepted all of Hester's $1,000,000, only the $600,000 would be used when he died.

 Like all the devices discussed in this chapter, disclaimers are complicated and technical. To include one in your trust or estate plan, you need the services of an experienced lawyer.

5. Irrevocable Income Tax Savings Trusts

Irrevocable trusts once were commonly used to reduce income taxes. No longer. Congress has eliminated most of the ways irrevocable trusts were used as tax dodges.

Now, a non-charitable trust will reach the 28% tax bracket, the tax rate which applies to all regular income, when its taxable income exceeds $5,000. So the maximum income tax saving obtained by transferring property to a tax savings trust is $650.

Income from trusts created after March 1, 1986 is taxed to the trust's creator "if the principal may revert back to the creator, or his spouse, and the actuarial value of that reversion exceeds 5% of the trust's original value." What this means in English is that short-term income tax savings trusts have been eliminated. There's no longer any tax advantage to creating what was called a "Clifford Trust" (no relation) which lasted for 10 years and a day, after which the trust principal reverted to the settlor.

C. Trusts for the Management of Property

ONGOING TRUSTS can be used to provide for the management and control of property when a person doesn't want to turn that property over to the beneficiary outright. Some beneficiaries, such as minors or persons who have been declared legally incompetent, aren't legally permitted to own substantial amounts of property outright. Or sometimes the trust creator (settlor) believes the beneficiary is a spendthrift or is otherwise unable to handle property responsibly. And seriously disabled people may also need someone to manage property for them.

A trust settlor can even decide that he himself no longer wants the burdens of administering his own property and turn that task over to someone else. More realistically, a settlor may know he's old and ill and that it's sensible to arrange for others to handle his finances. A managerial trust is one way to do this. Purchasing an annuity from an insurance company is a second. Preparing a durable power of attorney is a third and often the simplest. (See Chapter 18.) Sometimes people prefer a trust, however, because it is a more traditional legal form.

Selection of the trustee is particularly vital with a managerial trust. The trustee will have an ongoing relationship with the beneficiaries. Usually, the trustee will have important decisions to make, such as how to invest trust money and whether to spend some of the trust principal for the beneficiary's needs.

The more complex and sophisticated the financial responsibilities of the trustee, the more you need a trustee with business experience. Some people with considerable sums of money or property in these trusts use banks or other financial institutions as trustees. My strong preference, as I've stated before, is for personal trustees, if you know someone who can do the job. It's usually much better for the beneficiaries to deal with a human being. Banks can become mighty impersonal, perhaps paying little attention to any trust with less than many millions, or treating a beneficiary as a nuisance. In addition, they charge small (and sometimes not so small) fees for every tiny act, which taken together can cost a bundle.

Following are examples of commonly-used managerial trusts.

1. Trusts for Persons With Special Needs

Parents or others concerned with a person with special needs—who is physically disabled or emotionally disadantaged—can face difficult estate planning problems. If that person cannot sensibly manage property, property must be left in a managerial trust that is carefully drafted so the trustee has flexibility to deal with the beneficiary's needs, both expected and unexpected.

A major concern here is the effect property given to a disadvantaged person may have on eligibility for government assistance such as Supplemental Security Income (SSI) or medical aid. A disadvantaged person who is the legal owner of any substantial amount of property is usually ineligible for continued governmental assistance

until that property is used up.[2] So even if the property is worth a lot, it will probably be used up fairly quickly. The disadvantaged person will then be eligible again for governmental assistance, but none of the property will remain for emergencies or the many needs governmental assistance doesn't provide for.

What can a parent, or other concerned adult, do? They can, of course, not give any property to the disadvantaged person in the first place. But this can feel heartless, and rejecting. Also, most parents are rightly skeptical of relying on public programs to provide total care for a child with special needs. As various U.S. government reductions in safety net programs have taught us, even those with disabilities can't securely rely on governmental assistance, safe from cutbacks (unless the "disabled" is a weapons system).

Establishing a managerial trust for the benefit of the disabled person can avoid this unhappy result. Under Social Security Administration (SSA) guidelines, trust property doesn't affect eligibility if the beneficiary *cannot*:

• control the amount or frequency of trust payments, or

• revoke the trust and use the property.

In addition, some SSA offices require that the trust document show that the trust creator didn't "intend" the trust property to be used as the primary source of aid or income for the disadvantaged person. In other words, out there in the real world, each local office has wide latitude in interpreting the SSA guidelines for trusts to benefit a disadvantaged person.

 Thus, the key to drafting a trust for a disadvantaged person is up-to-date knowledge of SSA rules, court interpretation of them, and local SSA practices. All these can change rapidly, so the services of an expert are essential. Be sure you find someone who knows this field particularly well; it's a definite speciality.

---

[2]In some circumstances, the government may even demand reimbursement for past benefits.

National organizations, such as the Alliance For the Mentally Ill, are concerned with these problems, but, at present, no self-help or other informational material is available.

2. Spendthrift Trusts

A spendthrift trust is designed to minimize the opportunities for the beneficiary to squander or waste trust income and principal.

Pierre wants to leave money to his son, Maurice, a charming fellow who spends money like it's going out of style. So Pierre creates an ongoing "spendthrift" trust (to take effect after Pierre dies) for the benefit of Maurice, which will dole trust income out to Maurice on the first of each month. The trust will be managed by Pierre's prudent bourgeois brother Jean-Paul. Under the terms of the trust, Maurice cannot obtain the trust principal, or legally pledge his expected trust income to obtain credit. The trust will end when Maurice becomes 50, by which point Pierre hopes he'll have learned financial prudence.

But suppose Maurice dies before he reaches 50—what happens to the trust property then? What happens if Maurice truly needs more money than the monthly stipend? Does the trustee have the power to spend trust principal if Maurice becomes ill? And suppose Maurice sees the error of his scandalous ways and decides to give up the race track and go to dental school. Can the trustee use the principal to pay Maurice's tuition? These concerns must be resolved when the trust is drafted, and illustrate why drafting this sort of trust inevitably gets complicated.

3. Trust for Children's Education

One common type of managerial trust provides for the college, graduate school or other educational expenses of the beneficiaries.

Rick wants to provide for all of his nine grandnieces and grandnephews who go to college. Rick is 77, healthy, and has a substantial estate. His grandnieces and grandnephews range in ages from twelve years to six weeks. Here are some of the questions Rick must resolve before finalizing a trust:

- *What are the tax consequences of establishing the trust now or when Rick dies? If he creates the trust now, the property he gives to the trust will be a gift. However, the gift won't be subject to tax, because it's for educational costs (see Chapter 15, Gifts). If the trust is established when Rick dies, all property in the trust will be included in his taxable estate.*

- *If the trust is established now, does Rick want to be the trustee or appoint someone else? And in either case, who are the successor trustees to take over when Rick dies? And if the trust is created later, when Rick dies, who are the trustees and successor trustees?*

- *Does a student have to attend college or school full time to receive trust benefits? What's "full time?" What's a college or school? If a child discovers another honest way to learn—for example, becomes an apprentice to a metal sculptor—does he or she get trust benefits?*

- *Can unequal payments be made to different beneficiaries? If one attends Columbia Medical School, while the other goes to a non-tuition community college, their expenses will vary greatly. Lawyers call a trust where different amounts of principal or income can be paid to different family beneficiaries a "pot" trust—all the dough is in one pot. If that's not what Rick wanted, he'd set up distinct individual trusts for each beneficiary.*

- *What happens to the trust income when no beneficiaries attend college or school? Can it be used for beneficiaries "emergencies?" What kinds?*

• *When does the trust end? What happens to the money left when it does?*

As these questions highlight, a managerial educational trust needs to be created with the help of an expert.

4. Second Marriages: Marital Life Estate Trusts Used to Control Property

Marital life estate trusts can be used to impose controls over the property in the trust, not just to save on estate taxes. For instance, sometimes a spouse in a second marriage wants to insure that his own property goes, eventually, to his children and doesn't want the surviving spouse to be able to change that decision.

Ilana and George, both in their 50's, marry, each for the second time. Ilana has a son from her first marriage. George has two daughters from his. Ilana and George purchase, equally, an $800,000 house. If one dies, each wants the other spouse to be able to live in the house for the reminder of his or her life. But after both have died, each wants his or her share of the house to go to the children of their first marriages. So both Ilana and George create marital life estate trusts, allowing the surviving spouse full use of the house until his or her death. Then half the house goes to Ilana's son, and the other half to George's two daughters.

Many different types of controls can be imposed. For example, someone other than the surviving spouse can be named a successor trustee, to manage the marital life estate trust; the successor trustee—whoever it is—can be required to make periodic reports to the final beneficiaries, usually the deceased spouse's children; the successor trustee can be prohibited from selling any property in the marital life estate trust.

5. Powers of Appointment

Someone who wants to provide maximum flexibility for gifts can use something called a "power of appointment." With a power of appointment, one person legally authorizes another to decide what shall be done with that first person's property.

Tim states in his living trust that "I appoint Henry Neale with the general power of appointment to distribute all my musical instruments as he sees fit." After Tim's death, Henry can then give Tim's musical instruments to any people or organizations he chooses—including himself. This is called a "general" power of appointment. A "special" or "limited" power of appointment would limit Henry's power, prohibiting him from giving the instruments to himself, or to his estate or creditors.

Sue wants to assist her "worthy" grandchildren, but not the "rotten" ones (if any). They're all under age 10 now, so Sue isn't sure who will prove worthy. Rather than try to resolve this herself, and keep her estate plan up-to-date with each change, Sue, in her will, gives her daughter a special power of appointment to decide, after Sue dies, which grandchildren are worthy to receive some of Sue's property, and how much.

I've rarely had clients who decided to include a power of appointment in their estate plan. Most knew who they wanted their beneficiaries to be. Even if they were in Sue's situation, they'd decide to aid all their grandchildren and not try to distinguish among "worthy" and "rotten" ones.

 If you do want to use or investigate using powers of appointment in your estate plan, it should be no surprise to learn you'll need to consult a knowledgeable attorney

PART V

Wills

CHAPTER 17

CHAPTER 17

Wills

CHAPTER 17

Wills

A WILL IS what many people think of when they first consider estate planning. Most know what a will is: a document which specifies who gets your property when you die.

After reading this far, you're surely aware of a major problem caused by leaving property by a will—the legal requirement that most wills must go through probate. Indeed, a substantial portion of this book is devoted to explaining methods of avoiding this expensive time-consuming process. However, despite the downside of probate, a will should still be part of every estate plan, at least as a back-up to probate avoidance devices.

A thorough estate plan, the type this book encourages, avoids probate. With this kind of plan, you normally need only a very simple back-up will, which is exactly what this chapter presents. This back-up will enables you to:

- make up to three specific gifts,

- name a residuary beneficiary and alternate for any property subject to your will that is not specifically given to other named beneficiaries,

- name personal and property guardians and alternates for your minor children, and

- name your executor.

Warning: The will forms discussed in this chapter (and set out in the Appendix) are not suitable for those who, despite the specter of probate, decide to make a will the center of their estate plan. For example, these wills are not designed to make a number of major gifts or to establish children's trusts for property left to minor children. If, for any of the reasons discussed in Section B below, you want to use a will to leave the bulk of your property, you will want to use far more detailed will forms. Nolo publishes these in *Nolo's Simple Will Book* and the computer program *WillMaker*. As noted in the order section at the back of this book, Nolo extends a 25% discount on these will resources to all purchasers of this book.

A. Why Prepare a Will?

IF YOU PREPARE AN ESTATE PLAN, including a living trust designed to avoid probate, do you need a back-up will at all? Yes. It's always sensible to have a back-up will as part of your estate plan for one or probably more of the following reasons:

- **To name a personal guardian for your minor children.** You need a will to achieve the vital goal of naming a personal guardian for your minor children. You can't use a trust to appoint a personal guardian. Also, in your will you can appoint a property guardian for them to manage any of their property not otherwise legally supervised by an adult. (As discussed in Chapter 6, Section C, it's generally preferable to leave your minor children property as part of a children's trust rather than relying on a property guardian named in a will, which you name only as a back-up.) As discussed in Section B below, younger people with minor children, who don't have much property, may decide that because naming a personal guardian is the primary thing they're worried about, a simple will is all the estate planning they currently need.

- **To dispose of suddenly-acquired property.** Anyone may end up acquiring valuable property at or shortly before death, such as a sudden gift or inheritance, a lottery prize or a share of joint tenancy property because of simultaneous death. Under the will forms in the Appendix, that property will go to the person you've named as your residuary beneficiary. Unfortunately, there's no easy way to make gifts of these kinds of property through a living trust, since property must be formally added to the trust for it to be subject to the trust provisions.

- **To dispose of property not transferred by a probate avoidance device.** If you buy property after preparing your estate plan, but don't get around to planning probate avoidance for it (by placing it in your living trust, for example), a will is a valuable back-up device, ensuring that the property will go to who you want to have it (your residuary beneficiary), and not pass under the intestate laws. Similarly, if somehow you've failed to transfer some of your existing property to a probate avoidance device—either intentionally or because you didn't properly complete transfers of title—a will prevents that property from passing under the intestate laws.

- **To give away property someone left you that is still in probate.** If someone has left you property by will, and that property is still enmeshed in probate when you die, you can't arrange to transfer it by a probate avoidance device. Since you don't have title to the property, you have no legal right to transfer it. But again, under your will, that property goes to your residuary beneficiary.

- **To disinherit a child (or children).** As explained in Chapter 6, Section E(1), to functionally disinherit a child using a will form from the Appendix, you leave that child only the $1 the will provides, and nothing more.

- **To name your executor.** In your will, you name your executor, the person with legal authority to supervise distribution of property left by your will, and to represent your estate. It can be a good idea to have an executor even if you have also set up a living trust and named a successor trustee to manage it when you die, because banks and other institutions are often reassured to know an executor exists. The successor trustee and executor are often the same person.

- **In case probate is not required.** As explained in Chapter 13, some states don't require probate, or greatly simplify probate, for small or modest estates. If your estate qualifies for simplified treatment, there's no need to use a series of probate avoidance devices— a will is all you need. And in some states, even larger estates can make use of simplified probate. For example, California allows personal property worth up to $60,000 to be transferred by a will without any probate. Property transferred by probate avoidance methods doesn't count toward this $60,000 limit. So, in California (and in some other states), a will can be a useful method for making small gifts—that treasured sea-captain's chest to a close friend, the antique clock to a niece, or $3,000 to a fondly-remembered employee, etc., once you have placed the bulk of your estate in a living trust.

B. People Who Need a More Complex Will

TO REPEAT, the wills in the Appendix are designed as a back-up to probate avoidance devices. For this reason, these wills are truly barebones. If you decide not to engage in extensive estate planning at this time, and have more than a modest estate (roughly over $50,000 worth of property) or minor children, you will most likely need a more complex will than the ones provided in this book.

Despite the costs and delays associated with probate, many people decide to make a will the centerpiece of their estate plan. These include:

- People, no matter what their age or health, who simply don't want the bother of more extensive estate planning. Quite a few people say, "Yes, I guess I should probably do full-scale estate planning, but I never get around to it, so I'd better at least make a will now and think about the full-scale plan later." After all, a simple will easily achieves their basic goal of distributing their property as they see fit, with as little disturbance to themselves as possible. Sure a will is likely to lead to probate, but the goal of probate avoidance, as sensible as it is, should never obscure the more important goal of seeing to it that your property will go to the people and organizations you want to receive it.

- Healthy younger people who know that, statistically, they're unlikely to die for decades. These people primarily want to be certain their basic wishes for their property are carried out in the very unlikely event they die unexpectedly. A will achieves this goal, with considerably less paperwork than does a living trust. Accordingly, many younger people rely primarily on a will and make a probate-avoiding estate plan when they're older and more settled.

- Parents of minor children. The primary estate planning goal of many young parents—single or in couples—is to ensure, to the best of their abilities, that if they die, their children are well provided for and cared for. A will allows parents to name a personal guardian (something that can't be done in a living trust), while also allowing them to establish a simple children's trust to delay the age at which the kids get their hands on the money. Years later, of course, if the parents accumulate considerable property, they may want to engage in more thorough estate planning.

C. Options If You Decide You Want a More Complex Will

If you decide to prepare a more complex will, you can either draft one yourself or hire a lawyer. Happily, many—indeed most—people who need a more complex will than the ones in the Appendix can safely prepare their own, without the cost of a lawyer. I've mentioned *Nolo's Simple Will Book,* a thorough manual which I authored to enable you to prepare a will covering most needs. Also, Nolo/Legisoft publishes an excellent computer software package, *WillMaker,* which allows you to draft and print out a valid will with surprising ease. If you have access to an Apple II series, IBM PC (or clone), or Macintosh computer, *WillMaker* could be exactly what you need.

With *Nolo's Simple Will Book* or *WillMaker,* you can do any of the following:

- make gifts of cash or specific items of property;
- name alternate beneficiaries for each gift;
- name a residuary beneficiary to receive all property subject to the will not given to other-named beneficiaries;
- name personal and property guardians for your minor children, and also name successor guardians, in case your first choices can't serve.
- name different personal or property guardians for different children (*Nolo's Simple Will Book* only);
- establish a basic trust for any property you leave to your children. This allows you to specify the age at which each child gets his or her property outright. In the meantime, the trustee can spend money for the child's basic needs, such as health, housing and education;
- disinherit a child;
- forgive debts;
- specify what assets you want used to pay death taxes or debts;
- give real estate free of a mortgage (*Nolo's Simple Will Book* only);
- establish a "no contest" clause which disinherits any beneficiary who unsuccessfully challenges your will.

Is there anything you could possibly want in a will that can't be accomplished by using *Nolo's Simple Will Book* or *WillMaker*? Yes.You can't use either to create an ongoing trust that may continue in force for years after your death to manage property for people other than your children, or for tax savings purposes. As explained in Chapter 16, ongoing trusts haven't yet been made the subject of a competent do-it-yourself book. If you want to create any type of ongoing trust in your will, such as a marital life estate trust or a trust for a person with special needs, you'll need to see a lawyer. Also, you can't use either *Nolo's Simple Will Book* or *WillMaker* to make a gift of either a "future interest"—a gift which takes effect a significant time after you die—or a "conditional" gift— one which may or may not occur, depending on whether the conditions necessary for it to be made occur.

D. General Information About Wills

BEFORE I GET TO THE FORMS and instructions necessary for you to create a back-up will, let's pause for a moment and consider wills generally. Many people have questions about wills—how they work, what you can or can't do with one, who you can disinherit, how a will can be challenged. Here I briefly discuss (and hopefully answer) some of these major questions—which apply to all wills, back-up or not.

1. What Makes a Will Legal?

Drafting a legal will isn't nearly as complicated as most people fear. The requirements are:

- You must be a legal adult (at least 18 years old in all states except Alabama, where you must be at least 19 to leave real estate by will);

- You must be of "sound mind." The fact that you're reading and understanding this book is, as a practical matter, sufficient evidence that you meet this test.

- Your will must comply with the technical will-drafting requirements of your state's law. In general, these requirements are very similar in all states, and are less onerous than many people imagine. These technical requirements are:

- The will must be typewritten or printed on a computer printer [see Section D(2) for a discussion of handwritten wills];

- The will must have at least one substantive provision. The most common one gives some, or all, of your property to whoever you want to have it;

- You must appoint at least one executor;

- You must date the will;

- You must sign the will in front of three witnesses— people who don't inherit under the will. Some states only require two witnesses, but using three ensures that you've met the requirements of every state and, in any case, is safer. Witnesses watch you sign your will and then sign it themselves. They must be told that it's your will they are signing, but they don't have to read or be told what the will contains.

Those are all the basic technical requirements. There's no requirement that a will be notarized,[1] recorded, or filed with any governmental agency. Years ago, when I was a partner in a small law firm, we learned that some

---

[1]However, in many states, having the witnesses sign what's called a "self-proving" affidavit, which is then notarized, can eliminate any need for a witness to testify at subsequent probate proceedings. "Self-proving" wills are explained in detail in *Nolo's Simple Will Book*, Chapter 13, Section D.

clients were disappointed that their wills didn't look more impressive. So we began stapling all wills in a blue cover-binder, and attaching a red ribbon and red wax seal. Some clients appreciated these touches—although they were not legally required. If you want extras like these, you can purchase what you need at most stationery stores, for far less than if you buy them from a lawyer.

2. Are Handwritten Wills Valid?

"Holographic" is legalese for handwritten. A holographic will must be written, dated and signed entirely in the handwriting of the person making the will. It needn't be witnessed. Holographic wills are recognized by about 25 states. I definitely don't recommend them, even in the states where they're legal, and therefore don't cover them in detail in this book.

Holographic wills aren't recommended because probate courts traditionally have been very strict when examining them after the death of the writer. One reason for this is that since a handwritten will isn't normally witnessed, judges sometimes fear that it might have been forged. Also, there's often the need to prove that the will was actually and voluntarily written by the deceased person, which sometimes isn't easy to do. In short, given the tiny bit of extra trouble it takes to type out a will and have it witnessed, it's reckless not to do it.

3. What Are 'Statutory Wills'?

A statutory will is a pre-printed, fill-in-the-blanks, check-the-boxes will form authorized by state law. California, Wisconsin, Michigan and Maine have statutory wills, and other states are considering them. In theory, statutory wills are an excellent idea—inexpensive, easy to complete, and reliable. Unfortunately, in practice, statutory wills are so limited in scope they aren't useful for most people. The choices provided in the statutory forms are quite narrow and cannot legally be changed—that is, you

can't customize them to fit your situation or, indeed, change them at all. For example, the California Statutory Will allows you to make one, and only one, cash gift. All your other property must go to your spouse or children. Thus, these statutory wills are useful to you only if you are married and want all your property to go to your spouse (or, if she predeceases you, in trust for your minor children). But even if you're married, if you want to use your will to leave some of your property, beyond one cash gift, to relatives or friends, you cannot use the statutory will.

4. What Other Types of Wills Are There?

There are no other types of wills useful for most people. But just to cover all the bases, some other kinds of wills that people occasionally ask about are:

- *Oral wills.* Oral wills (also called "nuncupative" wills) are valid in a minority of states and, even where valid, are acceptable only if made under special circumstances, such as the will maker's perception of imminent death. Some states impose far more restrictive limits. For example, in California, an oral will can be made only by someone serving in the Armed Forces, just before death, for personal property worth less than $1,000. Not much help there, obviously.

- *Video or film wills.* Video or film wills aren't valid under any state's law. But films of a person reciting who they give property to can be useful evidence if a will is challenged, to demonstrate that the will maker was competent and didn't appear crazy or duped.

 If you fear a will contest based on your lack of competence or the undue influence of a beneficiary, ask a lawyer about using videos or films.

- *Joint wills.* A joint will is one document made by two people, who are usually married. Each leaves everything to the other when the first one dies, and then the will goes on to specify what happens to the property when the second person dies. In effect, a joint will can prevent the surviving person from changing his mind regarding what should happen to the survivors. I don't recommend joint wills. They may tie up property for years, pending the second death. Also, even if circumstances change radically, it can be unclear whether the survivor can revoke any part of the will. If you want to impose controls over property you leave to your spouse, the sensible way to do it is through a marital life estate trust. (See Chapter 16, Section B.)

- *Contracts to make a will.* A contract to make a will—that is, to leave certain property to the other person who signs the contract—can be valid but is usually not wise. The usual case in which such contracts are made is where someone provides services—care, or live-in nursing—in return for an agreement that the person receiving the care will leave property to the person providing the care. Tying up your property like this so you cannot change your will, even if circumstances change, isn't desirable for many reasons. Most lawyers prefer to establish a trust for these situations.

 If you face a situation in which you want to guarantee now that someone will receive money from your estate, seea lawyer.

- *Living wills.* A living will (sometimes called a "Directive to Physicians") isn't a conventional will at all, but a document in which the writer states that she wants a natural death and doesn't want her life artificially prolonged by use of life support equipment. As discussed in Chapter 18, a better way to provide binding instructions regarding the termination of life support systems is by use of a durable power of attorney.

5. What Property Cannot Be Transferred by Will?

Throughout this book, I have emphasized the fact that property transferred by a binding probate avoidance device can't also be transferred by will. Another way to make this point is to emphasize that once property is placed in one of the following forms of ownership, listing it in a will has no force and affect. The following property cannot be transferred by will:

- *all* joint tenancy property—it automatically goes to the surviving joint tenants (but if all joint tenants die simultaneously, you can transfer your share by will);
- *all* property in a living trust—it goes to the beneficiaries under the trust;
- life insurance proceeds payable to a named beneficiary or beneficiaries—they go to the beneficiaries of the policy;
- retirement plans, pensions, IRAs, Keoghs, etc., payable to named beneficiaries—the beneficiaries in these programs get these assets no matter what your will says; and
- informal bank account trusts or pay-on-death accounts—the person you designate as beneficiary on the account document inherits.

6. Can My Will Be Successfully Challenged?

The fact that many people worry about the possibility of challenges to their wills (or other transfer documents such as a living trust), shows how fear-ridden estate planning has become. Fortunately, the reality is that will challenges, let alone successful ones, are exceedingly rare. The legal grounds for contesting a will are limited to extreme circumstances. Basically, your will can only be invalidated if you were under-age when you made it, were clearly mentally incompetent, or the will was procured by fraud, duress or undue influence.

A person has to be pretty far gone before a court will rule that she lacked the capacity to make a valid will. For example, forgetfulness or even the inability to recognize friends don't by themselves establish incapacity. Also, it's important to remember that courts will presume that the will writer was of sound mind, unless someone challenges this in a court proceeding—which is rare. Similarly, a will is rarely declared invalid on grounds it was procured by fraud, duress or undue influence; this requires proof that some evildoer manipulated a person in a confused or weakened mental or emotional state to leave his property in a way the person otherwise wouldn't have.

 If you think there's any possibility anyone might challenge your will or estate plan, see a lawyer. Or if there are special circumstances, such as a seriously debilitating illness, that you believe might raise questions about the validity of your will, it's prudent to see a lawyer. In practice, of course, this can mean having the lawyer come to see and perhaps even physically help you. For example, in many states, if you're too ill to sign your own name, you can direct that a witness or an attorney sign it for you. In any unusual physical or mental circumstances, it's prudent to have a lawyer's assistance, especially if substantial amounts of property are involved. It could always be claimed that someone too ill to sign her name wasn't mentally competent. In any subsequent court challenge to the will, the lawyer's testimony that the will maker appeared to be in full possession of his or her faculties could be very important.

7. Does Divorce Automatically Revoke Gifts in a Will Made to a Former Spouse?

Not in every state. In any case, you should always revise your will and bring your estate plan up to date after a divorce. (See Chapter 23.)

8. What Happens If I Have a Child or Marry After I Make a Will?

If you have a child or get married after you make your will, you must revise your will, and your estate plan, to reflect your new situation. If you don't, your estate may become entangled in laws designed to protect "afterborn children" and spouses married after a will and other estate planning documents were prepared. In any case, most people who have a child or get married after they make their will and estate plan want to revise those documents to provide for the new child or spouse.

9. Who Should I Name as Executor?

Your executor should be the person you trust the most— and who's willing to do the job. If you plan to prepare a living trust, it's best that your executor be the same person as the one you've chosen to be the successor trustee of your trust.

You can name co-executors, or even several executors, if you have good reason for it. As with successor trustees of a living trust, I generally recommend having only one trustee. However, there can be compelling reasons— family harmony is one example—for selecting more than one trustee.

One caution here: Some states require that your executor must either live in your state or, if she doesn't, must post a bond. This costs your estate money solely to provide a bond your estate won't need if your executor is honest. In any case, it's a good idea to name at least one executor who does live in your state.

10. Can I Give My Property as I Choose?

Pragmatically, you can leave property to anyone and for any purpose you choose, except that in common law states, your spouse has a right to a certain percentage of your property. (See Chapter 3, Section C.) The few other legal limits restricting your power to give away your property however you choose rarely apply. For example, there are limits on how long you can tie up property after you die. If you want to mandate that property remain in your family for generations, you've got problems. Also, you cannot leave money for some socially-disapproved purposes, such as a gift contingent on the divorce of the beneficiary.

11. Can I Disinherit Whomever I Wish?

Aside from the rights of a spouse mentioned above, you can disinherit anyone you choose. As previously discussed in Chapter 6, anyone but a child (or a grandchild, if your child is deceased) can be disinherited simply by omitting to name him or her as a beneficiary of your will or living trust. However, if you decide to disinherit a child or a child of a deceased child you must specifically state so in your will—for example, "I disinherit my son, Nero, and declare he shall receive nothing from my estate." You can also leave a child a minimal amount—$1 or so—which functions as a disinheritance. This method can be used with the will forms in the Appendix, which automatically leave $1 to each of your children. If you disinherit a child, evaluate the possibility that the child will challenge your will and estate plan.

 If you conclude that it's a serious risk (and especially if you are very ill or aged), discuss the matter with an expert before finalizing a decision to disinherit a child.

12. What Happens If I Move?

If you use a will form provided in this book, your will is valid in any state except Louisiana.[2] However, it's often advisable to draft a new will after a permanent move, because it's wise to appoint an executor of your will who is nearby. Also, if you're married and move from a common law property state to a community property state or vice versa, the marital property ownership laws of your new state may affect your will.

13. Can I Give Property to Minors in My Will?

As previously explained, minor children cannot own substantial amounts of property outright. Gifts to minors —your own children or someone else's—can be made by various legal methods: trusts, gifts, a gift made under the Uniform Transfers to Minors Act, or gifts managed by a property guardian. Making gifts to be supervised by a property guardian is generally the least desirable of these alternatives. (See Chapter 6, Section C.)

14. What Happens if My Spouse or Mate and I Die at the Same Time?

The will form for a married person contains a "simultaneous death" clause. The objective of this clause is to provide for what happens if a husband and wife die in the same accident and it can't be determined who died first. Under these circumstances, the clause creates the presumption that the will maker survives his or her spouse. If both husband and wife use a will from *Plan Your Estate*, the husband is presumed to survive the wife for purposes of his will property, and the wife is presumed to survive the husband for purposes of her will property. Although at first glance this clause may appear to be contradictory if contained in the wills of both spouses, it is a standard, well-accepted clause. Because each spouse's will is inter-

---

[2]Louisiana law is based on a different source (the Napoleonic Code) than the laws of the other states.

preted separately, the clause acts to distribute each spouse's property as his or her own will provides.

Signing and Witnessing Your Will

To be valid, your will must be signed and dated in front of three witnesses. Then, these witnesses must sign the will in your presence, and also in the presence of the other witnesses.

While state laws vary as to how many witnesses you need, three meets the requirements of every state. Even if your state only requires two witnesses, three is better because it provides one more person to establish that your signature is valid during probate, if that becomes necessary.

Witnesses need only be:

- Adults (usually over 18) and of sound mind;
- People who won't inherit under the will. That means anyone who is to receive of any gift in your will cannot be a witness;
- People who should be easy to locate in the event of your death. This usually means choosing people who aren't likely to move around a lot and who are younger than you are.

Here's how to go about arranging for signing and witnessing your will:

- Have the three witnesses assemble in one place.
- Tell them that the papers you hold is your will. They don't need to know what's in it.
- Sign the signature page in the witnesses' presence. Remember to sign the will using the exact spelling of your name as you typed in the heading. This should be the form of the name you use to sign such documents as deeds, checks and loan applications. This needn't necessarily be the way your name appears on your birth or marriage certificate.
- Have each witness sign the last page in the place indicated while the other witnesses are watching. The clause immediately preceding the witnesses' signatures states ("attests") that the events outlined just above have occurred.

Important: If a will doesn't comply with the technical requirements (say you had only one witness to your will), it cannot be validated by the probate court. It's not hard to do a will correctly. But it's wise to double-check to be sure you've done so!

E.   Preparing a Back-Up Will

IF YOU DECIDE a will from this book is appropriate for you, you'll actually prepare that will from either Form VI (for one person) or Form VII (for a member of a couple. Both members of a couple must each prepare a will). Instructions for preparing your will are given in this section. In Section E, you'll find an example of a will, drafted from the form for one person (Form VI) so you can see how a finished one looks.

Here are the steps necessary to prepare your own will from a will form in the Appendix:

- Read this chapter carefully.

- Read through the will form carefully. There are a number of blanks to fill in. The information called for is identified by the words below each line. Most of this is self-explanatory. For example, if you have minor children, you'll nominate a personal guardian for them. You choose this personal guardian in Chapter 6, Section A. With a few blanks, you'll see circled numbers, keyed to the following points:

- *Naming your children's property guardian.* This person is normally the same as the successor trustee of your living trust. Similarly, the alternate property guardian is normally the same as the alternate successor trustee.

- *Naming your executor.* This person is also normally the same as the successor trustee of your living trust. Similarly, the alternate executor is normally the same as the alternate successor trustee.

Use a pencil and fill in the blanks in the form. Draw a line through any printed material in the form you want to delete. If you delete an entire section, you may need to renumber subsequent sections;

Once you're satisfied that your will is what you want, have the final draft of your will carefully typed (or printed out if you use a computer), double-spaced, on good 8 1/2" x 11" paper. Proofread it carefully and make sure it's letter perfect. If you find mistakes, retype the entire document.

It's never advisable, and is illegal in many states, to make alterations on the face of your will by crossing something out and initialing the change. Once the will is signed and witnessed, you can only amend or revoke it by the legal methods described in Chapter 23. In any case, it's obviously not desirable to leave a will filled with corrections that might be misinterpreted later. Your will is an important document. Have a completely clean copy typed before you sign it.

Sign and date your will in front of three witnesses, and have the witnesses sign the will.

F.   Sample Draft Will

THE FOLLOWING SAMPLES show you: (1) what a will form from this chapter can look like when a draft has been completed and the will is ready to be typed and (2) the final will after it has been typed.

In this sample, the will writer is Benjamin Werrin, who is single and has one adult child, Eric, who is his residuary beneficiary. His executor (and alternate beneficiary, should Eric die before he does) is his best friend, Gil Nason. The portions of the will completed by Mr. Werrin are in handwriting, so you can readily distinguish between the printed portion of the will and those portions completed by Mr. Werrin. There's a handwritten line drawn through printed words which Mr. Werrin deleted, so you can see what has been crossed out, and how to cross it out. The final version of Mr. Werrin's will, including all handwritten materials, should, of course, be typed; the material crossed out in the draft would simply be omitted in the final.

Form VI. Basic Will for One Person

Will

of

Benjamin Werrin
~~your name~~

I, Benjamin Werrin ~~your name~~, a resident of Fairmont ~~city~~, Duchess ~~county~~, New York ~~state~~, declare that this is my will.

(1) I revoke all wills and codicils that I previously have made.

(2) (A) I am not married.

(B) I am the father ~~mother/father~~ of the children whose name is: Eric Werrin

---

There are ___ living children of my deceased child _____ name

whose names are:

(C) If at my death any of my children are minors, and a guardian is needed, I recommend that _____ name be appointed guardian of the person(s) of my minor children. If _____ name cannot serve as personal guardian, I recommend that _____ name be appointed personal guardian.

(D) I appoint _____ name ① as property guardian for my minor children. If _____ name ① cannot serve as property guardian, I recommend that _____ name ① be appointed property guardian.

(E) I direct that no bond be required of any guardian.

(3) (A) In addition to any other property I may give, by this will or otherwise to the person(s) listed in Section 2(B), I give each person listed there One Dollar ($1.00).

(B) I give all my cameras ~~property described~~ to Sid Tropinsky name, or if Sid Tropinsky ~~name~~ fails to survive me, to Nancy Werrin name.

On the date last written above, _Benjamin Werrin_ [your name] declared to us, the undersigned, that this instrument was _his_ [~~his/her~~] will, and requested us to act as witnesses to it. _He_ [~~he/she~~] thereupon signed this will in our presence, all of us being present at the same time. We now at _his_ [~~his/her~~] request and in _his_ [~~his/her~~] presence, and in the presence of each other, have signed such instrument as witnesses.

We declare under penalty of perjury that the foregoing is true and correct.

_____
witness signature

_____ , _____
city   county

_____
state

_____
witness signature

_____ , _____
city   county

_____
state

_____
witness signature

_____ , _____
city   county

_____
state

I give _____ [~~residuary beneficiary's name~~] _____ property described _____ to _____ , or if _____ name _____ fails to survive me, to _____ name.

I give _____ property described _____ to _____ , or if _____ name _____ fails to survive me, to _____ name.

(C) I give all my other property subject to this will to _Eric Werrin_ [~~residuary beneficiary's name~~], or if _he_ [~~he/she~~] fails to survive me, to _Gil Nason_ [~~alternate beneficiary's name~~].

(4) (A) I nominate _Gil Nason_ ② [~~executor's name~~] to serve as executor of my will, or, if _he_ [~~he/she~~] is unable to serve or to continue serving as executor, I nominate _Nancy Werrin_ ② [~~alternate executor's name~~] to serve as executor.

(B) No bond shall be required of any executor.

I subscribe my name to this Will this _____ day of _____ , 19__ at _Fairmont_ [~~city~~], _Duchess_ [~~county~~], _New York_ [~~state~~].

_____
your signature

Will

of

Benjamin Werrin

I, Benjamin Werrin, a resident of Fairmont, Duchess County, New York, declare that this is my will.

(1) I revoke all wills and codicils that I previously have made.

(2) (A) I am not married.

(B) I am the father of the child whose name is Eric Werrin.

(3) (A) In addition to any other property I may give to the person(s) listed in Section 2(B), by this will or otherwise, I give each person listed there One Dollar ($1.00).

(B) I give all my cameras to Sid Tropinsky, or if Sid Tropinsky fails to survive me, to Nancy Werrin.

(C) I give all my other property subject to this will to Eric Werrin, or if he fails to survive me, to Gil Nason.

(4) (A) I nominate Gil Nason to serve as executor of my will, or if he is unable to serve or continue serving as executor, I nominate Nancy Werrin to serve as executor.

(B) No bond shall be required of any executor.

I subscribe my name to this will this _____ day of _____,

19___, at Fairmont, Duchess County, New York.

On the date last written above, Benjamin Werrin declared to us, the undersigned, that this instrument was his will, and requested us to act as witnesses to it. He thereupon signed this will in our presence, all of us being present at the same time. We now at his request and in his presence, and in the presence of each other, have signed such instrument as witnesses.

We declare under penalty of perjury that the foregoing is true and correct.

_____
witness signature

_____ , _____
city   county

_____
state

_____
witness signature

_____ , _____
city   county

_____
state

_____
witness signature

_____ , _____
city   county

_____
state

PART VI

Practical Matters and Special Problems

CHAPTERS 18-21

Durable Powers of Attorney and Living Wills

CHAPTER 18

Durable Powers of Attorney
and Living Wills

WE TEND TO THINK of estate planning as something we do now to take care of what happens when we die. While this definition has the advantage of being neat and tidy, it's a bit too simple. As we grow older, many of us face the stern reality that before we die we may not be mentally or physically competent for some period of time, sometimes an extended period. I believe that a thorough estate plan must consider this possibility. If your health deteriorates and you become incompetent to make financial or medical decisions, there must be another adult with legal authority to make decisions for you.

There are two ways to deal with this possibility:

1. Do nothing, and, if you ever become incapacitated, let a judge appoint someone, called a conservator or guardian (depending on the state) to make decisions for you. Court proceedings for incapacitated persons are almost always undesirable, unless you have no choice. These are costly, time-consuming, and expose to public concern what most people prefer to keep private.

Sometimes, people simply ignore the requirement of court proceedings: a niece signs her ill aunt's name to the aunt's retirement check, for example. Unfortunately, there's an unpleasant legal term for this act—forgery. So ignoring the law isn't wise, and often not practical either. Over an extended period of time, it's hard to adequately manage another's affairs by continually signing his name to financial documents, especially if he owns different types of property.

2. Use a document called a "durable power of attorney" to make your own binding choice of who will have authority to act for you in the event of your incapacity. Creation of a durable power of attorney in advance is a sensible, inexpensive alternative to the risk of court proceedings. In some states, you can also create what is called a "living will" to specify what you want done regarding use of life support equipment and procedures.

The Power of Attorney Book, Clifford (Nolo Press), explains in detail how to prepare each of these documents, which vary from state to state. But because planning for possible incapacity is so inextricably related to estate planning, I also briefly review the issues involved here. Also, if you use one of the living trust forms in the Appendix, you will create a rough equivalent of a durable power of attorney with respect to the property placed in your trust.

A. An Overview of Durable Powers of Attorney

A POWER OF ATTORNEY is a legal document in which one person gives another person legal authority to act for him or her. A "durable" power of attorney remains legally effective until the death of the person who created it, even if that person becomes incapacitated. You can use a durable power of attorney to authorize someone to make medical and financial decisions for you if you are incapacitated and can't make them yourself.

The essence of a durable power of attorney is self-control. You, not some judge, determine who will have legal authority to act for you if you become incapacitated. You can retain all control over your affairs unless and until incapacity occurs. If it does, you have determined what restrictions and directions are imposed on the person you've named to act for you.

Other advantages of a durable power of attorney include:

- It's a reasonably short document and is normally not difficult to prepare.

- The person who creates it doesn't need to transfer title of her assets.

- It can always be revoked by the principal, unless the principal becomes incapacitated.

- No court review or approval is needed.

- Normally, it doesn't have to be filed or recorded with any governmental agency.

1. How Durable Powers of Attorney Work

The person creating a durable power of attorney is called the "principal." The person he appoints to act for him is called the "attorney-in-fact." You can also appoint someone to act for you in case your first choice can't, an "alternate attorney-in-fact." The attorney-in-fact can be any person the principal chooses, and most definitely doesn't have to be a lawyer. It's typical for one spouse to appoint the other, or a parent to appoint one or more trusted children, to fulfill this function.

A durable power of attorney can be prepared so that it goes into effect *only* if you become incapacitated. This is called a "springing" durable power of attorney. It is the kind most people want; they're healthy now, but they want to provide for what should be done if they later become incapacitated.

Donna is 80 and healthy, but worried about what might happen to her in future years. She prepares a springing durable power of attorney, authorizing her daughter Janette to make medical and financial decisions for her if (and only if) Donna becomes incapacitated and can't make those decisions for herself. She requires that her doctor determine that she's become incapacitated before the durable power of attorney can "spring" into effectiveness.

Another type of durable power of attorney becomes effective on signing. With this type, the attorney-in-fact immediately has authority to make decisions for the principal. This type of durable power of attorney might be advisable for someone with a life-threatening illness, or who is facing major surgery, or who knows he's declining into advanced stages of Alzheimer's disease.

Durable powers of attorney are used for two vital areas: finances and health care. In either, or both, areas, with very few limits, you can put in whatever specifications, qualifications and limitations you want on the powers you grant your attorney-in-fact to manage your financial affairs and make medical decisions.

Freidel, who is elderly and frail, prepares a springing durable power of attorney authorizing her niece, Patricia, to be her attorney-in-fact for medical and financial decisions in the event Freidel becomes incapacitated. Freidel trusts Patricia. However, Freidel is nevertheless fearful that, somehow, her home might be sold, even though Patricia has promised she would never do this. So Freidel writes into her durable power of attorney a provision that "In no event shall my attorney-in-fact have authority or power to sell, transfer or otherwise encumber my home at 222 Fern Street, Atlanta, Georgia."

Sara is seriously ill, faces major surgery, and knows that for some time she will be unable to make all her own medical and health care decisions. She prepares a durable power of attorney, delegating to her sister, Kendell, the authority to make health care decisions for her. To make sure that her own wishes are complied with, she inserts several restrictions regarding Kendell's power. Specifically, Sara wants to be operated on by Dr. June Lee at Mattan Hospital. So, in defining the attorney-in-fact's authority, she includes the following clause:

"My attorney-in-fact shall comply with my stated desire that all surgery performed on me be done at Mattan Hospital [address], by Dr. June Lee, unless Dr. Lee is unable to perform such surgery."

Theodore, who is ill, decides to appoint his son, Jason, as his attorney-in-fact to handle his financial affairs. Theodore has two other children, Nancy and Ed, who don't live in Theodore's state. Nancy and Ed aren't on the best of terms with Jason. To try to prevent suspicion or conflict between his children over Jason's handling of Theodore's finances, Theodore decides to require Jason to prepare quarterly reports of all financial transactions he engages in as attorney-in-fact and send them to Nancy and Ed. To accomplish this, Theodore inserts the following clause in his durable power of attorney:

"The attorney-in-fact shall prepare quarterly reports of all financial transactions he engages in for or with any asset of the Principal. A copy of each such report shall be mailed to Nancy Byrne and Edward Post within 14 days of preparation."

2. Living Trusts and Powers of Attorney

The living trust forms in the Appendix provide that your successor trustee will manage the trust property for you if you become incapacitated. Even if you use a durable power of attorney to appoint someone (your attorney-in-fact) to handle your property if you become incapacitated, property in your living trust still remains subject to your successor trustee, not the attorney-in-fact. This division is typically only one of terminology, not substance, as most people appoint the same person to handle both jobs.

Some people who plan to transfer all of their property under a living trust ask why they need bother with a durable power of attorney at all. There are two reasons. First, only by using a durable power of attorney can you appoint a person who you want to make health care decisions for you if you become incapacitated. Second, you are likely to receive income after you become incapacitated, from pensions, social security and other sources, and you will need an attorney-in-fact to deal with this money, and maintain your personal bank account, pay bills, etc.

B. Terminal Illnesses and Durable Powers of Attorney

WE ALL UNDERSTAND that modern medical technology often has the ability to keep an incurably ill person alive for an extended period of time. We also understand that the odds that this might happen to each of us are higher than we would like. One good indication that this is a serious possibility is that, currently, over 80% of all deaths in the United States occur in institutions (hospitals, old age homes), whereas only a generation ago it was less than 50%. To many, the possibility of being institutionalized and hooked up to a tangle of wire and tubes, helplessly dependent with no hope of recovering normal life, is a nightmare. Increasingly, many people feel this kind of "living" isn't life and isn't worth it. If they have an irreversible disease, they choose to die a "natural" death, rather than to prolong life artificially.

Fortunately, by using a durable power of attorney you can specify, in advance, what you want done regarding life support systems in the event you become incapacitated and unable to express your own desires.

Basically, you have three options in your durable power of attorney for health care:

1. Require the use of life support systems.

2. Prohibit the use of life support systems to artificially prolong life when you have been diagnosed as "incurably ill" or having a "terminal condition."

3. Delegate the decision regarding use of life support equipment to your attorney-in-fact.

Most people I've worked with have chosen the second option. Their intent is to prohibit use of life support systems and to allow themselves a "natural death" if extending life by artificial means is clearly pointless. An example of a durable owner of attorney for health care prepared by a New York resident, directing that no life support equipment be used if his condition is terminal, is shown below.

Before a hospital will discontinue life support systems of an incapacitated person who authorized it in a durable power of attorney, the person must have a "fatal,"

Springing Durable Power of Attorney for Health Care

1. Creation of Durable Power of Attorney

To my family, relatives, friends and my physicians, health care providers, community care facilities and any other person who may have an interest or duty in my medical care or treatment: I, __Martin O'Corbett__ [name],

being of sound mind, willfully and voluntarily intend to create by this document a durable power of attorney for my health care by appointing the person designated as my attorney in fact to make health care decisions for me in the event I become incapacitated and am unable to make health care decisions for myself. This power of attorney shall not be affected by my subsequent incapacity.

2. Designation of Attorney in Fact

The person designated to be my attorney in fact for health care in the event I become incapacitated is __Edward Finstowald__ [name], of __1711 Leprett Road, White Plains, NY__ [address]. If __he__, for any reason shall fail to serve or ceases to serve as my attorney in fact for health care, __Sue O'Corbett__ [name], of __55 Monk St., Queens, NY__ [address] shall be my attorney in fact for health care.

3. Effective on Incapacity

This durable power of attorney shall become effective in the event I become incapacitated and am unable to make health care decisions for myself, in which case it shall become effective as of the date of the written statement by a physician, as provided in Paragraph 4.

4. Determination of Incapacity

(a) The determination that I have become incapacitated and am unable to make health care decisions shall be made in writing by a licensed physician. If possible, the determination shall be made by __Dr. Phil Spats__ [name of physician], __St. Vincents Hospital, Queens, NY__ [address].

(b) In the event that a licensed physician has made a written determination that I have become incapacitated and am not able to make health care decisions for myself, that written statement shall be attached to the original document of this durable power of attorney.

5. Authority of My Attorney in Fact

My attorney in fact shall have all lawful authority permissible to make health care decisions for me, including the authority to consent, or withdraw consent or refuse consent to any care, treatment, service or procedure to maintain, diagnose or treat my physical or mental condition, EXCEPT _if I have a terminal condition, I direct that no life support procedures or equipment be used, and I be permitted a natural death._

6. Inspection and Disclosure of Information Relating to My Physical or Mental Health

Subject to any limitations in this document, my attorney in fact has the power and authority to do all of the following:

(a) Request, review, and receive any information, verbal or written, regarding my physical or mental health, including, but not limited to, medical and hospital records.

(b) Execute on my behalf any releases or other documents that may be required in order to obtain this information.

(c) Consent to the disclosure of this information.

7. Signing Documents, Waivers, and Releases

Where necessary to implement the health care decisions that my attorney in fact is authorized by this document to make, my attorney in fact has the power and authority to execute on my behalf all of the following:

(a) Documents titled or purporting to be a "Refusal to Permit Treatment" and "Leaving Hospital Against Medical Advice."

(b) Any necessary waiver or release from liability required by a hospital or physician.

8. Duration

I intend that this Durable Power of Attorney remain effective until my death, or until revoked by me in writing.

Executed this __7th__ day of __June__, 19__89__ at __White Plains, NY__.

__Martin O'Corbett__
Principal

"terminal" or "irreversible" disease or condition. Most people, including doctors, seem to have a good gut knowledge of what's meant by a "fatal" or "terminal" condition, but logically, things aren't so clear. After all, from one perspective, we all have a terminal condition. Functionally, though, the juxtaposition of the requirement that a person's condition be hopeless, and the inherent conservatism of doctors and hospitals, who insist on preserving life if there's even the slightest chance of recovery, seems to work well.

If you check in advance with your doctor and hospital to see what they require in a durable power of attorney form and how they feel about termination of life support equipment, you should increase your chances that your durable power of attorney will be honored. If they are dubious about durable powers of attorney, you may need to find new medical people.

C. Living Wills

A "LIVING WILL" is confusingly named. It isn't a form of a conventional will used to transfer your property after your death. Rather, a living will is a document you can use, in a majority of states, to express what you want done regarding life support systems should you be diagnosed as being terminally ill. State laws on living wills vary significantly. And the document itself can go by other names than a living will; it's sometimes called a "Directive to Physicians," for example.

In recent years, the durable power of attorney discussed above has come to be the primary legal device used to allow people to make binding decisions regarding health care matters, including use of life support systems.

As durable powers of attorney for health care have become widely accepted, use of living wills, which were the first legal device used to deal with the problems raised by life support systems, has declined. Despite the fact that a living will has a catchy name, a durable power of attorney is, generally, a preferable way of expressing your desires regarding use of life support equipment. A living will is more limited because:

- A living will is addressed only to physicians. You normally cannot use a living will to appoint someone to make health care decisions for you or, more importantly, to see to it that your wishes are, in fact, carried out.

- In many states, living wills are binding only if signed after you have been informed you have a "terminal condition."

- Living wills apply only to use of life support systems; other health care decisions can't be covered.

- To prepare a living will, you usually must use a statutorily-required form and cannot make any significant changes in that form. For instance, you generally cannot specify in your own words what you mean by "life support systems." Nor can you express any of your own detailed desires regarding medical treatment.

Still, if you are the cautious type, you may decide to prepare a living will as well as a durable power of attorney for health care. The desire not to have life unnaturally extended by life support systems is so vital to many people (and the right to a natural death is a new area of law and medicine), that it can't hurt to express your desires in more than one legal form. Just make sure any living will you prepare is consistent with what you've provided in your durable power of attorney.

Organ Donation, Funerals and Burials

CHAPTER 19

Organ Donation, Funerals and Burials

PEOPLE FACING THE GRIEF and reality that someone they love has died face other immediate problems—disposing of the body and arranging the ceremonies desired to mark the death. It's hard to even talk directly about a body once life has left it; the word "corpse" sounds unfeeling and "cadaver" is worse. Statutes often refer to a dead body as "the remains," a word technically accurate and almost as disturbing. Perhaps it's because we don't like to think about death that the language we have invented for it's so awkward. But, however it is described, the reality is the same: a dead body must, somehow, be removed from the place of death and disposed of, rapidly. And then, if desired, commemorative ceremonies need to be scheduled.

Most people die in hospitals or nursing homes. These institutions want a dead body removed fast—and legally. So it's near-inevitable, if no planning has been done, for family or friends to turn to "professionals"—funeral homes. Often this is done without reflection, or even much knowledge, of what the traditional funeral parlor burial is or what it costs. This passive approach often means family and friends pay far too much for a funeral they don't even like.

Grief, sorrow, religious conviction, doubt, or whatever else survivors are feeling often leave them distraught and confused. In these circumstances, the expense of practical problems can seem trivial. However, I feel it's no slight to the deceased, or to the feelings of those who survive, to suggest that nothing is gained by needless expense. Funerals are expensive. Indeed, the traditional funeral, which can easily cost thousands of dollars, is one of the most expensive items normally purchased by an American family. To many, including this author, this is a huge and unnecessary cost to comply with the biblical injunction: "Remember, man, thou art dust and to dust thou shall return."

A. Making Your Own Choices

MORE AND MORE people are reflecting on what they want to happen to their bodies when they die, and making choices that have emotional meaning for them, as well as saving their families needless expense.

Broadly viewed, there are four choices available:[1]

1. Donating the entire body to a medical school. This must be arranged beforehand. If this is done, there's no burial to worry about. Specific body organs can also be donated to an organ bank. If organs are donated, however, the body is normally returned (without the removed organs) to those responsible for burial, which means that you still must arrange for its disposal.

2. A traditional funeral service conducted by a commercial funeral home, with burial in a cemetery.

3. A simpler funeral service, without embalming of the body, provided either through membership in a cooperative funeral society or by independent arrangements,[2] with burial in a cemetery.

4. Cremation, which can be arranged through funeral homes, funeral societies, or commercial enterprises specializing in low-cost cremations (irreverently called "burn and scatter outfits" in the trade). Cremations can be combined with whatever other services or commemorations are desired.

Planning for the immediate, practical aspects of your death is essential to make sure your wishes are carried out. To take one example, if you wish to donate body parts or organs, it's almost essential to authorize it, in writing, before your death. Similarly, if you want a non-traditional funeral, such as cremation with your ashes scattered over the sea, it may not happen unless you arrange the details yourself. (Each state has rules governing how and where ashes may be scattered.) Even for a traditional commer-

---

[1] I don't cover some of the more esoteric options—cryonics (body freezing), for example.

[2] How to handle funeral/burial problems yourself, with organizational help, is discussed in detail in *Caring For Your Own Dead*, Carlson (Upper Access Books).

cial funeral, planning is usually desirable. Funeral homes no longer effectively maintain price-fixing. Costs for similar services vary widely. There's really no sensible reason to plan how to save money on probate fees or estate taxes and then toss a chunk of it away on an overpriced funeral. Equally important, there's no reason to dread thinking about what kind of death notice and ceremonial service will be fitting, if you want them.

B. Leaving Written Instruction

WHATEVER DECISIONS a person makes regarding the disposition of his body should be put in writing. Under a number of states' laws, written burial instructions of a deceased person are binding, assuming, of course, the instructions don't violate state laws on body disposition. Even where laws do not require that a deceased person's instructions be followed, they almost always are.

However, if there may be conflict over body disposition, it's important to know whether your state's laws make written burial instructions binding. For example, a person may want to insure that his unmarried mate, not family members, has legal authority to carry out his instructions. To learn your state's rules regarding burial instructions, you'll need to do your own research or see a lawyer (see Chapter 22).

Commonly, written instructions are included in a will. This may not be the best choice, because it may take time to find and read a will. A better approach can be to prepare your instructions in a separate document, and to also include them in your will. However they're drawn up, written instructions should be kept in a safe and readily accessible place, known to whoever will have the responsibility for implementing them.

If no legally binding written instructions are left by the decedent, the next of kin (the closest family relation) has legal control over the disposition of the body. This can pose insoluble problems for a friend or lover of the deceased, who knows the deceased wanted a specific type of disposition that the next of kin opposes. Without legally binding written instructions, the friend or lover is powerless to prevent the next of kin from controlling the disposition.

Death Certificates

Whenever a person dies, a physician must complete a death certificate shortly after the death and file it with the appropriate governmental agency, often a local registrar of health. Certified copies of the death certificate are needed to transfer certain types of property to those legally entitled to them. For example, to collect money from a decedent's pay-on-death bank accounts, to end a joint tenancy of real estate, or to wind up a living trust, the inheritors need a certified copy (or copies) of the death certificate.

C. Donating Your Body or Organs

IF YOU WANT to leave your body to help humanity, you have two choices:

1. You can leave your entire body to medical science, usually a medical school; or

2. You can donate certain of your body organs or tissues to transplant facilities.

You cannot do both, because medical schools generally won't accept a body from which any part has been removed (except sometimes for eye transplants).

The procedure for donating a body to a medical school is simple: contact the school, see if it needs bodies, and, if so, what legalities and forms it requires. Most medical facilities don't pay to obtain bodies and won't absorb the cost of transporting a body.

Many medical schools are currently not accepting whole body donations. By contrast, the need for many types of organ donations is great. Heart transplants get the most publicity, but many more organs, tissues, and bones can and are being transplanted, including middle ear, eyes, liver, lungs, pancreas, kidneys, skin tissue, bone and cartilage, pituitary glands, and even hip or knee joints. To take but one example, thousands of people are kept alive by dialysis machines as they wait for kidney transplants. A gift of a vital organ is one of the most precious and loving acts one can make. I know this well, as I have a friend who was saved from blindness by a cornea transplant.

Every state has adopted the Uniform Anatomical Gift Act. Under this act, any mentally competent adult can promise to make after-death organ donations. Obviously, to authorize this you have to sign the proper forms. Your doctor and local hospital should be aware of what is required in your state. Also, under the Act, a person's family can agree to organ donations if the person is brain dead, but body organs have been kept alive by a life support system.

Time is truly of the essence for the successful removal of donated body parts, so anyone desiring to have organs removed on death should make arrangements beforehand, including discussing his intentions with family and friends. This is a matter that can be easily put off. Many people probably think to themselves—since I'm sure I'll live until I'm at least 90, why bother now with planning to donate my organs? With donation of body parts, the limits of this logic of procrastination are starkly seen. We all know that the real truth is you never know.

D. Services and Ceremonies Following a Death

MANY PEOPLE WISH to have input about the ceremonies held after their death. You may have a favorite church or synagogue where you would like the service held, or a particular priest, pastor or rabbi to conduct it. You may know how you want the service to be conducted. Of course, in many religious and spiritual communities, the broad outlines of ritual that accompanies a death are well-established. In most instances, however, when it comes to the particular prayers to be read and songs to be sung, there's room for personal choice. If the service won't be held by a religious institution, individual input becomes more urgent. It's sad to attend, as I have, a funeral of a good friend held in a commercial funeral home where not one personal word was said about him.

If you do wish to have something to say about your funeral ceremonies, the best way to do it is in writing. Simply include a brief statement as part of your burial instructions (see Section B above).

E. Death Notices

WHEN SOMEONE DIES, one of the first things that most families do is notify others. For close friends and relatives, phone calls normally work. But what about notifying the many other people whose lives have been touched by the deceased, such as former neighbors, golf partners, sailing or bowling friends, retired business associates and other friends? Doing this promptly is important, as many of these people will wish to attend one or more of the events which usually occur very soon after death, such as a wake, lying-in, funeral or memorial ceremony, and others will wish to communicate with the family.

In most communities, notification is handled by a local newspaper, with either a death notice or an obituary.

Death notices generally must be paid for, and consist of small print listings of the date of death, names of survivors, and location of any services.

An obituary is a news item, prepared by the staff of the newspaper. It runs in standard type, contains a small headline (e.g., "Local school principal dies") and is free. In small towns, many local newspapers prepare obituaries for a large percentage of people who die, giving more space to those who were locally prominent. In metropolitan areas, however, very few people qualify for obituaries in the large daily papers, and even fairly prominent people have their deaths recorded in the paid death notices, if at all.

Death notice information must be submitted to newspapers promptly. This can raise a real problem for survivors. Just when they are beset by difficult emotions and serious practical problems, someone has to write a death notice and take or call it in to the newspaper office. While often a funeral home will help with this, and newspapers are commonly very understanding, it still isn't always easy. Common problems involve remembering or locating dates, parents' names, details of key events, correct spellings for clubs and other affiliations, to mention just a few.

One solution to this problem is to prepare your own death notice. This might sound a bit macabre, but it will probably only take you a little while, and those who are later spared the task will surely be appreciative. Just look at the appropriate newspaper, follow the general form it uses and write one out.

What about an obituary? At least for many local newspapers, you can help write the news story about your death in advance. The paper will have a form on which you can list all relevant biographical information, including your education and employment history, civic responsibilities, names of children, and so on. If this form is filled out in advance, it can be given to the paper immediately after death, and will be used to write the news story. In addition to completing this form, however, you may want to actually try your hand at writing your own obituary, leaving blank your date of death. Does this sound weird? Well, yes, a little, perhaps, but remember, if

you don't do it, someone you love may have to deal with a reporter when there are more pressing concerns occasioned by your death. To get an idea of what an obituary should look like, read a few in your local paper. In my experience, if a family submits a well-written, factual obituary immediately after a person's death, a local newspaper is likely to use a good part of it, or at least echo its major themes.

F. Funerals

FOR FUNERALS, you have two basic options—use a commercial funeral home or a non-profit funeral society. There's a wide range of choices offered by both types of institutions.

1. Commercial Funerals

The traditional American funeral, as provided by a commercial funeral home, normally includes the following:

- The funeral director takes care of the paperwork required for death and burial certificates, and removes the body from the place of death and embalms it.

- The deceased's embalmed body is shown at an open—or closed—casket ceremony. Many funeral parlors have their own chapels and encourage all services to be held there, rather than in churches.

The funeral business is crowded. There are over 20,000 funeral parlors in the United States, half of which average 60 funerals or less per year. Until recently, there has been very little price competition. Funeral directors are faced with the ultimate in what economists call an "inelastic market;" they have absolutely no way, short of arsenic in the soup or other disapproved methods, to increase the number of persons who need their services. So traditionally, they adhered to an "all-in-the-same-boat" philosophy, keeping their prices fixed and high and revealing as little as possible of their costs and operation. This has changed somewhat, and price competition does exist in many areas, spurred by the need to compete with funeral society and other non-traditional funerals.

Our funerals are products of our culture, which has long been ambivalent about funerals. In some ages, expensive funerals and burials were scorned as ostentatious, wasteful, and the norm was a simple, dignified and inexpensive service. In other times, as in 17th century England, expensive funerals and grand tombs were in vogue for those with status and wealth. Today, in the United States, many of us seem more familiar with the tradition that exalts the expense and show of the final resting place. We've read about Egyptian tombs and their regal splendor, or the well-equipped send-off for the voyage to the underworld in the *Iliad*,[3] or the elaborate coffins of Japanese and Chinese aristocrats. We're less familiar with the methods of cultures that don't insist on expensive burials. In Switzerland, for instance, there have been no private commercial undertakers since 1890. Every Swiss citizen has the right to a free funeral arranged by municipal personnel. The grave, coffin and hearse are also free.

There is no generally-accepted American cultural tradition concerning funerals and burials. Many Americans do hold ceremonies when a person dies, of course, and many ethnic and religious traditions survive, such as the Jewish custom of burial within 24 hours or the Irish wake, but, generally speaking, for those not close to their ethnic roots, there's still a significant cultural vacuum. As should come as no surprise, that vacuum has long been filled by business people.

Before the Civil War, burials in America were most often simple affairs—a religious ceremony, a plain pine box, and quick burial. Undertakers weren't a separate trade until roughly the 1860's; originally they practiced some other trade, often carpentry. During the Civil War, bodies of dead soldiers were embalmed so they could be shipped home for burial. Then, undertakers emerged as a

distinct trade; they later evolved into funeral directors and began to proclaim themselves professionals. With this, the plain pine box was transformed into a luxurious coffin. Funerals became theater, and their cost rose accordingly. Embalming the dead body and showing the embalmed remains became standard funeral parlor practice—a practice which obviously adds substantially to the cost of burial, and one not used (and indeed regarded as barbaric) in most other countries. The funeral industry also developed a rationalization for embalming. They claimed that viewing the embalmed body is useful for the living, because seeing a lifelike body enables the viewers to cope with their grief. The term they invented for this is "grief therapy."

As many people sense, at least vaguely, there's something odd, as well as expensive, about traditional American funerals. Much of this awareness stems from *The American Way of Death,* by Jessica Mitford (Simon Schuster), a fascinating examination of commercial American culture in one of its more rapacious and grotesque areas. Written with wit and grace, Mitford's book (now over two decades years old, but still influential) raised many questions about American funeral customs.[4] Partially as a result of her book, many beneficial legal changes have occurred, allowing alternatives to conventional funeral parlor practices. Legal reform has aided the growth of funeral societies, which, in turn, have introduced real price competition into the commercial funeral business. Now some commercial funeral homes have begun to advertise very inexpensive funerals, comparable to those offered by funeral societies. So, if you do want to patronize a traditional funeral parlor, shop around.

a. Embalming

The greatest expense of a traditional funeral is embalming the body. Generally, state law doesn't require embalming unless the body will be transported by common carrier, such as a commercial plane, or county health officials

---

[3]Cremation, as it turns out, was also common in ancient Greece.

[4]Another fine book is Ruth Harmer's *The High Cost of Dying* (Crowell-Collier Press).

order embalming as a protection against the spread of contagious disease (a *very* rare event). There are those who claim that embalming is a necessary health measure, but there's little evidence to support this. If a body must be preserved for a short time, refrigeration is at least as reliable, and far cheaper.

In embalming, preservative and disinfectant fluid (formaldehyde solution) is injected into the arterial system and body cavities, replacing blood. Embalmed bodies aren't preserved for eternities, though medical science can do this for exceptional reasons (keeping Lenin's body on display, for example). Generally, an embalmed body begins to decompose rapidly within a few weeks.

By embalming the body, a funeral parlor can preserve it sufficiently to allow open-casket viewing of the body at a funeral service, a popular practice with some Americans. How one feels about this is, of course, a private matter. The important point is to realize that open-casket viewing is far from an inevitable practice. The choice is up to survivors or anyone who makes plans for his own burial. Many commercial undertakers embalm a body unless they are explicitly instructed not to. The result is that many people don't consciously choose to have the body of a loved one embalmed, but by the time they realize that they had a choice, the funeral service with the embalmed body is long over.

b. Costs

A major factor in the total cost of a funeral is the price of the casket. Not surprisingly, funeral directors generally urge as expensive a casket as possible. Anyone who's ever been casket shopping can tell you it's a bit like visiting a car dealership. There's always a larger, fancier model available, with more expensive options. The question all too often becomes not how much a casket costs, but how much are you willing to pay.

The cost of a traditional funeral can easily add up to many thousands of dollars. In addition to the casket, there's normally a charge for each extra, and there are a lot of possible extras, including flowers, special burial

clothing, additional limousines, clergyman's honorarium, music and cards.

Flowers have become traditional at American funerals. A significant percentage of all flowers sold by commercial florists in America are sold for funerals. Not surprisingly, this big business (with an annual gross from flower sales of somewhere over $1 billion) resists any attempt to reduce the sending of flowers to funerals. Some people prefer that money which would have been spent on flowers be given to a particular charity. Sometimes funeral notices or announcements state "Please Omit Flowers." Whether flowers are a beautiful and moving statement or an unnecessary expense is a choice each person can make; again, the point is to realize that there's a choice.

Finally, transporting a body from a distant place of death, or to a distant burial place, is particularly expensive. If you must arrange for the return of a body from a distant place of death, it's usually much cheaper to have a local funeral parlor (or funeral society) arrange it, rather than having one at the place of death do it.

2. Funeral Societies

Funeral societies are private, non-profit organizations, open to any who wish to join. They are devoted to the concept of simple, dignified burial services for a reasonable cost. Funeral societies are, essentially, cooperatives, run (at least theoretically) by their members. There's usually a small membership fee for joining. Members are entitled to the burial programs offered through the society. In many states, funeral societies don't employ their own morticians, or own their own cemeteries; rather, they have contracts of varying types with cooperating local mortuaries and crematoriums.

At first, funeral societies were bitterly opposed by segments of the commercial funeral industry, and a new society often had considerable difficult finding any funeral director who would work with them. From modest beginnings, funeral societies have grown substantially in recent years. Although the relationship between funeral societies and the commercial funeral industry still isn't always amicable, the two groups have generally learned to co-exist. Partially, this is due to the growth and resulting economic clout of funeral societies.

Specific policies, funeral costs and options vary somewhat from organization to organization, but the basics are common to all. Dignified, simple funerals can be arranged for hundreds of dollars, not thousands. Members are concerned not only with reducing the excessive costs, but at least equally with what they believe are the excesses and lack of spiritual values inherent in many commercial funerals. As the literature of the funeral societies notes, in the traditional funeral the emphasis is on the dead body —lying in an open casket, the body embalmed, often painted, rouged, or otherwise altered cosmetically in the belief that the embalmer's skills will make a more lifelike body, and that viewing a lifelike dead body is a sign of respect or affection. Funeral societies are opposed to the cost of embalming, and equally so to the emphasis on the corpse laid out in an expensive coffin. They normally recommend a memorial service where the body isn't viewed, and the emphasis is on remembering the person.

Funeral societies want new members and readily provide information on their programs. You can easily check out a funeral society's membership rules, the type of services it offers (and what's not included), as well as the names of all cooperating mortuaries. In most states, funeral societies will either conduct any desired services themselves or cooperate with any religious or spiritual

ceremony that's planned. If you move, there's a good chance you can transfer your membership to another society; there are funeral societies in most urban areas of the United States.

To locate a funeral society near you, check the phone book or contact:

The Continental Association of Funeral
and Memorial Societies
1146 19th Street NW, 3rd Floor
Washington, D.C. 20036

G. Cremation

CREMATION means the burning of the body. Cremation is common in many parts of the world. For example, over half of those dying in England are cremated. It's opposed by certain religions, such as Muslims, and Greek and Jewish Orthodox creeds. Catholics are supposed to receive the permission of their local bishop to be cremated, but the Catholic Church no longer bans cremation outright.

Both funeral homes and funeral societies now normally handle cremation at low cost. In addition, there are several profit-making organizations established exclusively for cremations, with names like The Neptune Society, Teleophase, and Memorial Cremation Society. Except for their profit-making nature, they function like funeral societies. For a small membership fee, you join the organization and select a type of cremation service. The cost is comparatively low—usually between $200 and $300.

By law in many states, a crematorium cannot require that a casket (rather than a bag) be used in cremation. This makes sense, as it seems particularly needless to pay for an expensive wood casket that is almost immediately burned. Cheaper wood caskets are often used, by custom, if no contrary directions are given.

Whether and how ashes can be scattered depends on state law. Scatterings were rare a few generations ago, but there has been a marked increase in their number as the number of cremations has grown. Cremated remains can be removed from the place of cremation or inurnment and disposed of by scattering by the person with the legal right to control the remains. A permit is usually required for scattering, whether at sea or over private land. The crematorium, funeral parlor, or funeral society involved should handle the paperwork. Once again, giving specific instructions regarding disposition can save considerable trouble.

H. Burials

A BODY MUST BE DISPOSED OF in a lawful way. Unless it's cremated and the ashes scattered or kept in a licensed columbarium, it must be interred somewhere. Usually this means the remains must be buried in a cemetery (graveyard, if you prefer the more descriptive word).

Most American cemeteries are private businesses. To be buried in one you have to buy your way in. Cemeteries are normally separate businesses from funeral homes, although they often have working relationships with one another. Sometimes, though, they compete, and some cemeteries sell caskets. Usually, the fact that cemeteries are separate means only that there's one more transaction to arrange—buying a funeral plot. This purchase can often be arranged through a funeral society or a funeral home. If there's a specific cemetery you desire, you should be sure the funeral home or society can arrange for that particular purchase. Also, you might save money if you select your own cemetery as prices can vary significantly.

Probably the best known graveyard in the world is Forest Lawn Cemetery in Los Angeles. Evelyn Waugh's justly famous satire of Forest Lawn, *The Loved One,* hasn't diminished the success of this cemetery. Many people still choose (or their relatives choose) to be buried in its "splendor." Depending on how much splendor is desired, this can be quite expensive indeed.

Cemeteries as a private enterprise, operated for personal gain, are a rather unusual concept. In most other countries, cemeteries are usually maintained by the family, tribe, community, state, or religious institution. In this country, there's a wide variety of cemetery types, including profit-making ones, large mutually-owned ones, church burial grounds, small co-ops, municipal ones, and national cemeteries, in which most veterans and their spouses, are entitled to free burial.

Cemetery costs, like everything else, are going up. The minimum cost includes:

1. the plot;

2. the coffin enclosure, which normally consists of a vault or grave liner of concrete and steel. Cemetery owners sometimes say vaults are required to prevent the land bordering the grave from eventually collapsing. Although this danger is often nonexistent or exaggerated, yearly vault sales have recently been estimated to amount to nearly one-half billion dollars. Many vaults are bought through a funeral director, although they are usually cheaper if bought from a cemetery;

3. opening and closing the grave; and

4. upkeep.

Many cemeteries sell "perpetual care," which they claim means that the grave will be attended "for eternity." This sounds pretty grandiose until you realize that as graves don't require much care, what this really means is that the grass will be cut. And even this task is now made as simple as possible, since many modern urban cemeteries have eliminated the use of headstones, substituting plaques that are planted flush to the ground, so as not to interfere with the power mower.

You can purchase a "prepaid" (or "pre-need") plan from most cemeteries. This means you pay now and the cemetery reserves a space for your eventual burial. In *The American Way of Death,* Jessica Mitford depicts fast-buck hustlers in the pre-need cemetery business selling plots that might not even exist, or selling them in places not likely to remain a cemetery by the time they are to be used. While the worst of these practices have been curtailed, abuses still occur. So, if you're interested in a pre-need burial plot, be sure to check out the reliability of the cemetery involved. In addition, try to figure out just how much additional money the security of this pre-need plot is costing, or saving, you.

If you haven't got enough to worry about, you could worry about what will happen when we run out of cemetery land. It'll take a while, surely, although one expert suggests that in only 500 years, at the present rate of graveyard growth, all the land in the United States would be graveyards.

If there's to be a headstone or plaque, why not create your own epitaph? It's a final opportunity for self-expression.

Among my favorite epitaphs are:

Cast a cold eye, on life, on death. Horseman, pass by!

—Yeats

and the classic:

On the whole, I'd rather be in Philadelphia.

—W.C. Fields

Business Ownership and Estate Planning

Business Ownership and Estate Planning

IF YOU OWN AN INTEREST in a small business, whether you're a sole proprietor, a partner in a partnership or a shareholder in a small corporation, estate planning can get complicated fast. Indeed, if a substantial part of your estate is a profit-making business of significant value, there's seldom a "simple" estate plan. By definition, you need to plan carefully both at the business and personal level. Here I can only give you a brief introduction to what is involved. You should get help from an experienced estate planner with strong business and tax experience.

The special estate planning problems for small business owners usually break down into two broad areas:

- **Operation of the business.** If the business is a sole proprietorship, your estate planning problems are comparatively simple. The first question to ask is whether your beneficiaries want to continue the business. The second is whether they are up to it. If the answer to both questions is yes, you'll want to plan so there will be a smooth transfer of ownership and management. If the answer is no, you will have to arrange to have the business sold, or managed by a professional manager.

  If the business is a partnership or closely-held corporation with shared ownership, you must first take into account the rights of surviving co-owners regarding your share of the business. It is very common for the surviving principals of a business to have the right to purchase the share of a principal who dies. If co-owners do have this right, two important questions should be addressed: How will your share be valued, and how will the money be found to actually buy it? Obviously, the buy-out should be planned so as to not destroy the business or force it to be sold to outsiders.

- **Death tax and probate concerns.** Once you have dealt with any concerns about operation of the business, you will have to choose an estate planning device to actually transfer your share of the business to your inheritors. Of course, you'll want to reduce death taxes on your business assets to the extent possible. You also want to consider ways to have your business

interests avoid probate, not only to save on probate fees, but also to assure prompt transfer of ownership.

Before you consult a lawyer, CPA or estate planner, however, it's wise to learn at least the basics of your estate planning choices. In the next two sections, I help you to do this.

A. Practical Business Problems

THE DEATH OF THE SOLE OR PART OWNER of a small business is likely to seriously disrupt that business. If no planning has been done, the disruption can be catastrophic. Let's now look more thoroughly at how your business will be affected, depending on whether you own it yourself or with others.

1. Sole Proprietorships

It's rarely desirable to simply end a business immediately on the death of its owner, unless it's a one-person service business. Even if the inheritors will ultimately sell the business, you'll want them to have some flexibility in the timing of the sale—which means the business must be capable of continuing in a profitable fashion for a while. One way to achieve at least short-term continuity is for key employees, the owner and beneficiaries to agree in writing that these employees will stay around and continue to run the business for a set time after the owner dies, perhaps in exchange for a small portion of the eventual sale proceeds. Another way to accomplish this is to incorporate the business and make the key employees officers of the corporation and minority stockholders. (Obviously, the officers can still quit at any time, but they are less likely to do so if they have an equity interest in the business.)

If there's more than one beneficiary, questions commonly arise about what happens after the death of the original owner. Suppose one of the new owners wants to sell out and the others don't. Or suppose they all want to sell, but don't see eye to eye about how best to do it. Or suppose the new owners want to operate the business but disagree on how to proceed? If a business has any real value that is likely to survive its sole proprietor, questions such as these should be anticipated and resolved as part of the estate planning process.

In some situations, a sole proprietor wants the business to continue but doesn't trust his ultimate inheritor to run it. If there is a trusted employee who can manage the business, she may be the logical person to take over. This sort of situation can necessitate a fairly complex legal structure, and is a good illustration of why professional estate planning help is typically needed.

Hank Jackson is the sole proprietor of a thriving print shop. He wants to leave management of the company in the hands of his friend, trusted employee and longtime co-worker, Ed Brown, for Brown's life. When Ed dies, the business will be given to Hank's grandchildren, who, Hank knows, will almost surely decide to sell the business promptly. Jackson incorporates the business. As part of his living trust, he establishes an ongoing life estate trust and provides that, when he dies, his shares will be placed in this trust. Ed Brown is named as trustee of this ongoing trust, with power to control the shares and thus manage the corporation. The trust also provides that Brown is to receive 50% of the business's profits during his life, with the other 50% divided between Hank's grandchildren. After Brown dies, the trust will be dissolved and the business transferred to Jackson's grandchildren.

In this situation, Brown's rights as trustee are vital. If Brown is given broad power, he can hire himself to run the corporation at a good salary. Or, he can take a more back-seat role, paying someone else to run the business on a day-to-day basis and taking out only the profit left over.

Jackson will probably not want to try and dictate how Brown is to run the company, but may want to institute some controls, such as requiring reinvesting at least some profits back into the business. He might do this to protect against any possibility that Brown would be tempted to overemphasize policies that will prefer short-term profit (in which he shares) over the long-term value of the business (which goes to the grandchildren).

Jackson should also provide (in the trust document) for what happens if the grandchildren disagree about what to do with the business. Do some have the right to buy out others? If so, how is the sale price to be determined, and how is the money to be raised?

2. Shared Ownership Businesses

When a business has more than one owner, whether the form of that business is a partnership or a corporation, each co-owner must carefully consider the others' rights when engaging in estate planning.

a. How to Plan Ahead

It's common that a partnership agreement, corporate bylaws or a shareholder's agreement controls disposition of a deceased co-owner's interest in the business. If this is the case, each partner or shareholder must create a personal estate plan that is in harmony with this document.

In the absence of an agreement, the rights of surviving owners are determined by the laws of the state where the business is located. Put bluntly, it is not wise to rely on state laws. Applying laws mechanistically to your situation is unlikely to produce a result that will satisfy anyone. For instance, state laws generally require that a partnership must be dissolved on the death of a partner unless the partnership agreement provides differently. State laws often further define how partnership property is to be valued, in the absence of agreement between the partners. It's obviously unwise to leave such crucial issues up to state law. It is essential that co-owners of a business resolve, in writing, exactly what's to happen when one owner dies.

Partnerships: If your business is a partnership, you should state, in your partnership agreement, what will happen when a partner dies. Below are two examples of how partnerships agreements can be structured to do this. For more information on how to write a partnership agreement to deal with these issues, see *The Partnership Book*, Clifford and Warner (Nolo Press). This book provides a number of ready to use clauses designed to fit different needs.

Ned, a partner in "N.J.D," has agreed with his other two partners (J. and D.) that the survivors will continue the business after one of them dies. Ned wants the value of his ownership interest to go to his children. The other partners have similar wishes. To achieve the dual goals of keeping the business going and providing for inheritors, Ned and his partners decide that management of the partnership business will be kept legally separate from the ownership interest of the partner's inheritors. To do this, they agree in the partnership agreement that the partnership share of a deceased partner will be placed in a trust for the benefit of his inheritors. The surviving partners will serve as trustees, with power to manage the business as they see fit. A deceased partner's inheritors will have the right to one-third of the partnership profits. The surviving partners also can, at their option, buy out the inheritor's share of the partnership. A formula to value this share is established in the shareholders' agreement, along with a payment schedule. If the buy-out isn't completed in a defined period of time, the trust ends and the inheritors can sell the share to outsiders.

Jason and Pat are equal partners in the J-P Co. When he dies, Jason wants his partnership interest to go to his son. Pat wants her interest to be divided between her three children. Both Jason and Pat want to avoid probate. Equally important, both want the survivor to be able to continue the partnership business for the remainder of his life. Neither wants the children of the first partner to die to be able to liquidate the partnership.

Jason and Pat agree on the following estate plan. Each creates a living trust and places his interest in the partnership business in that trust. They check their partnership agreement and recall that each partner must approve the other's transfer of partnership interest, so each signs a document formally giving approval to the other's transfer to a living trust. Finally, they amend the partnership agreement to put in the solution they've worked out to allow the surviving partner to continue the business: The amended partnership rules provide that a partner with 51% ownership of the business has exclusive control over it. Another partner or his inheritor has rights to income from the partnership if it makes profits, but no rights to manage it or dissolve it. When a partner dies, the value of his 50% interest in the partnership will be determined by a carefully-defined appraisal method. Then the surviving partner has the right to buy 1% of that deceased partnership interest, for 1/50 (or 2%) of the appraised worth of that interest. Thus, the surviving partner will obtain 51% of the business and have exclusive control over it.

In this situation, it's important for all to be aware that a deceased partner's inheritors have no rights to manage or liquidate the business, and that their income from it depends entirely on the decisions of the surviving partner. So, for this sort of plan to work well for all concerned, each partner must totally trust the other (which is what partnerships should be about).

Corporations: Although the legal form of a corporation is different from a partnership, the same types of estate planning problems must be resolved by the owners: how to value the interest of a deceased owner, how to provide continuity, and how to protect the interests of both the surviving owners and inheritors. The shareholders should resolve these issues in a written agreement which is incorporated in corporate documents, typically either the bylaws or a separate shareholders' agreement.

Frederick Smith and Rachel Twardzick are co-owners of a thriving plant store and commercial plant rental business. They entered the business with a kiss and high hopes, and they have never gotten around to incorporating the business or creating a written partnership agreement.

After many years, and more than a few gray hairs, they decide it's time to discuss their respective estate planning needs. Each wants to leave a majority of ownership of the store to others, with some of it divided between their three adult children. They decide to incorporate the store as "Plants, Inc," and divide the stock equally. Each then creates a living trust to give two-thirds of his or her stock to the survivor and one-third to the three children, to be equally divided among them. The bylaws also create a detailed provision defining how each child's interest can be valued and purchased by the other children if they all desire that. But if they don't, it can't be sold to an outsider.

The corporate bylaws are also custom-designed to prevent the children from selling their stock as long as one parent lives. In addition, the bylaws give managerial control to the majority shareholder, the surviving spouse. Frederick and Rachel privately agree that the survivor will leave all his or her stock to the children, but they don't make a formal contract to require this, because they realize that binding the survivor to dispose of property is overly restrictive.

b. Valuation of a Deceased Owner's Interest

It's important to establish a method to value a deceased owner's interest in a business for several reasons. Someone who inherits an interest in a business may well want to sell that interest. As the previous examples indicate, in some cases sale is prohibited. But in most situations, the inheritors do have a right to sell, although the other owners often have the first option to buy out the inheritors. If co-owners of a business agree in advance

of an owner's death how interests in the business are to be valued, they can often avoid potential conflicts between surviving owners and those who inherit a share of the business. And even if the inheritors don't have the right to sell, they will probably need to know the worth of their inheritance for death tax or other purposes. Although the IRS is not bound by private valuations of a business, it is prone to accept a valuation, and valuation formula, that is reasonable, especially for a business with no readily ascertainable market value.

Any of the conventional methods for determining the value of a small business can be adopted in a partnership agreement or corporate bylaws (or shareholders' agreement) to evaluate a deceased owner's share.

The co-owners can agree to:

- Establish a fixed dollar amount for the deceased co-owner's share.

- Have the business interest appraised. This often means agreeing on an appraiser in advance and then abiding by the value of the post-death appraisal.

- Determine the book value of the business interest (the total value of all tangible assets of the business).

- Use the "capitalization" of net earnings formula. This is useful in some types of businesses where there are generally net earnings, and the numerical multiplier used to calculate the value of the business has been generally defined and accepted in the trade.

- Give the surviving owner the right to match any outside bona fide purchase price, sometimes called "the right of first refusal." For this method to work, there must be an outside offer. Since this can rarely be assured beforehand, it's sensible to have a back-up method for determining the worth of a deceased owner's interest also included in the partnership agreement, corporate bylaws or shareholders' agreement.

c. *Payment for a Deceased Owner's Interest*

Assuming a valuation method is chosen in advance, some means of actually paying the deceased's inheritors for their interest should also be agreed on by the business owners. Purchasing life insurance is one way to do this. Each owner can purchase life insurance on the other owner's life; the purchaser is the beneficiary of that policy. Or the business itself can purchase insurance for all owners, with proceeds paid to the surviving owner. Or the surviving owners can be allowed to pay the deceased's inheritors over time, and use income of the business to make the payments. Again, the key point is for the owners to agree, in writing, on their plan for buy-out payments.

If the business is a corporation, buy-out agreements can become quite complicated. For instance, if the business buys the deceased's stock, is that purchase price taxed to the deceased's estate as a dividend? It can be, under some circumstances. This is one more reason to check your estate planning carefully with an expert if you're a co-owner of a corporate business.

B. Avoiding Probate and Reducing Estate Taxes

ONCE PLANNING IS DONE at the business level, each business owner obviously needs to do personal estate planning, to find the best method to transfer his business interest while avoiding probate and minimizing estate taxes. Let's briefly look at what's involved for each.

1. Probate Avoidance

It's often disastrous for a small business to become enmeshed in probate. Aside from the cost, it can be burdensome, even destructive, to have to seek a probate court's approval for business decisions. If you doubt this, ask yourself if you want a judge supervising your business for the year or more probate typically takes. You can plan to avoid probate by using either joint tenancy or a living trust to transfer your business interest. For a number of tax and ownership reasons discussed in detail in Chapters 9 and 10, a living trust is usually the best choice. Let's look at how this might work for sole proprietorship and shared ownership businesses.

a. *Sole Proprietorships*

Placing your business in a living trust is commonly the best means to avoid probate of a solely-owned business, unless your business has many debts and creditors' claims, in which case probate may be desirable because it provides a convenient forum for having those claims resolved. (See Chapter 7 for more on this.) This, however, is unusual. Most business owners, even those with a defined list of known creditors, should plan to avoid probate.

Sam is the sole owner of a New York restaurant. The business is not incorporated. Sam conducts the business under his name "dba [doing business as] The Manhattan Bar and Grill," and has filed the appropriate business and tax forms with city licensing agencies. Sam will leave the business to his son, Theodore. Sam creates a living trust and names Theodore as the beneficiary to inherit the restaurant. Sam lists the restaurant on Schedule A of the trust: "The restaurant dba The Manhattan Bar and Grill...[street address]... and all assets, supplies, accounts receivable, good will or other property of the business." Sam then checks with the city licensing agencies, who inform him that they do not require any paperwork for the living trust to be effective. Of course, when Theodore inherits the business, he'll need to complete new d/b/a forms.

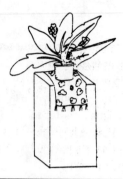

Natalie is sole owner of the Stay-Potted plant store. She wants to leave her interest in the store as follows:

30% to her close friend Donna;

25% to her niece Cindy;

15% to each of her three brothers.

After investigating her options, she decides to incorporate and then transfer the stock of the corporation into a living trust. The trust provides that each of its beneficiaries receives the percentage of shares of stock she's specified. Natalie also prepares the appropriate corporate records, according to the corporation's bylaws, to approve her actions. She decides she won't worry about management and continuity of the business after she dies. It's up to her inheritors. If they agree to run the business and can run it—fine. If that doesn't work out, they can sell the business.

b. Shared Ownership Businesses

For shared ownership, living trusts are normally the best probate avoidance devices. The partnership agreement, corporate bylaws or shareholders' agreement should specifically permit each owner to transfer her interest to a living trust. If the document does not provide for this, it should be amended or revised so that it does. Then, each owner creates her own living trust, consistent with any requirements of the partnership agreement, bylaws or shareholders' agreement (such as the right of surviving principals to buy out the deceased's share), and transfers her interest in the business to that trust. The trust then works like any other probate avoidance living trust, as

explained in Chapter 8. The business property transferred to the trust is listed on Schedule A.

"The settlor's shares in the ZT Corporation."

"The settlor's partnership interest in the AB partnership."

Then, any business asset with a document of title transferred to the living trust must be re-registered in the trust's name.

Vikki and Clint are partners in Go-Get-'Em, Inc. which owns two apartment houses. Both Vikki and Clint create living trusts for their business interest. Each must do the following to transfer his or her share of the business into their living trust:

- Prepare the appropriate corporate records and resolution authorizing and approving the transfer.

- Prepare new corporate shares, listing the living trust as owner.

2. Reducing Estate Taxes

There are special federal estate tax rules for small businesses (called "closely held" businesses in tax lingo) which can be used to lighten or reduce death taxes. To decide if the details of these rules apply to your business and whether it's sensible for you to plan to use them, you'll need to see a tax expert. Here's a summary of how these rules work:

- Estate taxes assessed against the value of a small business can be deferred five years and then paid in ten annual installments.

Steven Andrews owns the Ace Pharmacy, which has a net worth of $500,000. Andrews' total estate, including the pharmacy, is worth $1,000,000. The federal estate taxes assessed against the estate are $153,000. However, half the value of Andrews' estate is his small business, so half of these estate taxes can be postponed.

The principal IRS restriction here is that the value of the small business must be at least 35% of the total estate.

- Real estate used for a business or farm can be valued for estate tax purposes at its actual present use, rather than "highest yield" use. For example, a family farm doesn't have to be valued for its (possibly much higher) worth as a potential location for a shopping center or subdivision, but can be valued on the basis of its worth as a farm. This valuation rule can provide a real break for family businesses, as real estate valuation can be reduced up to a maximum of $750,000, the difference between "present use" and "best use." However, there are several requirements that must be met for the rule to apply:

- The value of the family business must be at least 50% of the overall estate.

- The value of the real estate of that business must be at least 25% of the overall estate.

- The decedent or a member of his family must have used the real estate for the business five of the preceding eight years.

- There are restrictions on sale or mortgage of the property and financial reporting for up to 15 years after the tax break.

- Significant income tax savings are permitted for corporate stock redeemed to pay estate taxes.

Social Security and Pensions

CHAPTER 21

Social Security and Pensions

UPON RETIREMENT, most people are entitled to payments from one or more retirement programs, such as social security payments, military benefits, private and public employee pensions, and union pension plans. Planning for retirement can be a complicated field, and I don't pretend to cover it in any depth here. There are many good books on the subject, including *Social Security, Medicare and Pensions*, Matthews (Nolo Press). However, retirement issues and estate planning are, obviously, related. For example, in drafting their estate plan, a married couple should consider each spouse's rights under pension plans. If a surviving spouse can expect to get generous monthly pension checks that will cover living expenses, with a little left over, the other spouse may sensibly decide to leave at least some money and property directly to children or friends. On the other hand, if a surviving spouse won't receive adequate pension income, the other spouse would more likely leave all property to him. And buying a life insurance policy on the life of a breadwinner makes great sense if there will be little continuing income should he die, and much less if a generous pension will be in the offing.

A related estate planning question is what happens if a family breadwinner dies before becoming eligible for retirement benefits. Do the benefits he would have received had he lived go to the surviving spouse or children? If so, how much, under what circumstances, and for how long? If you can't answer these questions, you don't have all the information you need to plan your estate. Start gathering information by checking your retirement program's survivors' benefit provisions. Social security and other public programs normally protect a covered worker's children and spouse. But there's no legal requirement that a private or union pension plan pay benefits to a surviving spouse or anyone else. Some are generous, some are miserly, and some don't even bother to say "tough luck, friend."

**Retirement Benefits:
Estate Tax and Probate Status**

Retirement program payments made to a surviving spouse or other beneficiary are normally exempt from probate. Also, these payments are not included in the deceased's taxable estate, and therefore are not counted in the property that may be subject to federal or state death taxes.

A. Social Security

THE MOST EXTENSIVE retirement program is the federal Social Security system. Despite periodic anxieties that the program will run out of money, it manages to make regular payments to millions and will surely continue to do so.

Social security provides payments to many categories of family survivors of covered wage earners, even if these people are not entitled to payments based on their own earnings record:

- A widower or widow who is 65 or older receives, for life, 100% of the deceased spouse's social security benefits if the deceased spouse was over 65 at death. If the surviving spouse is between ages 60 and 65, there is a reduction in benefits according to a set formula. (Remarriage after age 60 doesn't terminate benefits.) A surviving spouse cannot receive double benefits, both on the basis of the deceased spouse and because of his own social security contribution. However, the surviving spouse can choose to receive whichever payment is larger.

• Unmarried children up to 18 (or 19, if attending high school full time) receive benefits.

• Children disabled before age 22 can get benefits for as long as they're disabled. This program is of particular interest to the estate planning needs of parents with a mentally or physically disadvantaged child who will need continuing lifetime care. It allows them to create an ongoing trust [see Chapter 16, Section C(1)] to supplement social security income; they don't have to start from scratch.

• Divorced widows or widowers, if the marriage lasted at least 10 years, receive payment for life. It's possible for both a surviving spouse and an ex-spouse to collect social security based on the same deceased wage earner. A divorced widow or widower can receive full benefits at age 65, and reduced benefits from age 60.

• Under certain circumstances, grandchildren, great grandchildren, and dependent parents 62 or older may be eligible for payments.

In addition, social security pays one lump sum death payment of $255 to the surviving spouse or child eligible for benefits.

People under 70 who receive social security payments as the survivor of a deceased worker may have the payments reduced if they work and their earnings exceed "exempt amounts" set by law. The exempt amounts are $5,760 for people under 65 and $7,800 for people 65 through 69. Any amount can be earned by a person over 70 without a reduction in payment.

Under federal law the decedent's own last monthly social security check must be returned to the Social Security Administration. The amount is not pro-rated. Thus, if a person receives her social security check on the first of the month, and dies on the 20th of that month, her estate cannot keep any of her last check. The full monthly check must be given back to Social Security.

B. Keogh and IRA Retirement Programs

AS YOU DOUBTLESS KNOW, Keogh and IRA (Individual Retirement Account) plans are retirement plans you fund yourself from your own savings, without paying taxes on the money contributed. Income taxes are due when money is withdrawn after retirement.

Keogh and IRA plans were not intended as estate planning devices. In theory, at least, you create one to provide for yourself after retirement, not to make gifts after your death. However, in practice, IRAs and Keoghs often contain money when a person dies, and so become part (sometimes a significant part) of an estate plan.

An advantage of having money in an IRA or Keogh which many people don't consider is that any money left in the account at death goes to a named beneficiary free of probate. You simply specify the beneficiary on the account documents. The money can be paid in a lump sum, or in installments, in the form of an annuity. Money in an IRA or Keogh at a person's death is included in the deceased's taxable estate.

Because the federal government doesn't officially recognize IRAs and Keoghs as estate planning devices, it requires that you must begin to take money from your IRA account when you reach age 70 1/2. Then the percentage of the total that you must withdraw each year is determined by your age and statistical life expectancy. [For a thorough explanation of how IRAs work, see *IRA Investing Made Easy*, Hutchison (Eagle North Communications)].

C. Other Retirement Programs

THERE ARE MANY other types of benefits: military benefits, railroad retirement benefits, state and federal employment retirement, union pension plans, and so on. The benefits (if any) these programs provide survivors depend on the specific provisions of each program. To find out, you'll need to check the rules of each program that applies to you. Once you do, it shouldn't be difficult to integrate this information into your estate plan.

PART VII

Going Further

CHAPTERS 22 & 23

Going Further—Doing Your Own Research or Hiring Experts

Going Further—Doing Your Own Research or Hiring Experts

MANY, PROBABLY A MAJORITY of, readers will find the information set out in this book sufficient to plan their estate. However, as with any field where law intersects money, an almost infinite range of options and technicalities exist—more, certainly, than can be covered in one volume. So, for any one of a number of reasons, you may want to learn more about estate planning. Throughout the book I've identified a number of the areas likely to warrant further study. Here's a summary:

- Your estate is worth over $600,000 and you want to learn about more sophisticated techniques which might reduce federal estate taxes.

- You want to learn more about legal techniques designed to protect your combined assets from being totally consumed if you or your spouse become ill and need continuing care.

- You want to handle the details of making a relatively complex gift, such as a "marital life estate," to your spouse.

- You own a part of a valuable small business and have questions as to how you and the other owners can plan both to protect the surviving business owners and each owner's inheritors.

- You must make arrangements for long-term care and support of a mentally disadvantaged child or other relative who is likely to survive you by many years.

- You worry someone will challenge your living trust or will, and you want to be sure they are as unassailable as is humanly possible.

- You wish to leave as little money to your spouse as is legally possible.

- You want to establish an ongoing trust (other than the simple children's trust described in Chapters 6 and 9) that will continue after you die.

- You want to research a specific aspect of your state's laws, such as:

  - rules that exempt small estates from probate;

  - details of your state's Uniform Gifts (or Transfers) to Minors Act.

If you decide you want to learn more about any of these or other legal areas, you have three choices:

1. Do your own legal research;

2. See an expert; or

3. A combination of the two.

Often this third option is the wisest approach. By doing your own legal research you can understand at least the basics of your problems, and you may well be able to draft much of your own needed paperwork. Then, and only then, you pay for focused professional help to check your conclusions and be sure your paperwork is legal and will efficiently achieve your goals.

A. Doing Your Own Research

LEARNING HOW to do your own research into estate planning law often provides real benefits. Not only are you likely to save money on professional fees, you'll gain a sense of mastery over an area of law, generating a confidence that your estate plan really meets your needs and giving you a head start should you ever want to research other legal questions.

Fortunately, many aspects of estate planning law are fairly easy to research. For example, to answer questions concerning technical aspects of the state laws affecting wills or probate avoidance, you often need only to check the relevant statutes of your state to find the particular provision that concerns you.

In addition, if you want to try drafting a particular legal form, you may well find that it's easier than you think. Lawyers commonly draft forms largely by copying out fairly standard language (they call it "boilerplate") from legal form books. Indeed, once you take a look at these form books, you may be surprised to see how lawyers (or, typically, their paralegal assistants) can recycle "canned" language and charge hefty amounts for this limited service. For example, many wills and living trusts are copied by lawyers directly out of standard legal form books. Even in more complicated situations of will or trust drafting, all lawyers do, in many instances, is to check several standard legal form books. Obviously, you can do at least some of this for yourself, if you can locate the right books.

1. Research Aids

If you decide you want to do your own research, how do you go about it? First, you need an introduction to how law libraries work. If you can't hire your own law librarian, the best book explaining how to do your own legal work for nonlawyers is *Legal Research: How to Find and Understand the Law,* by Steve Elias (Nolo Press). It shows you, step-by-step, how to find answers in the law library and is, as far as I know, the only legal research book written specifically for non-professionals.

Next, locate a law library (or a public library with a good law collection). There's often one in your principal county courthouse, although its quality depends a lot on your state. County law libraries are normally supported by tax dollars or by the fees paid to file court papers. In my experience, their librarians are sensitive and generally most helpful and courteous to nonlawyers who want to learn to do their own legal research. If the county library is not adequate, your best bet is a law school library. Those in state colleges and universities supported by tax dollars are almost always open to the public.

Even with the assistance of a sympathetic law librarian and a research aid, digging into the law can be intimidating at first. I urge you to stay with it. After a while—probably much sooner than you anticipate—you'll understand the materials and how you can use them.

2. How to Approach Research Problems

In this section, I suggest a general strategy you can use when you want the answer to an estate planning legal question and must start from scratch. The basic nature of this strategy is easy to articulate: You start from the general and proceed to the specific. As you get more and more specific, you will arrive at a reasonably precise answer to your question. Of course, in theory there can be questions that have no answer, simply because they've never been decided by a court or legislature. But in reality, for most questions which are likely to affect your estate plan, there will be an answer, and it won't be too hard to find.

Note on Legal Research Short Cuts: As with any broad approach to problem-solving, doing systematic legal research—starting with the general and moving in an ordered way to the specific—isn't always necessary. For example, if all you want to do is find and read a statute, you won't need this strategy but rather will want to go right to the statute book. And I confess that I often use a less systematic, more hunt-and-peck approach in my own legal research. The method presented here is more comprehensive, designed to enable you to research an issue in depth and breath. For example, once you've located and read a statute, you may want to find out how courts have interpreted the statute. For this reason, I recommend that you understand the general research strategy presented here and be ready to plug into it as needed.

Step 1: Focus Your Issue

Focus on the basic subject you want to research. This will help you locate the right initial research resource. Does your question concern wills, trusts, or federal estate taxes? Take a little time to articulate your question to yourself. The sharper the focus of your inquiry, the easier it will be to obtain the answer. It may help you to discuss your problem with a law librarian. They are experts at pigeon-holing questions into the right categories for further research.

Step 2: Focus on Relevant Legal Language

The next step is to come up with some terms that will enable you to locate a basic resource book about your subject. Think of several key words or phrases that come up in your question or issue, using synonyms and related words where possible. If you have read this book carefully and use the Glossary, this shouldn't be difficult. For example, if you want to know more about leaving property in trust to a disadvantaged child, you could check "trusts," "irrevocable trusts," "children," "government benefits," and "disadvantaged" or "handicapped."

Step 3: Locate a Basic Resource

In a law library, use the card catalogue (or better yet, ask the law librarian) to locate a book that will provide basic information about your subject. This basic background reading will help you understand the law that applies to your issue, possibly provide some initial answers to your question, and give you reference to more specific sources.

As you look for books, keep in mind that any over a few years old are likely to contain information that is no longer current. The most useful materials are those that are updated regularly by new editions or "pocket part" inserts inside the back cover. Once you locate a basic resource, use its index to look up the terms you came up with in Step 2.

In the estate planning field, there are several categories of background books:

- **Overall estate planning.** There are many books covering estate planning in general. One of the best is Kess and Westlin, *The CCH Estate Planning Guide* (Commerce Clearing House). In reading these resources, please remember that they are written by attorney estate planners for attorneys and often have predictable prejudices against a do-it-yourself approach. So, you may need to ignore an author's attitude as you get to the solid legal information.

- **How-to-do-it estate planning books for lawyers.** Many states have estate planning books prepared for practicing lawyers. These books contain specific clauses and forms for wills or trusts, and many other "hands on" materials. For example, in California, the Continuing Education of the Bar (CEB) publishes several useful estate planning books, including *Drafting California Irrevocable Inter Vivos Trusts; Drafting California Revocable Inter Vivos Trusts; California Will Drafting;* and *Estate Planning for the General Practitioner.* Comparable books in New York are published by the Practicing Law Institute (PLI) and include:

  - *Estate Planning,* Manning
  - *Use of Trusts in Estate Planning,* Moore
  - *Stocker on Drawing Wills,* Stocker
  - *Income Taxation of Estates and Trusts,* Michaelson & Blattmaehr

In other states, the best way to locate this type of book for your state is to ask the law librarian or look in the subject-matter card catalog.

- **Comprehensive research books on one area of estate planning law.** There are legal treatises covering certain major aspects of estate planning. For example, for federal estate taxes there's *The CCH Federal Estate and Gift Tax Code* (and IRS Regulations); and for trusts, Cohan and Hemmerling, *Inter Vivos Trusts* (Shepard's Citations); and Peschel and Spurgeon, *Federal Taxation of Trusts; Grantors and Beneficiaries* (Warner, Gorham and Lamont). And there are a number of popular self-help tax guides.

- **Legal encyclopedias.** These provide an overview of virtually every legal topic. They are indexed by subject and can be used much the same way as a regular encyclopedia. Thus, they can give your research a little jump-start. There are two national legal encyclopedias: *American Jurisprudence* (Am.Jur.), generally the most up-to-date and better written, and *Corpus Jurum Secundum* (CJS) which contains numerous references to court decisions on any legal point.

There are also encyclopedias published for specific states (mostly the larger states). Unless you are dealing with a clearly federal topic (like federal estate and gift taxes), it is a good idea to first use a state encyclopedia. The material there is likely to be more specific than is an article in a national encyclopedia. Ask your law librarian whether there is an encyclopedia for your state.

- **Form books for lawyers.** Once you have read a discussion of your issue in one of the general research resources just discussed, you may want to tackle a lawyers' form book, especially if you are looking for a particular clause or language to put into a will, living trust, or durable power of attorney. Lawyers' form books are collections (often in many volumes) of sample legal forms and instructions, designed to accomplish many thousands of legal tasks. A law librarian will be able to direct you to the form books for your state. Unfortunately, often these books aren't very clear—you'll have to wade through some legalese.

- **Law review articles.** These are collections of articles published by law schools and various law-based organizations. The articles tend to focus on trends in the law or on important new statutes or court decisions. Thus, if your research topic involves issues that are current, or you want to know something about your state's new probate procedures, you stand a good chance of finding something relevant in a law review article. Don't expect practical advice from a law review article, though; they are written from an academic point of view and are usually fairly theoretical. *Legal Research: How to Find and Understand the Law*, mentioned above, gives thorough instructions on how to find and use law review articles.

Step 4: Read Statute or Case Referred to by Background Resource

Once you have read a basic background resource, you may have as much information as you need. However, if you want to be assured that the law is as it is represented to be in the book, you will need to check the source material. In other words, once you grasp the background of the law, you need to read the law itself.

Fortunately, almost all basic background resources are heavily footnoted. This means the resource will refer you to statutes and court opinions. Your next step, therefore, will be to read these law sources. Be warned, however, that many statutes are difficult to understand without considerable effort. The major research sources here are:

- **Federal statutes.** These are found in the volumes of the United States Code. The best research source here is called the U.S. Code Annotated (U.S.C.A.) which, after setting forth statutes, contains references to court decisions (cases) and other pertinent materials.

  Note on Federal Tax Statutes: Located in the United States Code, Title 26, the tax statutes are so abstruse and dense it is often impossible to determine their meaning, at least not without hours and hours of grueling effort. If you try to read the tax code, use it in conjunction with some of the more user-friendly tax treatises or guides listed above.

- **State laws (statutes).** State statutes contain detailed rules that affect estate planning, including probate, special probate exemptions, and trusts. State laws are called "codes," "laws," or "statutes," depending on the state. Usually, you want to locate the "annotated" version, which most states have; these contain both the statutes and summaries of relevant court decisions and cross-references to articles and commentaries, which you may want to read, too.

Once you have located the volumes that contain your state's laws, find and read the specific statute that concerns you, if you already have the numbered reference (citation) enabling you to find it. If you don't have a citation, check the index for the statutes covering the general subject that concerns you. In some states, the statutes are further divided into subject areas, often called "codes." If this is done, there will typically be a civil code, penal code, vehicle code, and so on. You will normally find the laws you want for estate planning in the volume of statutes dealing with your state's basic civil or probate laws.

Statutes are numbered sequentially. If they are divided into codes, numbers normally start over for each. In any case, once you locate the correct number (and if necessary, code) in the index, it's easy to find the statute you need. If you have trouble, the law librarian will usually be happy to help. And don't forget to check the supplement inside the back of the book, which contains recent law changes (if any) and court decisions about the statute.

- **Court opinions.** Court interpretations of statutes, and court decisions on matters that aren't covered by statute, are as much a part of our law as the statutes themselves. Court decisions are collected in bound volumes, and indexed in books called "digests," which a law librarian can help you find.

How do you know whether the courts have addressed the issue you are interested in? First, as mentioned, the background resources you read will most likely indicate significant court decisions in the area. If they do, you will almost always be given a case citation which tells you the volume and page number of the bound volume where the court case can be found.

Another source of relevant case citations is the annotated codes (statutes). The one-sentence summaries of court decisions that directly follow the statutes in these codes include citations to the cases. By skimming these summaries, you have an excellent chance of picking up on any case that may bear on your issue.

A third source of case citations is the subject matter index to state and national case digests (discussed in *Legal Research: How to Find and Understand the Law*).

Reading cases can be tricky. Basically, all cases set forth the facts that the court relied on to make its decision, the issue the court was asked to decide, the court's decision, and the reason for the decision. For a case to be applicable to your issue, its facts and the legal issue decided must be roughly the same as your situation.

Step 5: Make Sure Your Answers Are Up To Date

Law is always changing. When you find a case or statute that seems pertinent, your next question should be, "Is this still good law?" There are several techniques for bringing the fruits of your research up to date. For

statutes, the main technique is to check the pocket part, as explained in Step 4. If you want to be fanatical, you can also check to see whether your legislature has passed any new statutes on your subject since the pocket part was published.

The main technique for updating cases is a tool called *Shepard's Citations*. *Shepard's* tells you all the instances the case you are interested in has been referred to in other cases. This will tell your whether your case has been overruled or by subsequent cases. *Legal Research: How to Find and Understand the Law* covers how to use *Shepard's*.

B. Using Lawyers and Other Experts

IF YOU DO DETERMINE that you want an expert's assistance, obviously you don't want to hire a lawyer at random and say "tell me what to do." As an intelligent consumer, you want to gain as much knowledge about your problem as you conveniently can, which should enable you to determine if a lawyer or other expert is dealing with you in a straightforward way. You also want to be sure the person you hire is honest, knowledgeable and provides good service for your dollar.

One piece of advice: Your estate plan should express your intentions. No one else can know those intentions. Sometimes, when people think, or fear, that they need a lawyer, what they are really doing is longing for an authority figure (or believing one is required) to tell them what to do. Keep in mind that an estate planning expert is only your paid employee (advisor), not a mentor.

1. What Kind of Expert Do You Need?

The first question to decide if you want to consult an expert is what type you need: a lawyer, accountant or financial planner? Questions about federal estate taxes or how to calculate tax basis rules on the sale of appreciated property can normally be better answered by an experienced CPA than a lawyer. Similarly, for some financial decisions, such as what type of insurance to buy, you may be better off talking to a financial planner. But for many sophisticated estate planning concerns, you do need to see a lawyer. This would be the case, for instance, if you want to establish a marital life estate trust. It would also be advisable if your small business needs to customize its partnership agreement or corporate bylaws to allow for a surviving principal to buy out the shares of a deceased principal from his or her inheritors.

The type of lawyer right for you depends on what your problem is.[1] If you need fairly sophisticated estate planning, especially the creation of trusts, it's important that you see someone who specializes in the field. She may charge relatively high fees, but if she's good, she's worth it. Ongoing trusts are quite complex and technical; most general practice lawyers are simply not sufficiently educated in this field. For example, if you want to set up a trust for a child with special needs, and also protect that child's eligibility for government benefits, it's prudent to see a lawyer who specializes in this work. On the other hand, if your needs are more basic, such as a review of a garden variety living trust you've drafted from this book, or to check some provision of your state's laws, a competent attorney in general practice should be able to do a good job at a lower cost.

It's important that you feel a personal rapport with your lawyer. You want one who treats you as an equal.

---

[1] Ambrose Bierce defined a lawyer as "one skilled in circumvention of the law."

(Interestingly, the Latin root of the word "client" translates as "to hear, to obey.") When talking with a lawyer on the phone or at a first conference, ask specific questions that concern you. If the lawyer answers them clearly and concisely—explaining, but not talking down to you—fine. If he acts wise, but says little except to ask that the problem be placed in his hands (with the appropriate fee, of course), watch out. You are either talking with someone who doesn't know the answer and won't admit it (common), or someone who finds it impossible to let go of the "me expert, you peasant" way of looking at the world (even more common).

As you already know, lawyers are expensive. They charge fees usually ranging from $90 to $400 or more per hour. While fancy office trappings, three-piece suits and solemn faces are no guarantee (or even a good indication) that a particular lawyer will provide top notch service in a style you will feel comfortable with, this conventional style will almost always ensure that you will be charged at the upper end of the fee range. At Nolo, our experience tells us that high fees and quality service don't necessarily go hand in hand. Indeed, the attorneys I think most highly of tend to charge moderate fees (for lawyers, that is), and seem to get along very nicely without most stuffy law office trappings.

Be sure you've settled your fee arrangement—in writing—at the start of your relationship. Depending on the area of the county where you live, generally, I feel that fees in the range of $90 to $150 per hour are reasonable in urban areas, given the average lawyer's overhead. In rural counties and smaller cities, $75 to $125 is more like it. In addition to the amount charged per hour, you also want a clear commitment from the lawyer concerning how many hours he expects to put in on your problem.

2. Finding a Lawyer

All this sounds good, you may think, but how do you find a lawyer? Believe me, it isn't difficult. Indeed, ours is such a lawyer-ridden society that it's unusual if one hasn't already found you. There is a growing surplus of lawyers; one out of every 280 Americans will be one by 1995. (If we just look at white males, the figure is less than one out of 100.) The trick, of course, is not just finding a lawyer, but retaining one who is trustworthy, competent, and charges fairly. A few words of advice may be helpful.

When looking for a good lawyer, personal routes are the traditional, and probably best. If a relative or good friend found a lawyer he likes, chances are you'll like him too. Failing this, check with people you know in any political or social organization you're involved with, especially those with a large number of members over age 40. They may well know of a competent lawyer who handles routine estate planning matters and whose attitudes are similar to yours.

Another good approach is to ask the assistance of a lawyer you are personally acquainted with and think well of, even if she doesn't work in the estate planning area. Very likely she can refer you to someone trustworthy who does.

Also, check with people you respect who own their own small businesses. Almost anyone running a small business has a relationship with a lawyer, and chances are they've found one they like.

If you are a member of a legal insurance plan, you may be offered sophisticated estate planning assistance from a referral panel member at a reduced fee. Some of these referrals may be to excellent lawyers. In my experience, however, too often lawyers who sign up to do cut-rate work are not the best alternative. Excellent lawyers tend very quickly to get all the work they can handle, and thus don't need to cut fees to gain clients.

Also, be cautious when dealing with bar association referral panels. Never assume a listing on a referral panel is a seal of approval. While lawyers are supposed to be screened as to their specialty to get on these panels, screening is usually perfunctory. Often the main qualification is that the lawyer needs business.

Finally, don't hesitate to question any lawyer you are referred to; make your own judgments. If the expert is uncomfortable because you've done some of the work yourself, back off. You need an expert who's open and sympathetic to people who want to actively participate in handling their own legal affairs. And always keep in mind that in any field there are good high-priced experts and bad ones. It's all too easy to get a mumbo-jumbo speaking lawyer who confuses you at first, and enrages you later, when you receive his exorbitant bill for what may even turn out to be needless work. Don't be afraid to keep looking until you find a lawyer you like. Many people who have had unhappy experiences with lawyers (and we all know some) only wish they had done so.

Ater Your Estate Plan Is Completed

CHAPTER 23

After Your Estate Plan is Completed

YOUR ESTATE PLANNING IS DONE. Now what? First, congratulate yourself. You've completed a tough job. A celebration isn't out of place. Why not gather those you love, break out your favorite beverage and toast—"To Life!"

A. Storing Your Estate Planning Documents

COMPLETION OF AN ESTATE PLAN means that you have created some important documents: a will, probably a living trust, and quite possibly other forms, such as a durable power of attorney, joint tenancy deed, and perhaps business ownership documents or written instructions for your funeral or donations of body parts. Obviously, you want to keep these documents in a safe place, where you can readily find them. Any secure place can be used for storage: a safe in your house or office, or even a locked drawer in your home file cabinet.

In addition, while you may want at least some of these documents to be private while you live, you will also surely want them to be immediately accessible to whomever will handle your affairs at your death. Settle on a sensible storage place and let that person know what you've decided. If the documents are kept in a locked drawer in your house, be sure that person has ready access to that drawer. Similarly, if you store these documents in a safe deposit box, be sure that your executor or successor trustee has legal access to that box. Documents that deal with your wishes as to organ transplants and funeral or burial instructions must also be immediately available.

Is it sensible to make copies of your estate planning documents? That's entirely up to you. Often people do want copies—to give to their executor or successor trustee, family members or friends, or institutions that require them, such as a stock brokerage company, in order to transfer an account into the name of a living trust. If you do make copies, follow this approach:

- Photocopy the documents you want people to see. These are not legal originals.

- Never sign a copy. If you do, it could legally qualify as a "duplicate original." If you later decide to change, amend or revoke the document, you have to change each duplicate original as well.

- To be extra safe, mark "copy" in ink on each page. This isn't legally required, but it insures that no one can claim a copy is an original.

B. Revisions

ESTATE PLANS SHOULDN'T be changed frequently. If impromptu changes ("I'll show her, I'll cut her out of my estate!") occur often, you have an underlying family or personal problem to examine. Major life events, however, obviously can call for estate planning changes. For example, if any of the following events occur, you should review your plan:

- You sell or otherwise dispose of any property you've specifically mentioned in your will or living trust.

- Marriage. This one is particularly important, as your new spouse will have a right to inherit a share of your estate determined by law if you don't update your will.

- Divorce.

- Birth of a child. The rule here is similar to that for marriage.

- Death of a beneficiary.

- Your financial situation changes significantly.

- You move to a new state. This is particularly necessary if you are married and move from a common law property state to a community property state or vice versa. See Chapter 3 for a detailed discussion of the issues that should concern you.

- You acquire or sell substantial property.

- You want to change the successor trustee of your living trust, or the executor (personal representative) of your will.

• You want to change the personal guardian you have named for your minor children or, if you have established a children's trust, the person or institution you have named as trustee.

If you do decide to change your estate plan, you must decide whether you need, or want, to create entirely new documents or simply modify your existing ones. This can depend both on how complex your changes are and the estate planning document involved.

1. Property You No Longer Own at Your Death

Estate planning transfer devices, such as wills or living trusts, don't become binding until your death. Before then, you can sell, transfer or give away any property you own (except as limited by marital property law; see Chapter 3). So what happens when you dispose of property but don't change your will or trust? For example, what happens if your will leaves your son your 1988 Chevy, but by the time you die, you've already sold it and purchased a 1989 Buick?

To summarize what can be a complicated area of law: if you've given someone a specific piece of property (say the Chevy) but you no longer own it when you die, that beneficiary is out of luck. The fact that you own a Buick doesn't help the beneficiary. Lawyers call this "ademption"; people who don't inherit the property in question are often heard to use an earthier term. Obviously, the way to avoid creating this type of problem is to keep your estate plan up to date. If you've sold or transferred any item that is also specifically given away in your will or living trust, revise those documents.

2. Living Trusts

Living trusts can be revised by the following methods:

• Adding property to the trust, by listing it on the trust schedule and taking title to that property in the trust's name. This method does not automatically require you to name a new beneficiary for this new trust property. If you don't, it will go to your residuary beneficiary unless you've provided that "all property" on the trust schedule goes to some other beneficiary. If you only add property to a trust schedule, you do not have to have the trust notarized again.

• Amend the trust. As discussed in Chapter 9, Section H, you can make a formal amendment to your trust, to add or delete beneficiaries, change gifts, or name new successor trustees. The amendment must be notarized.

• Revoke the old trust and prepare a new one, reflecting your current intentions. This means you'll have to get the new trust document notarized.

3. Wills

There are only two ways to change a formal witnessed will:

• Prepare a formal witnessed codicil to the will.

• Destroy the old will and make a new one.

Let's briefly examine each procedure.

a. Make a Codicil

A codicil is a formal legal method for making changes to a will after the will has been drafted, signed and witnessed. A codicil is a sort of legal "P.S." to the will. It should be typed, with a formal heading like "Codicil to Will of _____." The text of the codicil then identifies the date of the original will and defines the change made.

"I give $3,000 to my friend Al Smith;" or "I give my silver tea set to Bertha Weinstock, and revoke my gift of that tea set to Mary Warbler, now deceased."

The codicil then must be prepared, signed and witnessed with all the formalities of a will. In other words, it should be signed and dated by the will maker in the presence of three witnesses, who are told that it's the maker's will and then sign their names. The witnesses don't have to be the same as those for the original will, though it's a good idea to use the original witnesses if they're available. Sample codicil forms are contained in *Nolo's Simple Will Book*.

b. Make a New Will

If a major revision of the will is desired, it's better to draft a new will and revoke the old one than to use a codicil. A will that has been substantially re-written by a codicil is an awkward document and can be confusing. It may not always be clear what the relationship of the codicil to the original will provisions means. One advantage of using a computer will program (such as Nolo's *WillMaker*) is that it's quite easy to make changes and print out a whole new will.

If you make a new will, your old will should be revoked (cancelled). This can be done as long as you are alive and mentally competent. You can do this by either:

- destroying the will itself (and all copies, if you can get your hands on them)—rip 'em up and throw 'em out; *and*

- stating in the new document you prepare that you revoke all previous or earlier wills you have made.

I strongly recommend that you do both.

4. Joint Tenancy

Once you've established a joint tenancy, you're pretty much stuck with shared ownership, unless all joint tenants agree to end it. One joint tenant can normally transform the joint tenancy into a tenancy in common,

which eliminates the right of the other co-owners to automatically inherit, but it takes agreement of all the joint tenants to allow any one to become the sole owner of the property. If all joint tenants agree to end a joint tenancy, they can sign a document (a deed, for real estate) transferring the property into whatever new form of ownership is desired.

 If you want to transfer your share of joint tenancy property into tenancy in common, and the other owner(s) don't consent, you'll need to see a lawyer to learn the procedures required in your state.

5. Informal Bank Account Trusts

You can revoke an informal bank account trust (pay-on-death account) at any time. This can be done formally either by closing it or removing (or changing) the beneficiary. It can also be done informally, by spending all the money it contains. If the account is empty when you die, obviously the beneficiary gets nothing.

6. Insurance

If you are the owner of an insurance policy, you can cancel the policy or change the beneficiary of that policy. If, as discussed in detail in Chapter 12, Section E, you are not the legal owner of the policy, you have no right to cancel the policy or change the beneficiary, even if the policy insures your own life.

PART VIII

Sample
Estate
Plans

Some Estate Plans

Some Estate Plans

THIS CHAPTER PRESENTS seven different estate plans. Each discusses the needs of a person or couple and the estate plan they decide upon. As I stated at the beginning of this book, I don't believe that relying on pre-set formula plans is a sensible way for anyone to form a personal plan. Rather, the purpose of providing these plans is to illustrate how the estate planning methods discussed in this book can be assembled into a coherent plan.

Other Nolo Resources

Some of the plans discussed in this chapter recommend a form contained in another publication of Nolo Press. I apologize for referring you to other books, but it is necessary. This book, *Plan Your Estate,* is Nolo's overview book on estate planning. As you can see, it is undoubtedly big enough. Of necessity then, a number of detailed forms and instructions are only set out in the Nolo books that focus more deeply on an individual component of the estate planning process. These include:

- *Nolo's Simple Will Book* (contains far more detailed wills than the one included in Chapter 17)

- *The Power of Attorney Book* (complete forms and instructions necessary to prepare your own durable power of attorney)

- *WillMaker* software package (a computer software package which allows you to prepare a will which addresses a number of concerns not covered in the back-up will included in Chapter 17.

As purchaser of *Plan Your Estate,* you are entitled to a 25% discount on all other Nolo estate planning books and software. A discount coupon is included at the back of the book.

A. A Couple in Their 50's

ABEL AND RACHEL Rublestam are in their 50's. They live in a non-community property state. They have two children, Isaiah and Rebecca. Isaiah is married and has two young children, one of whom has a severe physical handicap. Rebecca is attending college.

Their property: The Rublestams share ownership of all their property. Their estate consists of a coop apartment worth $350,000 ($100,000 equity), stocks and savings worth $80,000, life insurance on each spouse which pays $200,000 on death, and their one-third ownership of the R-S corporation, a family business. It's hard to determine the exact value for their business interest. As a rough guess, they decide it's worth $500,000.

Their estate planning goals: The Rublestams want to plan now to avoid probate. They also realize that their net estate is worth more than $600,000, and that the estate of the second spouse to die would face a federal estate tax. Nevertheless, each wants to leave all their property outright to the other. At their ages, neither wants the restrictions a marital life estate trust imposes [see Chapter 16, Section B(1)]. After all, if one unexpectedly dies soon, the survivor, who will have a life expectancy of 25 to 30 years, may well need all the property they have both accumulated, not just the income. They decide to postpone estate tax planning until later in their lives, accept the risk that if one dies prematurely, it may increase the eventual estate taxes on the property they leave to their children.

Their plan: To avoid probate, the Rublestams prepare a marital living trust (see Chapter 9). They use their trust to leave each other their apartment, stocks and corporation shares. Each names both children as alternate beneficiaries, in case both spouses die together. They carefully transfer title to these assets to the trust's name, having already checked that the bylaws of their co-op apartment association and the R-S corporation permit this.

Each spouse names the other spouse as beneficiary of their life insurance policy.

The Rublestams each prepare a back-up will (see Chapter 17). Each also signs a durable power of attorney for heath care authorizing the other spouse to make health care decisions if one becomes incapacitated. Each durable power of attorney specifically authorizes a spouse to terminate life support equipment if the other has a terminal illness (see Chapter 18).

If they become wealthier when they are older, the Rublestams intend to investigate how they can create a trust to benefit their disadvantaged grandchild. They also plan to eventually make tax-free gifts of $10,000 per year each to their children, but decide that it's premature to do it now.

B. A Wealthy Couple in Their 70's

ROBERT AND TERESA Casswell are a prosperous married couple in their mid-70's. Both are retired and live comfortably on their savings, assets and retirement payments. They live in a non-community property state and share ownership of all their property equally. The Casswells have four children.

Their property: A house worth $350,000 (all equity; they paid off the mortgage years ago), a summer home worth $125,000 ($75,000 equity), stocks worth $300,000, art works valued at $90,000, jewelry valued at $50,000, savings of $160,000, and miscellaneous personal property worth a total of $45,000. Their total net worth is $1,070,000, all of which is in both their names.

Their estate planning goals: Robert and Teresa each want to leave most of their property to the surviving spouse and then to their four children in equal shares. They also want to make small gifts to friends, relatives and charities. Because their combined estate is relatively large, they also want to plan to avoid probate and reduce estate taxes to the extent feasible.

Their plan: Robert and Teresa decide to establish a marital living trust to avoid probate. This trust will be combined with a marital life estate trust to reduce eventual estate taxes (see Chapter 14, Section B). Each spouse puts the bulk of his or her one-half of the marital property in the living trust. When the first spouse dies, his or her property will be turned over to a life estate trust, with the income going to the other spouse for his or her life. On the death of the second spouse, both this life estate trust

property and the bulk of one-half of the community property belonging to the second spouse will be divided equally between the four children.

In the living trust, each spouse also specifies several personal gifts to friends and charities. The successor trustee for the trust, after both spouses die, will be the Casswells' eldest daughter, a stable, savvy woman who lives near them and is respected by the other children. They have discussed this with her and mentioned it to the other children; happily, none of the others objected.

The Casswells work out the basic ideas of how they want their combined living trust and marital life estate trust to work. They see a lawyer to draft and prepare the actual trust. Because the marital life estate trust is an ongoing one which may last a number of years after the first spouse dies, how-to details are not covered in this book.

The Casswells also prepare back-up wills (see Chapter 12) and durable powers of attorney for health care (see Chapter 18).

By establishing a marital life estate trust (rather than leaving their property outright to the surviving spouse), Robert and Teresa effectively keep their total property in two piles, worth $535,000 each. Because up to $600,000 may be transferred at death free of federal estate tax (assuming no taxable gifts have been made earlier), the result is no federal estate tax. They won't need to do any more sophisticated planning unless their total estate grows to over $1,200,000. If this occurs, or perhaps just because they don't need more property, the Casswells might consider making gifts to their children. Each can give $10,000 per year to each child gift tax-free, for a combined total of $80,000 annually.

Because they combined their life estate trusts with a marital living trust, the Casswells' property will avoid probate.

C. A Widow in Her 80's

IDA GRANT, a widow, lives in California. She wants to leave the bulk of her estate to her one child, Carla. She also has a four-year-old Irish terrier, which she loves and wants to provide care for after she dies. Finally, she wants to make a number of small gifts to friends and charities.

Her property: Mrs. Grant's estate consists of a house that she and her husband bought in 1937 for $5,000. It now has a market value of $460,000. Mrs. Grant has household furnishings worth $20,000, a car worth $5,000, and savings of $200,000. She lives primarily on interest from her savings and social security.

Her estate planning goals: Mrs. Grant values simplicity. She wants to transfer her gifts by the simplest means possible, but she also wants to avoid probate.

Her plan: Mrs. Grant considers transferring her house into joint tenancy with her daughter Carla, who she trusts absolutely, because this seems to provide the simplest probate-avoidance transfer method (see Chapter 10). However, Mrs. Grant learns there will be serious disadvantages if she uses joint tenancy. The IRS will require that a gift tax return be filed because Mrs. Grant is giving a half-interest in the house to her daughter. No tax will actually be paid because the house is worth less than $600,000, but still, it's a hassle to prepare and file the tax return. Worse, if the house is transferred into joint tenancy, only half of it will receive a "stepped-up" tax basis[1] when Mrs. Grant dies. Since the house has risen so dramatically in price, losing half the stepped-up basis would substantially increase Carla's income tax liability should she ever sell the house after inheriting it.

Mrs. Grant decides to use a living trust for her house. This allows the house to avoid probate at the same time it delays the transfer until Mrs. Grant's death, so that Carla gets the benefit of the stepped-up tax basis. When she prepares the living trust following the instructions in Chapter 9, Mrs. Grant names Carla as the trust's beneficiary and successor trustee. She then signs and records a deed transferring the house from herself to the trust. When listing the house as part of the trust property on the trust schedule, Mrs. Grant includes "all household furnishings" as part of the trust property, so her daughter will receive this property outside of probate as well.

Mrs. Grant considered establishing an ongoing trust to provide care for her dog. However, when she checked this possibility out,[2] she learned that trusts for animals are not legal. A better approach, she learned, is to handle the problem informally. Mrs. Grant discussed it with Carla, who was not a dog lover. Carla suggested that the dog, and a sum of money necessary to care for it, be left to Betty Planquee, a good friend who had indicated she would accept the responsibility.

Mrs. Grant learns that, under California law she can transfer property worth less than $60,000 by her will free of probate (see Chapter 13, Section D). She has her savings in two money market accounts. She divides the money in those accounts so that one contains less than $60,000. She changes title to the other, larger account into an informal bank trust account, naming her daughter as beneficiary, and so avoids probate of that account (see Chapter 11). Then, using the back-up will in Chapter 17, she prepares a will making several cash gifts to close friends:

> *"I give the sum of $20,000 to my good friend and long-time veterinarian, Arthur Pedronnzi.*
>
> *"I give the sum of $5,000 to my good friend and faithful gardener, William Service.*
>
> *"I give the sum of $5,000 and my dog Cherry Blossom to my friend Betty Planquee.*
>
> *"I give the sum of $2,500 to my friend Mary Bale.*
>
> *"I give the sum of $2,500 to my friend Roberta Anthony."*

She included in her will a residuary clause stating: "I give all my remaining property subject to this will to my daughter, Carla." Under this clause, any of her property not specifically transferred under the terms of her living

---

[1]See Chapter 10, Section D(2) for a discussion of the basis rules and joint tenancy.

[2]*Dog Law*, by Randolph (Nolo Press) has a detailed discussion of how best to provide for a dog which may survive its owner.

trust or will would go to Carla. This includes any property she might get after the will was prepared.

Notice that Mrs. Grant didn't name any alternate beneficiaries. She wanted to keep her will simple, and decided that if any of her friends died before her, she wanted that money to go to her daughter under the terms of the residuary clause. And she doesn't even want to consider the possibility that her daughter could die before her.

Mrs. Grant also prepares two durable powers of attorney, one for health care and one for finances, naming her daughter Carla in both as her attorney-in-fact, to act for her if she becomes incapacitated and can't make medical or financial decisions herself (see Chapter 18).

D. A Couple in Their 30's

MARK RYAN AND ALICIA LOPEZ are married, in their 30's, with two young children. Mark is employed as a carpenter; Alicia works part-time as a proofreader for a publisher. They live in Texas, a community property state.

Their property: They own their house (heavily mort-gaged) in joint tenancy. It's the only major asset of their estate. They also own two cars, an old Ford and an older VW station wagon, the well-used furnishings of their home, personal possessions such as clothing, books and electronic equipment, and two savings accounts—one shared with $2,000, and another with $6,000 in Mark's name, an account he had before they were married.

Their estate planning goals: Mark and Alicia's main concern is providing for their children's care, both financial and personal, if both parents die. They don't need to worry about federal estate taxes, because their estate is well below the $600,000 minimum subject to federal tax. And because their house is owned in joint tenancy, their major asset will avoid probate, unless they die simultaneously.

Their plan: Mark and Alicia decide they don't want to create probate-avoiding living trusts now, as they don't have a lot of property and, statistically, are unlikely to die for many years. They prepare wills leaving all their non-joint tenancy property except Mark's savings account to each other. They name their children as alternate bene-ficiaries, to receive all property covered by the wills and the house, in case both parents die simultaneously.

Mark and Alicia learn, to their mutual surprise, that they disagree on what should be done with Mark's $6,000 savings account. Alicia believes it should be handled like all their other property; indeed, she points out that Mark can officially convert the account to community property by simply depositing it in their joint account. Mark states that he wants to keep exclusive control over the account, as his own separate property. Further, he wants to use his will to give it to his brother, Herb, a struggling artist who he is very close to. Alicia, who has long felt Herb was a no-goodnik, becomes upset that Mark wants to hold out on his own family. After all, if Mark died, she and the kids would need every cent they could get their hands on. As Mark starts to get angry, Alicia realizes they need to slow down and talk it out.

It takes a couple of days, but finally they arrive at a compromise. Mark will transfer $3,000 of his account into their shared account. He can give the other $3,000 to Herb in his will.

Only after they resolve their problem do Mark and Alicia approach the issue they both agree is most important—providing for their two children as best they can if the unlikely occurs and they die simultaneously.

They agree on who should be the children's personal guardian (named in their wills)—Alicia's sister Joan, who has stated that she's willing to do the job. They also name Joan as the children's property guardian. They decide that some life insurance is necessary (see Chapter 12), at least until their savings increase and the children are older. They decide to purchase $150,000 term life policies on each of their lives, realizing that because both work and the family needs two incomes to get by, it's not enough just to insure Mark's life. In case they both die simultaneously, they establish a children's trust in both their wills. If both parents die, the insurance proceeds will be paid to the trust and managed for the children's benefit until they become 35. The trusts can be set up in their wills. As Alicia has use of a computer at work, they use *WillMaker* to prepare wills that accomplish their goals.[3] (The back-up wills set out in this book don't contain children's trusts.)

Finally, Mark and Alicia prepare durable powers of attorney for health care, each naming the other to make health decisions in case he or she becomes incapacitated.

E. A Single Man in His 60's

DICK DAUGHTERTY, a lifelong bachelor, wants to leave some of his property to his sister, some to her three children, and much to many friends.

His property: Dick has personal possessions worth $75,000, two extremely valuable antique cars worth a total of $120,000, jewelry worth $25,000, a limited partnership business interest in a real estate venture worth $60,000, stocks now worth $47,000 and savings of $45,000. He doesn't own any real estate.

His estate planning goals: Dick is most concerned with who gets his property, not how they get it. He spends considerable time evaluating exactly who gets

what, making several lists and numerous revisions before he decides how it's best to distribute his property.

Since Dick's estate is worth less than $600,000, he doesn't have to worry about federal estate taxes (see Chapter 14). However, he definitely doesn't want his estate to have to pay probate fees.

His plan: Dick creates a probate-avoiding living trust using the form for one person in the Appendix. In his trust, he specifies the many beneficiaries he's chosen, identifying each item of property that goes to each. Then he transfers all his property, except his savings account, to the living trust. Specifically, he goes to the Department of Motor Vehicles and re-registers his cars in the trust's name. Likewise, he writes the Office of the General Partner for the limited partnership and instructs it to re-register ownership of his shares under the trust's name.

Dick changes his savings account into an informal bank trust account and names his three best friends as equal beneficiaries of the account.

Next, he makes out and signs a back-up will, although, at present, none of his property will be transferred by will. The will covers the possibility he may subsequently acquire property which he isn't able to transfer to his trust before he dies (see Chapter 17).

Then he prepares durable powers of attorney for health care and finances, and names his best friend, Al, to be his attorney-in-fact and another friend, Jacqueline, to be alternate attorney-in-fact if Al can't serve (see Chapter 18). Dick is particularly concerned about health care decisions. If he's incapacitated, he wants to be treated by his personal doctors. If he needs to be hospitalized, he wants to be taken to a specific local hospital. And he does not want life support technology used to artificially extend his life if he has a fatal, irreversible disease. With the aid of *The Power of Attorney Book*, he drafts a durable power of attorney that incorporates all his specific desires, making them legal and mandatory.

Finally, Dick prepares his funeral plan and instructions and gives them to Al, to insure they're carried out (see Chapter 19).

---

[3]Alicia and Mark could also use *Nolo's Simple Will Book* if they prefer a typewriter to a computer.

F. A Couple in Their 60's, In a Second Marriage

MIRIAM AND IRA Bloom are a married couple in their 60's. It's the second marriage for each. Miriam has one child, now 32, from her first marriage; Ira has two, who are 33 and 36, from his first marriage. They live in New York, a common law state.

Their property: Miriam and Ira share ownership of a $200,000 house ($160,000 equity), savings of $30,000, stocks worth $15,000, and miscellaneous furnishings worth approximately $15,000. Each separately owns a car. Ira owns, as his separate property, real estate worth $340,000 ($250,000 equity), limited partnership interests worth $80,000, and savings of $40,000. Miriam owns a coin collection worth $5,000 and stocks worth $110,000.

Their estate planning goals: Both Miriam and Ira want to provide for each other but also ensure that each's separate property eventually goes to their own children. Neither's estate is large enough to be subject to federal estate taxes, but they do want to avoid probate fees.

Their plan: Miriam and Ira agree that each will leave their shared ownership property outright to the other. Any New York state death taxes assessed against either's estate will be paid from this shared property. Each's separate property will be left in a marital life estate trust for the other spouse, with the property in the trust to ultimately go to the deceased spouse's children. Then they see a lawyer to draw up the trust document. The surviving spouse will be the trustee of the life estate trust. Each spouse fully trusts the other to manage the trust property, and is confident he or she will conserve the trust principal for their children. But both spouses know that their children are somewhat mistrustful of this arrangement. So, the spouses agree that the surviving spouse will send the deceased spouse's children yearly reports of the trust's financial status (a copy of the trust's annual tax return will suffice) to reassure them that the property isn't being squandered.

Because one of Ira's children still needs financial support for education, he places $20,000 of his separate savings in an informal bank account trust (pay-on-death

account) for her, so she will immediately get money, without delay, should he die before she graduates. If the daughter completes her education with Ira's help before he dies, he can, if he wants to, revoke the informal bank account trust and place the account in his living trust.

The Blooms also execute durable powers of attorney for health care and finances, naming the other spouse as the attorney-in-fact (see Chapter 18).

Finally, the Blooms sign simple back-up wills (see Chapter 17).

G. An Unmarried Couple in Their 40's

PAT AND MERCEDES have lived together for 13 years. They have no children. They have a written living together contract, stating that they share ownership of their house and its furnishings, and that all other property of each is his or her separate property. They've also recorded a deed to the house, listing their shared ownership.

Their estate planning goals: Each wants to leave his or her interest in the house and furnishings to the other. Each wants to leave separate property to family and friends. Each wants to avoid probate of all their property. Neither's estate will be subject to federal estate taxes. And each wants to insure that the other can make medical and financial decisions if one becomes incapacitated.

Their plan: They decide to create three living trusts: one for their shared property and one each for separate property (see Chapter 9). This, they conclude, will be clearer than lumping all their property into one trust. In each trust, they refer to their written property agreement and state that it remains binding when one—or both—die. In their shared trust, each gives his or her interest in the house and furnishings to the other. In their individual living trusts, they make the gifts of their own property to the beneficiaries they've chosen. Both of them leave much of their property to each other, but also make several other gifts. When their trusts are complete, they both complete all paperwork necessary to transfer all assets with title (ownership) documents to the trust.

Each also prepares a catch-all will and leaves all property subject to those wills (none now) to the other (see Chapter 17).

Finally, Pat and Mercedes each prepare durable powers of attorney for health care and finances, naming the other as their attorney-in-fact, with authority to make decisions if one becomes incapacitated (see Chapter 18).

Glossary

PART OF THE HOLD that the legal profession has over us has to do with its use of specialized language. It is easy to be intimidated and uncomfortable when we don't know what lawyers and judges are talking about. It is only beginning to dawn on many of us that legal language is sometimes consciously, and occasionally even cynically, used to keep us intimidated, and that the concepts behind the obtuse language are often easily understandable. I'd rather use only plain English throughout this book and eliminate legalistic jargon altogether, but unfortunately we are stuck with a legal system that often creaks into motion best when "magic" (sometimes four-syllabic) words are used. (Lawyers call such words "terms of art.")

If you don't find a confusing term defined here, try a standard dictionary, but be sure to read the entire definition, as specialized legal meanings are often listed last. Or check Nolo's legal dictionaries, the *Intellectual Property Law Dictionary* or the *Family Law Dictionary*. As a last resort, try *Black's Law Dictionary*, available in all law libraries.

Note: Definitions in quotes and with the symbol (B.) following are taken from Ambrose Bierce's *The Devil's Dictionary*.

A/B trust: A lawyer's phrase for a "marital life estate trust."

Abatement: Cutting back certain gifts under a will when it is necessary to create a fund to meet expenses, pay taxes, satisfy debts, or take care of other bequests which are given a priority under law or under the will.

Accumulation Trust: A trust where trust income is retained, and not paid out to beneficiaries until certain conditions occur.

Acknowledgment: A statement in front of a person who is qualified to administer oaths (e.g., a Notary Public) that a document bearing your signature was actually signed by you.

Ademption: The failure of a specific bequest of property to take effect because the property is no longer owned by the person who made the will at the time of his death.

Administration (of an estate): The court-supervised distribution of the probate estate of a deceased person. The person who manages the distribution is called the executor if there is a will. If there is no will, this person is called the administrator. In some states, the person is called "personal representative" in either instance.

Adopted Children: Any person, whether an adult or a minor, who is legally adopted as the child of another in a court proceeding.

Adult: Any person over the age of 18. All states allow all competent adults to make wills, except that in Georgia, you must be 19 to leave real estate.

Affidavit: A written statement made under oath.

Annuity: Payment of a fixed sum of money to a specified person at regular intervals.

Augmented Estate: A method used in a number of states following the common law ownership of property system to measure a person's estate for the purpose of determining whether a surviving spouse has been adequately provided for. Generally, the augmented estate consists of property left by the will plus certain property transferred outside of the will by gifts, joint tenancies and living trusts. In the states using this concept, a surviving spouse is generally considered to be adequately provided for if he or she receives at least one-third of the augmented estate.

Autopsy: Examination of the body of a deceased person to determine the cause of death.

Basis: This is a tax term which has to do with the valuation of property for determining profit or loss on sale. If you buy a house (or a poodle) for $20,000, your tax basis is $20,000. If you later sell it for $35,000, your taxable profit is $25,000. A "stepped-up" basis means that you have been able to raise this basic amount from which taxes are computed.

Beneficiary: A person or organization who is legally entitled to receive gifts made under a legal document such as a will or trust. Except when very small estates are involved, beneficiaries of wills only receive their benefits after the will is examined and approved by the probate court. Beneficiaries of living trusts receive their benefits outside of probate, as provided in the document establishing the trust. A primary beneficiary is a person who directly and certainly will benefit from a will or trust. A contingent beneficiary is a person who might or might not become a beneficiary, depending on the terms of the will or trust and what happens to the primary beneficiaries. For example, a contingent beneficiary might get nothing until and unless the primary beneficiary dies, with a portion of the trust corpus still remaining.

Bequest: An old legal term for a will provision leaving personal property to a specified person or organization. In this book it is called a "gift."

Bond: A document guaranteeing that a certain amount of money will be paid to those injured if a person occupying a position of trust does not carry out his or her legal and ethical responsibilities. Thus, if an executor, trustee or guardian who is bonded (covered by a bond) wrongfully deprives a beneficiary of his or her property (say by blowing it during a trip in Las Vegas), the bonding company will replace it, up to the limits of the bond. Bonding companies, which are normally divisions of insurance companies, issue a bond in exchange for a premium, usually about 10% of the face amount of the bond. Under *Plan Your Estate*, executors, trustees and guardians are appointed to serve without the necessity of purchasing a bond. This is because the cost of the bond would have to be paid out of the estate, and the beneficiaries would accordingly receive less. You should take care to select trustworthy people in the first place.

Children: For the purposes of *Plan Your Estate*, one's children are: (1) the biological offspring of a will maker, (2) persons who were legally adopted by a will maker, (3) children born out of wedlock if the will maker is the mother, (4) children born out of wedlock if the will maker is the father and has acknowledged the child as being his as required by the law of the particular state, or (5) children born to the will maker after the will is made, but before his or her death.

Codicil: A separate legal document which, after it has been signed and properly witnessed, changes an existing will.

Community and Separate Property: Eight states follow a system of marital property ownership called "community property," and Wisconsin has a very similar "marital property" law. Very generally, all property acquired after marriage and before permanent separation is considered to belong equally to both spouses, except for gifts to and inheritances by one spouse, and, in some community property states, income from property owned by one spouse prior to marriage.

In most marriages, the main property accumulated is a family home, a retirement pension belonging to one or both spouses, motor vehicles, a joint bank account, a savings account, and perhaps some stocks or bonds. So long as these were purchased during the marriage with the income earned by either spouse during the marriage, they are usually considered to be community property, unless the spouses have entered into an agreement to the contrary. If the property was purchased with the separate property of a spouse, it is separate property, unless it has been given to the community (the couple) by gift or agreement.

If separate property and community property are mixed together (commingled) in a bank account and expenditures made from this bank account, the goods purchased are usually treated as community property unless they can be specifically linked with the separate property (this is called "tracing").

Under the law of community property states, a surviving spouse automatically receives one-half of all community property. The other spouse has no legal power to affect this portion by will or otherwise. Thus, the property which someone may leave by will or other method consists of his or her separate property and one-half of the community property.

Conditional Gift: A gift which passes only under certain specified conditions or upon the occurrence of a specific event. For example, if you leave property to Aunt Millie provided she is living in Cincinnati when you die, and otherwise to Uncle Fred, you have made a "conditional gift." *Plan Your Estate* does not encourage or provide clauses for conditional gifts.

Contract: An agreement between two or more people to do something. A contract is normally written, but can be oral if its terms can be carried out within one year and it doesn't involve real estate. A contract is distinguished from a gift in that each of the contracting parties pledges to do something in exchange for the promises of the other.

Creditor: As used in this book, this means a person or institution to whom money is owed. A creditor may be the person who actually lent the money, or he may be a lawyer or bill collector who is trying to collect the money for the original creditor.

Curtesy: See **Dower and Curtesy**.

Custodian: A person named to care for property left to a minor under the Uniform Gifts (or Transfers) to Minors Act.

Death Taxes: Taxes levied on the property of a person who died. Federal death taxes are called Estate Taxes. State death taxes (if any) go by various names, including Inheritance Tax.

Debtor: A person who owes money.

Decedent: A person who has died.

Deed: The legal document by which one person (or persons) transfers title (recorded ownership) to real estate to another person or persons. If the transfer is by a grant deed, the person transferring title makes certain guarantees or warranties as regards the title. If the transfer is by quitclaim deed, the person transferring does not make any guarantees, but simply transfers to the other persons all the interest he has in the real property.

Descendant: A person who is an offspring, however remote, of a certain person or family.

Devise: An old English term for real estate given by a will. In this book, it is called a "gift."

Domicile: The state, or country, where one has his or her primary home.

Donor: One who gives a gift. A **donee** is one who receives a gift.

Dower and Curtesy: The right of a surviving spouse to receive or enjoy the use of a set portion of a deceased spouse's property (usually one-third to one-half) in the event the surviving spouse is not left at least that share and chooses to take against the will. Dower refers to the title which a surviving wife gets, while curtesy refers to what a man receives. Until recently, these amounts differed in a number of states. However, since discrimination on the basis of sex is now illegal in most cases, states generally provide the same benefits regardless of sex.

Durable Power of Attorney: A power of attorney which remains effective even if the person who created it (called the "principal") becomes incapacitated. The person authorized to act (called the "attorney-in-fact") can make health care decisions and handle financial affairs of the principal.

Encumbrances: If property is used as collateral for payment of a debt or loan, the property is "encumbered." The debt must be paid off before title to the property can pass to a new owner. Generally, the value of a person's ownership in such property (called the "equity") is measured by the market value of the property less the sum of all encumbrances.

Escheat: I put this in here because it's one of my favorite legal words; it means property that goes to a state government because there are no legal inheritors to claim it.

Estate: Generally, all the property you own when you die. There are different ways to measure your estate, depending on whether you are concerned with tax reduction (the taxable estate), probate avoidance (the probate estate) or net worth (the net estate).

Estate Planning: What this book is about—the art of continuing to prosper when you're alive, then dying with the smallest taxable estate and probate estate possible, and passing your property to your loved ones with a minimum of fuss and expense.

Estate Taxes: Taxes imposed on your property as it passes from the dead to the living. The federal government exempts $600,000 of property and all property left to a surviving spouse. Taxes are only imposed on property actually owned by you at the time of your death. Thus, estate planning techniques designed to reduce taxes usually concentrate on the legal transfer of ownership of your property while you are living, to minimize the amount of such property you own at your death.

Equity: The difference between the current fair market value of your real and personal property and the amount you owe on it, if any.

Executor: The person named in your will to manage your estate, deal with the probate court, collect your assets and distribute them as you have specified. In some states this person is called the "personal representative." If you die without a will, the probate court will appoint such a person, who is called the "administrator" of the estate.

Financial Guardian: See **Guardian of the Minor's Property.**

Funeral: "A pageant whereby we attest to our respect to the dead by enriching the undertaker, and strengthen our grief by an expenditure that deepens our groans and doubles our tears." (B.)

Future Interest: A right to property which cannot be enforced in the present, but at some future time.

Gifts: As used in *Plan Your Estate*, any property you give to another person or organization, either during your lifetime, or by will or living trust after your death.

Gift Taxes: Taxes levied by governments on gifts made during a person's lifetime.

Guardian of the Minor's Property: Termed "property guardian" in this book, this is the person you name in your will to care for property of your minor child not supervised by some other legal method, such as a minor's trust. Also sometimes called "the Guardian of the Minor's Estate," or "Financial Guardian."

Guardian of the Person: An adult appointed or selected to care for a minor child in the event no biological or adoptive parent (legal parent) of the child is able to do so. If one legal parent is alive when the other dies, the child will automatically go to that parent, unless the best interests of the child require something different, or (in some states) the court finds the child would suffer detriment.

Hearse: "Death's baby carriage." (B.)

Heirs: Persons who are entitled by law to inherit your estate if you don't leave a will or other device to pass property at your death.

Holographic Will: A will that is completely handwritten by the person making it. While legal in many states, it is never advised except as a last resort.

Incidents of Ownership: All (or any) control over a life insurance policy.

Inherit: To receive property from one who dies.

Inheritance Taxes: Taxes some states impose on property received by inheritors from a deceased's estate.

Inheritors: Persons or organizations who inherit property.

Instrument: Legalese for document; often used to refer to the document which creates a trust.

Insurance: "An ingenious modern game of chance in which the player is permitted to enjoy the comfortable conviction that he is beating the man who keeps the table." (B.)

Inter Vivos Trusts: See **Living Trusts.**

Intestate: To die without a will or other valid estate transfer device.

Intestate Succession: The method by which property is distributed when a person fails to distribute it in a will. In such cases, the law of each state provides that the property be distributed in certain shares to the closest surviving relatives. In most states, these are a surviving spouse, children, parents, siblings, nieces and nephews, and next of kin, in that order. The intestate succession laws are also used in the event an heir is found to be pretermitted (not mentioned or otherwise provided for in the will).

Irrevocable Trust: Means what it says. Once you set it up, that's it. Unlike a revocable, probate-avoidance trust, you can't later revoke it, amend it, or change it in any way.

Issue: Legalese for one's direct descendants—children, grandchildren, etc.

Joint Tenancy: A way to take title to jointly owned real or personal property. When two or more people own property as joint tenants, and one of the owners dies, the other owners automatically become owners of the deceased owner's share. Thus, if a parent and child own a house as joint tenants, and the parent dies, the child automatically becomes full owner. Because of this "right of survivorship," a joint tenancy interest in property does not go through probate, or, put another way, is not part of the probate estate. Instead it goes directly to the surviving joint tenant(s) once some tax and transfer forms are completed.

Placing property in joint tenancy is a common tool used in estate planning designed to avoid probate. However, when property is placed in joint tenancy, a gift is made to any persons who become owners as a result. Thus, if Tom owns a house and places it in joint tenancy with Karen, Tom will have made a gift to Karen equal to one-half the house's value. This may have gift tax consequences.

Lawful: "Compatible with the will of a judge having jurisdiction." (B.)

Lawyer: "One skilled in circumvention of the law." (B.)

Legacy: "A gift from one who is legging it out of this vale of tears." (B.)

Letters Testamentary: The term for the document issued by a probate court authorizing the executor to discharge her responsibilities.

Life Beneficiary: A person who can receive use of trust property, and benefit of trust income for his or her life, but who doesn't own the trust property itself (the "principal") and has no power to dispose of the trust property upon his or her own death.

Life Estate: The right to use trust property, and receive income from it, during one's lifetime.

Liquid Assets: Cash or assets that can readily be turned into cash.

Living Trusts: Trusts set up while a person is alive and which remain under the control of that person until death. Also referred to as "inter vivos trusts," living trusts are an excellent way to minimize the value of property passing through probate. This is because they enable people (called "settlors") to specify that money or other property (called the "trust corpus") will pass directly to their beneficiaries at the time of their death, free of probate, and yet allow the trustors to continue to control the property during their lifetime and even end the trust or change the beneficiaries if they wish.

Living Will: A document where you provide that you do not want to have your life artificially prolonged by technical means, but choose a natural death.

Marital Life Estate Trust: As used in *Plan Your Estate*, a trust giving a surviving spouse (or mate) a life estate interest in property of a deceased spouse or mate. This sort of trust is designed to save on eventual estate taxes by giving a surviving spouse (or member of an unmarried couple) the income from the property of the first spouse to die (not the property itself). It can also be called an "A/B trust," or "spousal bypass trust," or an "exemption trust."

Marriage: A specific status conferred on a couple by the state. In most states, it is necessary to file papers with a county clerk and have a marriage ceremony conducted by an authorized individual in order to be married. However, in a minority of states called "common law marriage" states you may be considered married if you have lived together for a certain period of time and intended to be husband and wife. These states are: Alabama, Colorado, District of Columbia, Georgia, Idaho, Iowa, Kansas, Montana, Oklahoma, Pennsylvania, Rhode Island, South Carolina and Texas.

Unless you are considered legally married in the state where you claim your marriage occurred, you are not married for purposes of *Plan Your Estate*.

Marital Deduction: A deduction allowed by the federal estate tax law for all property passed to a surviving spouse. This deduction (which really acts like an exemption) allows anyone, even a billionaire, to pass his or her entire estate to a surviving spouse without any tax at all. This might be a good idea if the surviving spouse is relatively young and in good health.

If the surviving spouse is likely to die in the near future, however, tax problems are usually made worse by relying on the marital exemption. This is because the second spouse to die will normally benefit from no marital deduction, which means the combined estate, less the standard estate tax exemption, will be taxed at a fairly high rate. For this reason, many older couples with ade-quate resources do not leave large amounts of property to each other, but rather, leave it directly to their children so that each can qualify for a separate tax exemption.

Mausoleum: "The final and funniest folly of the rich." (B.)

Minor: In most states, persons under 18 years of age. A minor is not permitted to make certain types of decisions (for example, enter into most contracts). All minors are required to be under the care of a competent adult (parent or guardian) unless they qualify as emancipated minors (in the military, married, or living independently with court permission). This also means that property left to a minor must be handled by a guardian or trustee until the minor becomes an adult under the laws of the state.

Mopery: Not genuine legalese, but a humorous facsimile; e.g., "indicted on two counts of mopery."

Net Taxable Estate: The value of all your property at death less all encumbrances and your other liabilities.

Next-of-Kin: The closest living relation.

Personal Property: All property other than land and buildings attached to land. Cars, bank accounts, wages, securities, a small business, furniture, insurance policies, jewelry, pets, and season baseball tickets are all personal property.

Pour-over trust: A pour-over trust is simply a trust that receives property from ("poured over" from) some other source. Some lawyers recommend using a will that "pours over" into a trust, instead of establishing a living trust in the first place. This means all the trust property must first go through probate, which commonly benefits no one but the lawyers.

Power of Appointment: Having the legal authority to decide who shall receive someone else's property, usually property held in a trust.

Power of Attorney: A legal document where you authorize someone else to act for you. See **Durable Power of Attorney.**

Pretermitted Heir: A child (or the child of a deceased child) who is either not named or (in some states) not provided for in a will. Most states presume that persons want their children to inherit. Accordingly, children, or the children of a child who has died who are not men-tioned or provided for in the will (even by as little as $1) are entitled to a share of the estate.

Probate: The court proceeding in which: (1) the authen-ticity of your will (if any) is established, (2) your executor or administrator is appointed, (3) your debts and taxes are paid, (4) your heirs are identified, and (5) your property in your probate estate is distributed according to your will (if there is a will).

Probate Estate: All of your property that will pass through probate. Generally, this means all property owned by you at your death less any property that has been placed in joint tenancy, a living trust, a bank account trust, or in life insurance.

Probate Fees: Because probate is so laden with legal formalities, it is usually necessary to hire an attorney to handle it. The attorney will take a substantial fee from the estate before it is distributed to the heirs.

Proving a Will: Getting a probate court to accept the fact after your death that your will really is your will. In many states this can be done simply by introducing a properly signed and witnessed will. In others, it is necessary to produce one or more witnesses (or their affidavits) in court, or offer some proof of the will maker's handwriting. Having the will maker and witnesses sign an affidavit before a notary public stating that all willmaking formalities were complied with usually allows the will to "prove" itself without the need for the witnesses to testify, or other evidence.

Q-tip Trust: A type of trust that allows a surviving spouse to postpone, until her death, paying estate taxes that were assessed on the death of the other spouse.

Quasi-Community Property: A rule that applies to married couples who have moved to Idaho or California. Laws in those states require all property acquired by people during their marriage in other states to be treated as community property at their death.

Real Estate: A term used by *Plan Your Estate* as a synonym for the legalese "real property."

Real Property: All land and items attached to the land, such as buildings, houses, stationary mobile homes, fences and trees are real property or "real estate." All property which is not real property is personal property.

Residual Beneficiary: Can have various meanings, including: a person who receives any property left by will or trust not otherwise given away by the document; a person receiving the property of a trust after the life beneficiary dies.

Residue, Residuary Estate: All property given by your will or trust to your residuary beneficiary after all specific gifts of property have been made—that is, what's left.

Rule Against Perpetuities: A rule of law which limits the durations of trusts (except charitable ones). The workings of the rule are very complicated, and have baffled law students for generations. Very roughly, a trust cannot last longer than the lifetime of someone alive when the trust is created, plus 21 years.

Separate Property: In states which have community property, all property which is not community property. See **Community and Separate Property**.

Settlor: The person who establishes a trust; also called "grantor" or "trustor," or "creator."

Sprinkling Trust: A trust that authorizes the trustee to decide how to distribute trust income or principal among different beneficiaries.

Spouse: In *Plan Your Estate*, your spouse is the person to whom you are legally married. If you later remarry, you will need to make a new estate plan, with new documents, if you wish to leave property to your new spouse.

Taking Against the Will: The ability of a surviving spouse to choose a statutorily allotted share of the deceased spouse's estate instead of the share specified in his or her will. In most common law property states, the law provides that a surviving spouse is entitled to receive a minimum percentage of the other spouse's estate (commonly one-third to one-half). If the deceased spouse leaves the surviving spouse less than this in, or outside of, the will, the surviving spouse may elect the statutory share instead of the will provision ("take against the will"). If the spouse chooses to accept the share specified in the will, it is called "taking under the will." See **Dower and Curtesy**.

Taxable Estate: The portion of your estate that is subject to federal or state estate taxes.

Tenancy in Common: A way of jointly owning property in which each person's share passes to his or her heirs or beneficiaries. The ownership shares need not be equal.

Tenancy by the Entirety: In some states, joint tenancy between spouses.

Title: Document proving ownership of property.

Totten Trust: A simple savings bank trust, revocable at any time before the death of the depositor (also called "pay-on-death" account).

Testamentary Trust: A trust created by a will.

Testate: Someone who dies leaving a valid will, or other valid property transfer devices, dies "testate."

Testator: A person making a will.

Trust: A legal arrangement under which one person or institution (called a "trustee") controls property given by another person (called a "settlor" or "trustor") for the benefit of a third person (called a "beneficiary"). The property itself can be termed the "corpus" of the trust.

Trust Corpus or Res: The property transferred to a trust. For example, if a trust is established (funded) with $250,000, that money is the corpus or res.

Trust Merger: Occurs when the sole trustee and sole beneficiary are the same person. Then, there's no longer the separation between the trustee's legal ownership of trust property from the beneficiary's interest, which is the essence of a trust. So, the trust "merges" and ceases to exist.

Trustee Power: The provisions in a trust document defining what the trustee may and may not do.

Trustee: The people or institutions who manage a trust and trust property under the terms of the trust.

Uniform Gifts/Transfers to Minors Act: A series of state statutes that provide a method for transferring property to minors.

Usufruct: Included because it's another of my favorite legal words, meaning the right to use property, or income from it, owned by another.

Will: A legal document in which a person states various binding intentions about what he or she wants done with his or her property after death.

Estate Forms

Form I: *Basic Living Trust for One Person*

The _____① Trust
<small>your name</small>

DECLARATION AND INSTRUMENT OF TRUST

I. Trust Name

This trust shall be known as The _____① Trust.
<small>your name</small>

II. Trust Property

(A) _____①, called the "settlor" or "trustee," declares
<small>your name</small>

that _____ has set aside and holds in the _____① Trust,
<small>he/she</small>   <small>your name</small>

all _____ interest in that property described in the attached Schedule A.②
<small>his/her</small>

The trust property shall be used for the benefit of the trust beneficiaries, and shall be

administered and distributed by the trustee in accordance with this trust instrument.

(B) Additional or after-acquired property may be added to the trust by listing it on the

appropriate schedule.

III. Reserved Powers of Settlor

(A) The settlor reserves the power to amend or revoke this trust at any time during

_____ lifetime, without notifying any beneficiary.
<small>his/her</small>

(B) Until the death of the settlor, all rights to income, profits, or control of the trust property shall be retained by or distributed to the settlor.

⑤(C) If at any time, as certified in writing by a licensed physician, the settlor has become physically or mentally incapacitated, the successor trustee shall manage this trust, and shall apply for the benefit of the settlor any amount of trust income, or trust principal, necessary in the trustee's discretion for the proper health care, support, maintenance, comfort or welfare of the settlor, in accordance with _____ accustomed manner of living, until the settlor, as

his/her

certified by a licensed physician, is again able to manage _____ own affairs, or until

his/her

_____ death.

his/her

Any income in excess of amounts applied for the benefit of the settlor shall be accumulated and added to the trust property.

(D) After the death of the settlor, this trust becomes irrevocable and may not be altered or amended in any respect unless specifically authorized by this instrument, and may not be terminated except through distributions permitted by this instrument.

IV. Trustees

(A) The trustee of The _____ ① Trust and

your name

all subtrusts created pursuant to Paragraph VI of this trust shall be

_____ ①. Upon the death of the trustee, or
                 your name

_____ incapacity as certified by a licensed physician, the successor trustee shall be
  his/her

_____ ⑥, or if _____ is
                 name   he/she

unable to serve, or continue serving, as successor trustee, the successor trustee shall be

_____ ⑥.
                 name

(B) Any trustee shall have the right to appoint, in writing which shall be notarized,

additional successor trustees to serve in the order nominated if all successor trustees named in

Paragraph IV(A) cannot serve as trustee.

(C) As used in this instrument, the term "trustee" shall include any successor trustee.

(D) No bond shall be required of any trustee.

(E) Except as provided in Paragraph VI(D)(2), no trustee shall receive any compensation.

V. Beneficiaries

(A) Upon the death of the settlor, the specific beneficiaries of the

_____ ① Trust shall be:
                 your name

1. _____ ⑦ shall be given
                    beneficiary

_____ or, if
                 property identified

_____ doesn't survive the settlor, that property shall
              beneficiary

be given to _____.
                    alternate beneficiary

2. _____⑦ shall be given
                          beneficiary

_____ or, if
                property identified

_____ doesn't survive the settlor, that property shall
                beneficiary

be given to _____.
                        alternate beneficiary

3. _____⑦ shall be given
                          beneficiary

_____ or, if
                property identified

_____ doesn't survive the settlor, that property shall
                beneficiary

be given to _____.
                        alternate beneficiary

4. _____⑦ shall be given
                          beneficiary

_____ or, if
                property identified

_____ doesn't survive the settlor, that property shall
                beneficiary

be given to _____.
                        alternate beneficiary

5. _____⑦ shall be given
                          beneficiary

_____ or, if
                property identified

_____ doesn't survive the settlor, that property shall
                beneficiary

be given to _____.
                        alternate beneficiary

(B) The residuary beneficiary of the trust shall be _____ ⑦

who shall be given all trust property not disposed of by Paragraph V(A), or if

_____ ⑦ doesn't survive the settlor, the alternate residuary
residuary beneficiary

beneficiary shall be _____.
alternate residuary beneficiary

(C) Upon the death of the settlor, the trustee shall distribute the trust property outright to

the beneficiaries named in Paragraphs V(A) and V(B), unless a beneficiary is a minor at the

time of distribution, in which case that beneficiary's property shall be retained in trust according

to the terms of Paragraph VI.

VI. Minor Beneficiaries

All trust property given in Paragraph V to any of the minor beneficiaries listed below in

Section A shall be retained in trust for each such beneficiary in a separate subtrust of this

_____ ① Trust. The following terms shall apply to
your name

each subtrust:

(A) Subtrust Beneficiaries and Age Limits

Each subtrust shall end when the beneficiary of that subtrust listed below becomes 30,

except as otherwise specified in this section:

⑧Trust for   Shall end at age

_____   _____

_____   _____

_____   _____

_____   _____

_____   _____

(B) Distribution of Subtrust Funds

1. Until a subtrust ends, the trustee may distribute from time to time to or for the benefit of

the beneficiary as much, or all, of the net income or principal of the subtrust, or both, as the

trustee deems necessary for the beneficiary's health, support, maintenance or education.

Education includes, but is not limited to, college, graduate, postgraduate and vocational

studies, and reasonably related living expenses.

2. In deciding whether to make a distribution to the beneficiary, the trustee may take into

account the beneficiary's other income, resources, and sources of support.

3. Any subtrust income which is not distributed to a beneficiary by the trustee shall be

accumulated and added to the principal of the subtrust administered for that beneficiary.

(C) Termination of Subtrust

A subtrust shall terminate when any of the following events occurs:

1. The beneficiary of that subtrust becomes the age specified in Paragraph V(A).

2. The beneficiary of that subtrust dies before becoming the age specified in Paragraph V(A).

3. The subtrust is exhausted through distribution allowed under these provisions.

If the subtrust terminates for reason (1), the remaining principal and accumulated net income of the subtrust shall be given outright to the beneficiary of that subtrust. If the subtrust terminates for reason (2), the remaining principal and accumulated net income of the subtrust shall pass to that subtrust beneficiary's heirs.

(D) Subtrust Administrative Provisions

1. The interests of subtrust beneficiaries shall not be transferable by voluntary or involuntary assignment or by operation of law and shall be free from the claims of creditors and from attachments, execution, bankruptcy or other legal process to the fullest extent permitted by law.

2. Any trustee of a subtrust created under this Paragraph VI shall be entitled to reasonable compensation out of the subtrust assets for ordinary and extraordinary services, and for all services in connection with the termination of any subtrust.

VII. Trustee's Powers and Duties

(A) To carry out the provisions of The _____ ① Trust,

your name

and any subtrust created pursuant to Paragraph VI, the trustee shall have all authority and

powers allowed or conferred on a trustee under _____ law
your state

and subject to the trustee's fiduciary duty to the settlor and the beneficiaries.

(B) The settlor's debts and death taxes shall be paid by the trustee from the following trust

property:

_____⑨

_____

_____

If this property is insufficient to pay all the settlor's debts and death taxes, the trustee shall

determine how such debts and death taxes shall be paid.

VIII. General Administrative Provisions

(A) The validity of The _____① Trust and the
your name

construction of its beneficial provisions shall be governed by the laws of _____.
your state

(B) If any provision of this Declaration of Instrument of Trust is held to be unenforceable,

the remaining provisions shall be nevertheless carried into effect.

Executed on _____
            date

_____
    your signature

I certify that I have read this Declaration of Trust and that it correctly states the terms and conditions under which the trust estate is to be held, managed, and disposed of by the trustee. I approve the Declaration of Trust.

Dated: _____

_____, Settlor and Trustee
              your signature

State of _____

County of _____

On _____, 19_____, before me, a notary public for the State of

_____ personally appeared _____①,
    your state   your name

known to me to be the trustee and settlor of the trust created by the above instrument, and to be the person whose name is subscribed to the instrument, and acknowledged that it was executed as settlor and trustee.

IN WITNESS WHEREOF, I have set my hand and affixed my official seal the day and year first above written.

_____

NOTARY PUBLIC for

the State of _____

My commission expires _____, 19___

Schedule A ③

Form II: Basic Living Trust for a Married Couple

The _____ ① Trust
your names

DECLARATION AND INSTRUMENT OF TRUST

I. Trust Name

This trust shall be known as The _____ ① Trust.
your names

II. Trust Property

(A) _____ ①, called the "settlors" or "trustees," declare
your names

that they have set aside and hold in the _____ ① Trust, all
your names

their interest in the property described in the attached Schedules A, B and C.②

The trust property shall be used for the benefit of the trust beneficiaries, and shall be

administered and distributed by the trustees in accordance with this trust instrument.

(B) Either settlor, or both, may add additional or after-acquired property to the trust at any

time by listing it on the appropriate schedule.

(C) All trust property listed on Schedule A:④

_____
identify the character of propety listed in Schedule A

_____

_____

_____

The trust property listed on Schedule B shall remain the separate property of

_____. The trust property listed on Schedule C shall
                wife's name

remain the separate property of _____.
                                                husband's name

(D) As long as both settlors live, either settlor may revoke The

_____ ① Trust in writing, at any time, without
                your names

notifying any beneficiary.

(E) As long as both settlors live, The _____ ① Trust
                                                          your names

may be altered, amended or modified only by joint action in writing by both

_____ ①.
                your names

III. Trustees

(A) The trustees of The _____ ① Trust,
                                          your names

and all subtrusts created pursuant to Paragraph V of this trust, shall be

_____ ①. Either trustee may act for, and
                your names

represent, the trust in any transaction.

(B) The first settlor or trustee to die shall be called the "deceased spouse." The living settlor

or trustee shall be called the "surviving spouse."

(C) Upon the death of the deceased spouse, the surviving spouse shall serve as sole trustee.

(D) Upon the death of the deceased spouse, the trustee shall divide the property of The

_____ ① Trust listed on Schedule A, B and
                    your names

C into two separate trusts, Trust #1 and Trust #2, as defined in Paragraph VI of this trust. Trust

#1 shall consist of all the property of The _____ ①
                                                          your names

Trust owned by the deceased spouse and become irrevocable. Trust #2 shall consist of all the

property of The _____ ① Trust owned by the
                            your names

surviving spouse and shall remain revocable until the death of the surviving spouse. The surviv-

ing spouse shall serve as trustee of Trust #1 and Trust #2.

(E) Upon the death or incapacity of the surviving spouse, the successor trustee for Trust #1

and Trust #2 shall be _____ ⑥. If _____ is unable
                                    name   he/she

to serve or to continue serving as successor trustee, the successor trustee shall be

_____ ⑥.
                name

(F) As used in this instrument, the term "trustee" shall include any successor trustee.

(G) Any trustee shall have the right to appoint, in writing which shall be notarized, addi-

tional successor trustees to serve, in the order nominated, as trustee, if all the successor trustees

named in this trust instrument cease or are unable to serve as trustee.

(H) No bond shall be required of any trustee.

(I) Except as provided in Paragraph V(D)(2), no trustee shall receive any compensation.

IV. Beneficiaries

(A) Until the death of the deceased spouse, the settlors retain all rights to income, profits,

or control of the property in The _____ ① Trust.
your names

(B) Upon the death of _____, the beneficiaries of the trust property
husband's name

owned by _____ as his share of the trust property listed on Schedule A
husband's name

and separate property listed on Schedule C shall be:

1. Specific Beneficiaries

a. _____ ⑦ shall be given
beneficiary

_____ or, if _____
property identified   beneficiary

doesn't survive _____, that property shall be given to
husband's name

_____.
alternate beneficiary

b. _____ ⑦ shall be given
beneficiary

_____ or, if _____
property identified   beneficiary

doesn't survive _____, that property shall be given to
husband's name

_____.
alternate beneficiary

c. _____ ⑦ shall be given
                              beneficiary

_____ or, if _____
            property identified   beneficiary

doesn't survive _____, that property shall be given to
                              husband's name

_____.
        alternate beneficiary

d. _____ ⑦ shall be given
                              beneficiary

_____ or, if _____
            property identified   beneficiary

doesn't survive _____, that property shall be given to
                              husband's name

_____.
        alternate beneficiary

e. _____ ⑦ shall be given
                              beneficiary

_____ or, if _____
            property identified   beneficiary

doesn't survive _____, that property shall be given to
                              husband's name

_____.
        alternate beneficiary

2. Residuary Beneficiary

The residuary beneficiary of all the trust property owned by _____
                                                                        husband's name

as his share of the trust property listed on Schedule A or as his separate property listed on

Schedule C, and not specifically and validly disposed of by Paragraph IV(B)(1), shall be

_____ ⑦ or, if _____
        residuary beneficiary   residuary beneficiary

doesn't survive _____, the residuary beneficiary shall be

_____.
       alternate residuary beneficiary

    (C) Upon the death of _____, the beneficiaries of the trust
                                     wife's name

property owned by _____ as her share of the trust property
                           wife's name

listed on Schedule A and as her separate property listed on Schedule B shall be:

    1. Specific Beneficiaries

    a. _____⑦ shall be given
                   beneficiary

_____ or, if _____
        property identified   beneficiary

doesn't survive _____, that property shall be given to
                    wife's name

_____.
    alternate beneficiary

    b. _____⑦ shall be given
                   beneficiary

_____ or, if _____
        property identified   beneficiary

doesn't survive _____, that property shall be given to
                    wife's name

_____.
    alternate beneficiary

    c. _____⑦ shall be given
                   beneficiary

_____ or, if _____
        property identified   beneficiary

doesn't survive _____, that property shall be given to
                    wife's name

_____.
    alternate beneficiary

d. _____⑦ shall be given
          beneficiary

_____ or, if _____
          property identified   beneficiary

doesn't survive _____, that property shall be given to
                              wife's name

_____.
     alternate beneficiary

e. _____⑦ shall be given
          beneficiary

_____ or, if _____
          property identified   beneficiary

doesn't survive _____, that property shall be given to
                              wife's name

_____.
     alternate beneficiary

2. Residuary Beneficiary

The residuary beneficiary of the trust property owned by _____
                                                                              wife's name

as her share of the trust property listed on Schedule A and separate property listed on Schedule

B, and not specifically and validly disposed of by Paragraph IV(C)(1), shall be

_____ ⑦ or, if _____ doesn't
          residuary beneficiary   residuary beneficiary

survive _____, the residuary beneficiary shall be
                     wife's name

_____.
     alternate residuary beneficiary

V. Minor Beneficiaries

All trust property given by either settlor in Paragraph IV to any of the minor beneficiaries

listed below in Section A shall be retained in trust for each such beneficiary in a separate

subtrust of this _____① Trust. The following terms shall
                                your names

apply to each subtrust:

(A) Subtrust Beneficiaries and Age Limits

Each subtrust shall end when the beneficiary of that subtrust listed below becomes 30,

except as otherwise specified in this section:

⑧Trust for   Shall end at age

_____   _____

_____   _____

_____   _____

_____   _____

_____   _____

(B) Distribution of Subtrust Funds

1. Until a subtrust ends, the trustee may distribute from time to time to or for the benefit of

the beneficiary as much, or all, of the net income or principal of the subtrust as the trustee

deems necessary for the beneficiary's health, support, maintenance or education.

Education includes, but is not limited to, college, graduate, postgraduate and vocational studies, and reasonably related living expenses.

2. In deciding whether to make a distribution to the beneficiary, the trustee may take into account the beneficiary's other income, resources, and sources of support.

3. Any subtrust income which is not distributed to a beneficiary by the trustee shall be accumulated and added to the principal of the subtrust administered for that beneficiary.

(C) Termination of Subtrust

A subtrust shall terminate when any of the following events occurs:

1. The beneficiary of that subtrust becomes the age specified in Paragraph V(A);

2. The beneficiary of that subtrust dies before becoming the age specified in Paragraph V(A);

3. The subtrust is exhausted through distribution allowed under these provisions.

If the subtrust terminates for reason (1), the remaining principal and accumulated net income of the subtrust shall be given outright to the beneficiary of that subtrust. If the subtrust terminates for reason (2), the remaining principal and accumulated net income of the subtrust shall pass to that subtrust beneficiary's heirs.

(D) Subtrust Administrative Provisions

1. The interests of subtrust beneficiaries shall not be transferable by voluntary or involuntary

assignment or by operation of law and shall be free from the claims of creditors and from attach-

ments, execution, bankruptcy or other legal process to the fullest extent permitted by law.

2. Any trustee of a subtrust created under this Paragraph V shall be entitled to reasonable

compensation out of the trust assets for ordinary and extraordinary services, and for all services

in connection with the termination of any subtrust.

VI. Administration of Trust Property

(A) Until the death of the deceased spouse, the trust property shall be administered as

provided in Paragraph IV(A).

(B) Upon the death of the deceased spouse, the trustee shall divide the trust property into

Trust #1 and Trust #2 as specified in Paragraph III(D).

(C) Trust #1 shall be administered as follows:

After the death of the deceased spouse, Trust #1 becomes irrevocable and the trust property

owned by the deceased spouse shall be distributed to the beneficiaries listed in Paragraph IV(B)

or Paragraph IV(C), except as otherwise provided by Paragraph V.

(D) Trust #2 shall be administered as follows:

1. The surviving spouse reserves the power to amend or revoke Trust #2 at any time during

his or her lifetime, without notifying any beneficiary.

2. Until the death of the surviving spouse, all rights to income, profits or control of property in Trust #2 shall be retained by or distributed to the surviving spouse.

3. Upon the death of the surviving spouse, Trust #2 becomes irrevocable, and the property in Trust #2 shall be distributed to the beneficiaries listed in Paragraph IV(B) or Paragraph IV(C), except as otherwise provided by Paragraph V.

⑤(E) If both settlors of The _____① Trust become
your names

physically or mentally incapacitated, as certified in writing by a licensed physician, the successor trustee shall manage The _____① Trust, and shall apply for
your names

the benefit of the settlors any amount of trust income or trust principal necessary in the successor trustee's discretion, for the proper health care, support, maintenance, comfort and welfare of the settlors, in accordance with their accustomed standard of living, until a licensed physician certifies that the settlors, or either of them, are again able to manage their own affairs, or until their deaths.

Any income in excess of amounts applied for the benefit of the settlors shall be accumulated and added to the property of The _____① Trust.
your names

⑤(F) If, after the death of the deceased spouse, the surviving spouse becomes physically or mentally incapacitated, as certified in writing by a licensed physician, the successor trustee shall:

Manage Trust #2, and shall apply for the benefit of the surviving spouse any amount of trust income or trust principal necessary in the successor trustee's discretion, for the proper health care, support, maintenance, comfort and welfare of the surviving spouse, in accordance with his or her accustomed standard of living, until a licensed physician certifies that the surviving spouse is again able to manage his or her own affairs, or until his or her death.

Any income in excess of amounts applied for the benefit of the surviving spouse shall be accumulated and added to the property of Trust #2.

VII. Trustee's Powers and Duties

(A) To carry out the provisions of this trust instrument, and to manage the trust property of

The _____ ① Trust, Trust #1 and Trust #2, and any subtrust
                             your names

created pursuant to Paragraph V, the trustee shall have all authority and power allowed or

conferred under _____ law and subject to the trustee's fiduciary duty to
                            your state

the settlors and the beneficiaries.

(B) Any debts or death taxes of _____ shall be paid by the
                                     husband's name

trustee from the following trust property:

_____ ⑨

_____

_____

_____

Any debts or death taxes of _____ shall be paid by the
wife's name

trustee from the following trust property:

⑨ _____

_____

_____

_____.

If specified property is insufficient to pay the debts and death taxes, the trustee shall deter-

mine how such debts and death taxes shall be paid.

VIII. General Administrative Provisions

(A) The validity of this trust and the construction of its beneficial provisions shall be

governed by the laws of _____.
your state

(B) If any provision of this Declaration and Instrument of Trust is held to be unenforceable,

the remaining provisions shall be nevertheless carried into effect.

Executed at _____, on _____, 19__.
place   date

_____
your signature

_____
your signature

We certify that we have read this Declaration and Instrument of Trust and that it correctly

states the terms and conditions under which the trust property is to be held, managed and

disposed of by the trustees, and we approve the Declaration and Instrument of Trust.

Dated: _____

_____
your signatures

_____

Settlors and Trustees

State of _____

County of _____

On _____, 19__, before me, a notary public for the State of

_____, personally appeared _____① ,
your state   your names

known to me to be the settlors and trustees of the trust created by the above instrument, and to

be the persons whose names are subscribed to the instrument, and they acknowledged and

executed the same as settlors and trustees.

   IN WITNESS WHEREOF, I have set my hand and affixed my official seal the day and year

first above written.

                                        _____

                                        NOTARY PUBLIC for

                                        the State of _____

                                        My commission expires _____, 19__

Schedule A ③

list shared marital or community property placed in trust

Schedule B ③

list wife's separate property placed in trust

Schedule C ③

list husband's separate property placed in trust

Form III: *Amendment to Living Trust for One Person*

This Amendment to The _____① Living Trust is made

your name

this _____ day of _____, 19__ by _____①,

your name

the settlor and trustee of the trust. Under the power of amendment reserved to the settlor by

Paragraph III(A) of the trust, the settlor amends the trust as follows:

1. The following is added to the trust:

_____

set out new language added to trust and identify precisely where it is added

_____

2. The following is deleted from the trust:

_____

identify precisely all language deleted from the trust

_____

[Repeat as needed]

In all other respects, the trust as executed on _____, 19___ by the settlor is hereby

date

affirmed.

Executed at _____, on _____, 19__.

_____

your signature

Settlor and Trustee

Notary's Acknowledgement

State of _____

County of _____

On _____, 19__, before me, a notary public for the State of _____,
your state

personally appeared _____,① known to me to be the
your name

trustee and settlor of the Amendment to living trust created in the above document, and to be

the person whose name is subscribed to the document, and acknowledged that it was executed

as settlor and trustee.

IN WITNESS WHEREOF, I have set my hand and affixed my official seal the day and year

first above written.

_____

NOTARY PUBLIC for

the State of _____

My commission expires _____, 19__

Form IV: Amendment to Living Trust for a Married Couple

This Amendment to The _____ ① Living Trust is made

                         your names

this _____ day of _____, 19__ by _____ and

                                        wife's name

_____ , the settlors and trustees of the Trust. Under the power of

          husband's name

amendment reserved to the settlors by Paragraph II(E) of the trust, the settlors amend the trust

as follows:

    1. The following is added to the trust:

_____

         set out new language added to trust and identify precisely where it is added

_____

    2. The following is deleted from the trust:

_____

             identify precisely all language deleted from the trust

_____

[Repeat as needed]

    In all other respects, the trust as executed on _____, 19___ by the settlors is hereby

affirmed.

Executed at _____ , on _____, 19__.

_____

        your signatures

_____

Settlors and Trustees

Notary's Acknowledgement

State of _____

County of _____

On _____, 19__, before me, a notary public for the State of _____,
<small>your state</small>

personally appeared _____,① known to me to be the
<small>your names</small>

trustees and settlors of the Amendment to Living Trust created in the above document, and to

be the persons whose names are subscribed to the document, and acknowledged that it was

executed as settlors and trustees.

IN WITNESS WHEREOF, I have set my hand and affixed my official seal the day and year

first above written.

_____

NOTARY PUBLIC for

the State of _____

My commission expires _____, 19__

Form V: Living Trust Revocation

On _____, 19___, _____ created a written revocable inter vivos trust,

called "The _____ Trust"
your name(s)

with _____ as the trustee(s);
name(s)

and under the terms of the trust, _____ reserved to _____the full power to
I/we   myself/ourselves

revoke the trust.

According to the terms of the trust, and the laws of the State of _____,
your state

_____ revoke the trust created by _____ in the document entitled The
I/we   me/us

_____ Trust and state that the trust is
your name(s)

completely revoked and all property transferred by _____ to the trust shall be
me/us

returned to _____ and legally owned by _____.
me/us   me/us

Dated: _____

_____
your signature(s)

_____

Notary's Acknowledgement

State of _____

County of _____

On _____, 19___, before me, a notary public for the State of _____
your state

personally appeared _____ ① known to me to be the trustees and
your names

settlors of the Amendment to Living Trust created in the above document, and to be the

persons whose names are subscribed to the document, and acknowledged that it was executed as

settlors and trustees.

IN WITNESS WHEREOF, I have set my hand and affixed my official seal the day and year

first above written.

_____

NOTARY PUBLIC for

the State of _____

My commission expires _____, 19___

Form VI: Basic Will for One Person

Will

of

_____
your name

I, _____, a resident of _____,
        your name   city

_____, _____, declare that
                    county   state

this is my will.

(1) I revoke all wills and codicils that I previously have made.

(2) (A) I am not married.

    (B) I am the _____ of children whose names are:
                                        mother/father

_____

_____

_____

_____

_____

There are _____ living children of my deceased child _____
                                                                              name

whose names are:

_____

_____

_____

(C) If at my death any of my children are minors, and a guardian is needed, I recommend

that _____ be appointed guardian of the person(s) of my
                        name

minor children. If _____ cannot serve as personal guardian,
                                    name

I recommend that _____ be appointed personal guardian.
                                name

(D) I appoint _____① as property guardian for my
                                    name

minor children. If _____① cannot serve as property
                                    name

guardian, I recommend that _____① be appointed property guardian.
                                        name

(E) I direct that no bond be required of any guardian.

(3) (A) In addition to any other property I may give, by this will or otherwise to the

person(s) listed in Section 2(B), I give each person listed there One Dollar ($1.00).

(B) I give _____ to
                                property described

_____, or if _____ fails to
                        name   name

survive me, to _____.
                                name

I give _____ to
　　　　　　　　　　property described

_____, or if _____ fails to
　　　　　　　name　　　　　　　　　　　　　　　　　　　name

survive me, to _____.
　　　　　　　　　　　　　name

I give _____ to
　　　　　　　　　　property described

_____, or if _____ fails to
　　　　　　　name　　　　　　　　　　　　　　　　　　　name

survive me, to _____.
　　　　　　　　　　　　　name

(C) I give all my other property subject to this will to

_____, or if _____ fails to survive me,
　　residuary beneficiary's name　　　　　　　　　he/she

to _____.
　　　alternate beneficiary's name

(4) (A) I nominate _____ ② to serve as executor of my
　　　　　　　　　　　executor's name

will, or, if _____ is unable to serve or to continue serving as executor, I nominate
　　　　　　he/she

_____ ② to serve as executor.
　　alternate executor's name

(B) No bond shall be required of any executor.

I subscribe my name to this Will this _____ day of _____, 19 __ at

_____, _____,
　　　　　　city　　　　　　　　　　　　　　county

_____.
　　　　state

_____
　　　　　　　　your signature

On the date last written above, _____ declared to us, the
your name

undersigned, that this instrument was _____ will, and requested us to act as
his/her

witnesses to it. _____ thereupon signed this will in our presence, all of us being
he/she

present at the same time. We now at _____ request and in _____
his/her   his/her

presence, and in the presence of each other, have signed such instrument as witnesses.

We declare under penalty of perjury that the foregoing is true and correct.

_____
witness signature

_____ , _____ ,
city   county

_____
state

_____
witness signature

_____ , _____ ,
city   county

_____
state

_____
witness signature

_____ , _____ ,
city   county

_____
state

Form VII: Basic Will for a Member of a Couple

Will

of

_____
your name

I, _____, a resident of _____,
your name   city

_____, _____, declare that
county   state

this is my will.

(1) I revoke all wills and codicils that I previously have made.

(2) (A) I am married to_____.

(B) I am the _____ of children whose names are:
mother/father

_____

_____

_____

_____

_____

There are _____ living children of my deceased child _____
name

whose names are:

_____

_____

_____

(C) If at my death any of my children are minors, and a guardian is needed, I recom-

mend that _____ be appointed guardian of the person(s) of
name

my minor children. If _____ cannot serve as personal
name

guardian, I recommend that _____ be appointed personal guardian.
name

(D) I appoint _____① as property guardian for my
name

minor children. If _____① cannot serve as property guard-
name

ian, I recommend that _____① be appointed property guardian.
name

(E) I direct that no bond be required of any guardian.

(3)(A) In addition to any other property I may give, by this will or otherwise to the

person(s) listed in Section 2(B), I give each person listed there One Dollar ($1.00).

(B) I give _____ to
property described

_____, or if _____ fails to
name   name

survive me, to _____.
name

I give _____ to
                          property described

_____, or if _____ fails to
                name   name

survive me, to _____.
                              name

I give _____ to
                          property described

_____, or if _____ fails to
                name   name

survive me, to _____.
                              name

(C) I give all my other property subject to this will to _____,
                                                        residuary beneficiary's name

or if _____ fails to survive me, to _____.
              he/she   alternate beneficiary's name

(4) (A) I nominate _____ ② to serve as executor of my
                              executor's name

will, or, if _____ is unable to serve or to continue serving as executor, I nominate
            he/she

_____ ② to serve as executor.
          alternate executor's name

(B) No bond shall be required of any executor.

(5) If my spouse and I should die simultaneously, or under such circumstances as to render it

difficult or impossible to determine who predeceased the other, I shall be conclusively presumed

to have survived my spouse for purposes of this will.

I subscribe my name to this Will this _____ day of _____, 19 __ at

_____, _____,
                city   county

_____.
          state

_____
              your signature

On the date last written above, _____ declared to us, the
                                            your name

undersigned, that this instrument was _____ will, and requested us to act as
                                              his/her

witnesses to it. _____ thereupon signed this will in our presence, all of us being
                      he/she

present at the same time. We now at _____ request and in _____
                                            his/her   his/her

presence, and in the presence of each other, have signed such instrument as witnesses.

We declare under penalty of perjury that the foregoing is true and correct.

_____
         witness signature

_____ , _____ ,
              city   county

_____
            state

_____
         witness signature

_____ , _____ ,
              city   county

_____
            state

_____
         witness signature

_____ , _____ ,
              city   county

_____
            state

APPENDIX II

State Death Tax Rules

Chart 1. Inheritance Taxes

Following are the rules for each state which imposes inheritance taxes:

Connecticut

Class AA: Surviving spouse

Class A: Parent, grandparent, adoptive parent or natural or adopted descendant

Class B: Son or daughter-in-law of child (natural or adopted) who has not remarried. Stepchild, brother or sister (full or half or adopted), brother or sister's children (descendants, natural or adopted)

Class C: All other persons

	Taxable Amount			Tax Rate
Class AA				No Tax
Class A	50,000	to	150,000	3%
	150,000	to	250,000	4%
	250,000	to	400,000	5%
	400,000	to	600,000	6%
	600,000	to	1,000,000	7%
	1,000,000		And Over	8%
Class B	6,000	to	25,000	4%
	25,000	to	150,000	5%
	150,000	to	250,000	6%
	250,000	to	400,000	7%
	400,000	to	600,000	8%
	600,000	to	1,000,000	9%
	1,000,000		And Over	10%
Class C	1,000	to	25,000	8%
	25,000	to	150,000	9%
	150,000	to	250,000	10%
	250,000	to	400,000	11%
	400,000	to	600,000	12%
	600,000	to	1,000,000	13%
	1,000,000		And Over	14%

Computation:

1. Calculate the tax due according to the table based on the aggregate transfer to each beneficiary

2. Multiply the tax according to the table by 1.43

3. An exception is made for farm land passed to natural or adoptive descendant in which case the tax from the table is multiplied by 1.30 instead of 1.43

Delaware

Class A: Spouse

Class B: Parent, grandparent, child (by birth or adoption), son- or daughter-in-law, lineal descendant, or stepchild

Class C: Brother, sister, their descendants; aunt, uncle, their descendants

Class D: All others

	Taxable Amount			Tax Rate
Class A	70,000	to	100,000	2%
	100,000	to	200,000	3%
	200,000		And Over	4%
Class B	25,000	to	50,000	2%
	50,000	to	75,000	3%
	75,000	to	100,000	4%
	100,000	to	200,000	5%
	200,000		And Over	6%
Class C	5,000	to	25,000	5%
	25,000	to	50,000	6%
	50,000	to	100,000	7%
	100,000	to	150,000	8%
	150,000	to	200,000	9%
	200,000		And Over	10%
Class D	1,000	to	25,000	10%
	25,000	to	50,000	12%
	50,000	to	100,000	14%
	100,000		And Over	16%

Idaho

Class 1:   Husband, wife, lineal ancestor, lineal issue (direct descendants) or adopted child

Class 2:   Brother or sister, or descendant of brother or sister, daughter- or son-in-law

Class 3:   Uncle or aunt or their children

Class 4:   All others

	Taxable Amount			Tax Rate
Class 1	0	to	25,000	2%
	25,000	to	50,000	4%
	50,000	to	100,000	6%
	100,000	to	200,000	8%
	200,000	to	500,000	10%
	500,000		And Over	15%
Class 2	0	to	25,000	4%
	25,000	to	50,000	6%
	50,000	to	100,000	8%
	100,000	to	200,000	12%
	200,000	to	500,000	16%
	500,000		And Over	20%
Class 3	0	to	25,000	6%
	25,000	to	50,000	9%
	50,000	to	100,000	12%
	100,000	to	200,000	15%
	200,000	to	500,000	20%
	500,000		And Over	25%
Class 4	0	to	25,000	8%
	25,000	to	50,000	14%
	50,000	to	100,000	20%
	100,000		And Over	30%

Exemptions:

1. All: Contributions to charitable organizations

2. Spouse: Community property

3. Spouse or minor child of descendant: $50,000

4. Class 1 persons other than spouse or minor child of descendant: $30,000

5. Class 1: Property received by deceased from another Class 1 deceased not more than four years before his death where inheritance tax was paid in Idaho

6. Classes 2-4 persons: $10,000

Indiana

Class A: Spouse, parents, children, grandchildren

Class B: Sibling, nieces and nephews, son- or daughter-in-law

Class C: All others

	Taxable Amount			Tax		
				Base Tax	Plus %	Of Amt Over
Class A	0	to	25,000	0 +	1%	0
	25,000	to	50,000	250 +	2%	25,000
	50,000	to	200,000	750 +	3%	50,000
	200,000	to	300,000	5,250 +	4%	200,000
	300,000	to	500,000	9,250 +	5%	300,000
	500,000	to	700,000	19,250 +	6%	500,000
	700,000	to	1,000,000	31,250 +	7%	700,000
	1,000,000	to	1,500,000	52,250 +	8%	1,000,000
	1,500,000		And Over	92,250 +	10%	1,500,000
Class B	0	to	100,000	0 +	7%	0
	100,000	to	500,000	7,000 +	10%	100,000
	500,000	to	1,000,000	47,000 +	12%	500,000
	1,000,000		And Over	107,000 +	15%	1,000,000
Class C	0	to	100,000	0 +	10%	0
	100,000	to	1,000,000	10,000 +	15%	100,000
	1,000,000		And Over	145,000 +	20%	1,000,000

Exemptions:

1. Spouse: All tax

2. Child under 21 at death: $10,000

3. Child over 21 at death: $5,000

4. Parents: $5,000

5. Other Class A: $2,000

6. Class B: $500

7. Class C: $100

Iowa

Class 1:   Spouse, parent, child

Class 2:   Sibling, son- or daughter-in-law, stepchild

Class 3:   All others

	Taxable Amount			Tax Rate
Class 1				No Tax
Class 2	0	to	12,500	0%
	12,500	to	25,000	5%
	25,000	to	50,000	6%
	50,000	to	75,000	7%
	75,000	to	100,000	8%
	100,000	to	150,000	9%
	150,000	And Over		10%
Class 3	0	to	50,000	10%
	50,000	to	100,000	12%
	100,000	And Over		15%

Exemptions:

1. Each son and daughter: $50,000

2. Father or mother: $15,000

3. Any other lineal descendant: $15,000

Kansas

Class A: Lineal ancestors and descendants; stepparents, stepchildren, adopted children, lineal descendants of adopted child or stepchild, spouse or surviving spouse of son or daughter, spouse or surviving spouse of an adopted child or stepchild

Class B: Siblings

Class C: All others

	Taxable Amount			Tax Rate
Class A	0	to	25,000	1%
	25,000	to	50,000	2%
	50,000	to	100,000	3%
	100,000	to	500,000	4%
	500,000	And Over		5%
Class B	0	to	25,000	3.0%
	25,000	to	50,000	5.0%
	50,000	to	100,000	7.5%
	100,000	to	500,000	10.0%
	500,000	And Over		12.5%
Class C	0	to	100,000	10%
	100,000	to	200,000	12%
	200,00	And Over		15%

Exemptions: *(Taxable amount begins after taking applicable exemption)*

1. Spouse: All tax

2. Class A: $30,000

3. Class B: $5,000

Kentucky

Class A: Parent, spouse, child, stepchild, adopted child, or grandchild

Class B: Sibling, nephew or niece, daughter- or son-in-law, aunt or uncle

Class C: All others

	Taxable Amount			Tax Rate
Class A	0	to	20,000	2%
	20,000	to	45,000	4%
	45,000	to	60,000	5%
	60,000	to	100,000	6%
	100,000	to	200,000	7%
	200,000	to	500,000	8%
	500,000		And Over	10%
Class B	0	to	10,000	4%
	10,000	to	20,000	5%
	20,000	to	30,000	6%
	30,000	to	45,000	8%
	45,000	to	60,000	10%
	60,000	to	100,000	12%
	100,000	to	200,000	14%
	200,000		And Over	16%
Class C	0	to	10,000	6%
	10,000	to	20,000	8%
	20,000	to	30,000	10%
	30,000	to	45,000	12%
	45,000	to	60,000	14%
	60,000		And Over	16%

Exemptions:

1. Spouse: All tax

2. Infant/child: $20,000

3. Mentally disabled child: $20,000

4. Parent: $5,000

5. Child: $5,000

6. Grandchild: $56,000

7. Class B: $1,000

8. Class C: $500

Louisiana

Class 1: Spouse, descendants, lineal ancestors

Class 2: Collateral relatives (siblings, their children)

Class 3: All others

	Taxable Amount			Tax Rate
Class 1	0	to	20,000	2%
	20,000		And Over	3%
Class 2	0	to	1,000	No Tax
	1,000	to	21,000	5%
	21,000		And Over	7%
Class 3	0	to	500	No Tax
	500	to	5,000	5%
	5,000		And Over	10%

Exemptions:

1. Spouse: All tax if death in 1992 or after

2. Class 1: $25,000 if death is in 1987 or after

Maryland

Class 1: Spouse, parent, children, grandparent, descendants, stepchild, stepparent

Class 2: All others

	Taxable Amount	Tax Rate
Class 1	All Amounts	1%
Class 2	All Amounts	10%

Exemptions:

1. Spouse: First $100,000 of personal property; all real property

Special tax rates:

2. Spouse of descendant: 1% for first $2,000 of jointly-owned savings; thereafter at 10%

Michigan

Class 1:   Spouse, parent, grandparent, sibling, son- or daughter-in-law, children and adopted children

Class 2:   All others

	Taxable Amount			Tax Rate
Class 1	0	to	50,000	2%
	50,000	to	250,000	4%
	250,000	to	500,000	7%
	500,000	to	750,000	8%
	750,000	And Over		10%
Class 2	0	to	50,000	12%
	50,000	to	500,000	14%
	500,000	And Over		17%

Exemptions:

1. Spouse: All tax

2. All other Class 1: $10,000

Montana

Class 1:   Spouse, lineal descendant or child, and lineal ancestor

Class 2:   Siblings, their offspring, son- or daughter-in-law

Class 3:   Uncle, aunt, or first cousins

Class 4:   All others

	Taxable Amount			Tax Rate
Class 1	0	to	25,000	2%
	25,000	to	50,000	4%
	50,000	to	100,000	6%
	100,000	And Over		8%
Class 2	0	to	25,000	4%
	25,000	to	50,000	8%
	50,000	to	100,000	12%
	100,000	And Over		16%
Class 3	0	to	25,000	6%
	25,000	to	50,000	12%
	50,000	to	100,000	18%
	100,000	And Over		24%
Class 4	0	to	25,000	8%
	25,000	to	50,000	16%
	50,000	to	100,000	24%
	100,000	And Over		32%

Exemptions:

1. Spouse or child: All tax

2. Lineal ancestors: $7,000

3. Class 2: $1,000

Nebraska

Class 1: Spouse, parent, child, son- or daughter-in-law

Class 2: Uncle, aunt, niece, nephew or their descendants or spouses

Class 3: All others

	Taxable Amount			Tax Rate
Class 1	0	to	1,000	No Tax
	1,000		And Over	1%
Class 2	0	to	2,000	No Tax
	2,000	to	60,000	6%
	60,000		And Over	9%
Class 3	0	to	5,000	6%
	5,000	to	10,000	9%
	10,000	to	20,000	12%
	20,000	to	50,000	15%
	50,000		And Over	18%

Exemptions:

1. Spouse: All tax

2. Class 1: $10,000

3. Class 2: $2,000

4. Class 3: $500

New Hampshire

Class 1: Spouse, lineal ancestors, and descendants, their spouses and all adopted children in descendant's line of succession

Class 2: All others

	Taxable Amount	Tax Rate
Class 1	Any Amount	No Tax
Class 2	Any Amount	15%

Exemptions:

1. Property left to care for cemetery lots

2. Contributions to charities

3. Children of deceased (must have lived with deceased from age 5-15): All taxes

4. Step-children and their spouses: All taxes

New Jersey

Class A: Spouse, parent, grandparent, children of children, step-children

Class B: Sibling, daughter- or son-in-law

Class C: All others

	Taxable Amount			Tax Rate
Class A				No Tax
Class B	0	to	1,100,000	11%
	1,100,000	to	1,400,000	13%
	1,400,000	to	1,700,000	14%
	1,700,000		And Over	16%
Class C	0	to	700,000	15%
	700,000		And Over	16%

Exemptions:

Class B: First $25000

North Carolina

Class A: Spouse, lineal descendants, ancestor, stepchild, adopted child, or son- or daughter-in-law whose spouse is not entitled to any beneficiary interest in property of deceased

Class B: Sibling, their issue, aunt or uncle

Class C: All others

	Taxable Amount			Tax Rate
Class A	0	to	10,000	1%
	10,000	to	25,000	2%
	25,000	to	50,000	3%
	50,000	to	100,000	4%
	100,000	to	200,000	5%
	200,000	to	500,000	6%
	500,000	to	1,000,000	7%
	1,000,000	to	1,500,000	8%
	1,500,000	to	2,000,000	9%
	2,000,000	to	2,500,000	10%
	2,500,000	to	3,000,000	11%
	3,000,000	And Over		12%
Class B	0	to	5,000	4%
	5,000	to	10,000	5%
	10,000	to	25,000	6%
	25,000	to	50,000	7%
	50,000	to	100,000	8%
	100,000	to	250,000	10%
	250,000	to	500,000	11%
	500,000	to	1,000,000	12%
	1,000,000	to	1,500,000	13%
	1,500,000	to	2,000,000	14%
	2,000,000	to	3,000,000	15%
	3,000,000	And Over		16%
Class C	0	to	10,000	8%
	10,000	to	25,000	9%
	25,000	to	50,000	10%
	50,000	to	100,000	11%
	100,000	to	250,000	12%
	250,000	to	500,000	13%
	500,000	to	1,000,000	14%
	1,000,000	to	1,500,000	15%
	1,500,000	to	2,500,000	16%
	2,500,000	And Over		17%

Exemptions:

1. Spouse: All tax

2. Other Class A: $26,150 tax credit

Oklahoma

Class 1: Parent, child, child of spouse, descendant

Class 2: All others

	Taxable Amount			Tax Rate
Class 1	0	to	10,000	No Tax
	10,000	to	20,000	1.0
	20,000	to	40,000	1.5
	40,000	to	60,000	2.0
	60,000	to	100,000	2.5
	100,000	to	250,000	3.0
	250,000	to	500,000	6.5
	500,000	to	750,000	7.0
	750,000	to	1,000,000	7.5
	1,000,000	to	3,000,000	8.0
	3,000,000	to	5,000,000	8.5
	5,000,000	to	10,000,000	9.0
	10,000,000	And Over		10.0
Class 2	0	to	10,000	1.0
	10,000	to	20,000	2.0
	20,000	to	40,000	3.0
	40,000	to	60,000	4.0
	60,000	to	100,000	5.0
	100,000	to	250,000	6.0
	250,000	to	500,000	13.0
	500,000	to	1,000,000	14.0
	1,000,000	And Over		15.0

Exemptions: *(Taxable amount begins after taking applicable exemption)*

1. Spouses: All tax

2. Other Class 1: $175,000

Pennsylvania

Class A: Grandparents, parents, spouse, lineal descendants, widower or widow of child, spouse of child

Class B: All others

	Taxable Amount	Tax Rate
Class A	All Amounts	6%
Class B	All Amounts	15%

Exemptions:

1. Spouse: All property held jointly

2. Family: $2,000

South Dakota

Class 1: Issue, adopted child, child

Class 2: Ancestor or descendant

Class 3: Sibling or their issue or son- or daughter-in-law

Class 4: Aunt or uncle

Class 5: All others

Class 6: Sibling if in business with descendant for 10 or 15 years before death of descendant

	Taxable Amount			Tax Rate
Class 1	0	to	30,000	No Tax
	30,000	to	50,000	3.75%
	50,000	to	100,000	6.00%
	100,000		And Over	7.50%
Class 2	0	to	3,000	No Tax
	3,000	to	15,000	3.00%
	15,000	to	50,000	7.50%
	50,000	to	100,000	12.00%
	100,000		And Over	15.00%
Class 3	0	to	500	No Tax
	500	to	15,000	4.00%
	15,000	to	50,000	10.00%
	50,000	to	100,000	16.00%
	100,000		And Over	20.00%
Class 4	0	to	200	No Tax
	200	to	15,000	5.00%
	15,000	to	50,000	12.50%
	50,000	to	100,000	20.00%
	100,000		And Over	25.00%
Class 5	0	to	100	No Tax
	100	to	15,000	6.00%
	15,000	to	50,000	15.00%
	50,000	to	100,000	24.00%
	100,000		And Over	30.00%
Class 6	0	to	15,000	3.00%
	15,000	to	50,000	7.50%
	50,000	to	100,000	12.00%
	100,000		And Over	15.00%

Exemptions:

1. Spouse: All tax

Tennessee

Class A: Spouse, child, lineal ancestor or descendant, sibling, stepchild, son- or daughter-in-law, adopted child

Class B: All other and common law spouse

Taxable Amount			Tax		
			Base Tax	Plus %	Of Amt Over
Class A (*Deceased dying in 1989*)					
0	to	40,000	0	+ 5.5%	0
40,000	to	240,000	2,200	+ 6.5%	40,000
240,000	to	440,000	15,200	+ 7.5%	240,000
440,000	And Over		30,200	+ 9.5%	440,000
Class B (*Deceased dying in 1989*)					
0	to	40,000	0	+ 5.5%	0
40,000	to	240,000	2,200	+ 6.5%	40,000
240,000	to	440,000	15,200	+ 7.5%	240,000
440,000	And Over		30,200	+ 9.5%	440,000
All Classes *after 1989*					
0	to	10,000			No Tax
10,000	to	60,000	0	+ 6.5%	10,000
60,000	to	110,000	3,900	+ 9.5%	60,000
110,000	to	160,000	8,650	+12.0%	110,000
160,000	to	210,000	14,650	+13.5%	160,000
210,000	And Over		21,400	+16.0%	210,000

Exemptions: (*Taxable amount begins after taking applicable exemption*)

1. Class A: $600,000

2. Class B in 1989: $350,000

3. Class B after 1989: $600,000

Wisconsin

Class A: Lineal issue (descendant), lineal ancestor, wife or widow of son or husband or widower of daughter

Class B: Brother or sister or a descendant of brother or sister

Class C: Brother or sister of father or mother or a descendant of brother or sister of father or mother

Class D: All others of blood relation but not surviving spouse

	Taxable Amount			Tax Rate
Class A	0	to	25,000	2.5%
	25,000	to	50,000	5.0%
	50,000	to	100,000	7.5%
	100,000	to	500,000	10.0%
	500,000	And Over		12.5%
Class B	0	to	25,000	5.0%
	25,000	to	50,000	10.0%
	50,000	to	100,000	15.0%
	100,000	And Over		20.0%
Class C	0	to	25,000	7.5%
	25,000	to	50,000	15.0%
	50,000	And Over		20.0%
Class D	0	to	25,000	10.0%
	25,000	And Over		20.0%

Exemptions:

1. Class A: $50,000 if date of death is on or after July 1, 1985

2. Class B and C: $1,000

3. Class D: $500

Chart 2. Estate Taxes

Following are the rules for each state which imposes estate taxes.

Massachusetts

Taxable Amount			Tax Rate
0	to	200,000	No Tax
200,000	to	400,000	10%
400,000	to	600,000	11%
600,000	to	800,000	12%
800,000	to	1,000,000	13%
1,000,000	to	2,000,000	14%
2,000,000	to	4,000,000	15%
4,000,000	And Over		16%

Mississippi

Taxable Amount			Tax Rate
0	to	60,000	1.0%
60,000	to	100,000	1.6%
100,000	to	200,000	2.4%
200,000	to	400,000	3.2%
400,000	to	600,000	4.0%
600,000	to	800,000	4.8%
800,000	to	1,000,000	5.6%
1,000,000	to	1,500,000	6.4%
1,500,000	to	2,000,000	7.2%
2,000,000	to	2,500,000	8.0%
2,500,000	to	3,000,000	8.8%
3,000,000	to	3,500,000	9.6%
3,500,000	to	4,000,000	10.4%
4,000,000	to	5,000,000	11.2%
5,000,000	to	6,000,000	12.0%
6,000,000	to	7,000,000	12.8%
7,000,000	to	8,000,000	13.6%
8,000,000	to	9,000,000	14.4%
9,000,000	to	10,000.000	15.2%
10,000,000	And Over		16.0%

Exemption:

$175,625 - taxable amount begins after taking exemption

New York

Taxable Amount			Tax Rate
0	to	50,000	2%
50,000	to	150,000	3%
150,000	to	300,000	4%
300,000	to	500,000	5%
500,000	to	700,000	6%
700,000	to	900,000	7%
900,000	to	1,100,000	8%
1,100,000	to	1,600,000	9%
1,600,000	to	2,100,000	10%
2,100,000	to	2,600,000	11%
2,600,000	to	3,100,000	12%
3,100,000	to	3,600,000	13%
3,600,000	to	4,100,000	14%
4,100,000	to	5,100,000	15%
5,100,000	to	6,100,000	16%
6,100,000	to	7,100,000	17%
7,100,000	to	8,100,000	18%
8,100,000	to	9,100,000	19%
9,100,000	to	10,100,000	20%
10,100,000	And Over		21%

Tax credits:

Tax	Credit
$0 to $2,750,	Full credit (No tax)
$2,750 to $5,000	Difference between tax and $5,000
$5,000 or more	$500

Ohio

Taxable Amount			Tax Rate
0	to	40,000	2%
40,000	to	100,000	3%
100,000	to	200,000	4%
200,000	to	300,000	5%
300,000	to	500,000	6%
500,000	And Over		7%

Exemption:

Marital deduction for the lesser of the federal marital deduction or one-half of adjusted gross estates greater than $500,000

Rhode Island

Taxable Amount			Tax Rate
0	to	25,000	2%
25,000	to	50,000	3%
50,000	to	100,000	4%
100,000	to	250,000	5%
250,000	to	500,000	6%
500,000	to	750,000	7%
750,000	to	1,000,000	8%
1,000,000		And Over	9%

Exemptions:

1. Spouse: $175,000

2. All estates: $25,000

Tax reduced according to the following schedule:

Year	Percentage Reduction
1989	60%
1990	80%
1991	100%

South Carolina

Taxable Amount			Tax Rate
0	to	40,000	6%
40,000	to	100,000	7%
100,000		And Over	8%

Exemptions:

1. Spouse: All taxes

2. All estates: $120,000

INDEX

V

W

About Nolo Press

It's no secret that our legal system offers most Americans poor access to justice. Especially when it comes to relatively straightforward legal tasks, many people knew that too often lawyers charge too much, explain too little, and provide inadequate services.

Nolo Press, founded in 1971, pioneered a different approach: helping people gain the knowledge necessary to cope with their own routine legal problems. Nolo now publishes over 60 self-help law books and software programs. Our materials are affordable, they explain—in plain English—what the law says, and they show readers how to complete many routine legal tasks (including court appearances) without a lawyer.

Bar associations thundered against Nolo's first book, **How To Do Your Own Divorce in California,** claiming it was a "danger to consumers." In the next few years the public was repeatedly warned that doing your own legal paperwork, for even the simplest legal task, was akin to doing your own brain surgery. Fortunately, consumers took a hard look at the expensive alternatives the legal profession offered, examined Nolo books, and made up their own minds. Today, close to 60% of the uncontested divorces in California are done without lawyers, most of them with the help of Nolo's divorce book, which has sold close to half a million copies.

In the late 1970s, after publishing a dozen successful California self-help law books in areas as diverse as tenants' rights and incorporating a small business, Nolo broadened its focus to the whole country. We now have national books on wills, patents, estate planning, and partnerships, to mention just a few. In 1981 Nolo began publishing a quarterly self-help law newspaper, the **Nolo News—Access To Law**. It keeps readers up-to-date on law changes that affect our books, encourages new self-help approaches, and provides consumer information.

An important part of Nolo's purpose is to spread the word that our legal system can easily be made more affordable, accessible, and fair if it is redesigned to serve consumers instead of the legal profession. To take but one example, Nolo has repeatedly urged that competent non-lawyers (independent paralegals) be permitted to provide reasonably-priced legal form completion services.

More recently, Nolo expanded into self-help legal software with a number of easy-to-use programs, including **WillMaker** (with Legisoft). With over 100,000 sold, it's fair to estimate that **WillMaker** has made more wills than any law firm in history.

Currently, we're busy creating new programs, writing new books, and keeping our existing titles up to date. Nolo has grown from a home-base business with a couple of part-time employees to one that employs close to 50 people.

One thing that hasn't changed since Nolo's undeniably humble beginnings is our commitment to quality. Our books and software are as clear, accurate, up-to-date and useful as we can make them. To help with this process we enclose a tear-out feedback card in this book and urge you to take a minute to give us the benefit of your suggestions. Every suggestion is read by a Nolo author or editor.

ABOUT THE AUTHOR

Denis Clifford is a lawyer who specializes in estate planning. He is the author of several Nolo Press books, including *Nolo's Simple Will Book* and *The Power of Attorney Book*. A graduate of Columbia Law School, where he was an editor of *The Law Review*, he has practiced law in various ways, and became convinced that people can do much of the legal work they need themselves.

SOFTWARE

willmaker

Nolo Press/Legisoft

Recent statistics say chances are better than 2 to 1 that you haven't written a will, even though you know you should. WillMaker makes the job easy, leading you step by step in a fill-in-the-blank format. Once you've gone through the program, you print out the will and sign it in front of witnesses. Because writing a will is only one step in the estate planning process, WillMaker comes with a 200-page manual providing an overview of probate avoidance and tax planning techniques.

National 3rd Ed.

Apple, IBM, Macintosh	$59.95
Commodore	$39.95

california incorporator

Attorney Mancuso and Legisoft, Inc.

About half of the small California corporations formed today are done without the services of a lawyer. This easy-to-use software program lets you do the paperwork with minimum effort. Just answer the questions on the screen, and California Incorporator will print out the 35-40 pages of documents you need to make your California corporation legal.

California Edition (IBM)	$129.00

for the record

By attorney Warner & Pladsen. A book/software package that helps to keep track of personal and financial records; create documents to give to family members in case of emergency; leave an accurate record for heirs, and allows easy access to all important records with the ability to print out any section

National Edition

Macintosh	$49.95

the california nonprofit corporation handbook—computer edition with disk

Attorney Anthony Mancuso

This is the standard work on how to form a nonprofit corporation in California. Included on the disk are the forms for the Articles, Bylaws and Minutes you will need, as wel as regular and special director and member minute forms. Also included are several chapters with line-by-line instructions explaining how to apply for and obtain federal tax exempt status. This is a critical step in the incorporation of any nonprofit organizaton and applies to incorporating in all 50 states.

California 1st Ed.

IBM PC 5 1/4 & 3 1/2	$69.00
Macintosh	$69.00

how to form your own texas corporation—computer edition with disk

AttorneyAnthony Mancuso

how to form your own new york corporation—computer edition with disk

AttorneyAnthony Mancuso

More and more business people are incorporating to qualify for tax benefits, limited liability status, the benefit of employee status and financial flexibility. These software packages contain all the instructions, tax information and forms you need to incorporate a small business, including the Certificate (or Articles) of Incorporation, Bylaws, Minutes and Stock Certificates. The manuals include instructions on how to incorporate a new or existing business; tax and securities law information; information on S corporations; Federal Tax Reform Act rates and rules; and the latest procedures to protect your directors under state law. All organizational forms are on disk.

1st Ed.

IBM PC 5 1/4 & 3 1/2	$69.00
Macintosh	$69.00

for the record

By attorney Warner & Pladsen. A book/software package that helps to keep track of personal and financial records; create documents to give to family members in case of emergency; leave an accurate record for heirs, and allows easy access to all important records with the ability to print out any section

National Edition

Macintosh	$49.95
IBM	$49.95

the california nonprofit corporation handbook

Attorney Anthony Mancuso

Used by arts groups, educators, social service agencies, medical programs, environmentalists and many others, this book explains all the legal formalities involved in forming and operating a nonprofit corporation. Included are all the forms for the Articles, Bylaws and Minutes you will need. Also included are complete instructions for obtaining federal 501(c)(3) exemptions and benefits. The tax information in this section applies wherever your corporation is formed.

California 5th Ed. $29.95

how to form your own corporation

Attorney Anthony Mancuso

More and more business people are incorporating to qualify for tax benefits, limited liability status, the benefit of employee status and the financial flexibility. These books contain the forms, instructions and tax information you need to incorporate a small business.

California 7th Ed.	$29.95
Texas 4th Ed.	$24.95
New York 2nd. Ed.	$24.95
Florida 1st Ed.	$19.95

1988 calcorp update package

Attorney Anthony Mancuso

This update package contains all the forms and instructions you need to modify your corporation's Articles of Incorporation so you can take advantage of new California laws. $25.00

the california professional corporation handbook

Attorney Anthony Mancuso

Health care professionals, marriage, family and child counsellors, lawyers, accountants and members of certain other professions must fulfill special requirements when forming a corporation in California. This edition contains up-to-date tax information plus all the forms and instructions necessary to form a California professional corporation. An appendix explains the special rules that apply to each profession.

California 3rd Ed. $29.95

marketing without advertising

Michael Phillips & Salli Rasberry

There are good ideas on every page. You'll find here the nitty gritty steps you need to–and can–take to generate sales for your business, no matter what business it is.—Milton Moskowitz, syndicated columnist and author of The 100 Best Companies to Work For in America

Every small business person knows that the best marketing plan encourages customer loyalty and personal recommendation. Phillips and Rasberry outline practical steps for building and expanding a small business without spending a lot of money.

National 1st Ed. $14.00

the partnership book

Attorneys Clifford & Warner

Lots of people dream of going into business with a friend. The best way to keep that dream from turning into a nightmare is to have a solid partnership agreement. This book shows how to write an agreement that covers evaluation of partner assets, disputes, buy-outs and the death of a partner.

National 3rd Ed. $18.95

nolo's small business start-up

Mike McKeever

...outlines the kinds of credit available, describing the requirements and pros and cons of each source, and finally shows how to prepare cashflow forecasts, capital spending plans, and other vital ideas. An attractive guide for would-be entrepreneurs.—ALA Booklist

Should you start a business? Should you raise money to expand your already running business? If the answers are yes, this book will show you how to write an effective business plan and loan package.

National 3rd Ed. $17.95

the independent paralegal's handbook: how to provide legal services without going to jail

Attorney Ralph Warner

Warner's practical guide highlights the historical background of self-help law, and then gives a great deal of nuts-and-bolts advice on establishing and maintaining a paralegal office ...Highly recommended...—Library Journal

A large percentage of routine legal work in this country is performed by typists, secretaries, researchers and various other law office helpers generally labeled paralegals. For those who would like to take these services out of the law office and offer them at a reasonable fee in an independent business, attorney Ralph Warner provides both legal and business guidelines.

National 1st Ed. $12.95

getting started as an independent paralegal (two audio tapes)

Attorney Ralph Warner

This set of tapes, approximately three hours in all, is a carefully edited version of Nolo Press founder Ralph Warner's Saturday Morning Law School class. It is designed for people who wish to go into business helping consumers prepare their own paperwork in uncontested actions such as bankruptcy, divorce, small business incorporations, landlord-tenant actions, probate, etc. Also covered are how to set up, run, and market your business, as well as a detailed discussion of Unauthorized Practice of Law. The tapes are designed to be used in conjunction with The Independent Paralegal's Handbook.

National 1st Ed. $24.95

collect your court judgment

Scott, Elias & Goldoftas

After you win a judgment in small claims, municipal or superior court, you still have to collect your money. Here are step-by-step instructions on hwo to collect your judgment from the debtor's bank accounts, wages, business receipts, real estate or other assets.

California 1st Ed. $24.95

chapter 13: the federal plan to repay your debts

Attorney Janice Kosel

For those who want to repay their debts and think they can, but are hounded by creditors, Chapter 13 may be the answer. Under the protection of the court you may work out a personal budget and take up to three years to repay a percentage of your debt and have the rest wiped clean.

National 3rd Ed. $17.95

make your own contract

Attorney Stephen Elias

If you've ever sold a car, lent money to a relative or friend, or put money down on a prospective purchase, you should have used a contract. Perhaps everything went without a hitch. If it didn't, though, you probably experienced a lot of grief and frustration.

Here are clearly written legal form contracts to: buy and sell property, borrow and lend money, store and lend personal property, make deposits on goods for later purchase, release others from personal liability, or pay a contractor to do home repairs.

National 1st Ed. $12.95

social security, medicare & pensions: a sourcebook for older americans

Attorney Joseph L. Matthews & Dorothy Matthews Berman

Social security, medicare and medicaid programs follow a host of complicated rules. Those over 55, or those caring for someone over 55, will find this comprehensive guidebook invaluable for understanding and utilizing their rightful benefits. A special chapter deals with age discrimination in employment and what to do about it.

National 4th Ed. $15.95

everybody's guide to small claims court

Attorney Ralph Warner

So, the dry cleaner ruined your good flannel suit. Your roof leaks every time it rains, and the contractor who supposedly fixed it won't call you back. The bicycle shop hasn't paid for the tire pumps you sold it six months ago. This book will help you decide if you have a case, show you how to file and serve papers, tell you what to bring to court, and how to collect a judgment.

California 7th Ed. $14.95
National 3rd Ed. $14.95

billpayers' rights

Attorneys Warner & Elias

Lots of people find themselves overwhelmed by debt. The law, however, offers a number of legal protections for consumers and Billpayers' Rights shows people how to use them.

Areas covered include: how to handle bill collectors, deal with student loans, check your credit rating and decide if you should file for bankruptcy.

California 8th Ed. $14.95

29 reasons not to go to law school

Ralph Warner & Toni Ihara

Lawyers, law students, their spouses and consorts will love this little book with its zingy comments and Thurber-esque cartoons, humorously zapping the life of the law.—Peninsula Times Tribune

Filled with humor and piercing observations, this book can save you three years, $70,000 and your sanity.

3rd Ed. $9.95

murder on the air

Ralph Warner & Toni Ihara

Here is a sure winner for any friend who's spent more than a week in the city of Berkeley...a catchy little mystery situated in the environs and the cultural mores of the People's Republic.—The Bay Guardian

Flat out fun...—San Francisco Chronicle $5.95

poetic justice

Ed. by Jonathan & Andrew Roth

A unique compilation of humorous quotes about lawyers and the legal system, from Socrates to Woody Allen.

$8.95

dog law

Attorney Mary Randolph

There are 50 million dogs in the United States—and, it seems, at least that many rules and regulations for their owners to abide by. *Dog Law* covers topics that everyone who owns a dog, or lives near one, needs to know about dispute about a dog injury or nuisance.

National 1st Ed. $12.95

the criminal records book

Attorney Warren Siegel

We've all done something illegal. If you were one of those who got caught, your juvenile or criminal court record can complicate your life years later. The good news is that in many cases your record can either be completely expunged or lessened in severity.

The Criminal Records Book takes you step by step through the procedures to: seal criminal records, dismiss convictions, destroy marijuana records, reduce felony convictions.

California 2nd Ed. $14.95

draft, registration and the law

Attorney R. Charles Johnson

This clearly written guidebook explains the present draft law and how registration (required of all male citizens within thirty days of their eighteenth birthday) works. Every available option is presented along with a description of how a draft would work if there were a call tomorrow.

National 2nd Ed. $9.95

fight your ticket

Attorney David Brown

At a trade show in San Francisco recently, a traffic court judge (who must remain nameless) told our associate publisher that he keeps this book by his bench for easy reference.

If you think that ticket was unfair, here's the book showing you what to do to fight it.

California 3rd Ed. $16.95

how to become a united states citizen

Sally Abel Schreuder

This bilingual (English/Spanish) book presents the forms, applications and instructions for naturalization. This step-by-step guide will provide information and answers for legally admitted aliens who wish to become citizens.

National 3rd Ed. $12.95

how to change your name

Attorneys Loeb & Brown

Wish that you had gone back to your maiden name after the divorce? Tired of spelling over the phone V-e-n-k-a-t-a-r-a-m-a-n   S-u-b-r-a-m-a-n-i-a-m?

This book explains how to change your name legally and provides all the necessary court forms with detailed instructions on how to fill them out.

California 4th Ed. $14.95

legal research: how to find and understand the law

Attorney Stephen Elias

Legal Research could also be called Volume-Two-for-all-Nolo-Press-Self-Help-Law-Books. A valuable tool for paralegals, law students and legal secretaries, this book provides access to legal information. Using this book, the legal self-helper can find and research a case, read statutes, and make Freedom of Information Act requests.

National 2nd Ed. $14.95

family law dictionary

Attorneys Leonard and Elias

Written in plain English (as opposed to legalese), the Family Law Dictionary has been compiled to help the lay person doing research in the area of family law (i.e., marriage, divorce, adoption, etc.). Using cross referencs and examples as well as definitions, this book is unique as a reference tool.

National 1st Edition $13.95

intellectual property law dictionary

Attorney Stephen Elias

This book uses simple language free of legal jargon to define and explain the intricacies of items associated with trade secrets, copyrights, trademarks and unfair competition, patents and patent procedures, and contracts and warranties.—IEEE Spectrum

If you're dealing with any multi-media product, a new business product or trade secret, you need this book.

National 1st Ed. $17.95

the people's law review: an access catalog to law without lawyers

Edited by Attorney Ralph Warner

Articles, interviews and a resource list introduce the entire range of do-it-yourself law from estate planning to tenants' rights. The People's Law Review also provides a wealth of background information on the history of law, some considerations on its future, and alternative ways of solving legal problems.

National 1st Ed. $8.95

how to do your own divorce

Attorney Charles E. Sherman

This is the book that launched Nolo Press and advanced the self-help law movement. During the past 17 years, over 400,000 copies have been sold, saving consumers at least $50 million in legal fees (assuming 100,000 have each saved $500—certainly a conservative estimate).

California 14th Ed. $14.95
Texas 2nd Ed. $12.95
(Texas Ed. by Sherman & Simons)

california marriage & divorce law

Attorneys Warner, Ihara & Elias

Most people marry only with the idea they are in love—that's not enough. This book should be a text in every California high school and college.—Phyllis Eliasberg, Consumer Reporter, CBS News

For a generation, this practical handbook has been the best resource for the Californian who wants to understand marriage and divorce laws. Even if you hire a lawyer to help you with a divorce, it's essential that you learn your basic legal rights and responsibilities.

California 9th Ed. $15.95

practical divorce solutions

Attorney Charles Ed Sherman

Written by the author of *How to Do Your Own Divorce* (with over 500,000 copies in print), this book provides a valuable guide both to the emotional process involved in divorce as well as the legal and financial decisions that have to be made.

Getting the "legal divorce," says Sherman, is "a ceremony you have to go through." The real divorce involves the many emotional and practical aspects of your life that are inevitably altered. To ensure the best possible outcome you must educate yourself. The worst thing you can do, he counsels, is to run directly to a lawyer and get involved in an uncontrolled battle.

California 1st Ed. $12.95

how to adopt your stepchild in california

Frank Zagone & Mary Randolph

For many families that include stepchildren, adoption is a satisfying way to guarantee the family a solid legal footing.This book provides sample forms and complete step-by-step instructions for completing a simple uncontested adoption by a stepparent.

California 3rd Ed. $19.95

how to modify and collect child support in california

Attorneys Matthews, Siegel & Willis

California has established landmark new standards in setting and collecting child support. Payments must now be based on both objective need standards and the parents' combined income.

Using this book, custodial parents can determine if they are entitled to higher child support payments and can implement the procedures to obtain that support.

California 2nd Ed. $17.95

a legal guide for lesbian and gay couples

Attorneys Curry & Clifford

The edge of the law... will be much less fearful for those who have this book. Full of clear language and concern for realistic legal expectations, this guide well serves and supports the spirit of the law.—Los Angeles Times

In addition to its clear presentation of "living together" contracts, A Legal Guide contains crucial information on the special problems facing lesbians and gay men with children, civil rights legislation, and medical/legal issues.

National 4th Ed. $17.95

the living together kit

Attorneys Ihara & Warner

Few unmarried couples understand the laws that may affect them. Here are useful tips on living together agreements, paternity agreements, estate planning, and buying real estate.

National 5th Ed. $17.95

your family records

Carol Pladsen & Attorney Denis Clifford

...a cleverly designed and convenient workbook that provides a repository for legal, financial and tax data as well as family history. —Los Angeles Times

Most American families keep terrible records. Typically, the checkbook is on a shelf in the kitchen, insurance policies are nowhere to be found, and jewelry and cash are hidden in a coffee can in the garage. Your Family Records is a sensible, straightforward guide that will help you organize your records before you face a crisis.

National 2nd Ed. $14.95

LANDLORDS, TENANTS & HOMEOWNERS

for sale by owner
George Devine
In 1986 about 600,000 homes were sold in California at a median price of $130,000. Most sellers worked with a broker and paid the 6% commission. For the median home that meant $7,800. Obviously, that's money that could be saved if you sell your own house. This book provides the background information and legal technicalities you will need to do the job yourself and with confidence.
California 1st Ed. $24.95

homestead your house
Attorneys Warner, Sherman & Ihara
Under California homestead laws, up to $60,000 of the equity in your home may be safe from creditors. But to get the maximum legal protection you should file a Declaration of Homestead before a judgment lien is recorded against you. This book includes complete instructions and tear-out forms.
California 6th Ed. $8.95

the landlord's law book:
vol. 1, rights & responsibilities
Attorneys Brown & Warner
Every landlord should know the basics of landlord-tenant law. Everything from the amount you can charge for a security deposit to terminating a tenancy, to your legal responsibility for the illegal acts of your manager is closely regulated by the law. In short, the era when a landlord could substitute common sense for a detailed knowledge of the law is gone forever. This volume covers: deposits, leases and rental agreements, inspections (tenants' privacy rights), habitability (rent withholding), ending a tenancy, liability, and rent control.
California 2nd Ed. $24.95

the landlord's law book: vol. 2, evictions
Attorney David Brown
Even the most scrupulous landlord may sometimes need to evict a tenant. In the past it has been necessary to hire a lawyer and pay a high fee. Using this book you can handle most evictions yourself safely and economically.
California 1st Ed. $24.95

tenants' rights
Attorneys Moskowitz & Warner
Your "security building" doesn't have a working lock on the front door. Is your landlord liable? How can you get him to fix it? Under what circumstances can you withhold rent? When is an apartment not "habitable?" This book explains the best way to handle your relationship with your landlord and your legal rights when you find yourself in disagreement.
California 10th Ed. $15.95

the deeds book:
how to transfer title to california real estate
Attorney Mary Randolph
If you own real estate, you'll almost surely need to sign a new deed at one time or another. The Deeds Book shows you how to choose the right kind of deed, how to complete the tear-out forms, and how to record them in the county recorder's public records. It also alerts you to real property disclosure requirements and California community property rules, as well as tax and estate planning aspects of your transfer.
California 1st Ed. $15.95

PATENTS, COPYRIGHTS & TRADEMARKS

how to copyright software
Attorney M.J. Salone
Copyrighting is the best protection for any software. This book explains how to get a copyright and what a copyright can protect.
National 2nd Ed. $24.95

the inventor's notebook
Fred Grissom & Attorney David Pressman
The best protection for your patent is adequate records. The Inventor's Notebook provides forms, instructions, references to relevant areas of patent law, a bibliography of legal and non-legal aids, and more. It helps you document the activities that are normally part of successful independent inventing.
National 1st Ed. $19.95

legal care for your software
Attorneys Daniel Remer & Stephen Elias
If you write programs you intend to sell, or work for a software house that pays you for programming, you should buy this book. If you are a freelance programmer doing software development, you should buy this book.—Interface
This step-by-step guide for computer software writers covers copyright laws, trade secret protection, contracts, license agreements, trademarks, patents and more.
National 3rd Ed. $29.95

patent it yourself
Attorney David Pressman
You've invented something, or you're working on it, or you're planning to start...Patent It Yourself offers help in evaluating patentability, marketability and the protective documentation you should have. If you file your own patent application using this book, you can save from $1500 to $3500.
National 2nd Ed. $29.95

COUPON

25% discount

Social Security, Medicare and Pensions
The Power of Attorney Book
How to Probate an Estate
Nolo's Simple Will Book
The Deeds Book

To receive the 25% discount on a future purchase of these listed books, simply cut out this coupon and attach it to the order form in the back of the book. Offer expires December 1991.

Social Security, Medicare & Pensions: A Sourcebook for Older Americans

Attorney J. L. Matthews & Dorothy Matthews Berman
This comprehensive resource guide provides invaluable information about rights and benefits available to Americans over 55. This revised edition includes detailed information on Social Security, age discrimination in employment, retirement rights and Medicare and Medicaid. A section has been added to explain the important Medicare Catastrophic Coverage Act of 1988.
National 4th Edition
Regular price: $15.95
Special discount: $11.97

Nolo's Simple Will Book

Attorney Denis Clifford
Most people need a will—to name a guardian for their children, give specific gifts to relatives, friends or charities, or to back up more sophisticated estate planning devices such as living trusts. It's easy to write a legally valid will using this book. And once you've done it yourself you'll know how to update it whenever necessary.
National 1st Edition
Regular price: $14.95
Special discount: $11.22

How to Probate an Estate

Julia Nissley
When a close relative dies, amidst the grieving there are financial and legal details to be dealt with. The natural response is to rely on an attorney, that response can be costly. With How to Probate an Estate, you can have the satisfaction of doing the work yourself and saving those fees.
California 3rd Edition
Regular price: $24.95
Special discount: $18.72

The Power of Attorney Book

Attorney Denis Clifford
The Power of Attorney Book concerns something you've heard about but probably would rather ignore: Who will take care of your affairs, make your financial and medical decisions, if you can't? With this book you can appoint someone you trust to carry out your wishes. The book includes the forms you need to formalize your choices: the Durable Power of Attorney and Living Will forms.
National 2nd Edition
Regular price: $17.95
Special discount: $13.47

The Deeds Book: How to Transfer Title to California Real Estate

Attorney Mary Randolph
If you own real estate, you'll need to sign a new deed when you transfer the property or put it in trust as part of your estate planning. The Deeds Book shows you how to choose the right kind of deed, complete the tear-out forms, and record them in the county recorder's public records. It also alerts you to real property disclosure requirements and California community property rules, as well as tax and estate planning aspects of property transfers.
California 1st Edition
Regular price: $15.95
Special discount: $11.97

nolo

SELF-HELP LAW BOOKS & SOFTWARE

ORDER FORM

Quantity	Title	Unit Price	Total

Sales Tax (CA residents only):

7%   Alameda, Contra Costa, San Diego, San
        Mateo & Santa Clara counties
6 1/2% Fresno, Inyo, LA, Sacramento, San Benito,
        San Francisco & Santa Cruz counties
6%   All others

Subtotal _____

Sales Tax _____

TOTAL_____

Method of Payment:

☐ Check enclosed

☐ VISA   ☐ Mastercard

Acct # _____ Exp._____

Signature _____

Phone (   ) _____

Ship to:

Name_____

Address _____

_____

Mail to:

NOLO PRESS
950 Parker Street
Berkeley CA 94710

**For faster service, use your credit card and
our toll-free numbers:**

Monday-Friday 8-5 Pacific Time

US   1-800-992-6656

CA   (outside 415 area)   1-800-445-6656

      (inside 415 area)   1-415-549-1976

General Information   1-415-549-1976

Prices subject to change

Please allow 1-2 weeks for delivery

Delivery is by UPS; no P.O. boxes, please

ORDER DIRECT AND WE PAY POSTAGE & HANDLING!

RECYCLE YOUR OUT-OF-DATE BOOKS & GET 25% OFF YOUR NEXT PURCHASE!

Using an old edition can be dangerous if information in it is wrong. Unfortunately, laws and legal procedures change often. To help you keep up to date we extend this offer. If you cut out and deliver to us the title portion of the cover of any old Nolo book we'll give you a 25% discount off the retail price of any new Nolo book. For example, if you have a copy of TENANT'S RIGHTS, 4th edition and want to trade it for the latest CALIFORNIA MARRIAGE AND DIVORCE LAW, send us the TENANT'S RIGHTS cover and a check for the current price of MARRIAGE & DIVORCE, less a 25% discount. Information on current prices and editions is listed in the NOLO NEWS. Generally speaking, any book more than two years old is of questionable value. Books more than four or five years old are a menace.

OUT OF DATE = DANGEROUS

This offer is to individuals only.

PYE 5/89

One Year Free!

Nolo Press wants you to have top quality and up-to-date legal information. The **Nolo News**, our "Access to Law" quarterly newspaper, contains an update section which will keep you abreast of any changes in the law relevant to **Plan Your Estate**. You'll find interesting articles on a number of legal topics, book reviews and our ever-popular lawyer joke column.

Send in the registration card below and receive FREE a one-year subscription to the **Nolo News** (normally $9.00).

Your subscription will begin with the first quarterly issue published after we receive your card.

NOLO PRESS
Plan Your Estate Registration Card

We would like to hear from you. Please let us know if the book met your needs. Fill out and return this card for a FREE one-year subscription to the *Nolo News*. In addition, we'll notify you when we publish a new edition of **Plan Your Estate.** (This offer is good in the U.S.only.)

Name _____

Address_____

City _____ State _____ Zip_____

Your occupation_____

Briefly, for what purpose did you use this book?

_____

_____

Did you find the information in the book helpful?
  (extremely helpful) 1 2 3 4 5 (not at all)

Where did you hear about the book?_____

Did you consult a lawyer? _____

Have you used other Nolo books?____Yes, ____No

Where did you buy the book?_____

Suggestions for improvement:_____

_____

_____

_____

_____

_____

_____

_____

_____

_____

_____

▲

[Nolo books are]..."written in plain language, free of legal mumbo jumbo, and spiced with witty personal observations."

—ASSOCIATED PRESS

▲

"Well-produced and slickly written, the [Nolo] books are designed to take the mystery out of seemingly involved procedures, carefully avoiding legalese and leading the reader step-by-step through such everyday legal problems as filling out forms, making up contracts, and even how to behave in court."

—SAN FRANCISCO EXAMINER

▲

"...Nolo publications...guide people simply through the how, when, where and why of law."

—WASHINGTON POST

▲

"Increasingly, people who are not lawyers are performing tasks usually regarded as legal work... And consumers, using books like Nolo's, do routine legal work themselves."

—NEW YORK TIMES

▲

"...All of [Nolo's] books are easy-to-understand, are updated regularly, provide pull-out forms...and are often quite moving in their sense of compassion for the struggles of the lay reader."

—SAN FRANCISCO CHRONICLE

----

affix
postage
here

NOLO PRESS

950 Parker St.
Berkeley, CA 94710